Knowledge and Social Capital

Resources for the Knowledge Based Economy Series

Knowledge and Social Capital: Foundations and Applications

Edited by
Eric L. Lesser

Boston   Oxford   Auckland   Johannesburg   Melbourne   New Delhi

GLOBAL
RELEAF
2000
AMERICAN FORESTS
Butterworth-Heinemann supports the efforts of American Forests and the Global ReLeaf program in its campaign for the betterment of trees, forests, and our environment.

Library of Congress Cataloging-in-Publication Data

Knowledge and Social Capital / edited by Eric L. Lesser.
   p. cm.
  Includes bibliographical references and index.
  ISBN

British Library Cataloguing-in-Publication Data
A catalogue record for this book is available from the British Library.

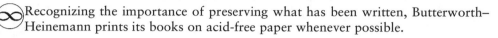

The publisher offers special discounts on bulk orders of this book.
For information, please contact:
Manager of Special Sales
Butterworth–Heinemann
225 Wildwood Avenue
Woburn, MA 01801–2041
Tel: 781-904-2500
Fax: 781-904-2620

For information on all Butterworth–Heinemann publications available, contact our World Wide Web home page at: http://www.bh.com

10 9 8 7 6 5 4 3 2 1

Printed in the United States of America

Table of Contents

Part III: Empirical Works

# Preface

This book is about relationships. Although it is unlikely that you will find it among the "How to Meet and Keep Your Future Life Partner" books scattered in the Self-Improvement section of your local bookstore, it addresses a topic that has become the interest of many: the role of relationships within and across organizations. Social capital, at its core, is about the value created by fostering connections between individuals. As organizations begin to recognize the importance of the tacit knowledge held by their employees, the need to share and leverage this knowledge takes on a higher priority. Social relationships between colleagues drive collaboration and knowledge sharing, provide important insight into internal and external labor markets, and lower transaction costs within and across firms.

The concept of social capital has a long tradition in the domain of the social sciences, including sociology, political science, anthropology, and economics. However, as the knowledge-based economy has focused the spotlight on this topic, more of the work in this area has begun to appear in both the academic and popular business literature. This compilation is an attempt to pull together some of the leading thinking from academicians, social scientists, and practitioners, and provide a resource for individuals trying to understand how they can effectively leverage social capital within their own organizations.

This book is divided into three sections. The first section, *Foundations*, addresses many of the underpinnings of social capital theory. The articles contained in this section include classic works, such as James Coleman's "Social Capital in the Creation of Human Capital," as well as newer perspectives from sociologists, business scholars, and practitioners. It is meant to give the reader a broad overview of the topic, highlighting the different dimensions of social capital that are being investigated today.

The second section, *Applications*, provides articles that address social capital theory in the context of other recent business issues. These topics include the linkages between social capital and organizational knowledge, the formation of cross-organization alliances, the development of virtual communities, and the governance of individual behavior. These articles focus on the importance of social capital in addressing fundamental issues of business strategy, organization design, knowledge management, and the introduction and implementation of new technology.

The final section, *Empirical Studies*, provides the reader with a number of approaches for measuring and identifying the impact social capital has on organizations. While some of these discussions may be somewhat technical, they serve as important reference points as individuals attempt to quantify social capital and its related benefits.

This book attempts to address the needs of a variety of audiences. For those who are new to social capital, there are several articles designed to provide a broad overview of the topic, and the various disciplines it reflects. Others more experienced with the subject will benefit from the variety of perspectives, as well as the mix of classic and new articles. In either case, these works should provide the reader with an appreciation for the topic and its applicability to the real world.

Acknowledgements

In developing this volume, a number of individuals need to be recognized. The IBM Institute for Knowledge Management provided significant assistance in making this book a reality. Larry Prusak, the Institute's Executive Director and resident thought leader, encouraged me to pursue this topic and has offered valuable insights along the way. Joseph Horvath, my compatriot at the Institute and frequent sounding board, helped jumpstart our initial research in this area. Another IBM colleague, Jim Cortada, played an important role in reviewing early drafts of my chapter and serving as my personal "publishing mentor" throughout the process. Finally, I would be remiss if I did not thank my wife, Leah, for her unmatched editing talents and overall support during the entire effort, and my parents, David and Sheila, who dedicated their careers to building relationships and sharing knowledge with thousands of emerging minds.

PART I

Foundations

Chapter 1

Leveraging Social Capital in Organizations

Eric L. Lesser
Executive Consultant, IBM Institute for Knowledge Management

INTRODUCTION

My most vivid encounter with social capital took place almost a decade prior to my introduction to the concept. Soon after graduating from college, I went to work for a Big Five management consulting firm. Part of the initial training was a three-week stint at the firm's corporate training complex located amidst the cornfields of central Illinois. During this time, new consultants from all over the world were brought together under the rubric of learning about the firm's methodology, rules and practices. While a significant amount of time was dedicated to listening to experienced consultants teach us about development standards and instructional design techniques, it also became quite clear that the course was about more than simply learning how to perform our new roles.

An underlying theme that was reinforced throughout the training was the importance of making connections. We were strongly encouraged to network and get to know our new-found colleagues—over meals, in the workout rooms, and even at the local bowling alley. Given the remoteness of the training location, and the interdependent nature of the class exercises, it was difficult *not* to get to know your neighbors. Another important component of the training experience was the communication of firm culture, values, and language. As part of our class content, and our frequent, late night sessions in the campus pub, we were often regaled with "war stories" from senior consultants. These stories not only shared insights about the firm culture, but also provided a window into the lives of more experienced professionals and how they had built their careers within the firm.

At the end of the three-week session, we emerged, a bit weary, but with more than just a series of certificates and binders. What arose from that course was a series of relationships that had been built among individuals who three weeks prior had been complete strangers. These relationships often continued

3

well beyond the training course, frequently taking the forms of voicemail messages, late night inquiries and occasional drinks in airport lounges across the world.

What I have come to realize today is that this particular firm took an active role in the promotion and development of social capital among its new recruits. As part of the initial rite of passage, we were engaged in a process that fostered the formation of a social network that individuals could tap into as they progressed through the firm. This social network was instrumental in answering tough, often sensitive questions ("How do I tell the project manager that the client is unhappy with his performance?"), identifying early opportunities in the firm's internal labor market ("I heard they are looking for senior consultants for a project in Switzerland"), and providing insight into the myriad of unspoken rules and regulations that govern life in a professional services firm. What this particular firm recognized was that the development of these relationships was critical to the success of individuals working in a fast-paced, distributed, and highly knowledge-intensive environment. Hence, the development of social capital was viewed by the organization as a critical piece in building competitive advantage in the marketplace.

SOCIAL CAPITAL: DEFINITIONS AND PERSPECTIVES

In the realms of political science, sociology, and economic development, there are a plethora of definitions for social capital (for an extensive list see Adler and Kwon).[1] According to *The Merriam-Webster Dictionary*, the term *capital* refers to "accumulated wealth, especially as used to produce more wealth."[2] Therefore, it is easiest to think about social capital as the wealth (or benefit) that exists because of an individual's social relationships. Within these social relationships, there are three primary dimensions that influence the development of these mutual benefits: the structure of the relationships, the interpersonal dynamics that exist within the structure, and the common context and language held by individuals in the structure.

The Structure of Relationships

In the social capital literature, there are two primary schools of thought that focus on the structural aspects of relationships. The first school is primarily concerned with the connections that individual actors have with one another. Sandefur and Laumann refer to this as the egocentric perspective on social networks, where "an individual's social capital is characterized by her direct

---

[1]   Adler, Paul and Seok-Woo Kwon, "Social Capital, The Good, The Bad and The Ugly," Paper submitted to the OMT Division of the Academy of Management, 1999, p. 2.
[2]   *Merriam Webster Dictionary*, 1974 edition, p. 115.

relationships with others and by the other people and relationships that she can reach through those to whom she is directly tied."[3]

For example, Mark has a series of relationships with people whom he works with on a regular basis. He often seeks the advice of these individuals on how to solve difficult problems, socializes with them during lunch and learns what kinds of behavior are acceptable or not acceptable within their broader community (for example, is it acceptable to sneak out at 4:30 P.M. on a Friday during the summer?). In this example, Mark is leveraging what is referred to in the literature as dense relationships. Writers, such as James Coleman, have written about the importance of these dense relationships emphasizing that "the strength of these ties make possible transactions in which trustworthiness is taken for granted and trade can occur with ease."[4] However these strong ties are not the only relationships that can provide value to an individual. Since strong ties, such as family members and close co-workers, typically share a common body of knowledge and contacts, they are often not useful in providing new sources of knowledge. Having so-called weak ties, such as friends of friends, may be useful for finding out new sources of information, such as finding a new job. Mark Granovetter, a leading writer on the subject of weak ties, states, "From an individual's point of view, then, weak ties are an important resource in making possible mobility opportunity. Seen from a more macroscopic vantage, weak ties play a role in effecting social cohesion."[5] Hence, both types of relationships, strong and weak, can provide value to individuals.

The second school is referred to as the sociocentric approach to understanding network structure.[6] This approach, based on the writings of thinkers such as Ronald Burt at the University of Chicago, believes that the social capital is based on a person's relative position within a given network, rather than the individual's direct relationship with people in the network. For example, imagine an organization consisting of software developers and software testers. Each of these groups consists of a dense network of individuals who have multiple, redundant connections to one another. Information flows freely within, but not across the groups. Then Sara, a new employee, is hired to serve as a liaison between the two groups. According to Burt and others, Sara is filling a "structural hole" that exists between the two divisions. Because Sara fills this structural hole, she increases her level of social capital because she now has the opportunity to obtain "information and control advantages of being the broker in relations

---

[3] Sandefur, Rebecca and Edward O. Laumann, "A Paradigm for Social Capital," *Rationality and Society*, 1998 (10:4), p. 484.

[4] Coleman, James S., "Social Capital in the Creation of Human Capital," *American Journal of Sociology*, 1988 (94 Supplement), p. s99.

[5] Granovetter, Mark S., "The Strength of Weak Ties," *American Journal of Sociology*, 1973 (78:6), p. 1373.

[6] Sandefur and Laumann, p. 484.

between people otherwise disconnected to the social structure."[7] It is her ability to bridge the gap between the software developers and testers, rather than her individual relationship with any one member that allows her to reap the benefits of her relationships.

Much of the literature approaches the network component of social capital from either the egocentric or sociocentric perspectives. Further, most studies tend to focus on the individual, and their role relative to other individuals within a network, as the primary unit of analysis. As part of a recent article, Gordon Walker, Bruce Kogut, and Weijan Shan have gone beyond this focus on the individual and have expanded the concept of social capital to include entire firms. In "Social Capital, Structural Holes and the Formation of an Industry Network," they examined whether the egocentric or sociocentric perspectives of social capital were relevant in understanding the formation of a network of biotechnology firms. Through their analysis, they found that biotech startups tended to be based on relationships with existing firms rather than the exploitation of structural holes in the industry.[8] They argued that the "long durations (associated with biotechnology research) entail extensive, ongoing interaction over a broad range of technical and commercial problems."[9] Thus, the development of these long-term relationships suggested the need for a relationship-based, rather than a structural hole, view of social capital.

The Interpersonal Dynamics within Relationships

For many writers, the development of social capital is not limited to the presence of contacts within a given network. Instead, it is the positive interactions that occur between individuals in the network that lead to the formation of social capital. In this context, issues such as trust and reciprocity become the focal point of social capital formation. Robert Putnam, a prominent political scientist who writes frequently about social capital, refers to this phenomenon as "norms of general reciprocity: I'll do this for you now, in the expectation that down the road you or someone else will return the favor."[10] Similarly, Jane Fountain, who has studied the role of social capital as an enabler of innovation in science and technology, states, "A key property of social capital rests on the transitivity of trust: A trusts C because B trusts C and A trusts B. Thus, relatively large networks may exhibit generalized trust without personal contact among

---

[7]   Burt, Ronald, "The Contingent Value of Social Capital," *Administrative Science Quarterly*, 1997 (42), p. 340.

[8]   Walker, Gordon, Bruce Kogut and Weijian Shan, "Social Capital, Structural Holes and the Formation of an Industry Network," *Organization Science*, March-April, 1997 (8:2), p. 118.

[9]   Ibid, p. 118.

[10]   Putnam, Robert D. "The Prosperous Community: Social Capital and Public Life," *The American Prospect*, 1993 (13), p. 37.

actors."[11] Francis Fukuyama, who has written extensively on the subject of trust, suggests that, "Social capital is the capability that arises from the prevalence of trust in a society or in certain parts of it. It can be embodied in the smallest and most basic social group, the family, as well as the largest of all groups, the nation, and in all the other groups in between."[12]

Common Context and Language

A third critical enabler of social capital is a common vernacular that individuals can use as part of their interactions. According to Janine Nahapiet at Oxford University and Sumantra Ghoshal at the London Business School, "To the extent that people share a common language, this facilitates their ability to gain access to people and their information. To the extent that their language and codes are different, this keeps people apart and restricts their access."[13] This use of common language includes, but goes beyond languages, such as English, Spanish, Japanese, et cetera. It also addresses the acronyms, subtleties and underlying assumptions that are the staples of day-to-day interactions. For example, as a management consultant in an information technology company, I frequently interact with software developers. While I have access to the network of these developers, and have developed positive relations with them, we have had to work hard to develop a common language and context with which we can transact our business. Without a shared understanding of common terms, activities, and outcomes, it becomes very difficult to reap the benefits associated with building social capital.

Comparing Social Capital with Other Forms of Capital

In a recent article, Paul Adler and Seok-Woo Kwon, professors at the Marshall School of Business at the University of Southern California, address an important issue: Is social capital truly a form of capital in the traditional sense of the word? They have identified four parallels where social capital demonstrates many of the characteristics that define other forms of capital, such as physical or financial capital:[14]

---

[11] Fountain, Jane, "Social Capital, A Key Enable of Innovation in Science and Technology," in L.M. Branscomb and J. Keller, eds., *Investing in Innovation: Towards a Consensus Strategy for Federal Technology Policy*, (Cambridge: The MIT Press, 1997, p. 3 (Internet version).

[12] Fukuyama, Francis, *Trust: The Social Virtues and the Creation of Prosperity*, (New York: Penguin Books, 1995), p. 26.

[13] Nahapiet, Janine and Sumantra Ghoshal, "Social Capital, Intellectual Capital and the Organizational Advantage," *Academy of Management Review*, 1998 (23:2), p. 253.

[14] Adler and Kwon, p. 4.

- *Social capital is a resource into which other resources can be invested with expectation of future, albeit uncertain, returns.* Much as money can be invested with the expectation that it will increase the production capacity of a machine, money can be invested in promoting social capital within a given network. An example of this might be an organization investing in a practitioner conference to enable people to build their informal networks and create the face-to-face interactions that lead to increased levels of trust.
- *Social capital is "appropriable" and to some degree "convertible."* Social capital can be used for a number of productive uses. It can make it easier to transfer a relevant practice from one part of an organization to another. Similarly, it can be used to find out information about a new job opening, a transferred supervisor, or a potential early retirement package. However, it is less "convertible" than other forms of capital: it is more difficult to "exchange" social capital for other forms of capital (though it could be argued in political circles that financial capital is used to obtain access and build positive relations all the time!)
- *Like physical and human capital, but unlike financial capital, social capital requires maintenance to remain productive.* Without providing time, energy, or other resources into social capital, the connections between individuals tend to erode over time, much like oxidation on a piece of steel. However, unlike human capital, maintaining social capital requires the participation of at least two parties; the recipient alone can not update it independently of others.
- *Like human capital, but unlike physical capital, social capital does not have predictable rate of depreciation.* Social capital, much like organizational knowledge, often grows and becomes more productive with use. Therefore, it tends to have increasing, rather than decreasing, returns over time. However, much as organizational knowledge can be rendered irrelevant (e.g. a revolutionary technology makes a current technology obsolete) social capital can rapidly lose its value unpredictably (e.g. an acquisition might reduce the value of social capital created within the acquired company if layoffs are expected).

However, they also note two key differences between social capital and other forms of capital:

- *Social capital is a public good.* It is not owned by one specific individual, but is dependent upon all members of the network. Other forms of capital tend to rely on either individual ownership or collective ownership in the form of shares. Much like public parks and conservation land, individuals can reap the benefits of social capital, but the responsibility for its maintenance rests with the collective. Since it is a public good, individuals may have a tendency to shirk its maintenance responsibility, relying on other members to ensure its upkeep.
- *Social capital is "located" not in the actors themselves, but in their relations with other actors.* Social capital can not exist in a vacuum; it is dependent on the interaction of individuals to create value. Therefore, a given person may have difficulty influencing the level of social capital in a group by him or herself. It may often require a collective action in order to create change to the status quo.

WHY ARE ORGANIZATIONS BECOMING INTERESTED IN SOCIAL CAPITAL?

While the presence of social capital is not a new phenomenon in organizations, recently it has received a great deal of attention from the academic and business press. This recent interest, I believe, is no accident. There are at least two primary drivers in today's business environment that are requiring individuals, organizations, and even governments to consider the impact of social capital and its effect on economic growth and organization success.

The Importance of the Knowledge-Based Organization

One of the primary drivers behind the interest in social capital is the rise of the knowledge-based organization. As knowledge begins to supplant land, labor, and capital as the primary source of competitive advantage in the marketplace, the ability to create new knowledge, share existing knowledge, and apply organizational knowledge to new situations becomes critical. As Larry Prusak and Thomas Davenport write in their influential book, *Working Knowledge: How Organizations Manage What They Know*, "Increasingly, companies will differentiate themselves on the basis of what they know."[15]

Knowledge in organizations is typically thought of as being either explicit (relatively easy to capture while maintaining its value) or tacit (difficult to articulate and document without losing its value). Social capital is necessary to enable the effective management of both explicit and tacit knowledge. Explicit knowledge, which is primarily found in books, articles, and procedure manuals, has been the focus of many knowledge management efforts in organizations. While technology has made it easier to scan, capture, house, and access forms of explicit knowledge through the use of electronic repositories, social capital plays a critical role in managing and maintaining this knowledge base.

The motivation for individuals to contribute to, and reuse explicit knowledge from such a repository-based system is largely dependent on the social capital of the members that use the system. For example, the extent to which documents are shared with others is based on issues around trust, obligation, and the perceived value of the intellect of others. If individuals feel that that they do not trust others with the knowledge, or believe that others will not be forthcoming with their knowledge, it is unlikely that they will take the time or energy to contribute. Similarly, if a person believes that the knowledge of others provides little value, or if the individual lacks the context necessary to understand the true nature of the document, the knowledge will likely remain unused. Therefore,

---

[15] Davenport, Thomas and Laurence Prusak. *Working Knowledge: How Organizations Manage What They Know*, (Cambridge, MA: Harvard Business School Press, 1997), p. 13.

while technology can facilitate the management of explicit knowledge, it is social capital that truly impacts the effectiveness of such efforts.

Even more important is the role of social capital in the sharing of tacit knowledge. Given that the most effective way of sharing tacit knowledge is through direct contact between the sender and receiver of the knowledge, then social capital plays a critical role in this transfer. Individuals must be able to identify individuals with expertise, build a relationship so that the sender is willing to share the knowledge with the receiver, and develop a sense of shared language that enables them to elucidate the required knowledge. Mentoring is an example of a process in which social capital is built with the express purpose of transferring tacit knowledge.

Nahapiet and Ghoshal have developed a conceptual model that illustrates this linkage between social capital and organizational knowledge. This model illustrates how social capital influences four variables that mediate the creation and sharing of organizational knowledge. These four variables include: access to parties for combining/exchanging intellectual capital, the anticipation of value through combining/exchanging intellectual capital, the motivation of individuals to combine/share intellectual capital, and the ability for the organization to change according to the needs of its outside environment.[16] They hypothesize that increasing the amount of social capital within an organization will positively influence the intermediate variables and subsequently impact the creation and sharing of organizational knowledge.

In a follow-up study, Ghoshal and Wenpin Tsai test this theoretical construct in a large multinational electronics company.[17] Using product innovation as a proxy for knowledge creation and sharing, the authors found that social capital had significant effects on the levels of resource exchange and combination within the organization. While this study was limited to the results of one organization, it further reinforced the concept that social capital has a significant impact on the way organizations create and share knowledge.

The importance of social capital in managing knowledge is reinforced by research on the transference of best practices within organizations. Gabriel Szulanski, an assistant professor at the Wharton School of Business, investigated 122 best practices transfers in 8 organizations. He found that the most relevant barriers to successfully transferring best practices were: a lack of absorptive capacity of the recipient, causal ambiguity (lack of understanding of the cause-effect relationship related to a new practice), and an arduous relationship between the source and recipient.[18] Based on these findings, we can extrapolate that social capital is a necessary ingredient to transfer best practices. Social capital is helpful

---

[16] Nahapiet and Ghoshal, p. 251.

[17] Tsai, Wenpin and Sumantra Ghoshal, "Social Capital and Value Creation: The Role of Intrafirm Networks," *Academy of Management Journal*, August, 1998 (41:4) p. 464.

[18] Szulanski, Gabriel, "Exploring Internal Stickiness: Impediments to the Transfer of Best Practice Within the Firm," *Strategic Management Journal*, 1996 (17) (Winter Special Issue), p. 36.

in building the positive relationship required by both the sender and the receiver of the new practice. Further, social capital can also minimize the effects of causal ambiguity. By providing a common context and background for the sender and receiver, it makes it easier for them to bridge the gap between what was accomplished in one setting and how it could be applied to another.

The Rise of the Networked Economy

Another important rationale for building social capital is the growth of strategic alliances and joint ventures. As more and more of the resources needed to complete a finished product lie outside of a single organization, the ability to build social capital across the network becomes more critical. One of the original scholars to write extensively on the subject, Robert Putnam, suggests that social capital across firms is often developed through extensive participation in local community affairs. This civic participation, which is built over long periods of time, directly carries over into the economic development of the businesses within the region. "The social capital embodied in norms and networks of civic engagement seems to be a precondition for economic development as well as for effective government."[19] He uses the example of local businesses in Northern Italy which, over time, banded together to cross-sell products, share common reservoirs of skilled labor, and even provide financial assistance to distressed companies.[20] As he states, "A society that relies on generalized reciprocity is more efficient than a distrustful society, for the same reason that money is more efficient than barter. Trust lubricates social life."[21]

Steven Cohen and Gary Fields, writing in the *California Management Review*, present another perspective of social capital across firms. In their analysis of social capital among firms in Silicon Valley, they argue that,

> There is no deep history, little in the way of family ties and little structured community. With its spatially isolated and spread-out residential patterns, its shopping strips and malls, its auto gridlock, its rapid demographic turnover, and the rampant individualism among its most talented workers, Silicon Valley would be hard-pressed to present the image of a close-knit civil society that, according to the social capital theorists, is the precondition of economic prosperity.[22]

Instead, trust in Silicon Valley is primarily performance, rather than community-based. "The main networks of social capital in Silicon Valley are not

[19] Putnam, p. 37.
[20] Pennar, Karen, "The Ties That Lead To Prosperity," *Business Week*, December 15, 1997, p. 155.
[21] Putnam, p. 37.
[22] Cohen, Stephen S. and Gary Fields, "Social Capital and Capital Gains in Silicon Valley" *California Management Review*, Winter, 1999 (41:2), p. 109.

dense networks of civic engagement, but focused interactions among . . . the great research universities, U.S. Government policy, venture capital firms, law firms, business networks, stock options, and the labor market."[23] The ability for multiple partners to come through for one another has more to do with creating value than the simple desire of firms to work towards a collective good. Given the mobility of workers in this region of the company, the sense of performance-based trust carries beyond the affiliation of a single firm—it moves with people as they work for various start-ups within the region.

CHALLENGES ASSOCIATED WITH BUILDING SOCIAL CAPITAL

At the same time as creation and maintenance of social capital within and across organizations has become more important, changes in the business environment have reduced the opportunity for individuals to build this valuable resource. In the age of vertical integration, the creation of social capital occurred naturally. As individuals tended to stay with one organization for a long period of time, they were able to develop strong informal networks through a series of rotational assignments through closely related divisions. Knowing Jack in the Electronics Division and Judy in Corporate Headquarters made it easier to get things done outside of the normal rules and formal communication channels. Similarly, many organizations also encouraged relationship building outside of working hours through the use of corporate clubs and other outside social activities.

However, this model is often the exception, rather than the rule, in today's organizations. As firms have become more global and virtual it has made it more difficult to get to know one's co-workers on a personal level. As individuals are expected to work on projects that are often comprised of multinational, cross-functional teams, it has become more difficult to build the common basis for understanding necessary to build constructive relationships. Sheer logistics make it challenging to even meet on a face-to-face basis, much less develop the positive interactions needed to build a common sense of trust and obligation.

Second, the reengineering undertaken by many organizations in the late 1980s and early 1990s often had a negative impact on the level of social capital in a number of ways. As individuals with significant experience within an organization were dismissed, the networks of relationships that were instrumental in performing day-to-day activity were quickly dismantled as well. Middle managers, many of whom played an informal role as knowledge brokers, were often the first ones targeted for dismissal. Further, the uncertainty associated with mass layoffs and "early retirements" made it extremely challenging to develop the mutual trust necessary to build social capital.

---

[23] Cohen and Fields, p. 110.

Finally, the changing nature of the employment contract has made it difficult to maintain intra-organizational networks. As moving from job to job becomes more common, it becomes more difficult to develop and maintain the informal networks that reduce transaction costs and make it easier to find expertise within the organization. Many of the organizations that I have recently worked with are struggling with this situation, especially as it relates to the use of contractors. These mobile employees often bring the requisite skills, but not necessarily the same motivation to develop relationships that are necessary to knowledge creation, sharing, and reuse. What many organizations are now realizing is that what they gain in staffing flexibility from the use of temporary employees, they often lose in terms of overall productivity and efficiency in the long run.

HOW ORGANIZATIONS CAN BUILD SOCIAL CAPITAL FOR COMPETITIVE ADVANTAGE

Foster the Development of Communities of Practice

One method for building social capital in organizations is to bring together informal groups of employees together to share knowledge and expertise. These "communities of practice," which can range from a few individuals to several hundred members, are built upon common ways of working. Individuals, looking for others with common experiences, work tools, and challenges, find each other and meet (either physically or virtually) to solve problems and build an affiliation to others with similar work interests. Communities of practice can help build social capital in a number of ways.[24]

- The community serves as an intra-network clearinghouse by identifying those with relevant knowledge and helping individuals within the community make connections with one another. This is particularly valuable as the organization grows and goes virtual and individuals find it increasingly difficult to know who knows what.
- The community acts as a reference mechanism, quickly enabling individuals to evaluate the knowledge of other members without having to contact each individual within the network.
- Communities of practice can help connect individuals from outside the network to those who are already identified as community members. This function can be critical, especially for new employees who are looking to identify individuals who hold the firm-specific knowledge needed to be successful in their new roles.
- By being able to bring people together to develop and share relevant knowledge, the community creates the condition where individuals can test the trustworthiness and the commitment of other community members. Through this process, the community builds its own form of informal currency, with norms and values

[24] Lesser, Eric and Laurence Prusak, "Communities of Practice, Social Capital and Organizational Knowledge," *Information Systems Review*, forthcoming.

that are commonly held and terms and conditions of payment that are generally accepted. It is through these repeated interactions that individuals can develop empathy for the situations of others and can develop the rapport with individuals in the community.

- Communities of practice help shape the actual terminology used by group members in everyday work conversations. In addition, they generate and share the knowledge objects or artifacts that are used by community members. Equally as important, communities generate stories that communicate the norms and values of the community and of the organization as a whole. These stories enable new members to take cues from more experienced personnel and allow the development of a community memory that perpetuates itself long after the original community members have departed.

Create Experiences that Build Trust Among Individuals

Influencing the level of trust in an organization is by far one of the most challenging endeavors an organization can set out upon. Intra-divisional rivalries, competition for promotions, and even common personality conflicts can breed mistrust among co-workers. However, in many disperse organization, trust never has the opportunity to form because individuals never have the opportunity to interact with individuals to achieve a common goal. When brought together to work on a specific task, or asked to share knowledge as part of an intellectual capital management system, individuals are hesitant to assist others simply because they don't have a shared history of interactions and common experiences that enable trust in the first place. Therefore, to influence the level of trust between people, often it is necessary to create experiences that enable individuals to determine whether or not others are trustworthy. For example, some firms use experiential learning classes, such as Outward Bound, to enable people to develop trust through achieving common physical goals. Other organizations may use training courses, similar to the ones described in the opening paragraphs, to create positive interactions in a safe environment. In either situation, individuals have the opportunity to evaluate the trustworthiness of others and make judgements prior to having to rely on those individuals in a more critical context.

Allow Time for People to Build Common Context and Understanding

Often times, in the haste to get started on a new idea or project, groups of people are thrust together and told to begin work. Often this has disastrous effects as individuals proceed without having a common working vision. Worse, members of the group often assume that the language they are using is agreed upon by all, giving the illusion that everybody is "reading off of the same page." Given the multitude of experiences that employees bring to any situation, it is more likely that individuals have very different assumptions about goals, priorities, final outputs, and expectations. This is especially true when these groups represent different functions, divisions, and especially different organizations. Therefore, at the beginning of any significant undertaking, time must be allocated to ensure that individuals have a common understanding of the task at hand and are familiar with the terminology and assumptions of others. By tackling the common challenges early in the effort, the organization can prevent misunderstandings that create rework and promote distrust among participants. These shared assumptions need to be validated on a regular basis to ensure that individuals remain in agreement and are able to maintain the overall shared vision.

Use Appropriate Technologies to Support Network Formation and Maintenance

Assuming that globalization and worker mobility are given conditions in today's economy, it is necessary to address the appropriate role of technology in creating and maintaining social capital. The use of collaborative technologies, such as shared repositories, chat rooms, and videoconferences can, when appropriately used, have a positive impact on the development of social capital. For example, expertise locators can help individuals make connections with others who may be located in other parts of the organization. This can help develop weak ties between individuals in distant offices, making it easier to locate sources of knowledge that might have previously remained undiscovered. Further, technologies such as the Internet and Lotus Notes can make it easier to share explicit knowledge representations, such as reports, e-mails, and other presentation materials. This ability to share may make it easier for individuals to conduct the multiple interactions deemed necessary to facilitate trust among individuals. Further, as highlighted by Blanchard and Horn in their discussion of virtual communities and social capital, collaborative technologies can highlight a single act of helping across a wide range of individuals.[25] According to the authors, ". . . small individual acts of helping can sustain a large virtual community because the act is seen by the entire group. Thus, a few group members' helpful actions will reinforce the group's concept of itself as being helpful to its members."[26]

However, the relationship between the development of social capital and the appropriate use of technology is still very much to be determined. It is possible to imagine that the use of technology could inhibit the development of trust between individuals who are not given the opportunity to meet face-to-face. As different types of communities and relationships are created in on-line environments, the ways in which social capital is developed within and across these groups remains to be fully understood. While technology can assist groups in

[25] Blanchard, Anita and Tom Horn, "Virtual Communities and Social Capital," *Social Science Computer Review*, Fall, 1998 (16:3), p. 298.
[26] Ibid, p. 298.

identifying and connecting members, it still is an open question to what extent virtual communities supplant or supplement relationships based on physical presence.

CONCLUSION

Social capital, by itself, is not a new phenomenon. Indeed, the importance of a strong network of trustworthy colleagues has always been regarded as a key factor in building a successful career. However, the changing nature of organizations requires us to look at social capital in a slightly different light. The emergence of knowledge as an untapped and powerful source of competitive advantage requires that we understand social capital in a more rigorous and comprehensive manner. Much as oil serves as the lubricant to ensure a vibrant and powerful engine, social capital acts as the fluid that enables the knowledge-intensive organization. Given the need to more effectively create, share, and use an organization's knowledge assets, the importance of being able to locate expertise, transfer best practices, and bring disparate parties together to collaborate becomes ever more critical.

The subject of social capital has been addressed by a range of academic disciplines, including economics, sociology, anthropology, and political science. The social science research in this area has been valuable in defining, analyzing, and providing a forum to discuss social capital related issues. Recently, the academic and popular business press have joined the discussion, identifying new frameworks, models, and examples that can be employed by modern organizations. From reviewing the literature, it is clear that significant research still needs to be performed to better understand how organizations can harness, cultivate, and measure social capital. However, one thing that is clear is the need for managers to be conscious of the importance of social capital and how it can be leveraged to improve individual and organizational performance.

Chapter 2

Social Capital in the Creation of Human Capital[*]

James S. Coleman[1]
University of Chicago

In this paper, the concept of social capital is introduced and illustrated, its forms are described, the social structural conditions under which it arises are examined, and it is used in an analysis of dropouts from high school. Use of the concept of social capital is part of a general theoretical strategy discussed in the paper: taking rational action as a starting point but rejecting the extreme individualistic premises that often accompany it. The conception of social capital as a resource for action is one way of introducing social structure into the rational action paradigm. Three forms of social capital are examined: obligations and expectations, information channels, and social norms. The role of closure in the social structure in facilitating the first and third of these forms of social capital is described. An analysis of the effect of the lack of social capital available to high school sophomores on dropping out of school before graduation is carried out. The effect of social capital within the family and in the community outside the family is examined.

There are two broad intellectual streams in the description and explanation of social action. One, characteristic of the work of most sociologists, sees the actor as socialized and action as governed by social norms, rules, and obligations. The principal virtues of this intellectual stream lie in its ability to describe action in social context and to explain the way action is shaped, constrained, and redirected by the social context.

[*] Reprinted with permission of The University of Chicago © 1988. All rights reserved.
[1] I thank Mark Granovetter, Susan Shapiro, and Christopher Winship for criticisms of an earlier draft, which aided greatly in revision. Requests for reprints should be sent to James S. Coleman, Department of Sociology, University of Chicago, Chicago, Illinois 60637.

The other intellectual stream, characteristic of the work of most economists, sees the actor as having goals independently arrived at, as acting independently, and as wholly self-interested. Its principal virtue lies in having a principle of action, that of maximizing utility. This principle of action, together with a single empirical generalization (declining marginal utility) has generated the extensive growth of neoclassical economic theory, as well as the growth of political philosophy of several varieties: utilitarianism, contractarianism, and natural rights.[2]

In earlier works (Coleman 1986a, 1986b), I have argued for and engaged in the development of a theoretical orientation in sociology that includes components from both these intellectual streams. It accepts the principle of rational or purposive action and attempts to show how that principle, in conjunction with particular social contexts, can account not only for the actions of individuals in particular contexts but also for the development of social organization. In the present paper, I introduce a conceptual tool for use in this theoretical enterprise: social capital. As background for introducing this concept, it is useful to see some of the criticisms of and attempts to modify the two intellectual streams.

CRITICISMS AND REVISIONS

Both these intellectual streams have serious defects. The sociological stream has what may be a fatal flaw as a theoretical enterprise: the actor has no "engine of action." The actor is shaped by the environment, but there are no internal springs of action that give the actor a purpose or direction. The very conception of action as wholly a product of the environment has led sociologists themselves to criticize this intellectual stream, as in Dennis Wrong's (1961) "The Oversocialized Conception of Man in Modern Sociology."

The economic stream, on the other hand, flies in the face of empirical reality: persons' actions are shaped, redirected, constrained by the social context; norms, interpersonal trust, social networks, and social organization are important in the functioning not only of the society but also of the economy. A number of authors from both traditions have recognized these difficulties and have attempted to impart some of the insights and orientations of the one intellectual stream to the other. In economics, Yoram Ben-Porath (1980) has developed ideas concerning the functioning of what he calls the "F-connection" in exchange systems. The F-connection is families, friends, and firms, and Ben-Porath, drawing on literature in anthropology and sociology as well as economics, shows the way these forms of social organization affect economic exchange. Oliver Williamson has, in a number of publications (e.g., 1975, 1981), examined the conditions under which economic activity is organized in different institutional forms, that is, within firms or in markets. There is a whole body of work in economics, the

---

[2] For a discussion of the importance of the empirical generalization to economics, see Black, Coats, and Goodwin (1973).

"new institutional economics," that attempts to show, within neoclassical economic theory, both the conditions under which particular economic institutions arise and the effects of these institutions (i.e., of social organization) on the functioning of the system.

There have been recent attempts by sociologists to examine the way social organization affects the functioning of economic activity. Baker (1983) has shown how, even in the highly rationalized market of the Chicago Options Exchange, relations among floor traders develop, are maintained, and affect their trades. More generally, Granovetter (1985) has engaged in a broad attack on the "undersocialized concept of man" that characterizes economists' analysis of economic activity. Granovetter first criticizes much of the new institutional economics as crudely functionalist because the existence of an economic institution is often explained merely by the functions it performs for the economic system. He argues that, even in the new institutional economics, there is a failure to recognize the importance of concrete personal relations and networks of relations—what he calls "embeddedness"—in generating trust, in establishing expectations, and in creating and enforcing norms.

Granovetter's idea of embeddedness may be seen as an attempt to introduce into the analysis of economic systems social organization and social relations not merely as a structure that springs into place to fulfill an economic function, but as a structure with history and continuity that give it an independent effect on the functioning of economic systems.

All this work, both by economists and by sociologists, has constituted a revisionist analysis of the functioning of economic systems. Broadly, it can be said to maintain the conception of rational action but to superimpose on it social and institutional organization—either endogenously generated, as in the functionalist explanations of some of the new institutional economists, or as exogenous factors, as in the more proximate-causally oriented work of some sociologists.

My aim is somewhat different. It is to import the economists' principle of rational action for use in the analysis of social systems proper, including but not limited to economic systems, and to do so without discarding social organization in the process. The concept of social capital is a tool to aid in this. In this paper, I introduce the concept in some generality, and then examine its usefulness in a particular context, that of education.

SOCIAL CAPITAL

Elements for these two intellectual traditions cannot be brought together in a pastiche. It is necessary to begin with a conceptually coherent framework from one and introduce elements from the other without destroying that coherence.

I see two major deficiencies in earlier work that introduced "exchange theory" into sociology, despite the pathbreaking character of this work. One was the limitation to microsocial relations, which abandons the principal virtue of economic theory, its ability to make the micro-macro transition from pair relations to system. This was evident both in Homans's (1961) work and in Blau's (1964) work. The other was the attempt to introduce principles in an ad hoc fashion, such as "distributive justice" (Homans 1964, p. 241) or the "norm of reciprocity" (Gouldner 1960). The former deficiency limits the theory's usefulness, and the latter creates a pastiche.

If we begin with a theory of rational action, in which each actor has control over certain resources and interests in certain resources and events, then social capital constitutes a particular kind of resource available to an actor.

Social capital is defined by its function. It is not a single entity but a variety of different entities, with two elements in common: they all consist of some aspect of social structures, and they facilitate certain actions of actors—whether persons or corporate actors—within the structure. Like other forms of capital, social capital is productive, making possible the achievement of certain ends that in its absence would not be possible. Like physical capital and human capital, social capital is not completely fungible but may be specific to certain activities. A given form of social capital that is valuable in facilitating certain actions may be useless or even harmful for others.

Unlike other forms of capital, social capital inheres in the structure of relations between actors and among actors. It is not lodged either in the actors themselves or in physical implements of production. Because purposive organizations can be actors ("corporate actors") just as persons can, relations among corporate actors can constitute social capital for them as well (with perhaps the best-known example being the sharing of information that allows price-fixing in an industry). However, in the present paper, the examples and area of application to which I will direct attention concern social capital as a resource for persons.

Before I state more precisely what social capital consists of, it is useful to give several examples that illustrate some of its different forms.

1. Wholesale diamond markets exhibit a property that to an outsider is remarkable. In the process of negotiating a sale, a merchant will hand over to another merchant a bag of stones for the latter to examine in private at his leisure, with no formal insurance that the latter will not substitute one or more inferior stones or a paste replica. The merchandise may be worth thousands, or hundreds of thousands, of dollars. Such free exchange of stones for inspection is important to the functioning of this market. In its absence, the market would operate in a much more cumbersome, much less efficient fashion.

Inspection shows certain attributes of the social structure. A given merchant community is ordinarily very close, both in the frequency of interaction and in ethnic and family ties. The wholesale diamond market in New York City, for example, is Jewish, with a high degree of intermarriage, living in the same community in Brooklyn, and going to the same synagogues. It is essentially a closed community.

Observation of the wholesale diamond market indicates that these close ties, through family, community, and religious affiliation, provide the insurance that is necessary to facilitate the transactions in the market. If any member of this community defected through substituting other stones or through stealing stones in his temporary possession, he would lose family, religious, and community ties. The strength of these ties makes possible transactions in which trustworthiness is taken for granted and trade can occur with ease. In the absence of these ties, elaborate and expensive bonding and insurance devices would be necessary—or else the transactions could not take place.

2. The *International Herald Tribune* of June 21–22, 1986, contained an article on page 1 about South Korean student radical activists. It describes the development of such activism: "Radical thought is passed on in clandestine 'study circles,' groups of students who may come from the same high school or hometown or church. These study circles . . . serve as the basic organizational unit for demonstrations and other protests. To avoid detection, members of different groups never meet, but communicate through an appointed representative."

This description of the basis of organization of this activism illustrates social capital of two kinds. The "same high school or hometown or church" provides social relations on which the "study circles" are later built. The study circles themselves constitute a form of social capital—a cellular form of organization that appears especially valuable for facilitating opposition in any political system intolerant of dissent. Even where political dissent is tolerated, certain activities are not, whether the activities are politically motivated terrorism or simple crime. The organization that makes possible these activities is an especially potent form of social capital.

3. A mother of six children, who recently moved with husband and children from suburban Detroit to Jerusalem, described as one reason for doing so the greater freedom her young children had in Jerusalem. She felt safe in letting her eight year old take the six year old across town to school on the city bus and felt her children to be safe in playing without supervision in a city park, neither of which she felt able to do where she lived before.

The reason for this difference can be described as a difference in social capital available in Jerusalem and suburban Detroit. In Jerusalem, the normative structure ensures that unattended children will be "looked after" by adults in the vicinity, while no such normative structure exists in most metropolitan areas of the United States. One can say that families have available to them in Jerusalem social capital that does not exist in metropolitan areas of the United States.

4. In the Kahn El Khalili market of Cairo, the boundaries between merchants are difficult for an outsider to discover. The owner of a shop that specializes in leather will, when queried about where one can find a certain kind of jewelry, turn out to sell that as well—or, what appears to be nearly the same thing, to have a close associate who sells it, to whom he will immediately take the customer. Or he will instantly become a money changer, although he is not a money changer, merely by turning to his colleague a few shops down. For some activities, such as bringing a customer to a friend's store, there are commissions; for others, such as money changing, merely the creation of obligations. Family relations are important in the market, as is the stability of proprietorship. The whole market is so infused with relations of the sort I have described that it can

be seen as an organization, no less so than a department store. Alternatively, one can see the market as consisting of a set of individual merchants, each having an extensive body of social capital on which to draw, through the relationships of the market.

The examples above have shown the value of social capital for a number of outcomes, both economic and noneconomic. There are, however, certain properties of social capital that are important for understanding how it comes into being and how it is employed in the creation of human capital. First, a comparison with human capital, and then an examination of different forms of social capital, will be helpful for seeing these.

HUMAN CAPITAL AND SOCIAL CAPITAL

Probably the most important and most original development in the economics of education in the past 30 years has been the idea that the concept of physical capital as embodied in tools, machines, and other productive equipment can be extended to include human capital as well (see Schultz 1961; Becker 1964). Just as physical capital is created by changes in materials to form tools that facilitate production, human capital is created by changes in persons that bring about skills and capabilities that make them able to act in new ways.

Social capital, however, comes about through changes in the relations among persons that facilitate action. If physical capital is wholly tangible, being embodied in observable material form, and human capital is less tangible, being embodied in the skills and knowledge acquired by an individual, social capital is less tangible yet, for it exists in the *relations* among persons. Just as physical capital and human capital facilitate productive activity, social capital does as well. For example, a group within which there is extensive trustworthiness and extensive trust is able to accomplish much more than a comparable group without that trustworthiness and trust.

FORMS OF SOCIAL CAPITAL

The value of the concept of social capital lies first in the fact that it identifies certain aspects of social structure by their functions, just as the concept "chair" identifies certain physical objects by their function, despite differences in form, appearance, and construction. The function identified by the concept of "social capital" is the value of these aspects of social structure to actors as resources that they can use to achieve their interests.

By identifying this function of certain aspects of social structure, the concept of social capital constitutes both an aid in accounting for different outcomes at the level of individual actors and an aid toward making the micro-to-macro transitions without elaborating the social structural details through which this occurs. For example, in characterizing the clandestine study circles of South

Korean radical students as constituting social capital that these students can use in their revolutionary activities, we assert that the groups constitute a resource that aids in moving from individual protest to organized revolt. If, in a theory of revolt, a resource that accomplishes this task is held to be necessary, then these study circles are grouped together with those organizational structures, having very different origins, that have fulfilled the same function for individuals with revolutionary goals in other contexts, such as the *Comités d'action lycéen* of the French student revolt of 1968 or the workers' cells in tsarist Russia described and advocated by Lenin ([1902] 1973).

It is true, of course, that for other purposes one wants to investigate the details of such organizational resources, to understand the elements that are critical to their usefulness as resources for such a purpose, and to examine how they came into being in a particular case. But the concept of social capital allows taking such resources and showing the way they can be combined with other resources to produce different system-level behavior or, in other cases, different outcomes for individuals. Although, for these purposes, social capital constitutes an unanalyzed concept, it signals to the analyst and to the reader that something of value has been produced for those actors who have this resource available and that the value depends on social organization. It then becomes a second stage in the analysis to unpack the concept, to discover what components of social organization contribute to the value produced.

In previous work, Lin (1988) and De Graf and Flap (1988), from a perspective of methodological individualism similar to that used in this paper, have shown how informal social resources are used instrumentally in achieving occupational mobility in the United States and, to a lesser extent, in West Germany and the Netherlands. Lin focused on social ties, especially "weak" ties, in this role. Here, I want to examine a variety of resources, all of which constitute social capital for actors.

Before examining empirically the value of social capital in the creation of human capital, I will go more deeply into an examination of just what it is about social relations that can constitute useful capital resources for individuals.

Obligations, Expectations, and Trustworthiness of Structures

If *A* does something for *B* and trusts *B* to reciprocate in the future, this establishes an expectation in *A* and an obligation on the part of *B*. This obligation can be conceived as a credit slip held by *A* for performance by *B*. If *A* holds a large number of these credit slips, for a number of persons with whom *A* has relations, then the analogy to financial capital is direct. These credit slips constitute a large body of credit that A can call in if necessary—unless, of course, the placement of trust has been unwise, and these are bad debts that will not be repaid.

In some social structures, it is said that "people are always doing things for each other." There are a large number of these credit slips outstanding, often on both sides of a relation (for these credit slips appear often not to be completely fungible across areas of activity, so that credit slips of B held by A and those of A held by B are not fully used to cancel each other out). The El Khalili market in Cairo, described earlier, constitutes an extreme case of such a social structure. In other social structures where individuals are more self-sufficient and depend on each other less, there are fewer of these credit slips outstanding at any time.

This form of social capital depends on two elements: trustworthiness of the social environment, which means that obligations will be repaid, and the actual extent of obligations held. Social structures differ in both these dimensions, and actors within the same structure differ in the second. A case that illustrates the value of the trustworthiness of the environment is that of the rotating-credit associations of Southeast Asia and elsewhere. These associations are groups of friends and neighbors who typically meet monthly, each person contributing to a central fund that is then given to one of the members (through bidding or by lot), until, after a number of months, each of the n persons has made n contributions and received one payout. As Geertz (1962) points out, these associations serve as efficient institutions for amassing savings for small capital expenditures, an important aid to economic development.

But without a high degree of trustworthiness among the members of the group, the institution could not exist—for a person who receives a payout early in the sequence of meetings could abscond and leave the others with a loss. For example, one could not imagine a rotating-credit association operating successfully in urban areas marked by a high degree of social disorganization—or, in other words, by a lack of social capital.

Differences in social structures in both dimensions may arise for a variety of reasons. There are differences in the actual needs that persons have for help, in the existence of other sources of aid (such as government welfare services), in the degree of affluence (which reduces aid needed from others), in cultural differences in the tendency to lend aid and ask for aid (see Banfield 1967) in the closure of social networks, in the logistics of social contacts (see Festinger, Schachter, and Back 1963), and other factors. Whatever the source, however, individuals in social structures with high levels of obligations outstanding at any time have more social capital on which they can draw. The density of outstanding obligations means, in effect, that the overall usefulness of the tangible resources of that social structure is amplified by their availability to others when needed.

Individual actors in a social system also differ in the number of credit slips outstanding on which they can draw at any time. The most extreme examples are in hierarchically structured extended family settings, in which a patriarch (or "godfather") holds an extraordinarily large set of obligations that he can call in at any time to get what he wants done. Near this extreme are villages in traditional settings that are highly stratified, with certain wealthy families who, because of their wealth, have built up extensive credits that they can call in at any time.

Similarly, in political settings such as a legislature, a legislator in a position with extra resources (such as the Speaker of the House of Representatives or the Majority Leader of the Senate in the U.S. Congress) can, by effective use of resources, build up a set of obligations from other legislators that makes it possible to get legislation passed that would otherwise be stymied. This concentration of obligations constitutes social capital that is useful not only for this powerful legislator but useful also in getting an increased level of action on the part of a legislature. Thus, those members of legislatures among whom such credits are extensive should be more powerful than those without extensive credits and debits because they can use the credits to produce bloc voting on many issues. It is well recognized, for example, that in the U.S. Senate, some senators are members of what is called "the Senate Club," while others are not. This in effect means that some senators are embedded in the system of credits and debits, while others, outside the "Club," are not. It is also well recognized that those in the Club are more powerful than those outside it.

Information Channels

An important form of social capital is the potential for information that inheres in social relations. Information is important in providing a basis for action. But acquisition of information is costly. At a minimum, it requires attention, which is always in scarce supply. One means by which information can be acquired is by use of social relations that are maintained for other purposes. Katz and Lazarsfeld (1955) showed how this operated for women in several areas of life in a midwestern city around 1950. They showed that a woman with an interest in being in fashion, but no interest in being on the leading edge of fashion, used friends who she knew kept up with fashion as sources of information. Similarly, a person who is not greatly interested in current events but who is interested in being informed about important developments can save the time of reading a newspaper by depending on spouse or friends who pay attention to such matters. A social scientist who is interested in being up-to-date on research in related fields can make use of everyday interactions with colleagues to do so, but only in a university in which most colleagues keep up-to-date.

All these are examples of social relations that constitute a form of social capital that provides information that facilitates action. The relations in this case are not valuable for the "credit slips" they provide in the form of obligations that one holds for others' performances or for the trustworthiness of the other party but merely for the information they provide.

Norms and Effective Sanctions

When a norm exists and is effective, it constitutes a powerful, though sometimes fragile, form of social capital. Effective norms that inhibit crime make it possible to walk freely outside at night in a city and enable old persons to leave their houses without fear for their safety. Norms in a community that support and provide effective rewards for high achievement in school greatly facilitate the school's task.

A prescriptive norm within a collectivity that constitutes an especially important form of social capital is the norm that one should forgo self-interest and act in the interests of the collectivity. A norm of this sort, reinforced by social support, status, honor, and other rewards, is the social capital that builds young nations (and then dissipates as they grow older), strengthens families by leading family members to act selflessly in "the family's" interest, facilitates the development of nascent social movements through a small group of dedicated, inward-looking, and mutually rewarding members, and in general leads persons to work for the public good. In some of these cases, the norms are internalized; in others, they are largely supported through external rewards for selfless actions and disapproval for selfish actions. But, whether supported by internal or external sanctions, norms of this sort are important in overcoming the public goods problem that exists in collectivities.

As all these examples suggest, effective norms can constitute a powerful form of social capital. This social capital, however, like the forms described earlier, not only facilitates certain actions; it constrains others. A community with strong and effective norms about young persons' behavior can keep them from "having a good time." Norms that make it possible to walk alone at night also constrain the activities of criminals (and in some cases of noncriminals as well). Even prescriptive norms that reward certain actions, like the norm in a community that says that a boy who is a good athlete should go out for football, are in effect directing energy away from other activities. Effective norms in an area can reduce innovativeness in an area, not only deviant actions that harm others but also deviant actions that can benefit everyone. (See Merton [1968, pp. 195–203] for a discussion of how this can come about.)

SOCIAL STRUCTURE THAT FACILITATES SOCIAL CAPITAL

All social relations and social structures facilitate some forms of social capital; actors establish relations purposefully and continue them when they continue to provide benefits. Certain kinds of social structure, however, are especially important in facilitating some forms of social capital.

Closure of Social Networks

One property of social relations on which effective norms depend is what I will call closure. In general, one can say that a necessary but not sufficient condition for the emergence of effective norms is action that imposes external effects on others (see Ullmann-Margalit 1977; Coleman 1987). Norms arise as attempts

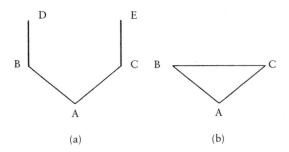

FIGURES 2.1(a) and **2.1(b)** Network without (*a*) and with (*b*) closure

to limit negative external effects or encourage positive ones. But, in many social structures where these conditions exist, norms do not come into existence. The reason is what can be described as lack of closure of the social structure. Figure 2.1 illustrates why. In an open structure like that of Figure 2.1*a*, actor *A*, having relations with actors *B* and *C*, can carry out actions that impose negative externalities on *B* or *C* or both. Since they have no relations with one another, but with others instead (*D* and *E*), then they cannot combine forces to sanction *A* in order to constrain the actions. Unless either *B* or *C* alone is sufficiently harmed and sufficiently powerful vis-à-vis *A* to sanction alone, *A*'s actions can continue unabated. In a structure with closure, like that of Figure 2.1*b*, *B* and *C* can combine to provide a collective sanction, or either can reward the other for sanctioning *A*. (See Merry [1984] for examples of the way gossip, which depends on closure of the social structure, is used as a collective sanction.)

In the case of norms imposed by parents on children, closure of the structure requires a slightly more complex structure, which I will call intergenerational closure. Intergenerational closure may be described by a simple diagram that represents relations between parent and child and relations outside the family. Consider the structure of two communities, represented by Figure 2.2. The vertical lines represent relations across generations, between parent and child, while the horizontal lines represent relations within a generation. The point labeled *A* in both Figure 2.2*a* and Figure 2.2*b* represents the parent of child *B*, and the point labeled *D* represents the parent of child *C*. The lines between *B* and *C* represent the relations among children that exist within any school. Although the other relations among children within the school are not shown here, there exists a high degree of closure among peers, who see each other daily, have expectations toward each other, and develop norms about each other's behavior.

The two communities differ, however, in the presence or absence of links among the parents of children in the school. For the school represented by Figure 2.2*b*, there is intergenerational closure; for that represented by Figure 2.2*a*, there is not. To put it colloquially, in the lower community represented by 2.2*b*, the parents' friends are the parents of their children's friends. In the other, they are not.

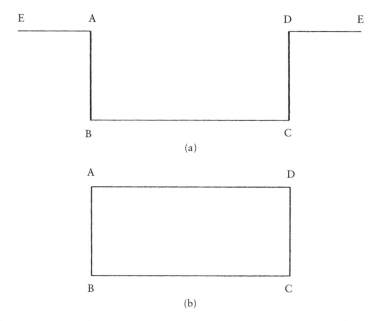

FIGURES 2.2(a) and **2.2(b)** Network Involving Parents (*A*, *D*) and Children (*B*, *C*) without (*a*) and with (*b*) Intergenerational Closure

The consequence of this closure is, as in the case of the wholesale diamond market or in other similar communities, a set of effective sanctions that can monitor and guide behavior. In the community in Figure 2.2*b*, parents *A* and *D* can discuss their children's activities and come to some consensus about standards and about sanctions. Parent *A* is reinforced by parent *D* in sanctioning his child's actions; beyond that, parent *D* constitutes a monitor not only for his own child, *C*, but also for the other child, *B*. Thus, the existence of intergenerational closure provides a quantity of social capital available to each parent in raising his children—not only in matters related to school but in other matters as well.

Closure of the social structure is important not only for the existence of effective norms but also for another form of social capital: the trustworthiness of social structures that allows the proliferation of obligations and expectations. Defection from an obligation is a form of imposing a negative externality or another. Yet, in a structure without closure, it can be effectively sanctioned, if at all, only by the person to whom the obligation is owed. Reputation cannot arise in an open structure, and collective sanctions that would ensure trustworthiness cannot be applied. Thus, we may say that closure creates trustworthiness in a social structure.

Appropriable Social Organization

Voluntary organizations are brought into being to aid some purpose of those who initiate them. In a housing project built during World War II in an eastern city of the United States, there were many physical problems caused by poor construction: faulty plumbing, crumbling sidewalks, and other defects (Merton, n.d.). Residents organized to confront the builders and to address these problems in other ways. Later, when the problems were solved, the organization remained as available social capital that improved the quality of life for residents. Residents had resources available that they had seen as unavailable where they had lived before. (For example, despite the fact that the number of teenagers in the community was smaller, residents were *more* likely to express satisfaction with the availability of teenage babysitters.)

Printers in the New York Typographical Union who were monotype operators formed a Monotype Club as a social club (Lipset, Trow, and Coleman 1956). Later, as employers looked for monotype operators and as monotype operators looked for jobs, both found this organization an effective employment referral service and appropriated the organization for this purpose. Still later, when the Progressive Party came into power in the New York Union, the Monotype Club served as an organizational resource for the Independent Party as it left office. The Monotype Club subsequently served as an important source of social capital for the Independents to sustain the party as an organized opposition while it was out of office.

In the example of South Korean student radicals used earlier, the study circles were described as consisting of groups of students from the same high school or hometown or church. Here, as in the earlier examples, an organization that was initiated for one purpose is available for appropriation for other purposes, constituting important social capital for the individual members, who have available to them the organizational resources necessary for effective opposition. These examples illustrate the general point, that organization, once brought into existence for one set of purposes, can also aid others, thus constituting social capital available for use.

It is possible to gain insight into some of the ways in which closure and appropriable social organization provide social capital by use of a distinction made by Max Gluckman (1967) between simplex and multiplex relations.[3] In the latter, persons are linked in more than one context (neighbor, fellow worker, fellow parent, coreligionist, etc.), while in the former, persons are linked through only one of these relations. The central property of a multiplex relation is that it allows the resources of one relationship to be appropriated for use in others. Sometimes, the resource is merely information, as when two parents who see each other as neighbors exchange information about their teenagers' activities; sometimes, it is the obligations that one person owes a second in relationship X,

---

[3] I am especially grateful to Susan Shapiro for reminding me of Gluckman's distinction and pointing out the relevance of it to my analysis.

which the second person can use to constrain the actions of the first in relationship Y. Often, it is resources in the form of other persons who have obligations in one context that can be called on to aid when one has problems in another context.

SOCIAL CAPITAL IN THE CREATION OF HUMAN CAPITAL

The preceding pages have been directed toward defining and illustrating social capital in general. But there is one effect of social capital that is especially important: its effect on the creation of human capital in the next generation. Both social capital in the family and social capital in the community play roles in the creation of human capital in the rising generation. I will examine each of these in turn.

Social Capital in the Family

Ordinarily, in the examination of the effects of various factors on achievement in school, "family background" is considered a single entity, distinguished from schooling in its effects. But there is not merely a single "family background"; family background is analytically separable into at least three different components: financial capital, human capital, and social capital. Financial capital is approximately measured by the family's wealth or income. It provides the physical resources that can aid achievement: a fixed place in the home for studying, materials to aid learning, the financial resources that smooth family problems. Human capital is approximately measured by parents' education and provides the potential for a cognitive environment for the child that aids learning. Social capital within the family is different from either of these. Two examples will give a sense of what it is and how it operates.

John Stuart Mill, at an age before most children attend school, was taught Latin and Greek by his father, James Mill, and later in childhood would discuss critically with his father and with Jeremy Bentham drafts of his father's manuscripts. John Stuart Mill probably had no extraordinary genetic endowments, and his father's learning was no more extensive than that of some other men of the time. The central difference was the time and effort spent by the father with the child on intellectual matters.

In one public school district in the United States where texts for school use were purchased by children's families, school authorities were puzzled to discover that a number of Asian immigrant families purchased two copies of each textbook needed by the child. Investigation revealed that the family purchased the second copy for the mother to study in order to help her child do well in school. Here is a case in which the human capital of the parents, at least as measured traditionally by years of schooling, is low, but the social capital in the family available for the child's education is extremely high.

These examples illustrate the importance of social capital within the family for a child's intellectual development. It is of course true that children are strongly affected by the human capital possessed by their parents. But this human capital may be irrelevant to outcomes for children if parents are not an important part of their children's lives, if their human capital is employed exclusively at work or elsewhere outside the home. The social capital of the family is the relations between children and parents (and, when families include other members, relationships with them as well). That is, if the human capital possessed by parents is not complemented by social capital embodied in family relations, it is irrelevant to the child's educational growth that the parent has a great deal, or a small amount, of human capital.[4]

I will not differentiate here among the forms of social capital discussed earlier, but will attempt merely to measure the strength of the relations between parents and child as a measure of the social capital available to the child from the parent. Nor will I use the concept in the context of the paradigm of rational action, as, for example, is often done in use of the concept of human capital to examine the investments in education that a rational person would make. A portion of the reason for this lies in a property of much social capital not shown by most forms of capital (to which I will turn in a later section): its public goods character, which leads to underinvestment.

Social capital within the family that gives the child access to the adult's human capital depends both on the physical presence of adults in the family and on the attention given by the adults to the child. The physical absence of adults may be described as a structural deficiency in family social capital. The most prominent element of structural deficiency in modern families is the single-parent family. However, the nuclear family itself, in which one or both parents work outside the home, can be seen as structurally deficient, lacking the social capital that comes with the presence of parents during the day, or with grandparents or aunts and uncles in or near the household.

Even if adults are physically present, there is a lack of social capital in the family if there are not strong relations between children and parents. The lack of strong relations can result from the child's embeddedness in a youth community, from the parents' embeddedness in relationships with other adults that do not cross generations, or from other sources. Whatever the source, it means that

---

[4] The complementarity of human capital and social capital in the family for a child's development suggests that the statistical analysis that examines the effects of these quantities should take a particular form. There should be an interaction term between human capital (parents' education) and social capital (some combination of measures such as two parents in the home, number of siblings, and parents' expectations for child's education). In the analysis reported, here, however, a simple additive model without interaction was used.

TABLE 2.1 Dropout Rates between Spring, Grade 10, and Spring, Grade 12, for Students whose Families Differ in Social Capital, Controlling for Human Capital and Financial Capital in the Family[a]

	Percentage Dropping Out	Difference in Percentage Points
1. Parents' presence:		
Two parents	13.1 }	6.0
Single parent	19.1 }	
2. Additional children:		
One sibling	10.8 }	6.4
Four siblings	17.2 }	
3. Parents and children:		
Two parents, one sibling	10.1 }	12.5
One parents, four siblings	22.6 }	
4. Mother's expectation for child's education:		
Expectation of college	11.6 }	8.6
No expectation of college	20.2 }	
5. Three factors together:		
Two parents, one sibling, mother expects college ...	8.1 }	22.5
One parent, four siblings, no college expectation ...	30.6 }	

[a] Estimates taken from logistic regression reported more fully in App. Table A1.

whatever *human* capital exists in the parents, the child does not profit from it because the *social* capital is missing.

The effects of a lack of social capital within the family differ for different educational outcomes. One for which it appears to be especially important is dropping out of school. With the *High School and Beyond* sample of students in high schools, Table 2.1 shows the expected dropout rates for students in different types of families when various measures of social and human capital in the family and a measure of social capital in the community are controlled statistically.[5] An explanation is necessary for the use of number of siblings as a measure of lack of social capital. The number of siblings represents, in this interpretation, a

[5] The analysis is carried out by use of a weighted logistic model with a random sample of 4,000 students from the public schools in the sample. The variables included in the model as measures of the family's financial, human, and social capital were socioeconomic status (a single variable constructed of parents' education, parents' income, father's occupational status, and household possessions), race, Hispanic ethnicity, number of siblings, number of changes in school due to family residential moves since fifth grade, whether mother worked before the child was in school, mother's expectation of child's educational attainment, frequency of discussions with parents about personal matters, and presence of both

dilution of adult attention to the child. This is consistent with research results for measures of achievement and IQ, which show that test scores decline with sib position, even when total family size is controlled, and that scores decline with number of children in the family. Both results are consistent with the view that younger sibs and children in large families have less adult attention, which produces weaker educational outcomes

Item 1 of Table 2.1 shows that, when other family resources are controlled, the percentage of students who drop out between spring of the sophomore year and spring of the senior year is 6 percentage points higher for children from single-parent families. Item 2 of Table 1 shows that the rate is 6.4 percentage points higher for sophomores with four siblings than for those with otherwise equivalent family resources but only one sibling. Or, taking these two together, we can think of the ratio of adults to children as a measure of the social capital in the family available for the education of any one of them. Item 3 of Table 2.1 shows that for a sophomore with four siblings and one parent, and an otherwise average background, the rate is 22.6%; with one sibling and two parents, the rate is 10.1%—a difference of 12.5 percentage points.

Another indicator of adult attention in the family, although not a pure measure of social capital, is the mother's expectation of the child's going to college. Item 4 of the table shows that, for sophomores without this parental expectation, the rate is 8.6 percentage points higher than for those with it. With the three sources of family social capital taken together, item 5 of the table shows that sophomores with one sibling, two parents, and a mother's expectation for college (still controlling on other resources of family) have an 8.1% dropout rate; with four siblings, one parent, and no expectation of the mother for college, the rate is 30.6%.

These results provide a less satisfactory test than if the research had been explicitly designed to examine effects of social capital within the family. In addition, Table 2.1(A1) in the Appendix shows that another variable that should measure social capital in the family, the frequency of talking with parents about personal experiences, shows essentially no relation to dropping out. Nevertheless, taken all together, the data do indicate that social capital in the family is a resource for education of the family's children, just as is financial and human capital.

parents in the household. The regression coefficients and asymptotic standard errors are given in the App. Table A1. An analysis with more extensive statistical controls, including such things as grades in school, homework, and number of absences, is reported in Hoffer (1986, table 25), but the effects reported in Table 1 and subsequent text are essentially unchanged except for a reduced effect of mother's expectations. The results reported here and subsequently are taken from Hoffer (1986) and from Coleman and Hoffer (1987).

Social Capital Outside the Family

The social capital that has value for a young person's development does not reside solely within the family. It can be found outside as well in the community consisting of the social relationships that exist among parents, in the closure exhibited by this structure of relations, and in the parents' relations with the institutions of the community.

The effect of this social capital outside the family on educational outcomes can be seen by examining outcomes for children whose parents differ in the particular source of social capital discussed earlier, intergenerational closure. There is not a direct measure of intergenerational closure in the data, but there is a proximate indicator. This is the number of times the child has changed schools because the family moved. For families that have moved often, the social relations that constitute social capital are broken at each move. Whatever the degree of intergenerational closure available to others in the community, it is not available to parents in mobile families.

The logistic regression carried out earlier and reported in Table 2.1(A1) shows that the coefficient for number of moves since grade 5 is 10 times its standard error, the variable with the strongest overall effect of any variable in the equation, including the measures of human and financial capital in the family (socioeconomic status) and the crude measures of family social capital introduced in the earlier analysis. Translating this into an effect on dropping out gives 11.8% as the dropout rate if the family has not moved, 16.7% if it has moved once, and 23.1% if it has moved twice.

In the *High School and Beyond* data set, another variation among the schools constitutes a useful indicator of social capital. This is the distinctions among public high schools, religiously based private high schools, and nonreligiously based private high schools. It is the religiously based high schools that are surrounded by a community based on the religious organization. These families have intergenerational closure that is based on a multiplex relation: whatever other relations they have, the adults are members of the same religious body and parents of children in the same school. In contrast, it is the independent private schools that are typically least surrounded by a community, for their student bodies are collections of students, most of whose families have no contact.[6] The choice of private school for most of these parents is an individualistic one, and, although they back their children with extensive human capital, they send their children to these schools denuded of social capital.

---

[6] Data from this study have no direct measures of the degree of intergenerational closure among the parents of the school to support this statement. However, the one measure of intergenerational closure that does exist in the data, the number of residential moves requiring school change since grade 5, is consistent with the statement. The average number of moves for public school students is 0.57; for Catholic school students, 0.35; and for students in other private schools, 0.88.

TABLE 2.2 Dropout Rates between Spring, Grade 10, and Spring, Grade 12, for Students from Schools with Differing Amounts of Social Capital in the Surrounding Community

	Public	Catholic	Other Private Schools
1. Raw dropout rates......................	14.4	3.4	11.9
2. Dropout rates standardized to average public school sophomore[a]...............	14.4	5.2	11.6
	Non-Catholic Religious		Independent
3. Raw dropout rates for students[b] from independent and non-Catholic religious private schools	3.7		10.0

[a]   The standardization is based on separate logistic regressions for these two sets of schools, using the same variables listed in n. 5. Coefficients and means for the standardization are in Hoffer (1986, tables 5 and 24).
[b]   This tabulation is based on unweighted data, which is responsible for the fact that both rates are lower than the rate for other private schools in item 1 of the table, which is based on weighted data.

In the *High School and Beyond* data set, there are 893 public schools, 84 Catholic schools, and 27 other private schools. Most of the other private schools are independent schools, though a minority have religious foundations. In this analysis, I will at the outset regard the other private schools as independent private schools to examine the effects of social capital outside the family.

The results of these comparisons are shown in Table 2.2. Item 1 of the table shows that the dropout rates between sophomore and senior years are 14.4% in public schools, 3.4% in Catholic schools, and 11.9% in other private schools. What is most striking is the low dropout rate in Catholic schools. The rate is a fourth of that in the public schools and a third of that in the other private schools. Adjusting the dropout rates for differences in student-body financial, human, and social capital among the three sets of schools by standardizing the population of the Catholic schools and other private schools to the student-body backgrounds of the public schools shows that the differences are affected only slightly. Furthermore, the differences are not due to the religion of the students or to the degree of religious observance. Catholic students in public school are only slightly less likely to drop out than non-Catholics. Frequency of attendance at religious services, which is itself a measure of social capital through intergenerational closure, is strongly related to dropout rate, with 19.5% of public school students who rarely or never attend dropping out compared with 9.1% of those who attend often. But this effect exists apart from, and in addition to, the effect of the school's religious affiliation. Comparable figures for Catholic school students are 5.9% and 2.6%, respectively (Coleman and Hoffer 1987, p. 138).

The low dropout rates of the Catholic schools, the absence of low dropout rates in the other private schools, and the independent effect of frequency of religious attendance all provide evidence of the importance of social capital outside the school, in the adult community surrounding it, for this outcome of education.

A further test is possible, for there were eight schools in the sample of non-Catholic private schools ("other private" in the analysis above) that have religious foundations and over 50% of the student body of that religion. Three were Baptist schools, two were Jewish, and three from three other denominations. If the inference is correct about the religious community's providing intergenerational closure and thus social capital and about the importance of social capital in depressing the chance of dropping out of high school, these schools also should show a lower dropout rate than the independent private schools. Item 3 of Table 2 shows that their dropout rate is lower, 3.7%, essentially the same as that of the Catholic schools.[7]

The data presented above indicate the importance of social capital for the education of youth, or, as it might be put, the importance of social capital in the creation of human capital. Yet there is a fundamental difference between social capital and most other forms of capital that has strong implications for the development of youth. It is this difference to which I will turn in the next section.

PUBLIC GOODS ASPECTS OF SOCIAL CAPITAL

Physical capital is ordinarily a private good, and property rights make it possible for the person who invests in physical capital to capture the benefits it produces. Thus, the incentive to invest in physical capital is not depressed; there is not a suboptimal investment in physical capital because those who invest in it are able to capture the benefits of their investments. For human capital also—at least human capital of the sort that is produced in schools—the person who invests the time and resources in building up this capital reaps its benefits in the form of a higher-paying job, more satisfying or higher-status work, or even the pleasure of greater understanding of the surrounding world—in short, all the benefits that schooling brings to a person.

But most forms of social capital are not like this. For example, the kinds of social structures that make possible social norms and the sanctions that enforce them do not benefit primarily the person or persons whose efforts would be necessary to bring them about, but benefit all those who are part of such a structure. For example, in some schools where there exists a dense set of associations among some parents, these are the result of a small number of persons, ordinarily mothers who do not hold full-time jobs outside the home. Yet these mothers

---

[7] It is also true, though not presented here, that the lack of social capital in the family makes little difference in dropout rates in Catholic schools—or, in the terms I have used, social capital in the community compensates in part for its absence in the family. See Coleman and Hoffer (1987, chap. 5).

themselves experience only a subset of the benefits of this social capital surrounding the school. If one of them decides to abandon these activities—for example, to take a full-time job—this may be an entirely reasonable action from a personal point of view and even from the point of view of that household with its children. The benefits of the new activity may far outweigh the losses that arise from the decline in associations with other parents whose children are in the school. But the withdrawal of these activities constitutes a loss to all those other parents whose associations and contacts were dependent on them.

Similarly, the decision to move from a community so that the father, for example, can take a better job may be entirely correct from the point of view of that family. But, because social capital consists of relations among persons, other persons may experience extensive losses by the severance of those relations, a severance over which they had no control.

A part of those losses is the weakening of norms and sanctions that aid the school in its task. For each family, the total cost it experiences as a consequence of the decisions it and other families make may outweigh the benefits of those few decisions it has control over. Yet the beneficial consequences to the family of those decisions made by the family may far outweigh the minor losses it experiences from them alone.

It is not merely voluntary associations, such as a PTA, in which underinvestment of this sort occurs. When an individual asks a favor from another, thus incurring an obligation, he does so because it brings him a needed benefit; he does not consider that it does the other a benefit as well by adding to a drawing fund of social capital available in a time of need. If the first individual can satisfy his need through self-sufficiency, or through aid from some official source without incurring an obligation, he will do so—and thus fail to add to the social capital outstanding in the community. Similar statements can be made with respect to trustworthiness as social capital. An actor choosing to keep trust or not (or choosing whether to devote resources to an attempt to keep trust) is doing so on the basis of costs and benefits he himself will experience. That his trustworthiness will facilitate others' actions or that his lack of trustworthiness will inhibit others' actions does not enter into his decision. A similar but more qualified statement can be made for information as a form of social capital. An individual who serves as a source of information for another because he is well informed ordinarily acquires that information for his own benefit, not for the others who make use of him. (This is not always true. As Katz and Lazarsfeld [1955] show, "opinion leaders" in an area acquire information in part to maintain their position as opinion leaders.)

For norms also, the statement must be qualified. Norms are intentionally established, indeed as means of reducing externalities, and their benefits are ordinarily captured by those who are responsible for establishing them. But the capability of establishing and maintaining effective norms depends on properties of the social structure (such as closure) over which one actor does not have control yet are affected by one actor's action. These are properties that affect the structure's capacity to sustain effective norms, yet properties that ordinarily do not enter into an individual's decision that affects them.

Some forms of social capital have the property that their benefits can be captured by those who invest in them; consequently, rational actors will not underinvest in this type of social capital. Organizations that produce a private good constitute the outstanding example. The result is that there will be in society an imbalance in the relative investment in organizations that produce private goods for a market and those associations and relationships in which the benefits are not captured—an imbalance in the sense that, if the positive externalities created by the latter form of social capital could be internalized, it would come to exist in greater quantity.

The public goods quality of most social capital means that it is in a fundamentally different position with respect to purposive action than are most other forms of capital. It is an important resource for individuals and may affect greatly their ability to act and their perceived quality of life. They have the capability of bringing it into being. Yet, because the benefits of actions that bring social capital into being are largely experienced by persons other than the actor, it is often not in his interest to bring it into being. The result is that most forms of social capital are created or destroyed as by-products of other activities. This social capital arises or disappears without anyone's willing it into or out of being and is thus even less recognized and taken account of in social action than its already intangible character would warrant.

There are important implications of this public goods aspect of social capital that play a part in the development of children and youth. Because the social structural conditions that overcome the problems of supplying these public goods—that is, strong families and strong communities—are much less often present now than in the past, and promise to be even less present in the future, we can expect that, ceteris paribus, we confront a declining quantity of human capital embodied in each successive generation. The obvious solution appears to be to attempt to find ways of overcoming the problem of supply of these public goods, that is, social capital employed for the benefit of children and youth. This very likely means the substitution of some kind of formal organization for the voluntary and spontaneous social organization that has in the past been the major source of social capital available to the young.

CONCLUSION

In this paper, I have attempted to introduce into social theory a concept, "social capital," paralleling the concepts of financial capital, physical capital, and human capital—but embodied in relations among persons. This is part of a theoretical strategy that involves use of the paradigm of rational action but without the assumption of atomistic elements stripped of social relationships. I have shown the use of this concept through demonstrating the effect of social capital in the family and in the community in aiding the formation of human capital.

The single measure of human capital formation used for this was one that appears especially responsive to the supply of social capital, remaining in high school until graduation versus dropping out. Both social capital in the family and social capital outside it, in the adult community surrounding the school, showed evidence of considerable value in reducing the probability of dropping out of high school.

In explicating the concept of social capital, three forms were identified: obligations and expectations, which depend on trustworthiness of the social environment, information-flow capability of the social structure, and norms accompanied by sanctions. A property shared by most forms of social capital that differentiates it from other forms of capital is its public good aspect: the actor or actors who generate social capital ordinarily capture only a small part of its benefits, a fact that leads to underinvestment in social capital.

APPENDIX

TABLE A1 Logistic Regression Coefficients and Asymptotic Standard Errors for Effects of Student Background Characteristics on Dropping Out of High School Between Sophomore and Senior Years, 1980–82, Public School Sample

	b	*SE*
Intercept	−2.305	0.169
Socioeconomic status	−0.460	0.077
Black	−0.161	0.162
Hispanic	0.104	0.138
Number of siblings	0.180	0.028
Mother worked while child was young	−0.012	0.103
Both parents in household	−0.415	0.112
Mother's expectation for college	−0.685	0.103
Talk with parents	0.031	0.044
Number of moves since grade 5	0.407	0.040

Source: Taken from Hoffer (1986).

REFERENCES

Baker, Wayne. 1983. "Floor Trading and Crowd Dynamics." Pp. 107–28 in *Social Dynamics of Financial Markets*, edited by Patricia Adler and Peter Adler. Greenwich, Conn.: JAI.

Banfield, Edward. 1967. *The Moral Basis of a Backward Society*. New York: Free Press.

Becker, Gary. 1964. *Human Capital*. New York: National Bureau of Economic Research.

Ben-Porath, Yoram. 1980. "The *F*-Connection: Families, Friends, and Firms and the Organization of Exchange." *Population and Development Review* 6: 1–30.

Black, R. D. C., A. W. Coats, and C. D. W. Goodwin, eds. 1973. *The Marginal Revolution in Economics*. Durham, N.C.: Duke University Press.

Blau, Peter. 1964. *Exchange and Power in Social Life*. New York: Wiley.

Coleman, James S. 1986a. "Social Theory, Social Research, and a Theory of Action." *American Journal of Sociology* 91:1309–35.

———. 1986b. *Individual Interests and Collective Action*. Cambridge: Cambridge University Press.

———. 1987. "Norms as Social Capital." Pp. 133–55 in *Economic Imperialism*, edited by Gerard Radnitzky and Peter Bernholz. New York: Paragon.

Coleman, J. S., and T. B. Hoffer. 1987. *Public and Private Schools: The Impact of Communities*. New York: Basic.

DeGraaf, Nan Dirk, and Hendrik Derk Flap. 1988. "With a Little Help from My Friends." *Social Forces*, vol. 67 (in press).

Festinger, Leon, Stanley Schachter, and Kurt Back. 1963. *Social Pressures in Informal Groups*. Stanford, Calif.: Stanford University Press.

Geertz, Clifford. 1962. "The Rotating Credit Association: A 'Middle Rung' in Development." *Economic Development and Cultural Change* 10:240–63.

Gluckman, Max. 1967. *The Judicial Process among the Barotse of Northern Rhodesia*, 2d ed. Manchester: Manchester University Press.

Gouldner, Alvin. 1960. "The Norm of Reciprocity: A Preliminary Statement." *American Sociological Review* 25:161–78.

Granovetter, Mark. 1985. "Economic Action, Social Structure, and Embeddedness." *American Journal of Sociology* 91:481–510.

Hoffer, T. B. 1986. *Educational Outcomes in Public and Private High Schools*. Ph.D. dissertation. University of Chicago, Department of Sociology.

Homans, George. 1974. *Social Behavior: Its Elementary Forms*, rev. ed. New York: Harcourt, Brace & World.

Katz, E., and P. Lazarsfeld. 1955. *Personal Influence*. New York: Free Press.

Lenin, V. I. (1902) 1973. *What Is To Be Done*. Peking: Foreign Language Press.

Lin, Nan. 1988. "Social Resources and Social Mobility: A Structural Theory of Status Attainment." In *Social Mobility and Social Structure*, edited by Ronald Breiger. Cambridge: Cambridge University Press.

Lipset, Seymour, M. Trow, and J. Coleman. 1956. *Union Democracy*. New York: Free Press.

Merry, Sally, E. 1984. "Rethinking Gossip and Scandal." Pp. 271–302 in *Toward a General Theory of Social Control*. Vol. 1, *Fundamentals*, edited by Donald Black. New York: Academic.

Merton, Robert K. 1968. *Social Theory and Social Structure*, 2d ed. New York: Free Press.

———. n.d. "Study of World War II Housing Projects." Unpublished manuscript. Columbia University, Department of Sociology.

Schultz, Theodore. 1961. "Investment in Human Capital." *American Economic Review* 51 (March): 1–17.

Ullmann-Margalit, Edna. 1977. *The Emergence of Norms*. Oxford: Clarendon.

Williamson, Oliver. 1975. *Markets and Hierarchies*. New York: Free Press.

————. 1981. "The Economics of Organization: The Transaction Cost Approach." *American Journal of Sociology* 87:548–77.

Wrong, Dennis. 1961. "The Oversocialized Conception of Man in Modern Sociology." *American Sociological Review* 26:183–93.

Chapter 3

Social Capital: Its Origins and Applications in Modern Sociology[*]

Alejandro Portes

Department of Sociology, Princeton University, Princeton, New Jersey 08540

KEY WORDS: *social control, family support, networks, sociability*

Abstract—*This paper reviews the origins and definitions of social capital in the writings of Bourdieu, Loury, and Coleman, among other authors. It distinguishes four sources of social capital and examines their dynamics. Applications of the concept in the sociological literature emphasize its role in social control, in family support, and in benefits mediated by extrafamilial networks. I provide examples of each of these positive functions. Negative consequences of the same processes also deserve attention for a balanced picture of the forces at play. I review four such consequences and illustrate them with relevant examples. Recent writings on social capital have extended the concept from an individual asset to a feature of communities and even nations. The final sections describe this conceptual stretch and examine its limitations. I argue that, as shorthand for the positive consequences of sociability, social capital has a definite place in sociological theory. However, excessive extensions of the concept may jeopardize its heuristic value.*

INTRODUCTION

During recent years, the concept of social capital has become one of the most popular exports from sociological theory into everyday language.

---

[*] With permission, from the *Annual Review of Sociology*, Volume 24, © 1998, by Annual Reviews (www.AnnualReviews.org).

Disseminated by a number of policy-oriented journals and general circulation magazines, social capital has evolved into something of a cure-all for the maladies affecting society at home and abroad. Like other sociological concepts that have traveled a similar path, the original meaning of the term and its heuristic value are being put to severe tests by these increasingly diverse applications. As in the case of those earlier concepts, the point is approaching at which social capital comes to be applied to so many events and in so many different contexts as to lose any distinct meaning.

Despite its current popularity, the term does not embody any idea really new to sociologists. That involvement and participation in groups can have positive consequences for the individual and the community is a staple notion, dating back to Durkheim's emphasis on group life as an antidote to anomie and self-destruction and to Marx's distinction between an atomized class-in-itself and a mobilized and effective class-for-itself. In this sense, the term social capital simply recaptures an insight present since the very beginnings of the discipline. Tracing the intellectual background of the concept into classical times would be tantamount to revisiting sociology's major nineteenth century sources. That exercise would not reveal, however, why this idea has caught on in recent years or why an unusual baggage of policy implications has been heaped on it.

The novelty and heuristic power of social capital come from two sources. First, the concept focuses attention on the positive consequences of sociability while putting aside its less attractive features. Second, it places those positive consequences in the framework of a broader discussion of capital and calls attention to how such nonmonetary forms can be important sources of power and influence, like the size of one's stock holdings or bank account. The potential fungibility of diverse sources of capital reduces the distance between the sociological and economic perspectives and simultaneously engages the attention of policy-makers seeking less costly, non-economic solutions to social problems.

In the course of this review, I limit discussion to the contemporary reemergence of the idea to avoid a lengthy excursus into its classical predecessors. To an audience of sociologists, these sources and the parallels between present social capital discussions and passages in the classical literature will be obvious. I examine, first, the principal authors associated to it. Then I review the various mechanisms leading to the emergence of social capital and its principal applications in the research literature. Next, I examine those not-so-desirable consequences of sociability that are commonly obscured in the contemporary literature on the topic. This discussion aims at providing some balance to the frequently celebratory tone with which the concept is surrounded. That tone is especially noticeable in those studies that have stretched the concept from a property of individuals and families to a feature of communities, cities, and even nations. The attention garnered by applications of social capital at this broader level also requires some discussion, particularly in light of the potential pitfalls of that conceptional stretch.

DEFINITIONS

The first systematic contemporary analysis of social capital was produced by Pierre Bourdieu, who defined the concept as "the aggregate of the actual or potential resources which are linked to possession of a durable network of more or less institutionalized relationships of mutual acquaintance or recognition" (Bourdieu 1985, p. 248; 1980). This initial treatment of the concept appeared in some brief "Provisional Notes" published in the *Actes de la Recherche en Sciences Sociales* in 1980. Because they were in French, the article did not garner widespread attention in the English-speaking world; nor, for that matter, did the first English translation, concealed in the pages of a text on the sociology of education (Bourdieu 1985).

This lack of visibility is lamentable because Bourdieu's analysis is arguably the most theoretically refined among those that introduced the term in contemporary sociological discourse. His treatment of the concept is instrumental, focusing on the benefits accruing to individuals by virtue of participation in groups and on the deliberate construction of sociability for the purpose of creating this resource. In the original version, he went as far as asserting that "the profits which accrue from membership in a group are the basis of the solidarity which makes them possible" (Bourdieu 1985, p. 249). Social networks are not a natural given and must be constructed through investment strategies oriented to the institutionalization of group relations, usable as a reliable source of other benefits. Bourdieu's definition makes clear that social capital is decomposable into two elements: first, the social relationship itself that allows individuals to claim access to resources possessed by their associates, and second, the amount and quality of those resources.

Throughout, Bourdieu's emphasis is on the fungibility of different forms of capital and on the ultimate reduction of all forms to economic capital, defined as accumulated human labor. Hence, through social capital, actors can gain direct access to economic resources (subsidized loans, investment tips, protected markets); they can increase their cultural capital through contacts with experts or individuals of refinement (i.e. embodied cultural capital); or, alternatively, they can affiliate with institutions that confer valued credentials (i.e. institutionalized cultural capital).

On the other hand, the acquisition of social capital requires deliberate investment of both economic and cultural resources. Though Bourdieu insists that the outcomes of possession of social or cultural capital are reducible to economic capital, the processes that bring about these alternative forms are not. They each possess their own dynamics, and, relative to economic exchange, they are characterized by less transparency and more uncertainty. For example, transactions involving social capital tend to be characterized by unspecified obligations, uncertain time horizons, and the possible violation of reciprocity expectations. But, by their very lack of clarity, these transactions can help disguise what otherwise would be plain market exchanges (Bourdieu 1979, 1980).

A second contemporary source is the work of economist Glen Loury (1977, 1981). He came upon the term in the context of his critique of neoclassical theories of racial income inequality and their policy implications. Loury argued that orthodox economic theories were too individualistic, focusing exclusively on individual human capital and on the creation of a level field for competition based on such skills. By themselves, legal prohibitions against employers' racial tastes and implementation of equal opportunity programs would not reduce racial inequalities. The latter could go on forever, according to Loury, for two reasons—first, the inherited poverty of black parents, which would be transmitted to their children in the form of lower material resources and educational opportunities; second, the poorer connections of young black workers to the labor market and their lack of information about opportunities:

> The merit notion that, in a free society, each individual will rise to the level justified by his or her competence conflicts with the observation that no one travels that road entirely alone. The social context within which individual maturation occurs strongly conditions what otherwise equally competent individuals can achieve. This implies that absolute equality of opportunity, . . . is an ideal that cannot be achieved. (Loury 1977, p. 176)

Loury cited with approval the sociological literature on intergenerational mobility and inheritance of race as illustrating his anti-individualist argument. However, he did not go on to develop the concept of social capital in any detail. He seems to have run across the idea in the context of his polemic against orthodox labor economics, but he mentions it only once in his original article and then in rather tentative terms (Loury 1977). The concept captured the differential access to opportunities through social connections for minority and nonminority youth, but we do not find here any systematic treatment of its relations to other forms of capital.

Loury's work paved the way, however, for Coleman's more refined analysis of the same process, namely the role of social capital in the creation of human capital. In his initial analysis of the concept, Coleman acknowledges Loury's contribution as well as those of economist Ben-Porath and sociologists Nan Lin and Mark Granovetter. Curiously, Coleman does not mention Bourdieu, although his analysis of the possible uses of social capital for the acquisition of educational credentials closely parallels that pioneered by the French sociologist.[1] Coleman defined social capital by its function as "a variety of entities with two elements in common: They all consist of some aspect of social structures, and they facilitate certain action of actors—whether persons or corporate actors—within the structure" (Coleman 1988a: p. S98, 1990, p. 302).

---

[1] The closest equivalent to human capital in Bourdieu's analysis is embodied cultural capital, which is defined as the habitus of cultural practices, knowledge, and demeanors learned through exposure to role models in the family and other environments (Bourdieu 1979).

This rather vague definition opened the way for relabeling a number of different and even contradictory processes as social capital. Coleman himself started that proliferation by including under the term some of the mechanisms that generated social capital (such as reciprocity expectations and group enforcement of norms); the consequences of its possession (such as privileged access to information); and the "appropriable" social organization that provided the context for both sources and effects to materialize. Resources obtained through social capital have, from the point of view of the recipient, the character of a gift. Thus, it is important to distinguish the resources themselves from the ability to obtain them by virtue of membership in different social structures, a distinction explicit in Bourdieu but obscured in Coleman. Equating social capital with the resources acquired through it can easily lead to tautological statements.[2]

Equally important is the distinction between the motivations of recipients and of donors in exchanges mediated by social capital. Recipients' desire to gain access to valuable assets is readily understandable. More complex are the motivations of the donors, who are requested to make these assets available without any immediate return. Such motivations are plural and deserve analysis because they are the core processes that the concept of social capital seeks to capture. Thus, a systematic treatment of the concept must distinguish among: *(a)* the possessors of social capital (those making claims); *(b)* the sources of social capital (those agreeing to these demands); *(c)* the resources themselves. These three elements are often mixed in discussions of the concept following Coleman, thus setting the stage for confusion in the uses and scope of the term.

Despite these limitations, Coleman's essays have the undeniable merit of introducing and giving visibility to the concept in American sociology, highlighting its importance for the acquisition of human capital, and identifying some of the mechanisms through which it is generated. In this last respect, his discussion of closure is particularly enlightening. Closure means the existence of sufficient ties between a certain number of people to guarantee the observance of norms. For example, the possibility of malfeasance within the tightly knit community of Jewish diamond traders in New York City is minimized by the dense ties among its members and the ready threat of ostracism against violators. The existence of such a strong norm is then appropriable by all members of the community, facilitating transactions without recourse to cumbersome legal contracts (Coleman 1988a: S99).

After Bourdieu, Loury, and Coleman, a number of theoretical analyses of social capital have been published. In 1990, W.E. Baker defined the concept as "a

---

[2] Saying, for example, that student A has social capital because he obtained access to a large tuition loan from his kin and that student B does not because she failed to do so neglects the possibility that B's kin network is equally or more motivated to come to her aid but simply lacks the means to do. Defining social capital as equivalent with the resources thus obtained is tantamount to saying that the successful succeed. This circularity is more evident in applications of social capital that define it as a property of collectivities. These are reviewed below.

resource that actors derive from specific social structures and then use to pursue their interests; it is created by changes in the relationship among actors" (Baker 1990, p. 619). More broadly, M. Schiff defines the term as "the set of elements of the social structure that affects relations among people and are inputs or arguments of the production and/or utility function" (Schiff 1992, p. 161). Burt sees it as "friends, colleagues, and more general contacts through whom you receive opportunities to use your financial and human capital" (Burt 1992, p. 9). Whereas Coleman and Loury had emphasized dense networks as a necessary condition for the emergence of social capital, Burt highlights the opposite situation. In his view, it is the relative absence of ties, labeled "structural holes," that facilitates individual mobility. This is so because dense networks tend to convey redundant information, while weaker ties can be sources of new knowledge and resources.

Despite these differences, the consensus is growing in the literature that social capital stands for the ability of actors to secure benefits by virtue of membership in social networks or other social structures. This is the sense in which it has been more commonly applied in the empirical literature although, as we will see, the potential uses to which it is put vary greatly.

SOURCES OF SOCIAL CAPITAL

Both Bourdieu and Coleman emphasize the intangible character of social capital relative to other forms. Whereas economic capital is in people's bank accounts and human capital is inside their heads, social capital inheres in the structure of their relationships. To possess social capital, a person must be related to others, and it is those others, not himself, who are the actual source of his or her advantage. As mentioned before, the motivation of others to make resources available on concessionary terms is not uniform. At the broadest level, one may distinguish between consummatory versus instrumental motivations to do so.

As examples of the first, people may pay their debts in time, give alms to charity, and obey traffic rules because they feel an obligation to behave in this manner. The internalized norms that make such behaviors possible are then appropriable by others as a resource. In this instance, the holders of social capital are other members of the community who can extend loans without fear of non-payment, benefit from private charity, or send their kids to play in the street without concern. Coleman (1988a: S104) refers to this source in his analysis of norms and sanctions: "Effective norms that inhibit crime make it possible to walk freely outside at night in a city and enable old persons to leave their houses without fear for their safety." As is well known, an excessive emphasis on this process of norm internalization led to the oversocialized conception of human action in sociology so trenchantly criticized by Wrong (1961).

An approach closer to the undersocialized view of human nature in modern economics sees social capital as primarily the accumulation of obligations from others according to the norm of reciprocity. In this version, donors provide privileged access to resources in the expectation that they will be fully repaid in the future. This accumulation of social chits differs from purely economic exchange in two aspects. First, the currency with which obligations are repaid may be different from that with which they were incurred in the first place and may be as intangible as the granting of approval or allegiance. Second, the timing of the repayment is unspecified. Indeed, if a schedule of repayments exists, the transaction is more appropriately defined as market exchange than as one mediated by social capital. This instrumental treatment of the term is quite familiar in sociology, dating back to the classical analysis of social exchange by Simmel ([1902a] 1964), the more recent ones by Homans (1961) and Blau (1964), and extensive work on the sources and dynamics of reciprocity by authors of the rational action school (Schiff 1992, Coleman 1994).

Two other sources of social capital exist that fit the consummatory versus instrumental dichotomy, but in a different way. The first finds its theoretical underpinnings in Marx's analysis of emergent class consciousness in the industrial proletariat. By being thrown together in a common situation, workers learn to identify with each other and support each other's initiatives. This solidarity is not the result of norm introjection during childhood, but is an emergent product of a common fate (Marx [1894] 1967, Marx & Engels [1848] 1947). For this reason, the altruistic dispositions of actors in these situations are not universal but are bounded by the limits of their community. Other members of the same community can then appropriate such dispositions and the actions that follow as their source of social capital.

Bounded solidarity is the term used in the recent literature to refer to this mechanism. It is the source of social capital that leads wealthy members of a church to anonymously endow church schools and hospitals; members of a suppressed nationality to voluntarily join life-threatening military activities in its defense; and industrial proletarians to take part in protest marches or sympathy strikes in support of their fellows. Identification with one's own group, sect, or community can be a powerful motivational force. Coleman refers to extreme forms of this mechanism as "zeal" and defines them as an effective antidote to free-riding by others in collective movements (Coleman 1990, pp. 273–82; Portes & Sensenbrenner 1993).

The final source of social capital finds its classical roots in Durkheim's ([1893] 1984) theory of social integration and the sanctioning capacity of group rituals. As in the case of reciprocity exchanges, the motivation of donors of socially mediated gifts is instrumental, but in this case, the expectation of repayment is not based on knowledge of the recipient, but on the insertion of both actors in a common social structure. The embedding of a transaction into such structure has two consequences. First, the donor's returns may come not directly from the recipient but from the collectivity as a whole in the form of status, honor, or approval. Second, the collectivity itself acts as guarantor that whatever debts are incurred will be repaid.

As an example of the first consequence, a member of an ethnic group may endow a scholarship for young co-ethnic students, thereby expecting not

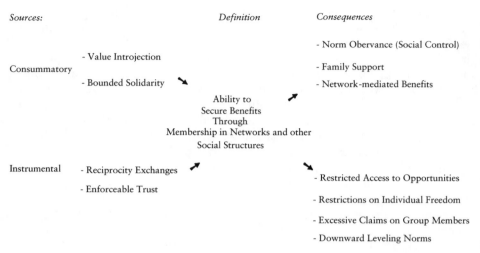

FIGURE 3.1 Actual and Potential Gains and Losses in Transactions Mediated by Social Capital

repayment from recipients but rather approval and status in the collectivity. The students' social capital is not contingent on direct knowledge of their benefactor, but on membership in the same group. As an example of the second effect, a banker may extend a loan without collateral to a member of the same religious community in full expectation of repayment because of the threat of community sanctions and ostracism. In other words, trust exists in this situation precisely because obligations are enforceable, not through recourse to law or violence but through the power of the community.

In practice, these two effects of enforceable trust are commonly mixed, as when someone extends a favor to a fellow member in expectation of both guaranteed repayment and group approval. As a source of social capital, enforceable trust is hence appropriable by both donors and recipients: For recipients, it obviously facilitates access to resources; for donors, it yields approval and expedites transactions because it ensures against malfeasance. No lawyer need apply for business transactions underwritten by this source of social capital. The left side of Figure 3.1 summarizes the discussion in this section. Keeping these distinctions in mind is important to avoid confusing consummatory and instrumental motivations or mixing simple dyadic exchanges with those embedded in larger social structures that guarantee their predictability and course.

EFFECTS OF SOCIAL CAPITAL: RECENT RESEARCH

Just as the sources of social capital are plural so are its consequences. The empirical literature includes applications of the concept as a predictor of, among others, school attrition and academic performance, children's intellectual development, sources of employment and occupational attainment, juvenile delinquency and its prevention, and immigrant and ethnic enterprise.[3] Diversity of effects goes beyond the broad set of specific dependent variables to which social capital has been applied to encompass, in addition, the character and meaning of the expected consequences. A review of the literature makes it possible to distinguish three basic functions of social capital, applicable in a variety of contents: (*a*) as a source of social control; (*b*) as a source of family support; (*c*) as a source of benefits through extrafamilial networks.

As examples of the first function, we find a series of studies that focus on rule enforcement. The social capital created by tight community networks is useful to parents, teachers, and police authorities as they seek to maintain discipline and promote compliance among those under their charge. Sources of this type of social capital are commonly found in bounded solidarity and enforceable trust, and its main result is to render formal or overt controls unnecessary. The process is exemplified by Zhou & Bankston's study of the tightly knit Vietnamese community of New Orleans:

> Both parents and children are constantly observed as under a "Vietnamese microscope." If a child flunks out or drops out of a school, or if a boy falls into a gang or a girl becomes pregnant without getting married, he or she brings shame not only to himself or herself but also to the family. (Zhou & Bankston 1996, p. 207)

The same function is apparent in Hagan et al's (1995) analysis of right-wing extremism among East German youth. Labeling right-wing extremism a subterranean tradition in German society, these authors seek to explain the rise of that ideology, commonly accompanied by anomic wealth aspirations among German adolescents. These tendencies are particularly strong among those from the formerly communist eastern states. That trend is explained as the joint outcome of the removal of social controls (low social capital), coupled with the long deprivations endured by East Germans. Incorporation into the West has brought about new uncertainties and the loosening of social integration, thus allowing German subterranean cultural traditions to re-emerge.

Social control is also the focus of several earlier essays by Coleman, who laments the disappearance of those informal family and community structures that produced this type of social capital; Coleman calls for the creation of formal institutions to take their place. This was the thrust of Coleman's 1992 presidential address to the American Sociological Association, in which he traced the decline of "primordial" institutions based on the family and their replacement by purposively constructed organizations. In his view, modern sociology's task is to

---

[3] The following review does not aim at an exhaustive coverage of the empirical literature. That task has been rendered obsolete by the advent of computerized topical searches. My purpose instead is to document the principal types of application of the concept in the literature and to highlight their interrelationships.

guide this process of social engineering that will substitute obsolete forms of control based on primordial ties with rationally devised material and status incentives (Coleman 1988b, 1993). The function of social capital for social control is also evident whenever the concept is discussed in conjunction with the law (Smart 1993, Weede 1992). It is as well the central focus when it is defined as a property of collectivities such as cities or nations. This latter approach, associated mainly with the writings of political scientists, is discussed in a following section.

The influence of Coleman's writings is also clear in the second function of social capital, namely as a source of parental and kin support. Intact families and those where one parent has the primary task of rearing children possess more of this form of social capital than do single-parent families or those where both parents work. The primary beneficiaries of this resource are, of course, the children whose education and personality development are enriched accordingly. Coleman (1988a: S110) thus cites approvingly the practice of Asian immigrant mothers who not only stay at home but often purchase second copies of school textbooks to help their offspring with their homework.

A second example of this function is in McLanahan & Sandefur's monograph *Growing Up with a Single Parent* (1994), which examines the consequences of single parenthood for school achievement and attrition, teenage pregnancy, and other adolescent outcomes. Social capital tends to be lower for children in single-parent families because they lack the benefit of a second at-home parent and because they tend to change residences more often, leading to fewer ties to other adults in the community. This deficit is not the only causal factor but certainly plays an important role in bringing about less desirable educational and personality outcomes among single-parent children. Along the same lines, Parcel & Menaghan (1994a,b) have conducted extensive quantitative analyses of national surveys to examine the effect of parental work on children's cognitive and social development. They conclude that parental intellectual and other resources contribute to the forms of family capital useful in facilitating positive children outcomes, but that common beliefs about a negative effect of maternal work during early infancy are overgeneralized.

A third example is Hao's (1994) analysis of kin support and out-of-wedlock motherhood. Like financial capital, social capital influences transfers made by parents to daughters and behavioral outcomes such as teen pregnancy, educational attainment, and labor force participation. Social capital is greater in two-parent families, those with fewer children, and those where parents have high aspirations for their young. These conditions foster greater parental attention, more hours spent with children, and the emergence of an achievement orientation among adolescents.

Two interesting final examples highlight the role of family support as a counterweight to the loss of community bounds. In their longitudinal study of adolescents in Toronto, Hagan et al (1996) confirm Coleman's finding about the deleterious effect of multiple family moves on children's emotional adjustment and educational achievement. Leaving a community tends to destroy established bonds, thus depriving family and children of a major source of social capital. These authors find, however, an interaction effect leading to an exacerbation of the loss among children whose parents provide them with weak support and to a partial neutralization among those in the opposite situation. Parental support leads to higher educational achievement, both directly and indirectly through compensating for the loss of community among migrants.

Along the same lines, Gold (1995) highlights the change in parental roles among Israeli immigrant families in the United States. In Israel, close community bonds facilitate supervision and rearing of children because other adults know the young and assume responsibility for their well-being. In the more anomic American environment, mothers are assigned the role of compensating for the lack of community ties with exclusive dedication to their children. Thus, female labor force participation is much greater in Israel than among Israelis in the United States as mothers endeavor to preserve an appropriate cultural environment for their young. Note that in both of these examples, reduction of social capital in its first form—community social bonds and control—is partially compensated by an increase of social capital in its second form, familial support.

By far, however, the most common function attributed to social capital is as a source of network-mediated benefits beyond the immediate family. This definition comes closest to that of Bourdieu (1979, 1980), for whom parental support of children's development is a source of cultural capital, while social capital refers to assets gained through membership in networks. This third function is illustrated by Anheier et al's (1995) use of blockmodeling techniques to map social ties among artists and intellectuals in the German city of Cologne. Results of their analysis show very strong networks among core members of the city's intellectual elite along with more restricted access to them for those in peripheral and commercial pursuits. From a methodological standpoint, this article is one of the most sophisticated applications of Bourdieu's ideas to the sociology of culture.

Yet, the most common use of this third form of social capital is in the field of stratification. It is frequently invoked here as an explanation of access to employment, mobility through occupational ladders, and entrepreneurial success. The idea that connections are instrumental in furthering individual mobility is central to Loury's analysis, as seen previously, and is also found among a number of authors who do not conceptualize it explicitly as social capital. Granovetter (1974), for example, coined the term "strength of weak ties" to refer to the power of indirect influences outside the immediate circle of family and close friends to serve as an informal employment referral system. The idea was original because it ran contrary to the commonsense notion that dense networks such as those available through family circles would be most effective in finding jobs. Almost two decades later, Burt (1992) built on Granovetter's insight by developing the concept of "structural holes." As we have seen, Burt did employ the term social capital and, like Bourdieu's, his definition is instrumental. In Burt's case, however, social capital is based on the relative paucity of network ties rather than on their density.

Another noteworthy early effort was by Nan Lin, Walter Ensel, and John C. Vaughn (1981), *Social Resources and Strength of Ties*, which points precisely in the opposite direction. Although Lin and his colleagues did not use the term social capital, Coleman (1988a) cites their work approvingly because of a common emphasis on dense networks as a resource. This alternative stance which, in contrast to Granovetter and Burt, may be labeled "the strength of strong ties" is also evident in other areas of the social-networks-and-mobility literature. One of the most noteworthy is the study of immigrant and ethnic entrepreneurship, in which networks and the social capital that flows through them are consistently identified as a key resource for the creation of small businesses. Light, for example, has emphasized the importance of rotating credit associations (RCAs) for the capitalization of Asian immigrant firms in the United States. RCAs are informal groups that meet periodically, with every member contributing a set amount to a common pool that is received by each in turn. Social capital in this case comes from the trust that each participant has in the continuing contribution of others even after they receive the pooled funds. Without such trust, no one will contribute and each will be deprived of this effective means to gain access to finance (Light 1984, Light & Bonacich 1988).

The role of social networks is equally important in studies of ethnic business enclaves and ethnic niches. Enclaves are dense concentrations of immigrant or ethnic firms that employ a significant proportion of their co-ethnic labor force and develop a distinctive physical presence in urban space. Studies of New York's Chinatown (Zhou 1992); of Miami's Little Havana (Portes 1987, Portes & Stepick 1993, Perez 1992); and of Los Angeles' Koreatown (Light & Bonacich 1988, Nee et al 1994) consistently highlight the role of community networks as a source of vital resources for these ethnic firms. Such resources include but are not limited to start-up capital; others are tips about business opportunities, access to markets, and a pliant and disciplined labor force.

Ethnic niches emerge when a group is able to colonize a particular sector of employment in such a way that members have privileged access to new job openings, while restricting that of outsiders. Examples documented in the literature range from restaurant work and garment factories all the way to police and fire departments and certain branches of the New York and Miami civil services (Waters 1994, Doeringer & Moss 1986, Bailey & Waldinger 1991, Waldinger 1996, Stepick 1989). As in the case of enclaves, mobility opportunities through niches are entirely network-driven. Members find jobs for others, teach them the necessary skills, and supervise their performance. The power of network chains is such that entry level openings are frequently filled by contacting kin and friends in remote foreign locations rather than by tapping other available local workers (Sassen 1995).

The opposite of this situation is the dearth of social connections in certain impoverished communities or their truncated character. Since publication of Carol Stack's *All Our Kin* (1974), sociologists know that everyday survival in poor urban communities frequently depends on close interaction with kin and friends in similar situations. The problem is that such ties seldom reach beyond the inner city, thus depriving their inhabitants of sources of information about employment opportunities elsewhere and ways to attain them. Wacquant & Wilson (1989) and Wilson (1987, 1996) also emphasize how the departure of both industrial employment and middle-class families from black inner city areas have left the remaining population bereft of social capital, a situation leading to its extremely high levels of unemployment and welfare dependency.

The same point is central to Mercer Sullivan's (1989) comparative ethnographies of Puerto Rican, black, and working-class white youth in three New York communities. Sullivan challenges blanket assertions about youth subcultures as determinants of deviant behavior by showing that access to regular jobs and participation in deviant activities are both network mediated. As Granovetter (1974) had noted earlier, teenagers seldom find jobs; instead jobs come to them through the mediation of parents and other adults in their immediate community. Sullivan shows how such networks are much feebler in the case of black youth because of the scarcity of occupants of influential positions in the adult generation. Thrown back on their own resources, black adolescents are seldom able to compete successfully for good regular jobs; thus they become available for alternative forms of income earning.

In her analysis of teenage pregnancy in Baltimore's ghetto, Fernandez-Kelly (1995) notes how the dense but truncated networks of inner-city black families not only cut off members from information about the outside world, but simultaneously support alternative cultural styles that make access to mainstream employment even more difficult. In this isolated context, teenage pregnancy is not the outgrowth of carelessness or excess sexuality but, more commonly, a deliberate means to gain adult status and a measure of independence.

Similarly, Stanton-Salazar & Dornbush (1995) have investigated the relationship between outside social networks and academic achievement and aspirations among Mexican high school students in the San Francisco area. They find positive correlations among these variables, although the strongest associations are with bilingualism, suggesting the role of cultural capital in status attainment. In a related article, Valenzuela & Dornbush (1994) highlight the role of family networks and a familistic orientation in the academic achievement of Mexican-origin students. Paralleling the studies of Hagan et al (1996) and Gold (1995), these articles suggest that immigrant families compensate for the absence of the third form of social capital—outside networks—with an emphasis on social capital in the form of familial support, including preservation of the cultural orientations of their home country.

As in the case of the various sources of social capital outlined in the last section, it is also important to keep in mind the differing functions of the concept both to avoid confusion and to facilitate study of their interrelationships. It is possible, for example, that social capital in the form of social control may clash with social capital in the form of network-mediated benefits, if the latter consists precisely on the ability to bypass existing norms. The capacity of authorities to enforce rules (social control) can thus be jeopardized by the existence of tight networks whose function is precisely to facilitate violation of those rules for private benefit. These paradoxical outcomes point to the need of a closer look at the actual and potential gainers and losers in transactions mediated by social capital. The right side of Figure 3.1 summarizes the previous discussion and that of the next section.

NEGATIVE SOCIAL CAPITAL[4]

The research literature on social capital strongly emphasizes its positive consequences. Indeed it is our sociological bias to see good things emerging out of sociability; bad things are more commonly associated with the behavior of homo economicus. However, the same mechanisms appropriable by individuals and groups as social capital can have other, less desirable consequences. It is important to emphasize them for two reasons: first, to avoid the trap of presenting community networks, social control, and collective sanctions as unmixed blessings; second, to keep the analysis within the bounds of serious sociological analysis rather than moralizing statements. Recent studies have identified at least four negative consequences of social capital: exclusion of outsiders, excess claims on group members, restrictions on individual freedoms, and downward leveling norms, I summarize them next.

First, the same strong ties that bring benefits to members of a group commonly enable it to bar others from access. Waldinger (1995) describes the tight control exercised by white ethnics—descendants of Italian, Irish, and Polish immigrants—over the construction trades and the fire and police unions of New York. Other cases include the growing control of the produce business by Korean immigrants in several East Coast cities, the traditional monopoly of Jewish merchants over the New York diamond trade, and the dominance of Cubans over numerous sectors of the Miami economy. In each instance, social capital generated by bounded solidarity and trust are at the core of the group's economic advance. But, as Waldinger (1995, p. 557) points out, "the same social relations that . . . enhance the ease and efficiency of economic exchanges among community members implicitly restrict outsiders."

Ethnic groups are not the only ones that use social capital for economic advantage. Two centuries ago, Adam Smith ([1776] 1979, p. 232) complained that meetings of merchants inevitably ended up as a conspiracy against the public. The public, of course, are all those excluded from the networks and mutual knowledge linking the colluding groups. Substitute for "merchants" white building contractors, ethnic union bosses, or immigrant entrepreneurs, and the contemporary relevance of Smith's point becomes evident.

The second negative effect of social capital is the obverse of the first because group or community closure may, under certain circumstances, prevent the success of business initiatives by their members. In his study of the rise of

---

[4]   This section is partially based on Portes & Sensenbrenner (1993) and Portes & Landolt (1996).

commercial enterprises in Bali, Geertz observed how successful entrepreneurs were constantly assaulted by job and loan-seeking kinsmen. These claims were buttressed by strong norms enjoining mutual assistance within the extended family and among community members in general (Geertz 1963). The result was to turn promising enterprises into welfare hotels, checking their economic expansion.

Granovetter (1995), who calls attention to this example, notes that it is an instance of the problem that classic economic development theory identified among traditional enterprises. Weber ([1922] 1965) made the same point when he stressed the importance of impersonal economic transactions guided by the principle of universalism as one of the major reasons for Puritan entrepreneurial success. Thus, cozy intergroup relations of the kind found in highly solidary communities can give rise to a gigantic free-riding problem, as less diligent members enforce on the more successful all kinds of demands backed by a shared normative structure. For claimants, their social capital consists precisely of privileged access to the resources of fellow members. In the process, opportunities for entrepreneurial accumulation and success are dissipated.[5]

Third, community or group participation necessarily creates demands for conformity. In a small town or village, all neighbors know each other, one can get supplies on credit at the corner store, and children play freely in the streets under the watchful eyes of other adults. The level of social control in such settings is strong and also quite restrictive of personal freedoms, which is the reason why the young and the more independent-minded have always left. Boissevain (1974) reports such a situation in his study of village life in the island of Malta. Dense, "multiplex"[6] networks tying inhabitants together created the ground for an intense community life and strong enforcement of local norms. The privacy and autonomy of individuals were reduced accordingly.

This is an expression of the age-old dilemma between community solidarity and individual freedom analyzed by Simmel ([1902] 1964) in his classic essay on "The Metropolis and Mental Life." In that essay, Simmel came out in favor of personal autonomy and responsibility. At present, the pendulum has swung back, and a number of authors are calling for stronger community networks and norm observance in order to re-establish social control. This may be desirable in many

---

[5] A related problem has been observed in inner city neighborhoods where kin networks form a key survival resource through mutual assistance and ready access to favors and small loans. By the same token, the norm that dictates that incoming resources (such as a money prize) be shared with relatives and friends effectively prevents any sustained accumulation or entrepreneurial investment by individuals. Those wishing to pursue that route must distance themselves from their former partners (see Uehara 1990, Fernandez-Kelly 1995, Stack 1974).

[6] Multiplexity refers to overlapping social networks where the same people are linked together across different roles. In small towns, for example, the same individuals may be simultaneously kin, neighbors, and co-workers thus intensifying the intensity and capacity for mutual monitoring of their ties (Boissevain 1974, p. 31–33).

instances, but the downside of this function of social capital must also be kept in mind.

Constraints on individual freedom may be responsible for Rumbaut's findings that high levels of familistic solidarity among recent immigrant students are negatively related to four different educational outcomes, including grades and standardized test scores. According to this author, "family ties bind, but sometimes these bonds constrain rather than facilitate particular outcomes" (Rumbaut 1977, p. 39).

Fourth, there are situations in which group solidarity is cemented by a common experience of adversity and opposition to mainstream society. In these instances, individual success stories undermine group cohesion because the latter is precisely grounded on the alleged impossibility of such occurrences. The result is downward leveling norms that operate to keep members of a downtrodden group in place and force the more ambitious to escape from it. In his ethnographic research among Puerto Rican crack dealers in the Bronx, Bourgois (1991, 1995) calls attention to the local version of this process, which singles out for attack individuals seeking to join the middle-class mainstream. He reports the views of one of his informants:

> When you see someone go downtown and get a good job, if they be Puerto Rican, you see them fix up their hair and put some contact lenses in their eyes. Then they fit in and they do it! I have seen it!. . . . Look at all the people in that building, they all "turn-overs." They people who want to be white. Man, if you call them in Spanish it wind up a problem. I mean like take the name Pedro—I'm just telling you this is an example—Pedro be saying (imitating a whitened accent) "My name is Peter." Where do you get Peter from Pedro? (Bourgois 1991, p. 32)

Similar examples are reported by Stepick (1992) in his study of Haitian American youth in Miami and by Suarez-Orozco (1987) and Matute-Bianchi (1986, 1991) among Mexican-American teenagers in Southern California. In each instance, the emergence of downward leveling norms has been preceded by lengthy periods, often lasting generations, in which the mobility of a particular group has been blocked by outside discrimination. That historical experience underlines the emergence of an oppositional stance toward the mainstream and a solidarity grounded in a common experience of subordination. Once in place, however, this normative outlook has the effect of helping perpetuate the very situation that it decries.

Notice that social capital, in the form of social control, is still present in these situations, but its effects are exactly the opposite of those commonly celebrated in the literature. Whereas bounded solidarity and trust provide the sources for socioeconomic ascent and entrepreneurial development among some groups, among others they have exactly the opposite effect. Sociability cuts both ways. While it can be the source of public goods, such as those celebrated by Coleman, Loury, and others, it can also lead to public "bads." Mafia families, prostitution and gambling rings, and youth gangs offer so many examples of how embeddedness in social structures can be turned to less than socially desirable ends. The point is particularly important as we turn to the more recent and more celebratory versions of social capital.

SOCIAL CAPITAL AS A FEATURE OF COMMUNITIES AND NATIONS[7]

As seen in previous sections, sociological analyses of social capital have been grounded on relationships between actors or between an individual actor and a group. Throughout, the focus has been on the potential benefit accruing to actors because of their insertion into networks or broader social structures. An interesting conceptual twist was introduced by political scientists who equate social capital with the level of "civicness" in communities such as towns, cities, or even entire countries. For Robert Putnam, the most prominent advocate of this approach, social capital means "features of social organizations, such as networks, norms, and trust, that facilitate action and cooperation for mutual benefit." The collective character of this version of the concept is evident in the next sentence: "Working together is easier in a community blessed with a substantial stock of social capital" (Putnam 1993, pp. 35–36).

In practice, this stock is equated with the level of associational involvement and participatory behavior in a community and is measured by such indicators as newspaper reading, membership in voluntary associations, and expressions of trust in political authorities. Putnam is not shy about the expected reach and significance of this version of social capital:

> This insight turns out to have powerful practical implications for many issues on the American national agenda—for how we might overcome the poverty and violence of South Central Los Angeles . . . or nurture the fledgling democracies of the former Soviet empire. (Putnam 1993: 36, 1996)

The prospect of a simple diagnosis of the country's problems and a ready solution to them has attracted widespread public attention. Putnam's article, "Bowling Alone: America's Declining Social Capital," published in the *Journal of Democracy* in 1995, created something of a sensation, earning for its author a tête-à-tête with President Clinton and a profile in *People* magazine. The nostalgic image evoked by the lonely bowler resonated with many powerful members of the American establishment and even inspired passages in Clinton's State of the Union address in 1995 (Pollitt 1996, Lemann 1996). Putnam buttressed his case with figures about rapidly declining levels of voting and membership in such organizations as the PTA, the Elks Club, the League of Women Voters, and the Red Cross. He then identified the immediate determinant of the decreasing

7   This section is partially based on Portes & Landolt (1996).

national stock of social capital, namely the passage from the scene of the civic generation active during the 1920s and 1930s and the succession of an uncivic generation—the baby boomers—born and raised after World War II:

> . . . the very decades that have seen a national deterioration in social capital are the same decades during which the numerical dominance of a trusting and civic generation has been replaced by this domination of post-civic cohorts. . . . Thus a generational analysis leads almost inevitably to the conclusion that the national slump in trust and engagement is likely to continue. (Putnam 1996, pp. 45–46)

Critics have focused on the question of whether voluntarism and civic spirit have actually declined in America and on the unacknowledged class bias in Putnam's thesis. Lay reviewers such as Lemann in *The Atlantic Monthly* and Pollitt in *The Nation* questioned whether American civic virtue is on the wane or has simply taken new forms different from the old-style organizations cited in Putnam's article. They also note the elitist stance of the argument, where responsibility for the alleged decline of social capital is put squarely on the leisure behavior of the masses, rather than on the economic and political changes wrought by the corporate and governmental establishment. In her trenchant review of Putnam's thesis, Skocpol (1996, p. 25) also stresses this point:

> How ironic it would be if, after pulling out of locally rooted associations, the very business and professional elites who blazed the path toward local civic disengagement were now to turn around and successfully argue that the less privileged Americans they left behind are the ones who must repair the nation's social connectedness . . . .

These critiques are valid but do not address a more fundamental problem with Putnam's argument, namely its logical circularity. As a property of communities and nations rather than individuals, social capital is simultaneously a cause and an effect. It leads to positive outcomes, such as economic development and less crime, and its existence is inferred from the same outcomes. Cities that are well governed and moving ahead economically do so because they have high social capital; poorer cities lack in this civic virtue. This circularity is well illustrated in passages like the following:

> Some regions of Italy . . . have many active community organizations. . . . These "civic communities" value solidarity, civic participation, and integrity. And here democracy works. At the other end are "uncivic" regions, like Calabria and Sicily, aptly characterized by the French term *incivisme*. The very concept of citizenship is stunted here. (Putnam 1993, p. 36)

In other words, if your town is "civic," it does civic things; if it is "uncivic," it does not.

Tautology in this definition of social capital results from two analytic decisions; first, starting with the effect (i.e. successful versus unsuccessful cities) and working retroactively to find out what distinguishes them: second, trying to explain all of the observed differences. In principle, the exercise of seeking to identify post-factum causes of events is legitimate, provided that alternative explanations are considered. In fairness to Putnam, he does this in his analysis of differences between the well-governed towns of the Italian north and the poorly governed ones of the south (Putnam 1993, Lemann 1996). Such retroactive explanations can only be tentative, however, because the analyst can never rule out other potential causes and because these explanations remain untested in cases other than those considered.

More insidious, however, is the search for full explanation of all observed differences because the quest for this prime determinant often ends up by relabeling the original problem to be explained. This happens as the elimination of exceptions reduces the logical space between alleged cause and effect so that the final predictive statement is either a truism or circular.[8] In Putnam's analysis of Italian cities, such factors as differences in levels of economic development, education, or political preferences proved to be imperfect predictors. Thus, the search for a prime determinant gradually narrowed to something labeled (following Machiavelli) *vertu civile* (civic virtue). It is present in those cities whose inhabitants vote, obey the law, and cooperate with each other and whose leaders are honest and committed to the public good (Putnam 1993, 1995).

The theory then goes on to assert that civic virtue is the key factor differentiating well-governed communities from poorly governed ones. It could hardly be otherwise given the definition of the causal variable. Thus, cities where everyone cooperates in maintaining good government are well governed. To avoid saying the same thing twice, the analyst of social capital must observe certain logical cautions: first, separating the definition of the concept, theoretically and empirically, from its alleged effects; second, establishing some controls for directionality so that the presence of social capital is demonstrably prior to the outcomes that it is expected to produce; third, controlling for the presence of other factors than can account for both social capital and its alleged effects; fourth, identifying the historical origins of community social capital in a systematic manner.

This task is doable, but time-consuming. Instead, the intellectual journey that transformed social capital from an individual property into a feature of cities and countries tended to disregard these logical criteria. The journey was fast, explaining major social outcomes by relabeling them with a novel term and then

---

[8] The method of analytic induction, popular in American sociology in the 1940s and 1950s, consisted precisely in this process of seeking to explain all cases and gradually eliminate all exceptions. It went rapidly out of favor when it was discovered that it basically gave rise to tautologies by redefining the essential characteristics of the phenomenon to be explained. The only way of guaranteeing closure or zero exceptions turns out to be an explanation that is a logical corollary of the effect to be explained. On analytic induction, see Turner (1953) and Robinson (1951).

employing the same term to formulate sweeping policy prescriptions. While I believe that the greatest theoretical promise of social capital lies at the individual level—exemplified by the analyses of Bourdieu and Coleman—there is nothing intrinsically wrong with redefining it as a structural property of large aggregates. This conceptual departure requires, however, more care and theoretical refinement than that displayed so far.[9]

CONCLUSION

Current enthusiasm for the concept reviewed in this article and its proliferating applications to different social problems and processes is not likely to abate soon. This popularity is partially warranted because the concept calls attention to real and important phenomena. However, it is also partially exaggerated for two reasons. First, the set of processes encompassed by the concept are not new and have been studied under other labels in the past. Calling them social capital is, to a large extent, just a means of presenting them in a more appealing conceptual garb. Second, there is little ground to believe that social capital will provide a ready remedy for major social problems, as promised by its bolder proponents. Recent proclamations to that effect merely restate the original problems and have not been accompanied so far by any persuasive account of how to bring about the desired stocks of public civicness.

At the individual level, the processes alluded to by the concept cut both ways. Social ties can bring about greater control over wayward behavior and provide privileged access to resources; they can also restrict individual freedoms and bar outsiders from gaining access to the same resources through particularistic preferences. For this reason, it seems preferable to approach these manifold processes as social facts to be studied in all their complexity, rather than as examples of a value. A more dispassionate stance will allow analysts to consider all facets of the event in question and prevent turning the ensuing literature into an unmitigated celebration of community. Communitarian advocacy is a legitimate political stance; it is not good social science. As a label for the positive effects of sociability, social capital has, in my view, a place in theory and research provided that its different sources and effects are recognized and that their downsides are examined with equal attention.

---

[9]   A promising effort in this direction has been made by Woolcock (1997), who seeks to apply the concept of social capital to the analysis of national and community development in Third World countries. After an extensive review of the literature, he notes that "definitions of social capital should focus primarily on its sources rather than its consequences since long-term benefits, if and when they occur, are the result of a combination of different . . . types of social relations, combinations whose relative importance will, in all likelihood, shift over time" (Woolcock 1997, p. 35).

ACKNOWLEDGMENTS

I acknowledge the assistance of Patricia Landolt and Clemencia Cosentino in the preparation of the article and the comments on an earlier version from John Logan and Robert K. Merton. Responsibility for the contents is exclusively mine.
Visit the Annual Reviews home page at http://www.AnnualReviews.org.

Alejandro Portes: Biographical Sketch

Alejandro Portes is professor of sociology at Princeton University and faculty associate of the Woodrow Wilson School of Public Affairs. He formerly taught at Johns Hopkins where he held the John Dewey Chair in Arts and Sciences, Duke University, and the University of Texas-Austin. In 1997 he held the Emilio Bacardi distinguished professorship at the University of Miami. In the same year he was elected president of the American Sociological Association. Born in Havana, Cuba, he came to the United States in 1960. He was educated at the University of Havana, Catholic University of Argentina, and Creighton University. He received his MA and PhD from the University of Wisconsin-Madison.

Portes is the author of some 200 articles and chapters on national development, international migration, Latin American and Caribbean urbanization, and economic sociology. His most recent books include *City on the Edge, the Transformation of Miami* (winner of the Robert Park award for best book in urban sociology and of the Anthony Leeds award for best book in urban anthropology in 1995); *The New Second Generation* (Russell Sage Foundation 1996); *Caribbean Cities* (Johns Hopkins University Press); and *Immigrant America, a Portrait*. The latter book was designated as a centennial publication by the University of California Press. It was originally published in 1990; the second edition, updated and containing new chapters on American immigration policy and the new second generation, was published in 1996.

LITERATURE CITED

Anheier, H. K., Gerhards, J., Romo, F. P. 1995. Forms of social capital and social structure in cultural fields: examining Bourdieu's social topography. *Am. J. Sociol.* 100: 859–903.

Bailey, T., Waldinger, R. 1991. Primary, secondary, and enclave labor markets: a training system approach. *Am. Sociol. Rev.* 56: 432–45.

Baker, W. E. 1990. Market networks and corporate behavior. *Am. J. Sociol.* 96: 589–625.

Blau, P. M. 1964. *Exchange and Power in Social Life.* New York: Wiley.

Boissevain, J. 1974. *Friends of Friends: Networks, Manipulators, and Coalitions.* New York: St. Martin's Press.

Bourdieu, P. 1979. Les trois états du capital culturel. *Actes Rech. Sci. Soc.* 30: 3–6.

Bourdieu, P. 1980. Le capital social: notes provisoires. *Actes Rech. Sci. Soc.* 31: 2–3.

Bourdieu, P. 1985. The forms of capital. In *Handbook of Theory and Research for the Sociology of Education*, ed. J. G. Richardson, pp. 241–58. New York: Greenwood.

Bourgois, P. 1991. *Search of respect: the new service economy and the crack alternative in Spanish Harlem*. Presented at Conf. Poverty, Immigr. Urban Marginality Adv. Soc., Maison Suger, Paris, May 10–11.

Bourgois, P. 1995. *In Search of Respect: Selling Crack in El Barrio*. New York: Cambridge Univ. Press.

Burt, R. S. 1992. *Structural Holes, The Social Structure of Competition*. Cambridge, MA: Harvard Univ. Press.

Coleman, J. S. 1988a. Social capital in the creation of human capital. *Am. J. Sociol.* 94: S95–121.

Coleman, J. S. 1988b. The creation and destruction of social capital: implications for the law. *Notre Dame J. Law, Ethics, Public Policy* 3: 375–404.

Coleman, J. S. 1990. *Foundations of Social Theory*. Cambridge: Belknap Press of Harvard Univ. Press.

Coleman, J. S. 1993. The rational reconstruction of society (1992 Presidential Address). *Am. Sociol. Rev.* 58: 1–15.

Coleman, J. S. 1994a. A rational choice perspective on economic sociology. In *Handbook of Economic Sociology*, ed. N. J. Smelser, R. Swedberg, pp. 166–80. Princeton, NJ: Princeton Univ. Press.

Coleman, J. S. 1994b. The realization of effective norms. In *Four Sociological Traditions: Selected Readings*, ed. R. Collins. pp. 171–89. New York: Oxford Univ. Press.

Doeringer, P., Moss, P. 1986. Capitalism and kinship: do institutions matter in the labor market? *Indust. Labor Relat. Rev.* 40: 48–59.

Durkheim, E. 1984. (1893). *The Division of Labor in Society*. New York: Free Press.

Frenández-Kelly, M. P. 1995. Social and cultural capital in the urban ghetto: implications for the economic sociology of immigration. See Portes 1995, pp. 213–47.

Geertz, C. 1963. *Peddlers and Princes*. Chicago: Univ. Chicago Press.

Gold, S. J. 1995. Gender and social capital among Israeli immigrants in Los Angeles. *Diaspora* 4: 267–301.

Granovetter, M. S. 1974. *Getting a Job: A Study of Contacts and Careers*. Cambridge, MA: Harvard Univ. Press.

Granovetter, M. S. 1995. The economic sociology of firms and entrepreneurs. See Portes 1995, pp. 128–65.

Hagan, J., Merkens, H., Boenhke, K. 1995. Delinquency and disdain: social capital and the control of right-wing extremism among East and West Berlin youth. *Am. J. Sociol.* 100: 1028–52.

Hagan, J., MacMillan, R., Wheaton, B. 1996. New kid in town: social capital and the life course effects of family migration in children. *Am. Sociol. Rev.* 61: 368–85.

Hao, L. 1994. *Kin Support, Welfare, and Out-of-Wedlock Mothers*. New York: Garland.

Homans, G. C. 1961. *Social Behavior: Its Elementary Forms*. New York: Harcourt, Brace & World.

Lemann, N. 1996. Kicking in groups. *Atlantic Mon.* 277(April): 22–26.

Light, I. 1984. Immigrant and ethnic enterprise in North America. *Ethn. Racial Stud.* 7: 195–216.

Light, I., Bonacich E. 1988. *Immigrant Entrepreneurs: Koreans in Los Angeles 1965–1982*. Berkeley: Univ. Calif. Press.

Lin, N., Ensel, W. M., Vaughn, J. C. 1981. Social resources and strength of ties: structural factors in occupational attainment. *Am. Sociol. Rev.* 46: 393–405.

Loury, G. C. 1977. A dynamic theory of racial income differences. In *Women, Minorities, and Employment Discrimination*, ed. P. A. Wallace, A. M. La Mond, pp. 153–86. Lexington, MA: Heath.

Loury, G. C. 1981. Intergenerational transfers and the distribution of earnings. *Econometrica* 49: 843–67.

Marx, K. 1967. (1894). *Capital*, Vol. 3. New York: International.

Marx, K., Engels, F. 1947. (1848). *The German Ideology*. New York: International.

Matute-Bianchi, M. E. 1986. Ethnic identities and patterns of school success and failure among Mexican-descent and Japanese-American students in California high school. *Am. J. Educ.* 95: 233–55.

Matute-Bianchi, M. E. 1991. Situational ethnicity and patterns of school performance among immigrant and non-immigrant Mexican-descent students. In *Minority Status and Schooling: A Comparative Study of Immigrant and Involuntary Minorities*, ed. M. A. Gibson, J. U. Ogbu, pp. 205–47. New York: Garland.

McLanahan, S., Sandefur, G. 1994. *Growing Up with a Single Parent: What Hurts, What Helps*. Cambridge, MA: Harvard Univ. Press.

Nee, V., Sanders, J. M., Sernau, S. 1994. Job transitions in an immigrant metropolis: ethnic boundaries and the mixed economy. *Am. Sociol. Rev.* 59: 849–72.

Parcel, T. L., Menaghan, E. G. 1994. *Parents' Jobs and Children's Lives*. New York: Aldine de Gruyter.

Parcel, T. L., Menaghan, E. G. 1994a. Early parental work, family social capital, and early childhood outcomes. *Am. J. Sociol.* 99: 972–1009.

Perez, L. 1992. Cuban Miami. In *Miami Now*, ed. G. J. Grenier, A. Stepick, pp. 83–108. Gainesville: Univ. Press Fla.

Pollitt, K. 1996. For whom the ball rolls. *The Nation* 262(April 15): 9.

Portes, A. 1987. The social origins of the Cuban enclave economy of Miami. *Sociol. Perspect.* 30: 340–72.

Portes, A. 1995, ed. *The Economic Sociology of Immigration*. New York: Russell Sage.

Portes, A., Landolt, P. 1996. The downside of social capital. *Am. Prospect* 26: 18–22.

Portes, A., Sensenbrenner, J. 1993. Embeddedness and immigration: notes on the social determinants of economic action. *Am. J. Sociol.* 98: 1320–50.

Portes, A., Stepick, A. 1993. *City on the Edge: The Transformation of Miami*. Berkeley: Univ. Calif. Press.

Portes, A., Zhou, M. 1993. The new second generation: segmented assimilation and its variants among post-1965 immigrant youth. *Ann. Am. Acad. Polit. Soc. Sci.* 530: 74–96.

Putnam, R. D. 1993. The prosperous community: social capital and public life. *Am. Prospect* 13: 35–42.

Putnam, R. D. 1995. Bowling alone: America's declining social capital. *J. Democr.* 6: 65–78.

Putnam, R. D. 1996. The strange disappearance of civic America. *Am. Prospect* 24: 34–48.

Robinson, W. S. 1951. The logical structure of analytic induction. *Am. Sociol. Rev.* 16: 812–18.

Rumbaut, R. G. 1977. Ties that bind: immigration and immigrant families in the United States. In *Immigration and the Family: Research and Policy on US Immigrants*, ed. A. Booth, A. C. Crouter, N. Landale, pp. 3–45. Mahwah, NJ: Erlbaum.

Sassen, S. 1995. Immigration and local labor markets. See Ports 1995, pp. 87–127.

Schiff, M. 1992. Social capital, labor mobility, and welfare. *Ration. Soc.* 4: 157–75.

Simmel, G. 1964. [1902]. The metropolis and mental life. In *The Sociology of Georg Simmel*, ed./transl. K.H. Wolff, pp. 409–24. New York: Free press.

Skocpol, T. 1996. Unraveling from above. *Am. Prospect* 25: 20–25.

Smart, A. 1993. Gifts, bribes, and guanxi: a reconsideration of Bourdieu's social capital. *Cult. Anthropol.* 8: 388–408.

Smith, A. 1979. (1776). *The Wealth of Nations*. Baltimore, MD: Penguin.

Stack, C. 1974. *All Our Kin*. New York: Harper & Row.

Stanton-Salazar, R. D., Dornbusch, S. M. 1995. Social capital and the reproduction of inequality: information networks among Mexican-origin high school students. *Social. Educ.* 68: 116–35.

Stepick, A. 1989. Miami's two informal sectors. In *The Informal Economy: Studies in Advanced and Less Developed Countries*, ed. A. Portes, M. Castells, L. A. Benton, pp. 111–34. Baltimore, MD: Johns Hopkins Univ. Press.

Stepick, A. 1992. The refugees nobody wants: Haitians in Miami. In *Miami Now*, ed. G. J. Grenier, A. Stepick, pp. 57–82. Gainesville: Univ. Fla. Press.

Suarez-Orozco, M. M. 1987. Towards a psychosocial understanding of hispanic adaptation to American schooling. In *Success or Failure? Learning and the Languages of Minority Students*, ed. H. T. Trueba, pp. 156–68. New York: Newbury House.

Sullivan, M. L. 1989. *Getting Paid: Youth Crime and Work in the Inner City*. Ithaca, NY: Cornell Univ. Press.

Turner, R. 1953. The quest for universals in sociological research. *Am. Sociol. Rev.* 18: 604–11.

Valenzuela, A., Dornbusch, S. M. 1994. Familism and social capital in the academic achievement of Mexican origin and anglo adolescents. *Soc. Sci. Q.* 75: 18–36.

Wacquant, L. J. D., Wilson, W. J. 1989. The cost of racial and class exclusion in the inner city. *Ann. Am. Acad. Polit. Soc. Sci.* 501: 8–26.

Waldinger, R. 1986. *Through the Eye of the Needle: Immigrants and Enterprise in the New York's Garment Trade*. New York: New York Univ. Press.

Waldinger, R. 1995. The "Other Side" of embeddedness: a case study of the interplay between economy and ethnicity. *Ethn. Racial Stud.* 18: 555–80.

Waldinger, R. 1996. *Still the Promised City? African-Americans and New Immigrants in Post-Industrial New York*. Cambridge, MA: Harvard Univ. Press.

Waters, M. 1994. West Indian immigrants, African Americans, and whites in the workplace: different perspectives on American race relations. Presented at Meet. Am. Sociol. Assoc., Los Angeles.

Weber, M. 1965. (1922, 1947.) *The Theory of Social and Economic Organization*. New York: Free Press. Originally published as *Wirtsch. Ges.*, Part I.

Weede, E. 1992. Freedom, knowledge, and law as social capital. *Int. J. Unity Sci.* 5: 391–409.

Wilson, W. J. 1996. *When Work Disappears: The World of the New Urban Poor*. New York: Knopf.

Wilson, W. J. 1987. *The Truly Disadvantaged: The Inner-City, the Underclass, and Public Policy*. Chicago: Univ. Chicago Press.

Woolcock, M. 1997. Social capital and economic development: towards a theoretical synthesis and policy framework. *Theory Soc.* In press.

Wrong, D. 1961. The oversocialized conception of man in modern sociology. *Am. Sociol. Rev.* 26: 183–93.

Zhou, M. 1992. *New York's Chinatown: The Socioeconomic Potential of an Urban Enclave*. Philadelphia: Temple Univ. Press.

Zhou, M., Bankston, C. L. 1996. Social capital and the adaptation of the second generation: the case of Vietnamese youth in New Orleans. In *The New Second Generation*, ed. A. Portes, pp. 197–220. New York: Russell Sage Found.

Chapter 4

A Paradigm for Social Capital[*]

Rebecca L. Sandefur and Edward O. Laumann

Abstract—*This paper reconsiders James S. Coleman's concept of social capital. The concept has gained wide use and acceptance in sociology since its first publication, but, Coleman's own writings on the subject remain to date its most extensive analytic treatment. We make two contributions to social capital theory. First, we recast social capital theory to focus on benefits rather than forms. We identify three benefits that forms of social capital may confer: information, influence and control, and social solidarity. In the context of a focus on benefits, we consider how a specific form of social capital may vary in the degree to which its benefits generalize to different kinds of goals, and how forms that are valuable for some purposes may be a liability for other purposes. Second, we emphasize social capital's origin in aspects of social structure that actors may appropriate to use in their interests. We suggest how changes in the social structure of which social capital is an aspect may affect the emergence and persistence of forms of social capital and may condition the value of given forms.*

KEY WORDS · social capital · information · influence and control · social solidarity

INTRODUCTION

The term 'social capital' has become a popular way of denoting many kinds of resources appropriable from interpersonal relationships. Since the publication

[*] Reprinted by permission of Sage Publications from Rebecca Sandefur and Edward O. Laumann, "A Paradigm for Social Capital" 1988, *Rationality and Society*, Vol. 10(4), pp. 481–501 Copyright © 1998 Sage Publications (London, Thousands Oaks. CA and New Delhi), Vol. 10(4): 481–501. [1043–4631(199811)10: 4; 481–501, 005901]

of James S. Coleman's first paper on the subject (Coleman 1988), the concept of 'social' capital has gained wide use and acceptance in sociology and related fields.[1] However, with notable exceptions, much empirical work employing the concept of social capital has been theoretically unreflective. Instead, the concept has been used largely as a metaphor that encompasses existing sociological ideas. In empirical analyses of its effects on outcomes of interest, social capital has been modeled as either present or absent: it has usually been treated as a qualitative characteristic of a given social system. Further, though social capital is an aspect of social structure, the social capital literature has largely ignored how social structural variation may affect social capital.

This paper reconsiders James S. Coleman's concept of social capital and the use it has received in the empirical literature. We make two contributions to social capital theory. First, we recast social capital theory to focus on benefits rather than forms. A focus on benefits has been characteristic of successful attempts to quantify individual's stocks of social capital. Second, we give explicit consideration to systemic properties of the social structures that constitute social capital. The paper proceeds from a discussion of Coleman's concept of social capital to the presentation of a paradigm for analyzing social capital. Drawing on examples from the empirical literatures on social capital, social resources, social support, network analysis and community studies, we illustrate the utility of the paradigm. Then, in the context of this paradigm, we turn to a consideration of how variation in a social system, of which a form of social capital is an aspect, may affect its productivity.

COLEMAN'S SOCIAL CAPITAL

According to Coleman, social capital is accumulated history in the form of social structure appropriable for productive use by an actor in the pursuit of her interests (Coleman 1990a, 300–3; see also Bourdieu 1986; Granovetter 1985; Zukin and DiMaggio 1990). In Coleman's rational actor framework, social structure itself emerges out of interactions entered by individuals in pursuit of their own interests (Coleman 1990a, 300). Such social structure may exist in relatively discrete forms, such as organizations (Coleman 1990a, 313), or in more diffuse forms, such as extended families, communities (Laumann and Pappi 1976) or other loosely bounded social systems (Sandefur et al. 1999). Always, social structure consists of relationships. These relationships may be components of formal organization, such as the relationships of classmate, department head, co-worker and instructor, or the relationships that constitute social structure may be defined by other criteria, such as the relationships of neighbor, lover, co-conspirator and friend-of-a-friend. These relationships may be characterized by both

---

[1] An electronic search in the Social Sciences Citation Index of articles published in the decade since the appearance of Coleman's paper reveals at least 210 articles citing Coleman's 1988 piece and 88 articles including the term 'social capital' in their title.

their structural form and the content that inheres in them, and aspects of both their form and their content will condition their productivity as social capital.

In Coleman's scheme, social structure becomes social capital when appropriable by an actor for effective use in the furtherance of her interests (Coleman 1990a, 302–5). Coleman's concept of social capital is thus defined by its function (Coleman 1990a, 305). Coleman chooses this method of definition because it permits him to 'account for different outcomes at the level of individuals [while] making the micro-to-macro transition without elaborating the social-structural details through which this occurs' (1990a, 305). In his essays on social capital (1988, 1990a, b), Coleman seeks simply to suggest the utility of his concept. He does so by presenting vignettes that illustrate various *forms* of social capital, such as trust, effective norms and voluntary organizations.

By this analytic tack—defining a concept by its function and illustrating its utility with exemplary vignettes—Coleman presents a compelling case for taking his concept seriously. However, this tack, by glossing the 'social-structural details', forgoes systematic analysis of the mechanisms through which social capital has its effects. Examination of these mechanisms gives insight into the workings of social capital, and suggests ways in which its multitude of forms can be fruitfully and parsimoniously differentiated.

Different types of social capital are useful in attaining different goals. The most successful empirical treatments of social capital have at least implicitly recognized this functional specificity of social capital's many forms. The paradigm we present later emphasizes three important characteristics of social capital: (i) A given *form* of social capital may provide one or more *benefits*. Three important benefits are information, influence and control, and social solidarity. (ii) A given form of social capital may confer benefits useful for a single goal of an actor, or the productive capacity of a form of social capital may generalize to aid in the attainment of many kinds of goals. That is, forms of social capital vary in the effective specificity of the benefits they confer. (iii) At the same the that a form of social capital may confer benefits useful for one or more purposes, it can confer liabilities as well. A form of social capital acquired to aid in one type of action may hinder other actions; thus, forms of social capital may be said to have a *valence*, contingent upon the goals which the actor wishes to attain.

A PARADIGM FOR SOCIAL CAPITAL

Our explication of social capital begins with three basic concepts: the concept of a social system, and egocentric and sociocentric perspectives on the relationships in social systems. Following Parsons, we define a social system as 'a plurality of individual actors interacting with each other in a situation which has at least a physical or environmental aspect' (Parsons 1951, 5). Thus, social systems are constituted by relationships of various types among actors, and may be large or small and tightly or loosely bounded.[2] Social systems may be nested within one another, as the social system of an academic department is nested with the social system of a college. And, any individual is at any time a member of more than one analytically identifiable social system.

An individual's potential stock of social capital consists of the collection and pattern of relationships in which she is involved and to which she has access, and further to the location and patterning of her associations in larger social space. That is, her potential social capital is both the contact she herself holds and the way in which those contacts link her to other patterns of relations. Two different traditions in network analysis serve to illustrate. In his classic paper on social contacts and white-collar job search success, Mark Granovetter (1973) demonstrates that 'weak ties' such as those to friends-of-friends were more useful to searchers than were 'strong ties' such as those to friends or relatives. The people to whom the searcher was strongly tied, as members of her own social circle, were likely to come in contact with the same information as the searcher was. However, since 'weak ties' linked the searcher to people more likely to move in social circles different from her own, the searcher was likely to hear of opportunities from them that were different from those 'strong ties' that she knew. The 'weak ties' approach exemplifies the *egocentric* perspective on social networks and the resources to which they give access: an individual's social capital is characterized by her direct relationships with others and by the other people and relationships that she can reach through those to whom she is directly tied.

Sociocentric approaches in network analysis examine patterns of relationships within a social system. Burt's (1992) 'structural hole' work demonstrates the costs and benefits of positions in a system of interpersonal contacts defined by multiple relationships between multiple actors. An individual actor's social capital is a by-product of how her relationships fit in to the larger pattern of relationships within the system. The analytic focus is not on the contacts held by the individual, but rather on the way the individual is situated in the social structure of interpersonal contacts. Thus, for instance, similar behavior is predicted for individuals located in the same social positions—individuals who are 'structurally equivalent'—regardless of the behavior of their close associates (Burt 1987).

In our paradigm, as in Coleman's theory, social capital's productive capacity extends beyond economic returns to any outcome of interest to a goal-directed actor. The social capital appropriated from social structure may provide benefits in any realm of interest to the individual, whether a promotion in his firm or more effective socialization of his children. We define the *benefit*[3] of a form of social capital as its particular usefulness to an actor in attaining a specified type of goal.

In this scheme, social capital's productive capacity results from three potential benefits: its ability to facilitate or hinder the flow of information (Burt 1992;

---

[2] See Laumann et al. (1983) for a discussion of how social networks may be bounded.
[3] We take the term 'benefit' from Burt (1992), who identifies two benefits of social capital, information and control.

Coleman 1990a; Laumann and Knoke 1987; Laumann and Marsden 1982) and the control of others and one's own autonomy (Coleman 1990a; Burt 1992; Seron and Ferris 1995), and the potential it provides for social solidarity (Coleman 1990a; Laumann and Pappi 1976; Portes and Sensenbrenner 1993; Suttles and Street 1970; Wellman and Wortley, 1990). We discuss each benefit provided by social capital—*information, influence and control, and social solidarity*[4]—in turn.

Information

Information benefits of social capital arise from the relevance, timeliness (Burt 1992) and trustworthiness (Laumann and Knoke 1987) of the information provided. Aspects of both the structural form and the content of relationships condition these qualities of the accessed information. Considered from an egocentric perspective, the formal properties of the social structure an individual can appropriate vary from a closed structure focused on a single target to a collection of diverse and disconnected contacts. These two extremes of structural form provide information useful for different kinds of goals. Access to diverse sources of information, also discussed as network range (Campbell et al. 1986; Marsden and Hurlbert 1988) and non-redundancy (Burt 1992), provides individuals with the opportunity to receive timely reports of relevant facts, which permits more effective instrumental action in competition with other actors. Analyses of the effects of 'social resources' on job search behavior and outcomes (Lin et al. 1981a, b) and socioeconomic attainment (Campbell et al. 1986; Marsden and Hurlbert 1988), as well as the demonstrated 'strength of weak ties' (Granovetter 1973), illustrate how diverse information available through wider social contacts, or contacts whose own circle of acquaintance is broad, increases the probability of earlier notification of opportunities and is thus instrumental for labor market success.

Among the best empirical studies of the information benefits of social capital in mobility contests among instrumental actors is presented by Burt. In a study of a large US high technology firm, Burt (1995) examines the effects of network constraint on the probability of early promotion for managers in the middle of the firm hierarchy (below the rank of vice-president). Constraint is a function of the size of each manager's network, as well as the cohesion of her contacts (her contacts' ties to each other), their contacts' structural equivalence (the degree to which they have similar ties to third parties) and her contacts' hierarchy (the degree to which her ties are directly or indirectly nested in a single individual). *Ceteris paribus*, those managers with lower network constraint were more likely to experience early promotion than those whose workplace networks

---

[4] Most empirical studies demonstrating evidence of social capital 'effects' argue or imply that social capital operates through some combination of its benefits. We distinguish between them analytically while recognizing that they covary empirically.

were more structurally limiting. Diverse networks provided access to more timely and relevant information about upcoming opportunities and about complications and contingencies managers might face in their work projects. This information permitted managers with lower network constraint to perform better than managers of equivalent skills and experience; their superior performance was rewarded with faster advancement in the firm. Burt's formulation of information benefits is elegantly structural. It gives little consideration to the content of relationships—for instance, whether trust is necessary for the sharing of sensitive (and, accordingly, sometimes more valuable) information, and whether relationships maintained by those managers whose networks were low in structural constraint were characterized by such arguably necessary trust.[5]

A different structure of relationships provides benefits to actors who seek detailed and comprehensive information about specific other actors or other specific targets: strong relationships with the others of interest and with their associates. The limiting case of this type of information access is complete structural closure around a target, which permits the mutually acquainted actors who constitute the closed structure better access to information about the individual at the center of that closed structure (Coleman 1988, S105–8). Parents who involve themselves with their children by investing the time necessary to develop strong relationships with them, their teachers, their friends, their friends' parents and other adults significant in their children's lives illustrate this type of social capital (Coleman 1988, 1990a, b). Not only the structural closure around the children, but also the mutual trust among the adults that arises from their shared interest in the children's welfare, support this type of effective surveillance. Parents involved in these closed structures of monitoring relationships have greater access to more timely, accurate, complete and trustworthy information about their children's behavior than those parents who are less involved in their children's lives. Parents with more of this type of social capital know more of what their children are doing, and have earlier and more complete knowledge of compliant and non-compliant behaviors.

The involved parents Coleman idealizes contrast starkly with Burt's successful managerial entrepreneurs. The network of concerned adults that makes for effective social control and socialization of children is characterized by both normative and structural closure. The children are structurally encircled by a network of adults linked to each other in a way that facilitates an easy exchange of information about the children. Inhering in the closed form of these relationships is some degree of normative agreement among the adults about how the children ought to act and, more fundamentally, that adults ought to be concerned about

[5]   In more recent work, Burt has considered the role of trust in entrepreneurial action (Burt 1996a). Burt's interest lies in entrepreneurial freedom and effectiveness; thus, he considers when the entrepreneur can or should trust the information she receives from others. The assumption appears to be either that colleagues share much information freely, or that the entrepreneur endowed with structural holes can manipulate her image as needed to gain others' trust (see Burt 1997a).

children's actions. The children thus face a united front of adults who share information about them and share a commitment to using that information to direct their behavior in particular ways. The networks of Burt's successful managerial entrepreneurs are defined by the very lack of others' capacity for this kind of surveillance and the apparent lack of normative agreement among other actors that colluding to monitor an entrepreneurial manager is a worthy end.

Between these two modalities lie less extreme cases of investment in specific types of relationships useful for the provision or blockage of particular types of information. One empirical example of such a middle state is provided by studies of misconduct among members of the professions. Studies of professional misconduct among lawyers find that private practice lawyers employed in large law firms have lower rates of both being charged with professional offenses and being convicted of them than do solo practitioners (Arnold and Kay 1995; Carlin 1966). Arnold and Kay interpret this finding as a result of the superior social capital to which lawyers working in law firms have access as a result of their formal organizational ties to other lawyers. The behavior of lawyers in firms can be more easily surveyed (and sanctioned, see later) by colleagues than that of solo practitioners, and lawyers in firms may have superior access to others who can collude to hide their misdeeds and buffer them from the professional consequences of their misconduct.

Various forms of social capital provide information benefit useful for different purposes. Involvement in the workplace analog of the social capital that makes for more effective surveillance of one's children hampers the entrepreneur of Burt's theory. Normative and structural closure aid only certain types of actions; they take on a negative valence when the individual's goal is her personal advancement in a competitive arena (see Burt 1995, 1996a; Portes and Sensenbrenner 1993). Even within a given context, social capital that is valuable for some purposes may be a liability at other times. While the adults who collude in monitoring the children gain from their involvement with each other, they do so at the cost of some of their own privacy, since any adult actor in the closed structure can potentially monitor the other adult actors. The social capital that permits parents to more effectively watch over their children also permits surveillance of other adults involved in childrearing. In analyses of social capital's effects, an accounting of both the multiple costs and the multiple benefits gives a better understanding of the mechanisms leading to different outcomes at the level of individuals.

Influence and Control

The influence and control benefits provided by social capital are in a sense obverse sides of one coin: the ability to influence others (Coleman 1990a) and the ability to be free of others' influence (Burt 1993, 1996b). In our discussion, we use the term 'influence' in a broad sense consonant with Coleman's exposition of social capital. Despite the concept's wide use, 'influence' has no agreed-upon meaning in the sociological literature; therefore, before discussing the influence benefits of social capital, we must clarify our use of the term. Parsons (1963) sets forth a typology of influence that informs our discussion here. The degree of influence, as broadly construed by Parsons, is something akin to Weber's 'imperative control . . . the probability that a given command with a given specific content will be obeyed by a given group of persons' (Weber 1946, 152). Parsons asserts that attempts to induce another to behave or think in a certain way may be classified in terms of two qualities: whether the proposed sanction is positive or negative in the perspective of the targeted individual, and whether the influencer appeals to the targeted individual's own motivations or orientations, or manipulates the targeted individual's situation. For Parsons, attempts to induce a certain behavior in another that constitute 'influence' occur when the influencer appeals to the targeted individual's pre-existing motivations or orientations to action through a 'positive' manipulation. That is, influence occurs when 'alter accepts ego's directions as his own because of his positive belief or trust in ego's superior competence or other attributes that commend ego's suggestion as worthy of being obeyed' (Laumann and Knoke 1987, 154).

Forms of social capital discussed by Coleman—in particular trust, obligations, and effective norms—are often bases of influence in this narrow sense. The classic interpretation of the relationship between a client and a professional typifies the Parsonsian concept of influence (Coleman 1990a, 313). A patient's trust in a physician and respect for her judgment may result in the doctor having considerable influence over the patient, a potential form of social capital for the doctor that is based in the patient's belief that trusting the doctor is the correct thing to do. (Of course, if the doctor is trustworthy and knowledgeable, the association may result in a positive outcome for the patient.) The capacity for Parsonsian influence also arises when a relationship or system of relationships contains sufficient outstanding obligations and certain effective norms about respecting them. For instance, when a doctor needs help or advice, she may rely on colleagues whom she has aided in the past, because she carries 'credit slips' with them from past favors (Coleman 1988, 1990a). The doctor can influence her colleagues to do what she wishes (use their expertise to advise her, for instance) because they already feel they 'owe' her. Norms governing certain kinds of relationships, such as the norm that students should assume teachers 'mean well by them' and so should be obeyed, can also be bases of this type of influence.

Parsons defines 'influence' in a relatively narrow sense. Other forms of pressure to act in a particular way are possible, and the capacity to influence others in this narrow Parsonsian sense does not necessarily coincide with the capacity to induce them to do what one wishes by other types of means. Coleman's concept of social capital includes Parsons' 'positive manipulations' (Coleman's 'effective norms' and 'trust') as well as an individual's activation of another's commitments or outstanding obligations, and threats of punishment as bases of the capacity for influence that social capital can provide.

As with the other benefits of social capital, aspects of both the content and the form of relationships condition an individual's capacity for influence and her freedom from the influence of others. Burt (1992, 1993, 1996b) argues that the structure of relationships in which an actor is involved can augment or restrain others' power to limit her actions and induce her to behave in desired ways. Structural constraint restructs an actor's autonomy, both of action and of cognition. 'Structural holes' exist between contacts who are non-redundant, in the sense of being neither directly nor indirectly strongly linked to one another, nor similarly located in the pattern of relationships in sociometric space. The presence of structural holes indicates that an actor has greater potential for freedom of decision and movement, that she is less likely to be required to act in ways desired by others because others cannot collude to restrict information nor present a unified front of normative pressure. Burt's (1995) early promotion findings for managers with networks rich in structural holes are one illustration of the entrepreneurial freedom and effectiveness that result when one is not in a position to be influenced, as well as strategically located to receive useful information early. Managers with networks rich in structural holes are argued to be more successful, *ceteris paribus*, because they can control the form of projects that bring together other parties: they gain from the increase in their ability to be effective brokers between their associates (Burt 1996a).

In other situations, involvement in strong and, therefore, in some ways restrictive ties may permit greater effectiveness with respect to one's occupational goals. In their study of lawyer misconduct, interview excerpts presented by Arnold and Kay (1995) suggest that some solo practitioners perceive that their lack of social capital (in the form of interested, engaged, admonitory colleagues) was involved in their downfall. Their professional failure arose in part because they were free from others' influence, and in part because they did not have access to others who could use their influence on their behalf (for instance, to sway a disciplinary committee's decision about disbarrment). The errant solo practitioners suffered from excessive amounts of autonomy and personal control, which left them both only weakly susceptible to others' influence and relatively powerless to mobilize others on their behalf.

The capacity to mobilize others for action—which often requires putting oneself in a position of obligation to those others—can be highly valuable. In a study of managers in Swedish firms, Meyerson (1994) presents results supportive of her thesis that strong ties are instrumental in increasing managers' income attainments, net of other productive characteristics.[6] Lin (1990, 1995) suggests that, for individuals at the top of a stratified, pyramidal system (for example, the vice-presidents and CEO of a firm), strong ties to other system members will be more effective for instrumental actions than weak ties, since weak ties to others in the system are likely to reach down the hierarchy to those with fewer resources. Similarly, if the members of the top tier of an organization are

---

[6] Burt (1996a) suggests that Meyerson may be modeling strong ties to disconnected structural holes, but notes that her data are not sufficiently detailed to be able to make an empirical determination of whether such is the case. Regardless, Meyerson's results indicate that, on average, managers benefit from strong ties.

required to compete as a team (say, against rivals for control of the organization), they may be well-served by strong and trusting relationships among themselves, as well as contacts with diverse information sources.

One can imagine each individual's relationships having an ideal empirical balance between cohesion and closure, and to access to diverse sources of information and influence. The ideal balance may well be different depending on where the individual is in the hierarchy of the social system, whether the context is characterized more by cooperation or competition, and, in competitive settings, on whether team competition or individual competition is the operative game. Here again, we see how the goals for which a form of social capital is activated condition its value.

Social Solidarity

Social solidarity obtains among two or more individuals when there exists a degree of mutual trust and commitment among them that is independent of any specific transaction; it is an 'emergent product of a particular situation' (Portes and Sensenbrenner 1993, 1322; cf. Burt 1992 on competition as a relation emergent). Social solidarity may exist among interrelated actors by fiat, as when cultural values, backed by effective norms, dictate that family members will look out for one another and care for one another. Or, solidarity may arise out of conditions of repeated interaction among the same actors over time, during which forms of social capital such as trust and mutual obligations accumulate. In the language of exchange theory, solidarity exists in circumstances of 'generalized reciprocity', when 'a helpful act is performed, not in response to any specific benefit received, but in honor of the social exchange relation itself' (Emerson 1981, 33). Solidary relationships are characterized by some degree of 'incorporation, in which . . . all . . . parties contribute to collective gain' (Emerson 1981, 34, italics removed).

A notable illustration of solidarity benefits is provided by a consideration of the effects of the advent of public aid programs on the social organization of poor communities. Suttles and Street (1970) examine how the shift from private to public provision of aid to the poor has affected the 'set of exchange relations which bind the poor to one another and to the wider society' (p. 744). In the era before the New Deal, aid to the poor consisted largely in voluntary transfers from wealthier individuals, and benevolent societies. The poor also relied on one another for 'meager', but nevertheless important benefits, 'rang[ing]' in value from the mere solace of understanding through small loans through free room and board' (p. 747). These exchanges enriched not only the individual recipients, but strengthened the community of exchangers:

> Without anyone intending it, then, an 'invisible hand' added value to the exchanges of the poor; as coresidents, they were very much dependent upon one another. In turn, each was forewarned not to offend the other. The

distinction between beneficiary and recipient was temporary at best. Within time, those most in need might become those most able to help, so that no firm line could be drawn between the two (Suttles and Street 1970, 747).

The exchanges both acted out and reinforced the poor's sense of being a community of common fate, bound together by mutual obligation, but also by a shared sense of precarious fortune (Suttles and Street 1970, 748). This sense of community had effects not only on the persistence of important informal relationships of social exchange, but on the capacity of the co-residents for social control of each other and of outsiders (Suttles and Street, 1970, 748–50; see also Suttles 1972).

A community-level focus, such as is exemplified by Suttles and Street's work on aid to the poor, is essentially a sociocentric perspective on the benefit of social solidarity. Empirical studies of social solidarity considered from an egocentric perspective abound in the literature on social support. Researchers investigating how individuals use social resources to deal with psychologically stressful events and situations regard social support as 'the resources that one actually uses in dealing with life's problems' (Pearlin 1989, 251). The empirical literature on social support is voluminous and we will not review it here (see Cohen and Syme 1985; House 1987; House et al. 1988; Lin et al. 1986). Some of this literature emphasizes the value of various kinds of close, trusting relationships and of social participation in the community in maintaining general physical and mental health, while other studies focus on the role of others' aid in coping with stressful life events.

In addition to providing social support conducive to maintaining health or coping with crises, relationships with trusted others can free an individual to use her energies more efficiently and effectively to attain desired goals. In academia, collaborative research projects are ideally characterized by co-investigators' mutual reliance on each others' judgment, specialized competence and good will. A division of labor grounded in trust permits greater productivity, as when faculty rely on research assistants to perform empirical analyses, or when one co-author elaborates a paper's general theoretical framework while the other performs sophisticated calculations. To consider a relationship perhaps less overtly instrumental, marriage often provides solidarity benefits to one or both of the partners. Seron and Ferris (1995) suggest that the social capital provided to male lawyers by wives who manage domestic work, grants the lawyers greater freedom both to put their human capital to more extensive use by expanding and more flexibly scheduling their work hours, and to accumulate more of other forms of social capital by participating in work-related leisure and social activities.[7]

---

[7] The paper is a thoughtful reinterpretation of the 'marriage premium' for men (cf. Daniel 1995). Seron and Ferris argue that gendered social capital is one of the institutional underpinnings of professional work such as work in the law. Coleman (1990a) also addresses the relationship with a spouse as social capital.

As with other forms of social capital, forms that confer social solidarity can become a liability. In a synthetic assessment of the ways in which the embeddedness of economic action in social relationships may affect economic success, Portes and Sensenbrenner (1993) examine both the positive and the negative effects of social solidarity on economic action. Reviewing research on immigrant and inner-city communities in the United States, they note that a sense of 'solidarity cemented on common adversity' can lead to 'leveling pressures' which 'conspir[e] directly against efforts toward individual mobility by [working] to keep members of downtrodden groups in the same situation as their peers' (p. 1342). The solidarity that leads to effective social control in a community can also stifle innovation and hamper individual mobility by 'restricting the scope of individual expression and the extent of extracommunity contact' (p. 1341). And, visibly successful members of a solidary group may become targets of less successful members who may wish to 'free-ride' on their success, and are able to do so because of norms that require successful individuals to aid less fortunate members of the group. Again, we see how a consideration of social capital's effectiveness in aiding an actor in attaining different goals gives insight into the sources of inequality at the level of individuals.

To sum briefly, we have differentiated forms of social capital by focusing on *benefits*—information, influence and control, and social solidarity—the mechanisms through which a form of social capital acts to increase an actor's capacity for action. This formulation in terms of benefits is consistent with Coleman's analytic decision to define social capital by its function. Implicit within our illustration of the three benefits of social capital has been a recognition of the varying *effective specificity* of any given form of social capital: forms of social capital vary in the degree to which their benefits are specific to one type of activity or goal or generalize to many. Forms of social capital valuable for one type of activity or in the attainment of one goal may be ineffective or detrimental to the attainment of other goals. Social capital can, in fact, become a liability. Since the value of a form of social capital can range from positive to negative depending on the goal in question, it may be said to have a *valence*.

The productive capacity of social capital—its value to an actor in attaining a goal—is thus conditioned by a number of factors specific to the goal of interest. However, a given form of social capital can also vary in its benefit to an actor because of variation in the social structure of which that form is an aspect. Changes in social structure can lead to the destruction of existing forms of social capital, the emergence of new forms, and changes in the value of persisting forms of social capital. We now turn to a brief consideration of variations in social structure and social capital.

SYSTEMIC VARIATION AND SOCIAL CAPITAL

Self-interested and otherwise purposive actors may strategically enter into certain kinds of relationships.[8] Coleman (1990a) cites several examples of individual's intentional creation of obligations, for instance, by the doing of unsolicited favors for others. These obligations become a basis for future influence and an entitlement to future social support. Uzzi's (1996) work on the garment industry provides strong evidence that suppliers and buyers, 'embedded' in relationships of trust and repeated exchange, behave in ways contrary to those predicted by models of short-term economic optimization in favor of sustaining longstanding relationships of mutual consideration and obligation. Uzzi finds that firms have a greater chance of survival as a result of their participation in these relationships.[9]

However, as Coleman notes, many, if not most, forms of social capital arise and decline as a by-product of activities engaged in for reasons other than the accumulation of social capital (Coleman 1988, 1990a). Systemic changes— changes in the social structure of which a particular form of social capital is an aspect—may affect the structure of relationships that constitute social capital, individuals' patterns of access to social capital, and the benefits of different forms of social capital. Because social capital is appropriable social structure, changes in the social structure will affect both its existence and its value.

Forms of social capital that confer solidarity benefits are perhaps those most obviously affected by systemic variation. Several examples serve to illustrate. As we saw previously in the work of Suttles and Street on the shift to public aid to the poor, formal, centralized aid programs can undermine indigenous social capital. In a reconsideration of international development efforts, Ostrom (1994) argues that development aid agencies ignore at their peril the social capital constituted by the self-consciously created rules that aid recipients use for allocating benefits from and assigning responsibility for physical facilities built with the funds provided by the aid agencies. These rules, which inhere in and are supported by existing relationships among indigenous aid recipients, are a form of social capital, which conditions the productivity of the physical facility built with the outside aid. Certain types of outside aid can change pre-existing patterns of relations among aid recipients, thereby 'reducing the recognition of mutual dependencies and patterns of reciprocity . . . that have long sustained the [existing] system' (Ostrom 1994, 553; see also Coleman 1988, 1990a).

---

[8] Interestingly, Burt et al. (in press) find little evidence of this for a sample of managers; as they say, the managers are 'innocent of network theory'. Nevertheless, Burt does finds 'entrepreneurial personality correlates' of structural holes among a sample of business school students (Burt 1997b); the valuable social capital of structural holes and the entrepreneurial mind set to exploit it seem to travel together.

[9] Uzzi (1996) finds a threshold effect of 'embeddedness'; beyond a certain degree of involvement, embeddedness becomes detrimental to survival, not least for reasons predicted by structural hole theory, such as constraint on exchanges.

Destruction of indigenous social capital can lead to gross inequality in the distribution of the costs and benefits of new facilities, and to instability in or eventual
collapse of the community the facility was built to aid.

Current interest in social capital's role in supporting democratic vitality and
active citizenship represents a concern with factors that affect social capital at the
level of the social system. Scholars such as Putnam (cf. 1993) attempt to measure
social integration by focusing on rates of social participation in activities such as
soccer teams, bowling leagues and Elks Clubs. Putnam suggests that high levels
of these types of social participation are indicative of a certain density of interaction that is instrumental in building mutual trust and commitment.[10] Individuals
who live in communities characterized by such patterns of social participation
are argued to receive certain kinds of social support, such as the confidence that
other, unrelated adults will 'keep an eye out for' their children (as in Coleman
1988, S99–100). System-level properties, such as rates of residential mobility,
place an upper bound on the possible degree of adult closure around children,
since some stability is required for the necessary acquaintance, trust and commitment to shared goals to arise among the adults (Coleman 1988; Hagan et al.
1996).

The previous examples concerned changes in the social structure that affect
the emergence and persistence of particular forms of social capital. Changes in
simple characteristics of social systems, such as changes in size, can have important consequences for the value of social capital, as well. Sandefur et al. (1999)
investigate changes in the income returns to rank-and-file lawyers of ties to elite
lawyers in the City of Chicago. They found evidence consistent with the hypothesis that the value of contacts with elite members of the social system of the bar
increased because of the growing scarcity of such contacts as the bar expanded in
size (see also Heinz et al. 1997).

Empirical studies of how variation in the structure of social systems affects
the capacity for action of the system and of individual actors within the system
have been rare, not least because data on multiple social systems and data from
multiple observations of single systems are difficult to come by. A sizable net-
work-analytic literature on community power and decision-making has investigated ways in which system-level properties affect network utility, or, in the
present paper's terms, social capital (Friedkin 1977; Heinz et al. 1997; Laumann
and Knoke 1987; Laumann and Marsden 1982; Laumann and Pappi 1976). In
this literature, specific patterns of social organization are argued to facilitate and
impede flows of information and influence in ways that affect the community's
ability both to make decisions and to act upon them, and that constrain the way
specific types of conflict will play themselves out in the community.

These observations about variations in social structure have two implications for social capital theory. First, system-level properties condition the capacity for action in a social system in ways that are sociologically relevant, but may
not be accessed when the analyst focuses solely on individual actors and the

[10] This work has been roundly criticized (cf. Levi 1996).

social capital those actors hold. Second, variation in system-level properties will affect the value of specific forms of social capital to particular individual actors. In comparisons of the workings of social capital in different contexts, attention to these system-level variations will be an essential task in understanding variation in social capital's productivity.

CONCLUSION

Coleman's concept of social capital provides a fruitful way to bring a concern with social structure into a framework of individual rational or purposive actors. We have suggested ways in which social capital may be differentiated in terms of its benefits, rather than its forms. This analytic tack permits better understanding of the mechanisms through which social capital has its effects and should, thus, permit more refined hypotheses about how social capital generates unequal outcomes at the level of individuals. A focus on benefits has been characteristic of the most successful attempts to quantify individuals' stocks of social capital. Such attempts have started with a focus on actors' goals and the specific benefits that would aid in the attainment of those goals, and then proceeded to construct measures of social structural properties that provide greater or lesser amounts of those benefits. Burt's 'structural hole' work is exemplary in this respect.

Variation in properties of the social structures from which individuals appropriate social capital affects the emergence, persistence and value of specific forms of social capital. Investigating this variation would further our understanding both of inequality in individual outcomes and of differences in the capacity of social systems to provide support for certain kinds of action. The analyses presented by Suttles and Street and Ostrom suggest compelling, real-life consequences of ignoring these kinds of system-level considerations.

As the social capital perspective has become an increasingly popular way of thinking about the resources that exist in different kinds of interpersonal relationships, the number and diversity of outcomes social capital has been hypothesized to affect has accordingly increased. Even in fairly narrow areas of inquiry, such as internal labor markets in a firm, certain forms of social capital that have been shown to be very valuable for some kinds of instrumental action, such as entrepreneurship and effective brokering, may be shown to be liabilities for other kinds of instrumental action, such as action that requires established trust or the capacity to mobilize others to act on one's behalf. As empirical evidence about the effects of various forms of social capital on different kinds of outcomes accumulates, social capital theory will no doubt develop richer and more subtle understandings of how resources that inhere in social structure produce and condition inequality. Attention to the existing literatures of related areas of inquiry—network analysis, social resources, social support and community studies, to suggest a few relevant fields—will add to this richness and subtlety.

NOTES

This paper is a revision and extension of a section of a paper presented at a conference in honor of James S. Coleman, Mannheim, Germany, 2 November 1996. This research was supported in part by grants from the American Bar Foundation and the National Science Foundation (#SBR-9411515). We thank Charles E. Bidwell, Ronald S. Burt, John P. Heinz, Ray Reagans, Ezra W. Zuckerman, Mary Brinton and two anonymous reviewers for helpful comments and suggestions. Gratitude is due, too, to Michael Reay for his patience. The views presented in this paper are the authors' alone, and they are responsible for any errors.

REFERENCES

Arnold, B. L. and F. M. Kay. 1995. 'Social Capital, Violations of Trust and the Vulnerability of Isolates: The Social Organization of Law Practice and Professional Self-Regulation.' *International Journal of the Sociology of Law* 23: 321–46.

Boudieu, Pierre. 1986. 'The Forms of Capital.' In *Handbook of Theory and Research for the Sociology of Education*, ed. J. Richardson, pp. 241–58. New York: Greenwood Press.

Burt, R. S. 1980. 'Autonomy in a Social Topology.' *American Journal of Sociology* 85: 892–925.

Burt, R. S. 1982. *Toward a Structural Theory of Action*. New York: Academic Press.

Burt, R. S. 1987. 'Social Contagion and Innovation: Cohesion versus Structural Equivalence.' *American Journal of Sociology* 92(May): 1287–1335.

Burt, R. S. 1992. *Structural Holes: The Social Structure of Competition*. Cambridge, MA: Harvard University Press.

Burt, R. S. 1993. 'Strategy: Predicting Social and Emotional Adaptive Structures from Underlying Constraint Structures.' Lecture, University of Chicago, Autumn.

Burt, R. S. 1995. 'Social Capital, Structural Holes and the Entrepreneur.' *Revue Francaise de Sociologie*, XXXVI-4.

Burt, R. S. 1996a. 'Entrepreneurs First and Third Parties' Prepared for presentation at Shared Cognition in Organizations. The Management of Knowledge Conference at the J. L. Kellogg Graduate School of Management, Northwestern University, November.

Burt, R. S. 1996b. 'Bent Preferences: Evidence on the Endogeneity of Beliefs and Preferences.' Social Organization of Competition Workshop Discussion Paper, Graduate School of Business and Department of Sociology, University of Chicago.

Burt, R. S. 1997a. 'The Contingent Value of Social Capital.' *Administrative Science Quarterly* 42(2): 339–65.

Burt, R. S. 1997b. 'A Note on Social Capital and Network Content.' *Social Networks* 19(4): 355–73.

Burt, R. S. 1998. 'The Gender of Social Capital.' *Rationality and Society* 10(1): 5–46.

Burt, R. S., J. E. Jannotta, Jr and J. T. Mahoney. In press. 'Personality Correlates of Structural Holes.' *Social Networks.*

Campbell, K. E., P. V. Marsden and J. S. Hurlbert. 1986. 'Social Resources and Socio-economic Status.' *Social Networks* 8: 97–117.

Carlin, J. 1966. *Lawyers' Ethics: A Survey of the New York City Bar.* New York: Russell Sage Foundation.

Cohen, S. and S. L. Syme (eds). 1985. *Social Support and Health.* Orlando, Fl.: Academic Press.

Coleman, J. S. 1988. 'Social Capital in the Creation of Human Capital.' *American Journal of Sociology* 94: S95–120.

Coleman, J. S. 1990a. *Foundations of Social Theory.* Cambridge, MA: The Belknap Press of Harvard University Press.

Coleman, J. S. 1990b. 'How Worksite Schools and Other School Reforms Can Generate Social Capital.' *American Educator* Summer: 35–6, 45.

Daniel, K. 1995. 'The Marriage Premium.' In *The New Economics of Human Behavior*, Ch. 7, ed. by M. Tommasi and K. Ierulli. Cambridge: Cambridge University Press.

Emerson, R. M. 1981. 'Social Exchange Theory.' In *Social Psychology: Sociological Perspectives*, eds by M. Rosenberg and R. Turner, pp. 30–65. New York: Basic Books.

Friedkin, N. 1977. 'The University and Corporate Organization in Basic Science.' Ph.D. Thesis, Department of Education, University of Chicago.

Granovetter, M. 1973. 'The Strength of Weak Ties.' *American Journal of Sociology* 78: 1360–80.

Granovetter, M. 1985. 'Economic Action and Social Structure: The Problem of Embeddedness.' *American Journal of Sociology* 91 (3): 481–510.

Hagan, J., R. MacMillan and B. Wheaton. 1996. 'New Kid in Town: Social Capital and the Life Course Effects of Family Migration on Children.' *American Sociological Review* 61(June): 368–85.

Heinz, J. P. and E. O. Laumann, R. L. Nelson and P. S. Schnorr. 1997. 'Elite Networks Among Urban Lawyers.' *Law and Social Inquiry* 31(3): 441–72.

House, J. S. 1987. 'Social Support and Social Structure.' *Sociological Forum* 2(1): 135–46.

House, J. S., D. Umberson and K. R. Landis. 1988. 'Social Structure and Processes of Support.' *Annual Review of Sociology* 14: 293–318.

Laumann, E. O. and D. Knoke. 1987. *The Organizational State: Social Choice in National Policy Domains*, Madison, WI: University of Wisconsin Press.

Laumann, E. O. and P. V. Marsden. 1982. 'Microstructural Analysis in Interorganizational Systems.' *Social Networks* 4: 329–48.

Laumann, E. O., P. V. Marsden and D. Prendai. 1983. 'The Boundary Specification Problem in Network Analysis.' In *Applied Network Analysis: A Methodological Introduction*, eds R. Burt and M. Minor. pp. 18–34. Beverly Hills: Sage Publications.

Laumann, E. O. and F. U. Pappi. 1976. *Networks of Collective Action: A Perspective on Community Influence.* New York: Academic Press.

Levi, M. 1996. 'Social and Unsocial Capital: A Review Essay of Robert Putnam's Making Democracy Work.' *Politics and Society* 24(1): 45–55.

Lin, N. 1990. 'Social Resources and Social Mobility: A Structural Theory of Status Attainment.' In *Social Mobility and Social Structure*, ed. Ronald L. Breiger, pp. 241–71. New York: Cambridge University Press.

Lin, N. 1995. 'Social Resources: A Theory of Social Capital.' *Revue Francaise de Sociologie* XXXVI-4.

Lin, N., A. Dean and W. M. Ensel. 1986. *Social Support, Life Events and Depression.* Orlando: Academic Press.

Lin, N., W. M. Ensel and J. C. Vaughn. 1981a. 'Social Resources and Occupational Status Attainment.' *Social Forces* 59(4): 1163–81.

Lin, N., J. C. Vaughn and W. M. Ensel. 1981b. 'Social Resources and Strength of Ties.' *American Sociological Review* 46(4): 393–405.

Marsden, P .V. and J. S. Hurlbert. 1988. 'Social Resources and Mobility Outcomes: A Replication and Extension.' *Social Forces* 66(4): 1038–59.

Meyerson, E. M. 1994. 'Human Capital, Social Capital and Compensation: the Relative Contribution of Social Contacts to Managers' Incomes.' *Acta Sociologica* 37: 383–99.

Ostrom, E. 1994. 'Constituting Social Capital and Collective Action.' *Journal of Theoretical Politics* 6(4): 527–62.

Parsons, T. 1951. *The Social System.* Glencoe, IL: The Free Press.

Parsons, T. 1963. 'On the Concept of Influence.' *Public Opinion Quarterly* 27(1): 37–62.

Pearlin, L. I. 1989. 'The Sociological Study of Stress.' *Journal of Health and Social Behavior* 30(3): 241–56.

Portes, A. and J. Sensenbrenner. 1993. 'Embeddedness and Immigration: Notes on the Social Determinants of Economic Action.' *American Journal of Sociology* 6(May): 1320–50.

Putnam, R. D. 1993. *Making Democracy Work: Civic Traditions in Modern Italy.* Princeton: Princeton University Press.

Sandefur, R. L., E. O. Laumann and J. P. Heinz. (1999). 'The Changing Value of Social Capital in an Expanding Social System: Lawyers in the Chicago Bar, 1975 and 1995'. In *Corporate Social Capital and Liability*, eds Roger Th. A.J. Leenders and Shaul M. Gabbay. Norwell, MA: Kluwer Academic Publishers.

Seron, C. and K. Ferris. 1995. 'Negotiating Professionalism: the Gendered Social Capital of Flexible Time.' *Work and Occupations* 22(1): 22–47.

Suttles, G. D. 1972. *The Social Construction of Communities.* Chicago: The University of Chicago Press.

Suttles, G. D. and D. Street. 1970. 'Aid to the Poor and Social Exchange.' In *The Logic of Social Hierarchies*, eds E. O. Laumann, P. M. Siegel and R. W. Hodge, Ch. 48. Chicago: Markham Publishing Company.

Uzzi, B. 1996. 'The Sources and Consequences of Embeddedness for the Economic Performance of Organizations: The Network Effect.' *American Sociological Review* 61(4): 674–98.

Weber, M. 1946. *The Theory of Social and Economic Organization.* Translated by A.M. Henderson and Talcott Parsons, ed. Talcott Parsons. New York: The Free Press.

Wellman, B. and S. Wortley. 1990. 'Different Strokes From Different Folks: Community Ties and Social Support.' *American Journal of Sociology* 96(3): 558–88.

Zukin, S. and P. DiMaggio, eds. 1990. *Structures of Capital: The Social Organization of the Economy*, Cambridge: Cambridge University Press.

REBECCA L. SANDEFUR is a PhD candidate in sociology at the University of Chicago. Her research concerns social stratification and inequality. Her dissertation investigates the relationship between career trajectories and inequality within the local labor market of a profession. With Edward O. Laumann and John P. Heinz, she has written 'The Changing Value and Character of Social Capital in an Expanding Social System' (forthcoming in a volume entitled *Corporate Social Capital*, edited by Shaul Gabbay and Roger Leenders).

EDWARD O. LAUMANN is the George Herbert Mead Distinguished Service Professor and Chairman of the Department of Sociology at the University of Chicago, and Director of the Ogburn Stouffer Center for Population and Social Organization. His research interests include social stratification, the sociology of professions, social network analysis, the analysis of elite groups and national policymaking, and the sociology of human sexuality. His eleven books include *The Organizational State: Social Choice in National Policy Domains* with David Knoke; *Chicago Lawyers: The Structure of the Bar* with John P. Heinz; and *The Social Organization of Sexuality* with John H. Gagnon, Robert T. Michael, and Stuart Michaels.

Chapter 5

Social Capital: The Good, the Bad, and the Ugly[*]

Paul S. Adler

Dept of Management and Organization, Marshall School of Business, University of Southern California, Los Angeles, CA 90089-1421

and

Seok-Woo Kwon

Dept of Management and Organization, Marshall School of Business, University of Southern California, Los Angeles, CA 90089-1421

Abstract—A growing number of sociologists, political scientists, development economists, and organizational theorists have invoked the concept of social capital in their search for answers to a broadening range of questions confronting their own fields. Seeking to clarify the utility of the concept for organizational theory, this paper synthesizes the theoretical research undertaken in these various disciplines and develops a common conceptual framework that identifies the sources, benefits, and risks of social capital.

INTRODUCTION

During recent years, the concept of social capital has become increasingly popular across a range of social science disciplines. A growing number of sociologists, political scientists, and development economists have invoked the concept of social capital in their search for answers to a broadening range of

---

[*] Reprinted with permission.

questions confronting their own fields. Social capital—understood broadly as the features of social structure that facilitates action—has informed the study of families and youth behavior problems, schooling and education, community life, democracy and governance, economic development, and general problems of collective action.

In organization studies, too, the concept of social capital is gaining currency. Researchers have used it to help explain phenomena such as career success (Burt, 1992; Podolny and Baron, 1997), organizational dissolution rates (Pennings, Lee, and van Witteloostuijn, 1998), the level of interunit resource exchange and product innovation (Tsai and Ghoshal, 1998), the creation of intellectual capital (Nahapiet and Ghoshal, 1998), CEO compensation (Belliveau, O'Reilly, and Wade, 1996), the network formation of start-up companies (Walker, Kogut, and Shan, 1997), and supplier relations (Baker, 1990). For a growing number of organizational researchers, the concept of social capital offers a way to bring more theoretical specificity to the broad range of phenomena that have long been at the heart of organization studies under the label "informal organization." The lineage can be traced back to the original Hawthorn studies (Roethlisberger & Dickson, 1939) which mapped cliques among workers and showed their influence on work norms and performance.

The growing interest in social capital has, however, not been matched by a corresponding degree of theoretical integration across the disciplines. In order to benefit from the insights into the sources, benefits, and risks of social capital developed by the various social science disciplines, we need a common conceptual framework. This paper proposes such a framework. We leave aside much of the empirical research on social capital to focus here on its conceptual foundations.

DEFINING SOCIAL CAPITAL

Over the years, social scientists have offered a number of definitions of social capital—see Table 5.1. These definitions fall into two broad types depending on whether they focus primarily the relations an actor maintains with other actors or the relations characterizing the internal structure of an organization.

The first group focuses primarily on social capital as a resource facilitating action by a focal actor, a resource that inheres in the social network tying that focal actor to other actors. This view, more common among sociologists, begins with the idea that the actions of individuals and groups can be greatly facilitated by their membership in social networks, specifically by their direct and indirect links to other actors in these networks. Under this view, social capital can help explain the differential success of individuals and firms in their competitive rivalry. Sociological social capital research has been strongly influenced by network theorists, and this view of social capital is reflected in the ego-centric variant of network analysis.

TABLE 5.1 Definitions of Social Capital

AUTHORS	DEFINITIONS OF SOCIAL CAPITAL	EXTERNAL VS INTERNAL
Baker	"a resource that actors derive from specific social structures and then use to pursue their interests; it is created by changes in the relationship among actors." (1990: 619).	external
Belliveau, O'Reilly, & Wade	"an individual's personal network and elite institutional affiliations" (1996: 1572).	external
Bourdieu	"the aggregate of the actual or potential resources which are linked to possession of a durable network of more or less institutionalized relationships of mutual acquaintance or recognition" (1985: 248). Social capital is "made up of social obligations ("connections"), which is convertible, in certain conditions, into economic capital and may be institutionalized in the form of a title of nobility" (1985: 243). "the sum of the resources, actual or virtual, that accrue to an individual or a group by a virtue of possessing a durable network of more or less institutionalized relations of mutual acquaintance and recognition" (Bourdieu and Wacquant, 1992: 119).	external
Boxman, et al.	"the number of people who can be expected to provide support and the resources those people have at their disposal" (1991: 52).	external
Burt	"friends, colleagues, and more general contacts through whom you receive opportunities to use your financial and human capital" (1992: 9). "the brokerage opportunities in a network" (1997: 355).	external
Coleman	"Social capital is defined by its function. It is not a single entity, but a variety of different entities having two characteristics in common: They all consist of some aspect of social structure, and they facilitate certain actions of individuals who are within the structure. Like other forms of capital, social capital is productive, making possible the achievement of certain ends that would not be attainable in its absence" (1990: 302).	external
Portes	"the ability of actors to secure benefits by virtue of membership in social networks or other social structures" (1998: 6).	external
Brehm & Rahn	"the web of cooperative relationships between citizens that facilitate resolution of collective action problems" (1997: 999).	internal

TABLE 5.1 *Continued*

Fukuyama	"the ability of people to work together for common purposes in groups and organizations" (1995: 10). "Social capital can be defined simply as the existence of a certain set of informal values or norms shared among members of a group that permit cooperation among them" (1997).	internal
Inglehart	"a culture of trust and tolerance, in which extensive networks of voluntary associations emerge" (1997: 188).	internal
Thomas	"those voluntary means and processes developed within civil society which promote development for the collective whole" (1996: 11).	internal
Portes and Sensenbrenner	"those expectations for action within a collectivity that affect the economic goals and goal-seeking behavior of its members, even if these expectations are not oriented toward the economic sphere" (1993: 1323).	internal
Putnam	"features of social organization such as networks, norms, and social trust that facilitate coordination and cooperation for mutual benefit" (1995: 67).	internal
Loury	"naturally occurring social relationships among persons which promote or assist the acquisition of skills and traits valued in the marketplace . . . an asset which may be as significant as financial bequests in accounting for the maintenance of inequality in our society" (1992: 100).	both
Nahapiet and Ghoshal	"the sum of the actual and potential resources embedded within, available through, and derived from the network of relationships possessed by an individual or social unit. Social capital thus comprises both the network and the assets that may be mobilized through that network" (1998: 243).	both
Pennar	"the web of social relationships that influences individual behavior and thereby affects economic growth" (1997: 154).	both
Schiff	"the set of elements of the social structure that affects relations among people and are inputs or arguments of the production and/or utility function" (1992: 160).	both
Woolcock	"the information, trust, and norms of reciprocity inhering in one's social networks" (1998: 153).	both

In contrast to this view of social capital as a resource located in the external linkages of a focal actor, other strands of social capital research focus on social capital as a feature of the internal linkages that characterize the structures of collective actors (groups, organizations, communities, regions, nations, etc. as distinct from individual actors) and give them cohesiveness and its associated benefits. This view is more common among political scientists and developmental economists. It is reflected in the socio-centric (Sandefur and Laumann, 1998) and much of the "whole-network" (Wellman, 1988: 26) variants of network sociology.

To a large extent, the distinction between the individual resource, external view and the collective characteristic, internal view is a matter of perspective and unit of analysis. Some definitions are therefore neutral on this dimension. Moreover, these two views are not mutually exclusive. A collective actor such as a firm is influenced by both its external linkages to other firms and institutions and the fabric of its internal linkages: its capacity for effective action is typically a function of both. Research on social capital has, however, tended to focus on one or the other (for a notable exception, see Gabbay and Zuckerman, 1998. We should note in passing that much of the more recent network theory has embodied a commitment to methodological individualism in theory-building, and is therefore skeptical of the explanatory as distinct from descriptive value of socio-centric analysis). We thus adopt a definition that allows such an integrated view:

> Social capital is a resource for individual and collective actors created by the configuration and content of the network of their more or less durable social relations.

THE RELATION OF SOCIAL CAPITAL TO OTHER FORMS OF CAPITAL

In what sense is this resource a form of capital? Baron and Hannan (1994) complain about the indiscriminate and metaphoric import of economic concepts into sociological literature and refer to the social capital literature as an example of "a plethora of capitals." Social capital exhibits a number of similarities with, as well as differences from, other forms of capital. We review these relations, starting with the commonalities and moving progressively towards the stronger differentiators.

First, like all other forms of capital, social capital is a resource into which other resources can be invested with the expectation of future, albeit uncertain, returns. Through investment in building their network of external relations, both individual and collective actors can augment their social capital and thereby gain access to valuable contacts and information; and by investing in the development of their internal relations, collective actors can strengthen their collective identity and augment their capacity for effective governance. While social capital can reasonably be assumed to be an exogenously given "endowment" for the purposes of some analyses, taking the longer and broader view, it is "constructible" (Evans, 1996; see also Sabel, 1993, on the constructibility of trust.)

Second, like other forms of capital, social capital is "appropriable" (Coleman, 1988) and "convertible" (Bourdieu, 1985). Like physical capital which can typically be used for different purposes (albeit not necessarily equally efficiently), social capital is appropriable in the sense that an actor's network of, say, friendship ties, can be used for other purposes, such as information or advice. Moreover, the advantages conferred by one's position in a social network can be converted to economic or other advantage. Among the many forms of capital identified by Bourdieu, economic capital is most liquid; it is readily convertible into human, cultural, and social capital. By comparison, the "convertibility rate" of social capital into economic capital is lower: social capital is less liquid and more "sticky" (Anheier, Gerhards, and Romo, 1995).

Third, like other forms of capital, social capital can be a substitute or a complement to other resources. As a substitute, actors can sometimes compensate for a lack financial or human capital by excellent "connections." More commonly, social capital is complementary to other forms of capital. For example, social capital can improve the efficiency of economic capital by reducing transaction costs.

Fourth, like physical capital and human capital but unlike financial capital, social capital needs maintenance. Social bonds have to be periodically renewed and reconfirmed, or else they lose efficacy.

Fifth, like human capital but unlike physical capital, social capital does not have a predictable rate of depreciation, and that for two reasons. First, while it may depreciate with non-use, as suggested in the previous paragraph, it does not depreciate with use. Like human capital and some forms of public goods such as knowledge, it normally grows and develops with use: trust demonstrated today will be reciprocated and amplified tomorrow. Second, while social capital is sometimes rendered obsolete by contextual changes (see Sandefur and Laumann, 1998, for examples), the rate at which this happens is most typically unpredictable, so that even conservative accounting principles cannot estimate a depreciation rate.

Sixth, like clean air and safe streets but unlike many other forms of capital, social capital of aggregate actors is a "collective good," in that it is not the private property of those who benefit from it (Coleman, 1988). Hence, it is vulnerable to "tragedy of the commons" risks. While it takes mutual commitment and cooperation from both parties to build social capital, a defection by only one party will destroy it.

Seventh, unlike all other forms of capital, social capital is "located" not in the actors but in their relations with other actors. This is perhaps the most general and fundamental difference. "No one player has exclusive ownership rights to social capital. If you or your partner in a relationship withdraws, the connection dissolves with whatever social capital it contained" (Burt, 1992: 58). (We might note in passing that in this sense, social capital echoes the Marxist concept of capital as a social relation: for Marx, productive capital creates value only because of its intimate, mutually-constitutive relation to wage-labor. Social capital, however, unlike Marxian capital, is not essentially asymmetrical.)

Notwithstanding these differences, the designation "capital" therefore seems appropriate. Solow (1997) objects to the dressing up social capital in the language and apparatus of capital theory: "what are those past investments in social capital? How could an accountant measure them and cumulate them

[even] in principle?" However, such measurement concerns do not constitute a conceptual critique. To Baron and Hannan (1994) complaint about "a plethora of capitals," we therefore respond that if research reveals more numerous sources of effective agency, such a proliferation is to be welcomed.

THE SOURCES OF SOCIAL CAPITAL

There is considerable confusion in the research to date on the sources of social capital. We present the various sources of social capital identified by different authors in Table 5.2. The views of the different authors appear to depend on their disciplinary background and on the questions they address with the social capital concept.

In the sociological literature, Coleman presents a network-based interpretation of the sources of social capital. Locating the source of social capital in the structure of social networks, Coleman highlights the way in which networks characterized by closure and multiplex ties facilitate the emergence of various forms of social capital such as obligations, information channels, trust, norms, and effective sanctions.

Portes (1998) shifts the explanatory focus from networks to norms, differentiating the sources of social capital according to actors' motivations to honor its obligations. In the first type of motivation, which he calls "consummatory," action is based on internalized norms. People feel an obligation to behave in certain ways because they have internalized the corresponding norms. These internalized norms can be engendered through socialization in childhood or through common experience later in life. The second type of motivation is "instrumental": it too is based on norms, but norms of the different kind, namely, the norms of reciprocity. Unlike consummatory motivation, instrumental motivation is more calculative and rational and is based on enforceable trust of others. Therefore, in Portes' version, social capital can be engendered either through noncalculative processes of generalized norms or through calculative processes of social exchange.

The political science and development economics literatures are more eclectic in their characterization of the sources of social capital. Putnam (1993) for example, lists network ties, norms, and trust. Other political scientists, criticizing Putnam's excessively "bottom-up" view of social capital, have stressed the "top-down" role of formal institutions, such as government structure and legal rules, in facilitating the emergence and maintenance of social capital and trust in civil society (e.g., Berman, 1997; Evans, 1996; Kenworthy, 1997; Levi, 1996; Pildes, 1996; Portney and Berry, 1997; Schneider, et al, 1997; Woolcock, 1998; Youniss, McLellan, and Yates, 1997). Synthesizing and summarizing this literature, Ostrom (1994) identifies four key sources of social capital: networks, norms, social beliefs, and rules.

TABLE 5.2 Source of Social Capital

AUTHORS	NETWORK	NORMS	BELIEFS	RULES AND FORMAL INSTITUTIONS
Nahapiet & Ghoshal (1998)	structural dimension	relational dimension	cognitive dimension	
Ostrom (1994)	networks	norms	social beliefs	rules
Portes (1988)		value interjection; norms of reciprocity	bounded solidarity	
Putnam (1993)	networks	norms		
Coleman (1988; 1990)	closure; multiplex ties			
Brehm & Rahn (1997)	civic participation			
Newton (1997)	networks	norms and values		
Evans (1996)				integrity and synergy of state
Pildes (1996)		social norms		formal state law
Woolcock (1998)	community integration and linkage			government integrity and state-society synergy
Berman (1997)				political institution
Schneider, et al (1997)				government institutions
Levi (1996)				government
Fellmeth (1996)				rule of law
Kenworthy (1997)				institutions
Minkoff (1997)				national-level social movement organizations
Portney and Berry (1997)				government
Youniss, McLellan, & Yates (1997)		values inculcated by schooling	beliefs inculcated by schooling	schooling
Greeley (1997)		religion	religion	
Burt (1997)	structural holes			

Finally in the organizational research literature, Nahapiet and Ghoshal (1998) discuss three dimensions of social capital: structural, relational, and cognitive. Under the structural dimension, they list network ties, network configuration, and appropriable organization. The cognitive dimension includes shared codes, language, and narratives. The relational dimension includes trust, norms, obligations, and identification.

We believe that these various accounts can be integrated within a single conceptual model without doing too much violence to their respective arguments. We propose to highlight the three primary direct sources of social capital most prominent in the extant theory: network, shared norms, and shared beliefs. Each of these sources makes a distinct contribution to the formation of social capital, although all three are mutually interdependent. Rules, or more generally formal institutions—government at the societal level, and formal structure at the organizational level—have a strong effect on all three direct sources of social capital, and may arguably also have a direct effect on social capital. The role of trust in this conceptual model is more complex, reflecting the considerable confusion in the literature as to whether the notion of social capital includes trust (per Fukuyama and Putnam) or social capital is the source of trust (per Coleman). In the subsections below, we review these factors in turn and identify a number of features within each.

Networks

Some authors focus on the social networks of individuals, groups, and organizations as the crucial source of social capital because social capital is essentially about the relationships between individuals and groups. For network sociologists, the focus on networks is also motivated by a prior commitment to basing explanation on behaviors rather than subjective phenomena such norms and beliefs (see Wellman, 1988: 23).

While many researchers cite networks as an important source of social capital, what they mean by networks varies considerably. Among such theorists as Putnam, Brehm and Rahn, Ostrom, and Evans, who have focused on internal ties within a given society, the term networks often simply means informal face-to-face interaction or membership in civic associations or social clubs. By contrast, network theorists argue that an understanding of social capital requires a finer-grained analysis of the specific structures of these networks.

According to network theorists, social networks influence a focal actor's social capital both through the actor's direct ties and through the indirect ties afforded them by virtue of the overall structure of the broader network within which they are embedded (Tichy, 1981; Scott, 1991). Burt (1992), Coleman (1988), Granovetter (1973), and Lin (1998), among others, point out that direct and indirect network ties provide access both to people who can themselves provide support and to the resources those people can mobilize through their own network ties.

In addition to the number of network ties, the structure of these network relationships have been studied by several researchers. Coleman's (1988) discussion of "closure" as a source of social capital is one such argument based on network structure. Coleman argues that closure of the network structure—the extent to which my contacts are themselves connected—facilitates the emergence of effective norms and maintains the trustworthiness of others, thereby strengthening social capital. In a more open structure, violations of norms are more likely to go undetected and unpunished. People will thus be less trusting of one another, weakening social capital. Putnam draws on Coleman's closure argument and argues that dense networks strengthen trust and shared norms, thus making democratic institutions function effectively.

In other research on the social capital effects of network structure, but in contrast with Coleman's focus on closure, Burt (1992) argues that a sparse network with few redundant ties often provides greater social capital benefits. If the opportunity to broker the flow of information between groups constitutes a central benefit of social capital, and if in general information circulates more within than between groups, then a key source of social capital is a network of ties characterized by many structure holes—linkages to groups not otherwise connected. One of the pioneers of the concept of social capital, Jane Jacobs (1993/1961) also notes the importance of brokers in public community life. She argues that brokers who interact with many different community members facilitate the circulation of news that is of interest to communities, without imposing extensive sociability among people.

In part, the difference between Coleman and Burt reflects the difference between their respective internal and external focii. Closure provides social capital's cohesiveness benefits within an organization or community; structural holes in the focal actor's external linkages provides cost-effective resources for action. We believe that both closure and sparse networks can yield benefits. Which is more valuable depends on the state of the other sources of social capital (e.g., norms, beliefs, and rules) and on the task and environment confronting the actor. We return to this and other interdependencies below.

Norms

Much network theory in sociology has worked towards Simmel's vision of a "formalistic sociology" which can reveal how the structure of social interaction generates its content (Wellman, 1988: 23): it has thus downplayed the importance of the content of network ties as an independent sources of social capital (Emirbayer and Goodwin, 1994). By contrast, research in other disciplines has emphasized the role of shared norms and beliefs in determining the amount of social capital embodied in these ties. As Edwards and Foley (1997: 671) put it, "it is precisely this sociocultural component of social capital that provides the context within which it acquires meaning and becomes available to individuals and groups in a way that can facilitate an individual or collective action not otherwise possible."

A number of theorists see social capital as primarily based on shared norms. Portes (1998) and Putnam (1993) focus on the norm of generalized reciprocity. As Putnam (1993) puts it, generalized reciprocity involves "not 'I'll do this for you, because you are more powerful than I,' nor even 'I'll do this for you now, if you do that for me now, but 'I'll do this for you now, knowing that somewhere down the road you'll do something for me.'" (pp. 182–183). This norm of generalized reciprocity resolves problems of collective action and binds communities. It thus serves to transform individuals from self-seeking and egocentric agents, with little sense of obligation to others, into members of a community with shared interests and a sense of the common good.

While Putnam and Portes focus on shared norms as a key source of social capital, there is some ambiguity in the literature as to exactly what it is about norms that makes them a source. In the classic study by Banfield (1958) of "amoral familism" in southern Italy, norms are strong and shared but are such as to undermine rather than create social capital. For other scholars, therefore, it is the specific nature of the shared norms that determines whether they function as a source of social capital. We return to this concern below.

Beliefs

In the literature on social capital, the role of beliefs has received relatively little attention. However, we find compelling the arguments for the inclusion of beliefs presented by Nahapiet and Ghoshal (1998) and Portes (1988).

Nahapiet and Ghoshal argue that beliefs, in the forms of shared strategic visions, interpretations, and systems of meaning, play a critical role in the generation of social capital, and that such beliefs are theoretically and practically distinct from normative value orientations. Social capital is unlikely to arise among people who do not understand each other. In the absence of shared meanings or goals, it is difficult to see why or how people would collaborate. Social capital stems in part from the availability of common belief system that allows participants to communicate their ideas and make sense of common experiences. Such communicative resources allow common world-views, assumptions, and expectations to emerge among people and facilitate their joint action.

Portes (1998) makes a similar argument. Shared experiences and the common beliefs that typically result from these experiences contribute to social capital because they create a strong sense of community and solidarity. For a prototypical example of such a story, Portes cites Marx's analysis of emergent class consciousness in the industrial proletariat: workers learn to identify with each other and support each other's initiatives because they are thrown together in a common situation of adversity and therefore form similar beliefs. In a case study of community organizing among low-income, ethnically diverse residents of Oakland, California, Wood (1997) found that not only shared values, but also symbol systems and assumptions about the world play a crucial role in determining the success of organizing.

As with norms, the specific content of the beliefs that are shared may also play a role in determining whether they add or detract from social capital and whether this social capital acts as a facilitator or constraint on action.

Rules

Formal institutions and rules also have a strong effect on social capital. It is therefore unfortunate—perhaps a function of what Nohria and Berkley (1994) called the "ideological foundation of network analysis"—that network theorists have largely ignored this effect. In organizational research, calls by Tichy (1981) to study this relationship have been echoed by Ibarra (1992) but have largely gone unanswered (Gittell and Weiss, 1998).

Formal institutions and rules can have a powerful indirect effect on social capital via their influence on the first three sources. They can also have a significant direct effect.

First, formal rules and institutions can shape the network structure and the content of the ties (Salancik, 1995). Podolny and Baron (1997) note that formal organization shapes and determines much of informal organization because many ties come with positions and are not voluntarily chosen. Such an impact of formal structure on network structure will in turn influence social capital.

Second, formal institutions can influence norms and beliefs. For example, we can reasonably conjecture that the passage of civil rights legislation contributed to setting in motion a process which—while complex and contradictory in its effects—led not only to a reduction in the extent of racial segregation in Americans' social networks but also and more directly to a reduction in the prevalence of racist norms and beliefs, all of which in turn increased American society's social capital.

Formal institutions can arguable also affect social capital more directly. In her criticism of Putnam's and Fukuyama's research, Levi (1996) argues that government is a major source of social capital: "governments provide more than the backdrop for facilitating trust among citizens; governments also influence civic behavior to the extent they elicit trust or distrust towards themselves" (p. 51). She argues that government with transparent and procedurally fair rules and mechanisms for ensuring the credibility of government actors' policy promises can create social capital (Levi, 1996: 51). Other political scientists (e.g., Berman, 1997; Kenworthy, 1997; Ostrom,1994; Pildes, 1996; Portney and Berry, 1997) all agree that strong government responsive to people's needs plays a direct role in building social capital in community.

We note in passing that if rules' effects on social capital were only indirect, this might encourage us to think of them as a distinct construct—as "institutional capital" (Hardin, 1998). If, however, rules also have a direct effect on social capital, such a distinction is less fruitful.

To characterize rules as source, direct or indirect, of social capital runs counter to a powerful anti-authoritarian ideology within social research. This ideology has tended to encourage the assumption that the effects of formal structure (such as bureaucracy within organizations and government within societies) on social capital (in the form of informal organization within organizations and civil society within societies) are primarily negative. A more objective assessment reveals the possibility of a positive contribution (see Hyden's, 1997, review of the literature on the different possible relations between civil society and state, and Evan's, 1996, contrast of crowding out vs. synergy views).

What features of formal institutions explain these positive vs. negative effects? Adler and Borys (1996) distinguish "enabling" and "coercive" forms of bureaucracy within organizations, and argue that these forms have contrasting effects on the employee commitment and the informal fabric of cooperation. They identify differences in the two forms in both how the formal structures are designed and how they are implemented. Their analysis parallels the work of Evans (1996) in development economics, who argues that the state can buttress rather than undermine civil society's social capital on two conditions: internally, its structure and process must display sufficient integrity, and externally, its relations with actors in civil society must display sufficient synergy. Clearly, these conditions are not always (perhaps not even often) met; but just as clearly, when they are met, rules act as a powerful source of social capital.

Trust

There is some confusion in the literature as to the relationship between trust and social capital. Some authors equate trust with social capital (Fukuyama, 1995, 1997); some see it as a source (Putnam, 1993); some as a form (Coleman, 1988). We believe that trust is conceptually distinct from social capital and that it is both a source and an effect.

Trust is conceptually distinct: it is a psychological state of individuals, whereas social capital is feature of social structure. Granovetter's (1973) demonstration of the importance of weak ties in facilitating access to jobs is simultaneously a demonstration that social capital—in this case, the strength of weak ties—does not require high trust—since these weak ties are characterized by levels of trust that are close to neutral.

We believe that trust and social capital are mutually reinforcing. Social capital often generates trusting relationships, and the trust generated will in turn produce social capital. Using indicators of trust and civic norms from the World Values Surveys from 29 countries, Knack and Keefer (1996) find that trust in people is correlated with civic norms. Using the General Social Survey data from 1972 to 1994, Brehm and Rahn (1997) also find that civic engagement as measured by membership in civic and political organizations and interpersonal trust are in a reciprocal relationship: "the more that citizens participate in their communities, the more that they learn to trust others; the greater trust that citizens hold for others, the more likely they are to participate" (pp. 1001–1002). Brehm and Rahn use structural modeling to tease out this reciprocal causality, and find that the relationship between civic engagement and trust is significant and positive in both directions, though the direction from civic engagement to trust is stronger than the reverse.

The positive correlation between trust and social capital is partially explained by the fact that the three sources of social capital also influence trust. Interpersonal trust is the result of familiarity, shared norms, and calculation, and it is buttressed by system trust (Adler, 1998; Lewicki and Bunker, 1995; Shapiro, Sheppard, and Cheraskin, 1992). There is therefore a close relationship between the sources of trust and the sources of social capital: familiarity as a source of trust refers to the central feature of network ties as a source of social capital; shared norms appear as a determinant of both; calculative trust rests on shared beliefs; and the buttressing role of system trust is close to the role we have ascribed to formal rules and institutions in the constitution of social capital.

Complementarities Between Social and Human Capital

We should note briefly that there are important complementarities between the various sources of social capital identified above and human capital.

First, human capital is complementary to networks in the formation of social capital. In his discussion of the role of social capital within the family in a child's intellectual development, Coleman argues that if human capital (in the form of parents' education) is not complemented by social capital (in the form of both parents in the home, greater number of siblings, and higher expectations by parents for the child's education), the parents' human capital contributes little to the child's educational growth (1988: S110). While human capital in the absence of social capital is not productive, Coleman argues, there are cases where social capital in the absence of human capital can be still productive: he cites the example of Asian immigrant families who have high expectations and investments for their children.

Second, human capital can considerably enhance the contribution of shared norms and beliefs to social capital. Nebus (1998) develops a conceptual model of the inter-unit technology transfer within multinational firms. He argues that this transfer is facilitated by shared norms and beliefs, and that the efficacy of these factors is considerably augmented by the characteristics of the respective actors. Reinterpreting his argument slightly, we can see that the actors' motivation and openness augment the effect of shared norms, and their absorptive and communicative abilities augment the effect of shared beliefs.

Finally, human capital can augment the contribution of formal rules to social capital. While the anti-authoritarian tradition of social theory has encouraged the assumption that strong rules and institutions substitute for human capital, a more plausible generalization is that the relationship is more often one of complementarity. Bureaucracy is more often associated with higher rather than lower levels of skill and professionality (Kohn and Schooler, 1983).

Social Capital and Market Relations

Before leaving the theme of the sources of social capital, we should at least note the importance of the question of whether market relations promote or undermine social capital. Several currents of social theory that have argued the market tends over time to corrode community and social capital. Hirschman (1982) reviews the many incarnations of this "self-destructive" view of market-based society expressed in both Marxist and classical reactionary thought as well as in numerous strands of sociological theory associated with Weber, Simmel, Durkheim to name but a few. In this view, the market undermines the traditional bonds of community and extended family, leading to the anonymity of urbanization.

Hirschman points out, however, that this self-destructive view has competed with another, more benign view of the effect of the market of society, a view he labels the "*doux commerce*" (Fr: gentle commerce) thesis. Thomas Paine in *The Rights of Man* (1951 [1792]: 215) expressed it in the proposition: "[Commerce] is a pacific system, operating to cordialise mankind, by rendering Nations, as well as individuals, useful to each other." Echoes of this view are heard in contemporary scientific and ideological discourse on the way economic "liberalization" fosters "democracy."

It is beyond the scope of the present article to attempt a synthesis of these two strands (for further discussion, see Adler, 1998). We note simply that research on social capital has varied in its sensitivity to this theoretically and historically broader framing of its significance. Organizational research might find opportunities to link to the broader concerns of historians and sociologists by considering this broader framing (for one fruitful linkage, see Howard, 1988).

BENEFITS OF SOCIAL CAPITAL

For our discussion of benefits, we draw on Sandefur and Laumann's (1998) distinction between information, influence and control, and social solidarity benefits. We will consider each of these benefits for the focal actors as well as positive externalities engendered for the broader aggregate. Table 5.3 summarizes our points.

For the focal actor, social capital facilitates access to broader sources of information at lower cost. Coleman (1988) illustrates this benefit with the example of a social scientist catching up on the latest research in related fields through everyday interaction with colleagues. Network research has shown that network ties help actors gain access to information about job opportunities (Boxman, De Graaf, and Flap, 1991; Burt, 1992; Fernandez and Weinberg, 1997; Granovetter, 1973; Lin, Ensel, and Vaughn, 1981; Meyerson, 1994), and about innovations (Rogers, 1995; Coleman, Katz, and Menzel, 1966). Research on ethnic entrepreneurs and ethnic firms (as reviewed in Portes and Sensenbrenner, 1993) has also

TABLE 5.3 The Benefits and Risks of Social Capital

	BENEFITS	RISKS
FOR THE FOCAL ACTOR	* Information access	* costs of creating and maintaining relationship
	* power	* tradeoff between power benefits and information benefits
	* solidarity	* overembedding due to excessive external ties * excessive claims * restrictions on freedom *lower creativity and innovation * downward leveling of norms
EXTERNALITIES FOR THE BROADER AGGRGATE	* information diffusion	* excessive brokering
	* task accomplishment adds to social welfare	* negative externalities of successful task accomplishment for broader aggregate
	* civic community/ organization citizenship behavior	* fragmentation of broader whole due to excessive identification with focal group * collusion by focal actors against broader aggregate interests * restricted access by outsiders to focal group's knowledge and resources

shown that the information provided by community ties are critical for the mobility opportunities of newly arrived immigrants. The informational benefits of social capital have also been studied in interorganizational research. Powell and Smith-Doerr (1994) and Podolny and Page (1998) review the research showing that interorganizational networks have a considerable benefit in helping firms acquire new skills and knowledge. Uzzi (1997) found that social embeddedness allows firms to exchange fine-grained information.

Information benefits at the focal group level can also lead to positive externalities for the broader aggregate. In Burt's (1997) view, social capital enables brokering activities that bring information from other actors to the focal actor; but if this brokering activity relies on a reciprocal outflow of information, the entire network will benefit from the diffusion of valuable information. Drawing on ethnographic fieldwork of apparel industry, Uzzi (1997) finds that transfer of fine-grained information among firms helps them all better to forecast future demands and anticipate customer preferences. Nebus (1998) argues that social capital between independent units within a multinational corporation facilitates the transfer of information, and Hansen (1998b) shows that weak ties facilitate the cost-effective search for new information and that strong ties facilitate the cost-effective transfer of complex information and tacit knowledge.

Power and influence is a second benefit of social capital. In Coleman's example of the "Senate Club," some senators are more powerful than others because they have built up a set of obligations from other senators and they can use those credits to get legislation passed (Coleman, 1988: S102). While Coleman looks at power benefits originating within the same social circles, Burt (1992) focuses on power benefits that accrue to entrepreneurs who bridge disconnected groups. Because these entrepreneurs have a say in whose interests are served by the bridge and can thus negotiate terms favorable to these interests, they become powerful actors. In a related study, Burt (1997) argues that managers spanning structural holes are more powerful because they can control the form of projects that connect other groups.

These power benefits can also have positive externalities for broader aggregate level. Power facilitates the completion of tasks. Power in the positive sense of the word enables people to lead others toward a common goal and facilitates collective action. The Senate Club is arguably a more effective legislative body than an ideal-typical egalitarian-collegial organization because some of its actors have accrued more power and can thus play a leadership role.

The third benefit of social capital is solidarity. Strong social norms and beliefs, associated with a high degree of closure of the social network, encourage compliance with local rules and customs, and reduce the need for formal controls. The effectiveness of rotating-credit associations (Geertz, 1962) and the low dropout rate among Catholic-school students (Coleman, 1988) illustrate these solidarity benefits. In the organizational culture literature, we find similar phenomena in organizations with strong culture and solidarity. Ouchi (1980) argues that clan organizations with strong shared norms benefit from lower monitoring costs and higher commitment. Nelson's (1989) study of intergroup ties in organizations supports this interpretation. He shows that frequent interactions among groups permits faster dispute resolution and prevents the accumulation of grievances and grudges. Krackhardt and Hanson (1988) point out that the trust network can transmit more sensitive and richer information than other types of networks because of its solidarity benefit.

For the broader aggregate, the positive externalities associated with a collective actor's internal solidarity include civic engagement at the societal level and organizational citizenship behavior at the organizational level. Putnam articulates these externalities in his analysis of the sources of civic engagement: "Internally, associations instill in their members habits of cooperation, solidarity, and public-spiritedness" (Putnam, 1993: 89–90) and these habits in turn spill over into members' involvement with other associations and more broadly into a higher level of generalized trust. In business organizations, such externalities would lead people working in more highly cohesive subunits to show higher commitment to the firm's superordinate goals.

RISKS OF SOCIAL CAPITAL

While a large body of research has focuses on the benefits of social capital, the literature on its risks is much sparser. However, social capital sometimes can be profoundly dysfunctional and counter-productive. As with physical capital, investments in social capital are not costlessly reversible or convertible, and therefore unbalanced investment or over-investment in social capital can transform a potentially productive asset into a constraint and a liability. This section explores the nature of these risks, using the same analytical structure as the previous section's discussion of benefits to distinguish the risks for the focal actors and the risks of negative externalities for the broader aggregate—respectively the bad and the ugly aspects of social capital referred to in this paper's title.

Let us begin with the risks for focal actors. First, building social capital requires considerable investment in establishing and maintaining relationships. As with any expensive investment, social capital investment may not be cost-efficient in certain situations. Hansen's (1998a) research on social capital's information benefit shows that project teams with too many direct ties with other units took longer to complete their tasks than those with fewer ties. Though these ties had information benefits, they were too costly to maintain. He argues that weak ties are more effective, not because they provide access to nonredundant information (as Granovetter would argue), but because they are less costly to maintain than strong ones.

Second, the information benefits of social capital may in some cases cancel out its power benefits. Ahuja (1998) argues that while an actor gains information benefits by having many contacts who themselves have many ties with many other contacts, the focal actors' direct contacts will be less dependent on the focal actor than if these direct contacts had few other contacts.

Third, for the focal actor, solidarity benefits may backfire in several ways. Strong solidarity with in-group members may overembed the actor in the relationship. Such overembeddedness reduces the flow of new ideas into the group, resulting in parochialism and inertia. As Powell and Smith-Doerr put it, "the ties that bind may also turn into ties that blind" (p. 393). Uzzi (1997) shows that overembeddedness increases feuding, blocks access to new information, and increases vulnerability of whole network to extinction from large-scale changes in the environment. Kern (1998) makes a similar argument about the current state of German industry. He notes that there is too much trust in Germany today to support radical innovation—firms are too loyal to established suppliers, and are thus slow to seek out and adopt more novel ideas.

In a similar vein, Portes (1998) notes that social capital may create free-riding problems and hinder entrepreneurship. Strong norms in a community may dictate the sharing of resources among extended family members, which may in turn reduce the incentives for entrepreneurial activity and thus slow the accumulation of capital. This argument is reflected in Uzzi's finding that, in overembedded relationships, "feelings of obligation and friendship may be so great between transactors that a firm becomes a 'relief organization' for the other firms in its network" (1997: 59).

For the broader aggregate too, social capital presents real risks of negative externalities. In Coleman's example, closure of the network of ties among children is bad for the broader community, because it weakens control by adults (parents, teachers, etc.) and increases dropout rates. Brokering for informational benefits for lower-level units may lead to a tragedy of the commons for the broader aggregate. Even if some reciprocity is required of the broker, there is no guarantee that what is offered in exchange for the information valuable to the subunit will be what the larger organization requires to thrive. Gabbay and Zuckerman's (1998) analysis of networks of R&D scientists suggests that in units whose effectiveness depends on broad sharing of information, excessive brokering by individuals may hamper innovation.

The risks of negative externalities to the focal actors' search for the power benefits of social capital are all too obvious. While some degree and configuration of power differentiation in the Senate Club may be effective, it is obvious that even slight changes from that optimal configuration can lead to gridlock or diversion.

Solidarity benefits for the lower-level too can have downsides for the aggregate. Strong identification with the focal group may contribute to the fragmentation of broader whole. The broader aggregate may split into "warring factions or degenerate into congeries of rent-seeking 'special interests'" (Foley and Edwards, 1996: 39). Portes (1998) points out that by bringing together dissatisfied actors, associational activity in civil society may deepen social cleavage. A gang derives considerable benefit from its social capital, but may use that social capital to exploit and weaken the surrounding community.

Woolcock's (1998) analysis of social capital in economic development provides a useful general framework that captures many of the points in the preceding paragraph. He constructs a two-by-two matrix of high versus low and internal versus external linkages. Obviously, the actors that have few internal or external ties will suffer from a low stock of social capital; and it is equally obvious that the high-high configuration holds great promise. The two off-diagonal cells point to two generic risks of social capital. First, strong internal linkages combined with sparse external linkages will create a situation where internal solidarity is likely to be detrimental to the actors' integration into the broader whole. Such configuration of ties may lead to isolation—such as reflected in the "Not Invented Here" (NIH) syndrome—and fragmentation of the whole. The other potentially dysfunctional configuration is one with high external ties but low internal ties. Durkheim's analysis of "anomie" provides an example: city life simultaneously increases contact with outsiders and undermines community solidarity.

While shared norms and beliefs are a source of the strength of social capital, this discussion reveals the extent to which the risks of social capital flow from the specific content of the norms and beliefs that are shared. Depending on its norms and beliefs, a group with strong internal ties but only few external ties can become insular and xenophobic or maintain an openness that affords the possibility of integration into the larger aggregate at a later date. Portes and Sensenbrenner (1993: 1343) note entrepreurship is often encouraged among Asian, Middle-Eastern, and other immigrant communities by social capital based on solidarity, but that in the inner city this solidarity has the opposite effect because it encourages a downward levelling of norms. Conversely, depending on their culture's norms and beliefs, some ethnic communities whose children develop strong external ties will assimilate rapidly while others manage to reproduce a collective identity.

The balance of positive and negative externalities also depends on the specific norms and beliefs that are the source of the subunit's social capital. Depending on the norms and beliefs that guide its action, the street gang can wreak havoc on the neighborhood or serve as a powerful force assisting its social integration. Adler (1998) distinguishes "modern" and "traditionalistic" forms of trust and argues that the latter will tend to induce rigidity for the focal actors and fragmentation of the broader aggregate.

CONTINGENCY FACTORS

The two previous sections outlined the key benefits and risks of social capital, but the net value of a given form of social capital depends in large measure on the context, and in particular on the tasks of the focal group and on its fit with environment. Both factors will influence the relative importance of social capital's benefits and risks.

Task Contingencies

In discussing informal networks in organizations, Krackhardt and Hanson (1993) write, "what matters is the fit, whether networks are in sync with company goals." We agree that the fit between the network features that contribute to social capital and the organization's objectives—its "task"—is critical to understanding the value of that social capital.

Task contingencies help explain, first, whether strong or weak ties are more valuable. Hansen (1998) provides a nice example in the study we have already cited, showing that weak ties facilitate the cost-effective search for new information and that strong ties facilitate the cost-effective transfer of complex information and tacit knowledge. Uzzi (1997) makes a similar point: if the task requires trust and cooperation, embedded ties with repeated exchange history is preferred, but if the task requires economic rationality and market competition, arm's length market relations are more effective. Depending on the mix of tasks facing a network of firms, strong social capital will be more of a blessing or a liability.

Second, a task-contingency view clarifies the tension between Coleman's thesis that the closure of social network is the key source of social capital and Burt's theory favoring sparse networks with many structural holes. Coleman's analysis highlights solidarity benefits, while Burt's focuses on information benefits, and depending on which benefit is more important in a given situation, one or the other network configuration will be more desirable. Gabbay and Zukerman's (1998) study of scientists' mobility in R&D settings illustrates this tradeoff nicely. They found that, in basic research units where individual contribution and autonomy are more critical, scientists with sparse network with many holes are more likely to be successful. In applied research and development units, where cooperation and group contribution are more important, individuals with high contact density are more likely to be successful.

Walker, Kogut, and Shan (1997) examine the changing value of social capital over the lifecycle of interfirm networks. They found that structural holes are more valuable during the early history of the network formation, since the key tasks facing the network at that stage are informational. However, as the network become better established, more densely connected, and stabilized, cooperative network relationships become more valuable than brokerage opportunities.

Third, task contingencies influence the relative value of internal and external linkages. Krackhardt and Stern (1988) show that friendship links extended across groups (external ties) facilitate interunit cooperation, whereas within-group friendships (internal ties) produce cooperation only within single units. Which is more important? It depends. When the task requires cross-unit organization-wide cooperation—such as in an organization-wide crisis—the relative value of the second form of social capital is reduced, and indeed it may become a liability, serving to anchor parochial resistance.

Symbolic Contingencies

Norms and beliefs figure in the analysis of social capital not only because they function as sources but also because the norms and beliefs in the surrounding environment influence the value of a given stock of social capital. For example, entrepreneurship may be seen as legitimate in one context whereas in another context such activities might be seen as opportunistic and self-seeking. In Burt's (1997) analysis of corporate managers, he finds that brokering by senior managers is perceived as legitimate and thus rewarded, but less senior managers may actually suffer if they engage in such activities. Similarly, in Gabbay and Zukerman's (1998) study, organizational settings where norms encourage cooperation often shun entrepreneurs, and brokering activities are less likely to rewarded. Fernandez and Gould (1994) also emphasize the role of norms and beliefs in determining the effectiveness of brokering: widely-shared norms in the US frown on advocacy by government agencies, so agencies' effectiveness in brokering new arrangements depends on their ability to preserve a neutral role.

These considerations remind us of the lesson of institutionalization theory: that the success of organizations depends on their ability to meet not only the tasks imposed on them but only the symbolic constraints. From this perspective, we can see that social capital theory and institutionalization theory are largely complementary. Whereas institutionalization theory is a story about how higher-level aggregates—through the diffusion and imposition via networks of norms, beliefs and rules—shape choices for lower-level aggregates (see Scott, 1995, pp. 141–143), social capital is a story about the networks, norms, beliefs, and rules provide social capital resources needed by lower-level aggregates—organizations within societies and individuals within organizations—in their efforts to reshape and renegotiate the higher-level aggregates.

CONCLUSION

In this article, we have attempted to synthesize the theoretical research undertaken in various disciplines and to develop a common conceptual framework that identifies the sources, benefits, and risks of social capital. Figure 5.1 summarizes our overall model. We have argued that the sources of social capital can be broadly summarized as networks, norms, beliefs, and rules. Each of these sources can lead to benefits and risks, both for the focal unit and in the form of externalities for the broader aggregate of which it is a part. And finally, the net value of social capital is further contingent on its fit with the task and symbolic environment.

Our synthesis has revealed a strong tendency of research to bifurcate between internal and external views of social capital. While both focii have

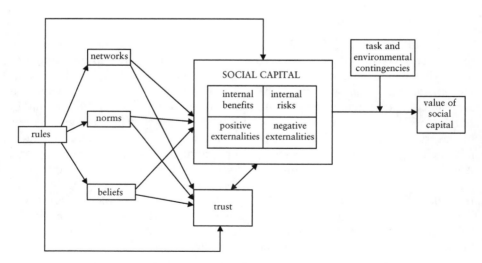

FIGURE 5.1 Sources, Benefits, and Risks of Capital

generated important insights, we conclude this paper with a call for more research that integrates them. The firm needs both kind of social capital. In the field of organizational studies, externally-oriented strategy research and internally-oriented organization research are tied at the hip.

REFERENCES

Adler, P. S. (1998). Market, hierarchy, and trust: The knowledge economy and the future of capitalism. University of Southern California, Working paper.

Adler, P. S., & Borys, B. (1996). Two types of bureaucracy: Enabling and coercive. *Administrative Science Quarterly, 41(1)*, 61–ß89.

Ahuja, G. (1998). Collaboration networks, structural holes and innovation: A longitudinal study. Paper presented at the Academy of Management, San Diego.

Anheier, H. K., Gerhards, J., & Romo, F. P. (1995). Forms of capital and social structure in cultural fields: Examining Bourdieu's social topography. *American Journal of Sociology, 100*, 859–903.

Baker, W. (1990). Market networks and corporate behavior. *American Journal of Sociology, 96*, 589–625.

Banfield, E. C. (1958). *The moral basis of a backward society*. Chicago: The Free Press.

Baron, J., & Hannan, M. (1994). The impact of economics on contemporary sociology. *Journal of Economic Literature, 32*, 1111–1146.

Belliveau, M. A., O'Reilly, C. A. I., & Wade, J. B. (1996). Social capital at the top: Effects of social similarity and status on CEO compensation. *Academy of Management Journal, 39(6)*, 1568–1593.

Berman, S. (1997). Civil society and political institutionalization. *American Behavioral Scientist, 40(5)*, 562–74.

Bourdieu, P. (1985). The forms of capital. In J. G. Richardson (Ed.), *Handbook of theory and research for the sociology of education* (pp. 241–58). N.Y.: Greenwood.

Bourdieu, P., & Wacquant, L. J. D. (1992). *An invitation to reflexive sociology*. Chicago: University of Chicago Press.

Boxman, E. A. W., Graaf, P. M. D., & Flap, H. D. (1991). The impact of social and human capital on the income attainment of Dutch Managers. *Social Networks, 13*, 51–73.

Brehm, J., & M. R. W. (1997). Individual-level evidence for the causes and consequences of social capital. *American Journal of Political Science, 41*, 999–1023.

Burt, R. S. (1992). *Structural holes: The social structure of competition*. Cambridge, Mass: Harvard University Press.

Burt, R. S. (1997). The contingent value of social capital. *Administrative Science Quarterly, 42(2)*, 339–365.

Coleman, J., Katz, & Menzel (1966). *Medical innovation: A diffusion study*. Indianapolis: Bobbs-Merrill Co.

Coleman, J. S. (1988). Social capital in the creation of human capital. *American Journal of Sociology, 94*, S95–S120.

Coleman, J. S. (1990). *Foundations of social theory*. Cambridge, Mass: Harvard University Press.

Edwards, B., & Foley, M. W. (1997). Social capital and the political economy of our discontent. *American Behavioral Scientist, 40*(5), 669.

Emirbayer, M., & Goodwin, J. (1994). Network analysis, culture, and the problem of agency. *American Journal of Sociology, 99 (6)*, 1411–54.

Evans, P. (1996). Government action, social capital and development: Reviewing the evidence on synergy. *World Development, 24*(6), 1119.

Fellmeth, A. X. (1996). Social Capital in the United States and Taiwan: Trust or Rule of Law? *Development Policy Review, 14*(2), 151.

Fernandez, R. M., & Gould, R. V. (1994). A dilemma of state power: Brokerage and influence in the National Health Policy Domain. *American Journal of Sociology, 99*, 1455–1491.

Fernandez, R. M., & Weinberg, N. (1997). Sifting and sorting: Personal contacts and hiring in a retail bank. *American Sociological Review*, 62 (Dec.), 883–902.

Foley, M. W., & Edwards, B. (1996). The paradox of civil society. *Journal of Democracy*, 7(3), 38–52.

Foley, M. W., & Edwards, B. (1997). Escape from politics? Social theory and the social capital debate. *American Behavioral Scientist, 40*(5), 550.

Fukuyama, F. (1995). *Trust: The social virtues and the creation of prosperity*. NY: Free Press.

Fukuyama, F. (1997). Social capital and the modern capitalist economy: Creating a high trust workplace. *Stern business*.

Gabbay, S. M., & Zuckerman, E. W. (1998). Social capital and opportunity in corporate R&D: The contingent effect of contact density on mobility expectations. *Social Science Research*, 27(2), 189–217.

Geertz, C. (1962). The rotating credit association: A 'middle rung' in development. *Economic Development and Cultural Change, 10*, 240–63.

Gittell, J. H., & Weiss, L. (1998). How organization design shapes networks: Toward a grounded theory of crossfunctional coordination, Working paper, Harvard Business School, Boston, MA.

Granovetter, M. S. (1973). The strength of weak ties. *American Journal of Sociology,* 78(6), 1360–1380.

Greeley, A. (1997). Coleman revisited: Religious structures as a source of social capital. *American Behavioral Scientist, 40*(5), 587.

Hansen, Morten T. (1998a). Combining network centrality and related knowledge: Explaining effective knowledge sharing in multiunit firms. Working paper, Harvard Business School, Boston, MA.

Hansen, Morten T. (1998b). The search-transfer problem: The role of weak ties in sharing knowledge across organization subunits. Working paper, Harvard Business School, Boston, MA.

Hardin, Russell. (1998). Social Capital. Working paper, New York University.

Howard, Leslie. (1988). Work and community in industrializing India. In B. Wellman & S. D. Berkowitz (Ed.), *Social structures: A network approach* (pp. 185–197). N.Y.: Cambridge University Press.

Hirschman, A.O., Rival Interpretations of Market Society: Civilizing, Destructive or Feeble? *Journal of Economic Literature*, 20, Dec. 1982: 1463–1484

Hyden, G. (1997). Civil society, social capital, and development dissection of a complex discourse. *Studies in Comparative International Development, 32*(1), 3–30.

Ibarra, H. (1992). Structural alignments, individual strategies, and managerial action: Elements toward a network theory of getting things done. In N. Nohria & R. G. Eccles (Ed.), *Networks and organizations: Structure, form, and action* (pp. 165–188). Boston, Mass: Harvard Business School Press.

Inglehart, R. (1997). *Modernization and post-modernization: Cultural, economic, and political change in 43 societies*. Princeton, NJ: Princeton University Press.

Jacobs, J. (1993/1961). *The death and life of great American cities*. N.Y.: Modern Library.

Kenworthy, L. (1997). Civic engagement, social capital, and economic cooperation. *American Behavioral Scientist, 40*(5), 645.

Kern, H. (1998). Lack of trust, surfeit of trust: Some causes of the innovation crisis in German industry. In C. Lane & R. Bachmann (Ed.), *Trust within and between organizations* (pp. 203–213). N.Y.: Oxford University Press.

Knack, S., & Keefer, P. (1996). Does social capital have an economic payoff?: A cross-country investigation. *The quarterly journal of economics, 112*(4), 1251.

Kohn, Melvin L., & Schooler, C. (1983). *Work and Personality: An Inquiry into the Impact of Social Stratification*. Norwood, N.J.: Ablex.

Krackhardt, D., & Hanson, J. R. (1993). Informal networks: The company behind the chart. *Harvard Business Review*, July-August, 104–111.

Krackhardt, D., & Stern, R. (1988). Informal networks and organizational crises: An experimental simulation. *Social Psychology Quarterly, 51*, 123–140.

Levi, M. (1996). Social and unsocial capital: A review essay of Robert Putnam's *Making Democracy Work. Politics and Society, 24*, 46–55.

Lewicki, R. J., & Bunker, B. B. (1995). Trust in relationships: A model of development and decline. In B. B. Bunker & J. Z. Rubin (Ed.), *Conflict, cooperation, and justice* (pp. 133–73). San Francisco: Jossey-Bass Inc.

Lin, N. (1998). *Social resources and social action*. N.Y.: Cambridge University Press.

Lin, N., Ensel, W. M., & Vaughn, J. C. (1981). Social resources and strength of ties: Structural factors in occupational status attainment. *American Sociological Review, 46*(4), 393–405.

Loury, G. (1992). The economics of discrimination: Getting to the core of the problem. *Harvard Journal for African American Public Policy, 1*.

Meyerson, E. M. (1994). Human capital, social capital and compensation: The relative contribution of social contacts to managers' incomes. *Acta Sociologica, 37*, 383–399.

Minkoff, D. C. (1997). Producing social capital: National social movements and civil society. *American Behavioral Scientist, 40*(5), 606.

Nahapiet, J., & Ghoshal, S. (1998). Social capital, intellectual capital, and the organizational advantage. *Academy of Management Review, 23*(2), 242–266.

Nebus, J. (1998). International teams: Their social capital and its effects on MNE knowledge creation and knowledge transfer. University of South Carolina, Working Paper.

Nelson, R. E. (1989). The strength of strong ties: Social networks and intergroup conflict in organizations. *Academy of Management Journal, 32(2)*, 377–401.

Newton, K. (1997). Social capital and democracy. *American Behavioral Scientist, 40(5)*, 575.

Nohria, N., & Berkley, J. D. (1994). The virtual organization: Bureaucracy, technology, and the imposition of control. In C. Heckscher & A. Donnellon (Ed.), *The post-bureaucratic organization: New perspectives on organizational change* (pp. 108–128). Thousand Oaks: Sage.

Ostrom, E. (1994). Constituting Social Capital and Collective Action. *Journal of Theoretical Politics, 6(4)*.

Ouchi, W. G. (1980). Markets, bureaucracies, and clans. *Administrative Science Quarterly, 25* (1), 129–141.

Paine, Thomas. (1792/1951). *The Rights of Man*, New York: E.P. Dutton.

Pennar, K. (1997, Dec. 15). The ties that lead to prosperity: The economic value of social bonds is only beginning to be measured. *Business Week*, pp. 153–5.

Pennings, J. M., Lee, K., & Witteloostuijn, A. V. (1998). Human capital, social capital, and firm dissolution. *Academy of Management Journal, 41(4)*, 425–440.

Pildes, R. H. (1996). The destruction of social capital through law. *University of Pennsylvania Law Review, 144(5)*, 2055.

Podolny, J. M., & Baron, J. N. (1997). Resources and relationships: Social networks and mobility in the workplace. *American Sociological Review, 62*, 673–693.

Podolny, J. M., & Page, K. L. (1998). Network forms of organization. *Annual Review of Sociology, 24*, 57–76.

Portes, A. (1998). Social capital: Its origins and applications in modern sociology. *Annual Review of Sociology, 24*, 1–24.

Portes, A., & Landolt, P. (1996). The downside of social capital. *The American Prospect* (May-June).

Portes, A., & Sensenbrenner, J. (1993). Embeddedness and immigration: Notes on the social determinants of economic action. *American Journal of Sociology, 98*, 1320–1350.

Portney, K. E., & Berry, J. M. (1997). Mobilizing minority communities: Social capital and participation in urban neighborhoods. *American Behavioral Scientist, 40(5)*, 632–644.

Powell, W. W., & Smith-Doerr, L. (1994). Networks and economic life. In N. J. Smelser & R. Swedberg (Ed.), *The handbook of economic sociology* (pp. 368–402). Princeton: Princeton University Press.

Putnam, R. D. (1993). *Making democracy work: civic traditions in modern Italy*. Princeton: Princeton University Press.

Putnam, R. D. (1995). Bowling alone: America's declining social capital. *Journal of Democracy, 6*, 65–78.

Roethlisberger, F. J., & Dickson, W. J. (1939). *Management and the worker*. Cambridge, Mass: Harvard University Press.

Rogers, E. M. (1995). *Diffusion of innovations*. NY: Free Press.

Sabel, C. F. (1993). Studied trust: Building new forms of cooperation in a volatile economy. *Human Relations, 46(9)*, 1133–1170.

Salancik, G. R. (1995). Wanted: A good network theory of organization. *Administrative Science Quarterly, 40*(2), 345–349.

Sandefur, R. L., & Laumann, E. O. (1988). A paradigm for social capital. *Rationality and Society, 10*(4), 481–.

Schiff, M. (1992). Social capital, labor mobility, and welfare: The impact of uniting states. *Rationality and Society, 4*, 157–75.

Schneider, M., Teske, P., Marschall, M., Mintrom, M., & Roch, C. (1997). Institutional Arrangements and the Creation of Social Capital: The effects of public school choice. *The American Political Science Review, 91(1)*, 82.

Scott, J. (1991). *Social network analysis: A handbook*. London: Sage Publications.

Scott, W. R. (1995). *Institutions and organizations*. Thousand Oaks: Sage.

Shapiro, D. L., Sheppard, B. H., & Cheraskin, L. (1992). Business on a handshake. *Negotiation Journal*, 365–377.

Solow, R. M. (1997). Tell me again what we are talking about. *Stern Business Magazine*.

Thomas, C. Y. (1996). Capital Markets, Financial Markets and Social Capital. *Social and Economic Studies, 45*(2–3), 1.

Tichy, N. (1973). An analysis of clique formation and structure in organizations. *Administrative Science Quarterly, 18*, 194–208.

Tichy, N. M. (1981). Networks in organizations. In P. C. Nystrom & W. H. Starbuck (Ed.), *Handbook of Organizational Design* (pp. 225–249). NY: Oxford University Press.

Tsai, W., & Ghoshal, S. (1998). Social capital and value creation: The role of intrafirm networks. *Academy of Management Journal, 41(4)*, 464–478.

Uzzi, B. (1997). Social structure and competition in interfirm networks: The paradox of embeddedness. *Administrative Science Quarterly, 42(1)*, 35–67.

Walker, G., Kogut, B., & Shan, W. (1997). Social capital, structural holes and the formation of an industry network. *Organization Science, 8(2)*, 109–125.

Wellman, B. (1988). Structural analysis: from method and metaphor to theory and substance. In B. Wellman & S. D. Berkowitz (Ed.), *Social structures: A network approach* (pp. 19–61). N.Y.: Cambridge University Press.

Woolcock, M. (1998). Social capital and economic development: Toward a theoretical synthesis and policy framework. *Theory and Society, 27(2)*, 151–208.

Youniss, J., McLellan, J. A., & Yates, M. (1997). What we know about engendering civic identity. *American Behavioral Scientist, 40*(5), 620–631.

PART II

Applications

Chapter 6

Social Capital, Intellectual Capital, and the Organizational Advantage [*]

Janine Nahapiet
Templeton College, University of Oxford

Sumantra Ghoshal
London Business School

Scholars of the theory of the firm have begun to emphasize the sources and conditions of what has been described as "the organizational advantage," rather than focus on the causes and consequences of market failure. Typically, researchers see such organizational advantage as accruing from the particular capabilities organizations have for creating and sharing knowledge. In this article we seek to contribute to this body of work by developing the following arguments: (1) social capital facilitates the creation of new intellectual capital; (2) organizations, as institutional settings, are conducive to the development of high levels of social capital; and (3) it is because of their more dense social capital that firms, within certain limits, have an advantage over markets in creating and sharing intellectual capital. We present a model that incorporates this overall argument in the form of a series of hypothesized relationships between different dimensions of social capital and the main mechanisms and processes necessary for the creation of intellectual capital.

[*]   Requested with permission of Academy of Management, PO Box 3020, Briar Cliff Manor, NY 10510–8020. "Social Capital, Intellectual Capital and the Organizational Advantage," J. Nahapiet & S. Ghoshal, *Academy of Management Review*, Vol. 23, No. 2. Reproduced by permission of the publisher via Copyright Clearance Center, Inc.

119

This research was supported in part by a grant from the Sundridge Park Research Fund. We are grateful to John Stopford, Peter Moran, Morten Hansen, Richard Pascale, Max Boisot, Wen-Pin Tsai, Nitin Nohria, Paul Willman, Anthony Hopwood, Tim Ambler, Martin Waldenstrom, and three anonymous referees for their helpful comments on earlier drafts of this article and in discussions of its subject matter.

Kogut and Zander recently have proposed "that a firm be understood as a social community specializing in the speed and efficiency in the creation and transfer of knowledge" (1996: 503). This is an important and relatively new perspective on the theory of the firm currently being formalized through the ongoing work of these (Kogut & Zander, 1992, 1993, 1995, 1996; Zander & Kogut, 1995) and several other authors (Boisot, 1995; Conner & Prahalad, 1996; Loasby, 1991; Nonaka & Takeuchi, 1995; Spender, 1996). Standing in stark contrast to the more established transaction cost theory that is grounded in the assumption of human opportunism and the resulting conditions of market failure (e.g., Williamson, 1975), those with this perspective essentially argue that organizations have some particular capabilities for creating and sharing knowledge that give them their distinctive advantage over other institutional arrangements, such as markets. For strategy theory, the implications of this emerging perspective lie in a shift of focus from the historically dominant theme of value appropriation to one of value creation (Moran & Ghoshal, 1996).

The particular capabilities of organizations for creating and sharing knowledge derive from a range of factors, including the special facility organizations have for the creation and transfer of tacit knowledge (Kogut & Zander, 1993, 1996; Nonaka & Takeuchi, 1995; Spender, 1996); the organizing principles by which individual and functional expertise are structured, coordinated, and communicated, and through which individuals cooperate (Conner & Prahalad, 1996; Kogut & Zander, 1992; Zander and Kogut, 1995); and the nature of organizations as social communities (Kogut & Zander, 1992, 1996). However, notwithstanding the substantial insights we now have into the attributes of organizations as knowledge systems, we still lack a coherent theory for explaining them. In this article we seek to address this gap and to present a theory of how firms can enjoy what Ghoshal and Moran (1996) have called "the organizational advantage."

Our theory is rooted in the concept of social capital. Analysts of social capital are centrally concerned with the significance of relationships as a resource for social action (Baker, 1990; Bourdieu, 1986; Burt, 1992; Coleman, 1988, 1990; Jacobs, 1965; Loury, 1987). However, as Putnam (1995) recently has observed, social capital is not a unidimensional concept, and, while sharing a common interest in how relational resources aid the conduct of social affairs, the different authors on this topic have tended to focus on different facets of social capital. In this article we (1) integrate these different facets to define social capital in terms of three distinct dimensions; (2) describe how each of these dimensions facilitates the creation and exchange of knowledge; and (3) argue that organizations, as institutional settings, are able to develop high levels of social capital in terms of all three dimensions. Our primary focus, however, is on the interrelationships between social and intellectual capital since, as we have already noted, there is already a clear stream of work that identifies and elaborates the significance of knowledge processes as the foundation of such organizational advantage. Our aim here is to provide a theoretical explanation of why this is the case.

SOCIAL CAPITAL

The term "social capital" initially appeared in community studies, highlighting the central importance—for the survival and functioning of city neighborhoods—of the networks of strong, crosscutting personal relationships developed over time that provide the basis for trust, cooperation, and collective action in such communities (Jacobs, 1965). Early usage also indicated the significance of social capital for the individual: the set of resources inherent in family relations and in community social organizations useful for the development of the young child (Loury, 1977). The concept has been applied since its early use to elucidate a wide range of social phenomena, although researchers increasingly have focused attention on the role of social capital as an influence not only on the development of human capital (Coleman, 1988; Loury, 1977, 1987) but on the economic performance of firms (Baker, 1990), geographic regions (Putnam, 1993, 1995), and nations (Fukuyama, 1995).

The central proposition of social capital theory is that networks of relationships constitute a valuable resource for the conduct of social affairs, providing their members with "the collectivity-owned capital, a 'credential' which entitles them to credit, in the various senses of the word" (Bourdieu, 1986: 249). Much of this capital is embedded within networks of mutual acquaintance and recognition. Bourdieu (1986), for example, identifies the durable obligations arising from feelings of gratitude, respect, and friendship or from the institutionally guaranteed rights derived from membership in a family, a class, or a school. Other resources are available through the contacts or connections networks bring. For example, through "weak ties" (Granovetter, 1973) and "friends of friends" (Boissevain, 1974), network members can gain privileged access to information and to opportunities. Finally, significant social capital in the form of social status or reputation can be derived from membership in specific networks, particularly those in which such membership is relatively restricted (Bourdieu, 1986; Burt, 1992; D'Aveni & Kesner, 1993).

Although these authors agree on the significance of relationships as a resource for social action, they lack consensus on a precise definition of social capital. Some, like Baker (1990), limit the scope of the term to only the structure of the relationship networks, whereas others, like Bourdieu (1986, 1993) and Putnam (1995), also include in their conceptualization of social capital the actual or potential resources that can be accessed through such networks. For our purposes here, we adopt the latter view and define social capital as the sum of the actual and potential resources embedded within, available through, and derived from the network of relationship possessed by an individual or social unit. Social capital thus comprises both the network and the assets that may be mobilized through that network (Bourdieu, 1986; Burt, 1992).

As a set of resources rooted in relationships, social capital has many different attributes, and Putnam (1995) has argued that a high research priority is to clarify the dimensions of social capital. In the context of our exploration of the role of social capital in the creation of intellectual capital, we suggest that it is useful to consider these facets in terms of three clusters: the structural, the relational, and the cognitive dimensions of social capital. Although we separate these three dimensions analytically, we recognize that many of the features we describe are, in fact, highly interrelated. Moreover, in our analysis we set out to indicate important facets of social capital rather than review such facets exhaustively.

In making the distinction between the structural and the relational dimensions of social capital, we draw on Granovetter's (1992) discussion of structural and relational embeddedness. Structural embeddedness concerns the properties of the social system and of the network of relations as a whole.[1] The term describes the impersonal configuration of linkages between people or units. In this article we use the concept of the structural dimension of social capital to refer to the overall pattern of connections between actors—that is, who you reach and how you reach them (Burt, 1992). Among the most important facets of this dimension are the presence or absence of network ties between actors (Scott, 1991; Wasserman & Faust, 1994); network configuration (Krackhardt, 1989) or morphology (Tichy, Tushman, & Fombrun, 1979) describing the pattern of linkages in terms of such measures as density, connectivity, and hierarchy; and appropriable organization—that is, the existence of networks created for one purpose that may be used for another (Coleman, 1988).

In contrast, the term "relational embeddedness" describes the kind of personal relationships people have developed with each other through a history of interactions (Granovetter, 1992). This concept focuses on the particular relations people have, such as respect and friendship, that influence their behavior. It is through these ongoing personal relationships that people fulfill such social motives as sociability, approval, and prestige. For example, two actors may occupy equivalent positions in similar network configurations, but if their personal and emotional attachments to other network members differ, their actions also are likely to differ in important respects. For instance, although one actor

---

[1]   We recognize that this terminology deviates from much that is customary in the field of network analysis. In particular, the focus of network analysis is relational data, but included under its heading are attributes that we label structural here. Scott, for example, describes network analysis as being concerned with "the contacts, ties and connections, the group attachments and meetings which relate one agent to another. . . . These relations connect pairs of agents to larger relational systems" (1991: 3). However, we justify our usage both through reference to Granovetter and because we believe this terminology captures well the personal aspect of this dimension.

may choose to stay in a firm because of an attachment to fellow workers, despite economic advantages available elsewhere, another without such personal bonds may discount working relationships in making career moves. In this article we use the concept of the relational dimension of social capital to refer to those assets created and leveraged through relationships, and parallel to what Lindenberg (1996) describes as behavioral, as opposed to structural, embeddedness and what Hakansson and Snehota (1995) refer to as "actor bonds." Among the key facets in this cluster are trust and trustworthiness (Fukuyama, 1995; Putnam, 1993), norms and sanctions (Coleman, 1990; Putnam, 1995), obligations and expectations (Burt, 1992; Coleman, 1990; Granovetter, 1985; Mauss, 1954), and identity and identification (Hakansson & Snehota, 1995; Merton, 1968).

The third dimension of social capital, which we label the "cognitive dimension," refers to those resources providing shared representations, interpretations, and systems of meaning among parties (Cicourel, 1973). We have identified this cluster separately because we believe it represents an important set of assets not yet discussed in the mainstream literature on social capital but the significance of which is receiving substantial attention in the strategy domain (Conner & Prahalad, 1996; Grant, 1996; Kogut & Zander, 1992, 1996). These resources also represent facets of particular importance in the context of our consideration of intellectual capital, including shared language and codes (Arrow, 1974; Cicourel, 1973; Monteverde, 1995) and shared narratives (Orr, 1990).

Although social capital takes many forms, each of these forms has two characteristics in common: (1) they constitute some aspect of the social structure, and (2) they facilitate the actions of individuals within the structure (Coleman, 1990). First, as a social-structural resource, social capital inheres in the relations between persons and among persons. Unlike other forms of capital, social capital is owned jointly by the parties in a relationship, and no one player has, or is capable of having, exclusive ownership rights (Burt, 1992). Moreover, although it has value in use, social capital cannot be traded easily. Friendships and obligations do not readily pass from one person to another. Second, social capital makes possible the achievement of ends that would be impossible without it or that could be achieved only at extra cost.

In examining the consequences of social capital for action, we can identify two distinct themes. First, social capital increases the efficiency of action. For example, networks of social relations, particularly those characterized by weak ties or structural holes (i.e., disconnections or nonequivalencies among players in an arena), increase the efficiency of information diffusion through minimizing redundancy (Burt, 1992). Some have also suggested that social capital in the form of high levels of trust diminishes the probability of opportunism and reduces the need for costly monitoring processes. It thus reduces the costs of transactions (Putnam, 1993).

Whereas the first theme could be regarded as illustrative of what North (1990) calls "allocative efficiency," the second theme centers on the role of social capital as an aid to adaptive efficiency and to the creativity and learning it implies. In particular, researchers have found social capital to encourage cooperative behavior, thereby facilitating the development of new forms of association and innovative organization (Fukuyama, 1995; Jacobs, 1965; Putnam, 1993). The concept, therefore, is central to the understanding of institutional dynamics, innovation, and value creation.

We should note, however, that social capital is not a universally beneficial resource. As Coleman observes, "[A] given form of social capital that is useful for facilitating certain actions may be useless or harmful for others" (1990: 302). For example, the strong norms and mutual identification that may exert a powerful positive influence on group performance can, at the same time, limit its openness to information and to alternative ways of doing things, producing forms of collective blindness that sometimes have disastrous consequences (Janis, 1982; Perrow, 1984; Turner, 1976).

The main thesis of the work we have reviewed thus far is that social capital inheres in the relations between and among persons and is a productive asset facilitating some forms of social action while inhibiting others. Social relationships within the family and wider community have been shown to be an important factor in the development of human capital (Coleman, 1988). In a parallel argument we suggest that social relationships—and the social capital therein—are an important influence on the development of intellectual capital. In elaborating this argument, we focus on the firm as the primary context in which to explore the interrelationships between social and intellectual capital. Later in the article we consider how our analysis may be extended to a wider range of institutional settings.

INTELLECTUAL CAPITAL

Traditionally, economists have examined physical and human capital as key resources for the firm that facilitate productive and economic activity. However, knowledge, too, has been recognized as a valuable resource by economists. Marshall, for example, suggests that "capital consists in a great part of knowledge and organization. . . . [K]nowledge is our most powerful engine of production" (1965: 115). He goes on to note that "organization aids knowledge," a perspective also central to the work of Arrow (1974). More recently, Quinn has expressed a similar view, suggesting that "with rare exceptions, the economic and producing power of the firm lies more in its intellectual and service capabilities than its hard assets—land, plant and equipment. . . . [V]irtually all public and private enterprises—including most successful corporations—are becoming dominantly repositories and coordinators of intellect" (1992: 241).

In this article we use the term "intellectual capital" to refer to the knowledge and knowing capability of a social collectivity, such as an organization, intellectual community, or professional practice. We have elected to adopt this terminology because of its clear parallel with the concept of human capital, which embraces the acquired knowledge, skills, and capabilities that enable persons to act in new ways (Coleman, 1988). Intellectual capital thus represents a valuable resource and a capability for action based in knowledge and knowing.

This orientation to intellectual capital builds on some central themes and distinctions found in the substantial and expanding literature on knowledge and knowledge processes. Many of these themes have a long history in philosophy and Western thought, dating back to Plato, Aristotle, and Descartes. Two issues are of particular relevance to our consideration of the special advantage of organizations as an institutional context for the development of intellectual capital. These are, first, debates about the different types of knowledge that may exist and, second, the issue of the level of analysis in knowledge processes, particularly the question of whether social or collective knowledge exists and in what form.

Dimensions of Intellectual Capital

Types of Knowledge

Arguably, the most persistent theme in writing about the nature of knowledge centers on the proposition that there are different types of knowledge. For example, a key distinction scholars frequently make is between practical, experience-based knowledge and the theoretical knowledge derived from reflection and abstraction from that experience—a distinction reminiscent of the debate of early philosophers between rationalism and empiricism (Giddens & Turner, 1987; James, 1950). Variously labeled "know-how" or "procedural knowledge," the former frequently is distinguished from know-that, know-what, or declarative knowledge (Anderson, 1981; Ryle, 1949). It concerns well-practiced skills and routines, whereas the latter concerns the development of facts and propositions.[2]

Perhaps the most-cited and influential distinction of this sort is Polanyi's identification of two aspects of knowledge: tacit and explicit. This is a distinction he aligns with the "knowing how" and "knowing what" of Gilbert Ryle (Polanyi, 1967). Polanyi distinguishes tacit knowledge in terms of its incommunicability, and Winter (1987) has suggested that it may be useful to consider tacitness as a variable, with the degree of tacitness a function of the extent to which the knowledge is or can be codified and abstracted (see also Boisot, 1995). However, close reading of Polanyi indicates that he holds the view that some knowledge will always remain tacit. In so doing, he stresses the importance of *knowing*, as well as knowledge, and, in particular, the active shaping of experience performed in the pursuit of knowledge.[3] Discussing the practice of science, he observes that "science is operated by the skill of the scientist and it is through the exercise of this skill that he shapes his scientific knowledge" (Polanyi, 1962: 49). This

---

[2] To this recent authors have added the concept of know-why (Hamel, 1991; Kogut & Zander, 1992).

[3] Indeed, his much-referenced chapter, in which he introduces the tacit dimension, is entitled "Tacit Knowing," not "tacit knowledge."

suggests both a view of knowledge as object and of knowing as action or enactment in which progress is made through active engagement with the world on the basis of a systematic approach to knowing.

Levels of Analysis in Knowledge and Knowing

Another equally fundamental cause for debate within philosophical and sociological circles centers on the existence, or otherwise, of particular phenomena at the collective level. That is, what is the nature of social phenomena that is different from the aggregation of individual phenomena (Durkheim, 1951; Gowler & Legge, 1982)? In the context of this article, the question concerns the degree to which it is possible to consider a concept of organizational, collective, or social knowledge that is different from that of individual organizational members.

Simon represents one extreme of the argument, stating that "all organizational learning takes place inside human heads; an organization learns in only two ways: (a) by the learning of its members, or (b) by ingesting new members who have knowledge the organization didn't previously have" (1991a: 176). In contrast, Nelson and Winter take a very different position, asserting that

> the possession of technical "knowledge" is an attribute of the firm as a whole, as an organized entity, and is not reducible to what any single individual knows, or even to any simple aggregation of the various competencies and capabilities of all the various individuals, equipments and installations of the firm (1982: 63).

A similar view is reflected in Brown and Duguid's (1991) analysis of communities of practice, in which shared learning is inextricably located in complex, collaborative social practices. Weick and Roberts (1993) also report research demonstrating collective knowing at the organizational level.[4] Our definition of intellectual capital reflects the second of these perspectives and acknowledges the significance of socially and contextually embedded forms of knowledge and knowing as a source of value differing from the simple aggregation of the knowledge of a set of individuals.

These two dimensions of explicit/tacit and individual/social knowledge have been combined by Spender (1996), who created a matrix of four different elements of an organization's intellectual capital. Individual explicit knowledge—what Spender labels "conscious knowledge"—is typically available to the individual in the form of facts, concepts, and frameworks that can be stored and retrieved from memory or personal records. The second element, individual tacit knowledge—what Spender labels "automatic knowledge"—may take many different forms of tacit knowing, including theoretical and practical knowledge of people and the performance of different kinds of artistic, athletic, or technical

---

[4] See also Walsh's (1995) comprehensive discussion of organizational cognition.

skills. Availability of people with such explicit knowledge and tacit skills clearly is an important part of an organization's intellectual capital and can be a key factor in the organization's performance, particularly in contexts where the performance of individual employees is crucial, as in specialist craft work (Cooke & Yanow, 1993).

The other two elements of an organization's intellectual capital are social explicit knowledge (what Spender calls "objectified knowledge") and social tacit knowledge ("collective knowledge," in Spender's terms). The former represents the shared corpus of knowledge—epitomized, for example, by scientific communities, and often regarded as the most advanced form of knowledge (Boisot, 1995). Across a wide range of organizations, we are currently witnessing major investments in the development of such objectified knowledge as firms attempt to pool, share, and leverage their distributed knowledge and intellect (Quinn, Anderson, & Finkelstein, 1996).

The latter represents the knowledge that is fundamentally embedded in the forms of social and institutional practice and that resides in the tacit experiences and enactment of the collective (Brown & Duguid, 1991). Such knowledge and knowing capacity may remain relatively hidden from individual actors but be accessible and sustained through their interaction (Spender, 1994). It is the type of knowledge frequently distinguishing the performance of highly experienced teams. This shared knowledge has been defined as "routines" by Nelson and Winter (1982), and it appears that much important organizational knowledge may exist in this form. For example, Weick and Roberts (1993) describe the complex, tacit, but heedful interrelating they observed between members of the flight operations team on aircraft carriers, which they suggest may characterize all high-reliability organizations.

For a given firm, these four elements collectively constitute its intellectual capital. Further, the elements are not independent, as Spender (1996) notes. However, in a stylized comparison of individuals working within an organization versus the same individuals working at arm's length across a hypothetical market (in the spirit of Conner and Prahalad's [1996] analysis), we use the two categories of social knowledge to provide the crux of our distinction: as Spender argues, "[C]ollective knowledge is the most secure and strategically significant kind of organizational knowledge" (1996: 52). Therefore, it is on the social explicit knowledge and the social tacit knowledge that we focus our analysis of organizational advantage. This is an important limitation of our theory because, by restricting the scope of our analysis only to social knowledge, we will be unable to capture the influences that explicit and tacit individual knowledge may have on the intellectual capital of the firm.

There is another important way in which we limit our analysis. The potential advantages of internal organization over market organization may arise from its superior abilities in both creating and exploiting intellectual capital (Kogut & Zander, 1993). We focus here only on the creation of intellectual capital and ignore the exploitation aspects. We have two reasons for imposing this constraint. First, comprehensive consideration of both processes would exceed the space available. Second, and more important, the benefits of intraorganizational exploitation of knowledge stem largely from missing, incomplete, or imperfect markets for such knowledge (Arrow, 1974; Teece, 1988; Williamson, 1975). Therefore, such advantages historically have been a part of the more traditional market-failure-based theories of the firm. Where we go beyond such theories is in our argument that internal organization may, within limits, be superior to market transactions for the creation of new knowledge.

The Creation of Intellectual Capital

How is new knowledge created? Following Schumpeter (1934), Moran and Ghoshal (1996) have argued that all new resources, including knowledge, are created through two generic processes: namely, combination and exchange. While this argument is yet to be widely scrutinized, and although it is possible there may be still other processes for the creation of new knowledge (particularly at the individual level), we believe that these two, indeed, are among the key mechanisms for creating social knowledge; therefore, we adopt this framework for our purposes.

Combination and the Creation of Intellectual Capital

Combination is the process viewed by Schumpeter as the foundation for economic development—"to produce means to combine materials and forces within our reach" (1934: 65)—and this perspective has become the starting point for much current work on organizations as knowledge systems (Boisot, 1995; Cohen & Levinthal, 1990; Kogut & Zander, 1992). In this literature scholars frequently identify two types of knowledge creation. First, new knowledge can be created through incremental change and development from existing knowledge. Schumpeter (1934), for example, talks of continuous adjustment in small steps, and March and Simon (1958) identify "localized search" and "stable heuristics" as the basis for knowledge growth. Within the philosophy of science, Kuhn (1970) sees development within the paradigm as the dominant mode of progression. Second, many authors also discuss more radical change: innovation, in Schumpeter's terms; double-loop learning, according to Argyris and Schon (1978); and paradigmatic change and revolution, according to Kuhn (1970). There appears to be a consensus that both types of knowledge creation involve making new combinations—incrementally or radically—either by combining elements previously unconnected or by developing novel ways of combining elements previously associated. "Development in our sense is then defined by the carrying out of new combinations" (Schumpeter, 1934: 66),[5] a view endorsed by the recent research of Leonard-Barton (1995).

---

[5]   In their theory of the knowledge-creating company, Nonaka and Takeuchi define combination as "a process of systematizing concepts into a knowledge system. This mode of

Exchange and the Creation of Intellectual Capital

Where resources are held by different parties, exchange is a prerequisite for resource combination. Since intellectual capital generally is created through a process of combining the knowledge and experience of different parties, it, too, is dependent upon exchange between these parties. Sometimes, this exchange involves the transfer of explicit knowledge, either individually or collectively held, as in the exchange of information within the scientific community or via the Internet. Often, new knowledge creation occurs through social interaction and coactivity. Zucker, Darby, Brewer, and Peng (1996) recently have shown the importance of collaboration for the development and acquisition of fine-grained collective knowledge in biotechnology. Their research endorses the significance of teamwork in the creation of knowledge, as identified much earlier by Penrose (1959). In developing her theory of the growth of the firm, Penrose proposed that a firm be viewed as "a collection of individuals who have had experience in working together, for only in this way can 'teamwork' be developed" (1959: 46).

There are many aspects to the learning embedded in such shared experience. They include the specific meanings and understandings subtly and extensively negotiated in the course of social interaction. Importantly, they also include an appreciation of the ways in which action may be coordinated. For, as Penrose observes, such experience

> develops an increasing knowledge of the possibilities for action and the ways in which action can be taken by . . . the firm. This increase in knowledge not only causes the productive opportunity of a firm to change . . . but also contributes to the "uniqueness" of the opportunity of each individual firm (1959: 53).

An interest in the ways in which such collective learning, especially concerning how to coordinate diverse production skills and to integrate several technology streams, has been at the heart of much recent discussion of core competence as the source of competitive advantage (Prahalad & Hamel, 1990) and is suggestive of the complex ways in which exchange contributes to the creation of intellectual capital.

knowledge conversion involves combining different bodies of explicit knowledge" (1995: 67). They prefer to use different terms for those forms of conversion involving tacit knowledge. However, following Polanyi (1967), we believe that all knowledge processes have a tacit dimension and that, fundamentally, the same generic processes underlie all forms of knowledge conversion. Therefore, our usage of the term "combination" in this context is more general and is rooted in our view of intellectual capital as embracing both the explicit knowledge and the tacit knowing of a collective and its members. Our view, thus, resembles more closely the concept of combinative capabilities discussed by Kogut and Zander (1992).

The Conditions for Exchange and Combination

In their analysis of value creation, Moran and Ghoshal (1996) identify three conditions that must be satisfied for exchange and combination of resources actually to take place. We believe that these conditions apply to the creation of new intellectual capital. In addition, however, we identify a fourth factor, which we regard as a prerequisite for the creation of intellectual capital.

The first condition is that the opportunity exists to make the combination or exchange. In our context we see this condition being determined by accessibility to the objectified and collective forms of social knowledge. A fundamental requirement for the development of new intellectual capital is that it is possible to draw upon and engage in the existing and differing knowledge and knowing activities of various parties or knowing communities (Boland & Tenkasi, 1995; Zucker et al., 1996). In the academic world the "invisible college" long has been recognized as an important social network giving valuable early access to distributed knowledge, facilitating its exchange and development, and thereby accelerating the advancement of science (Crane, 1972). Clearly, recent developments in technology, such as Lotus Notes and the Internet, have considerably increased the opportunities for knowledge combination and exchange. In addition, however, as the history of science demonstrates, the creation of new intellectual capital also may occur through accidental rather than planned combinations and exchanges, reflecting emergent patterns of accessibility to knowledge and knowledge processes.

Second, in order for the parties involved to avail themselves of the opportunities that may exist to combine or exchange resources, value expectancy theorists suggest that those parties must expect such deployment to create value. In other words, they must anticipate that interaction, exchange, and combination will prove worthwhile, even if they remain uncertain of what will be produced or how. Writing about the anticipated outcome of a conference of business practitioners and researchers, Slocum comments, "[E]ach of us expects to learn something of value as a result of our being here. None of us knows exactly what we are going to learn or what path we will take in the pursuit of this knowledge. We are confident, however, that the process works" (1994: ix). This anticipation of or receptivity to learning and new knowledge creation has been shown to be an important factor affecting the success or otherwise of strategic alliances (Hamel, 1991). It exemplifies Giddens' (1984) concept of intentionality as an influence on social action and, in so doing, also acknowledges the possibility that outcomes may turn out to be different from those anticipated.

The third condition for the creation of new resources highlights the importance of motivation. Even where opportunities for exchange exist and people anticipate that value may be created through exchange or interaction, those involved must feel that their engagement in the knowledge exchange and combination will be worth their while. Moran and Ghoshal (1996) see this as the expectation that the parties engaged in exchange and combination will be able to appropriate or realize some of the new value created by their engagement, even though, as noted previously, they may be uncertain about precisely what that value may be. For example, while having considerable potential, the availability of electronic knowledge exchange does not automatically induce a willingness to share information and build new intellectual capital. Quinn et al. (1996) found, in a study of Arthur Andersen Worldwide, that major changes in incentives and culture were required to stimulate use of its new electronic network, and they suggest that motivated creativity, which they describe as "care-why," is a fundamental influence in the creation of value through leveraging intellect. In his research on internal stickiness, Szulanski (1996) also found that lack of motivation may inhibit the transfer of best practice within the firm. However, Szulanski discovered that far more important as a barrier was the lack of capacity to assimilate and apply new knowledge.

Accordingly, we propose that there is a fourth precondition for the creation of new intellectual capital: combination capability. Even where the opportunities for knowledge exchange and combination exist, these opportunities are perceived as valuable, and parties are motivated to make such resource deployments or to engage in knowing activity, the capability to combine information or experience must exist. In their research on innovation, Cohen and Levinthal (1990) argue that the ability to recognize the value of new knowledge and information, but also to assimilate and use it, are all vital factors in organizational learning and innovation. Their work demonstrates that all of these abilities, which they label "absorptive capacity," depend upon the existence of related prior knowledge. Moreover, they suggest that an organization's absorptive capacity does not reside in any single individual but depends, crucially, on the links across a mosaic of individual capabilities—an observation that parallels Spender's (1996) discussion of collective knowledge.

Toward a Theory of the Creation of Intellectual Capital

By way of summary, we have argued the following. First, new intellectual capital is created through combination and exchange of existing intellectual resources, which may exist in the form of explicit and tacit knowledge and knowing capability. Second, there are four conditions that affect the deployment of intellectual resources and engagement in knowing activity involving combination and exchange. Third, in reviewing the burgeoning literature on knowledge and knowing, we have encountered much evidence in support of the view that the combination and exchange of knowledge are complex social processes and that much valuable knowledge is fundamentally socially embedded—in particular situations, in coactivity, and in relationships. As yet, we have uncovered no single theoretical framework that pulls together the various strands we can identify in this literature. For example, although a growing body of work exists in which scholars adopt an evolutionary perspective and identify the special capabilities of firms in the creation and transfer of tacit knowledge, this work has not yet produced a coherent theory explaining these special capabilities. Given the social embeddedness of intellectual capital, we suggest that such a theory is likely to be one that is primarily concerned with social relationships. Accordingly, we believe that social capital theory offers a potentially valuable perspective for understanding and explaining the creation of intellectual capital. It is to this theory we now return.

SOCIAL CAPITAL, EXCHANGE, AND COMBINATION

Social capital resides in relationships, and relationships are created through exchange (Bourdieu, 1986). The pattern of linkages and the relationships built through them are the foundation for social capital. What we observe is a complex and dialectical process in which social capital is created and sustained through exchange and in which, in turn, social capital facilitates exchange. For example, there is mounting evidence demonstrating that where parties trust each other, they are more willing to engage in cooperative activity through which further trust may be generated (Fukuyama, 1995; Putnam, 1993; Tyler & Kramer, 1996). In social systems, exchange is the precursor to resource combination. Thus, social capital influences combination indirectly through exchange. However, we argue below that several facets of social capital, particularly those pertaining to the cognitive dimension, also have a direct influence on the ability of individuals to combine knowledge in the creation of intellectual capital. Although our primary objective is to explore the ways in which social capital influences the development of intellectual capital, we recognize that intellectual capital may, itself, facilitate the development of social capital. Thus, later in the article we consider how the coevolution of these two forms of capital may underpin organizational advantage.

The main thesis we develop here is that social capital facilitates the development of intellectual capital by affecting the conditions necessary for exchange and combination to occur. To explore this proposition, we now examine some of the ways in which each of the three dimensions of social capital influences the four conditions for resource exchange and combination we presented earlier. The specific relationships we identify are summarized in Figure 6.1.

For the sake of clarity of exposition, we consider, in the following analysis, the impact of each dimension of social capital independently of the other dimensions. We recognize, however, that both the dimensions and the several facets of social capital are likely to be interrelated in important and complex ways. For example, particular structural configurations, such as those displaying strong symmetrical ties, have consistently been shown to be associated with such relational facets as interpersonal affect and trust (Granovetter, 1985; Krackhardt, 1992). Similarly, researchers have highlighted the often-complex interdependencies between social identification and shared vocabulary and language (Ashforth & Mael, 1995).

Moreover, not all dimensions of social capital are mutually reinforcing. For instance, an efficient network in structural terms may not be the best way to

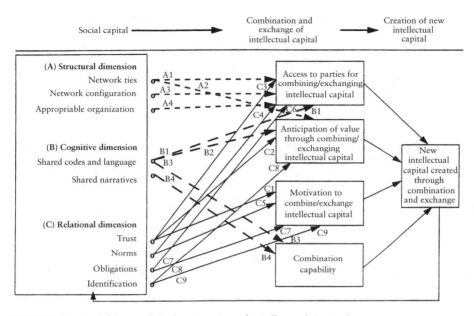

FIGURE 6.1 Social Capital in the Creation of Intellectual Capital

develop the strong relational or cognitive social capital that may be necessary to ensure the effective operation of such networks. Nohria and Eccles (1992), for example, highlight important differences between face-to-face and electronic exchange and propose that using electronically mediated exchange to help create a network organization requires more, not less, face-to-face communication. Our primary focus on the independent effects of these dimensions therefore limits the richness of the present exploration and identifies an important area for future work.

Exchange, Combination, and the Structural Dimension of Social Capital

Our main argument in this section is that, within the context of the framework of combination and exchange adopted by us in this article, the structural dimension of social capital influences the development of intellectual capital primarily (though not exclusively) through the ways in which its various facets affect access to parties for exchanging knowledge and participating in knowing activities. While recognizing that the structural facets also may be systematically associated with other conditions for the exchange and combination of knowledge, we believe that these associations are primarily derived indirectly, through the ways in which structure influences the development of the relational and cognitive dimensions of social capital. For example, the strong, symmetrical ties frequently associated with the development of affective relationships (both positive and negative) may, in turn, influence individuals' motivation to engage in social interaction and, thereby, exchange knowledge (Krackhardt, 1992; Lawler & Yoon, 1996). Similarly, stable networks characterized by dense relations and high levels of interaction are conducive to the development of the different facets of the cognitive social capital we discuss in this article (Boisot, 1995; Orr, 1990).

Network Ties

The fundamental proposition of social capital theory is that network ties provide access to resources. One of the central themes in the literature is that social capital constitutes a valuable source of information benefits (i.e., "who you know" affects "what you know"). Coleman (1988) notes that information is important in providing a basis for action but is costly to gather. However, social relations, often established for other purposes, constitute information channels that reduce the amount of time and investment required to gather information.

Burt (1992) suggests that these information benefits occur in three forms: access, timing, and referrals. The term "access" refers to receiving a valuable piece of information and knowing who can use it, and it identifies the role of networks in providing an efficient information-screening and distribution process for members of those networks. Thus, network ties influence both access to parties for combining and exchanging knowledge (A1 in Figure 6.1) and anticipation of value through such exchange (A2 in Figure 6.1). The operations of the invisible college provide an example of such networks.

"Timing" of information flows refers to the ability of personal contacts to provide information sooner than it becomes available to people without such contacts. This may well increase the anticipated value of such information (A2 in Figure 6.1), as demonstrated in research on job-seeking behavior (Granovetter, 1973). Such early access to information may be especially important in commercially oriented research and development, where speed to market may be a crucial factor in determining success.

"Referrals" are those processes providing information on available opportunities to people or actors in the network, hence influencing the opportunity to combine and exchange knowledge (A1 in Figure 6.1). They constitute a flow of information not only about possibilities but frequently include reputational endorsement for the actors involved—thereby influencing both the anticipated value of combination and exchange and the motivation for such exchange (see Granovetter, 1973, and Putnam, 1993). However, we believe that such reputational endorsement derives more from relational than structural factors, which we explore below.

Network Configuration

Ties provide the channels for information transmission, but the overall configuration of these ties constitutes an important facet of social capital that may impact the development of intellectual capital. For example, three properties of network structure—density, connectivity, and hierarchy—are all features associated with flexibility and ease of information exchange through their impact on the level of contact or the accessibility they provide to network members (A3 in Figure 6.1; Ibarra, 1992; Krackhardt, 1989).

Burt (1992) notes that a player with a network rich in information benefits has contacts established in the places where useful bits of information are likely to air and who will provide a reliable flow of information to and from those places. While acknowledging the importance of trust and trustworthiness as a factor in the choice of contacts, Burt (1992) devotes much more attention to the efficiency of different relationship structures, arguing, in particular, that the sparse network, with few redundant contacts, provides more information benefits. The dense network is inefficient in the sense that it returns less diverse information for the same cost as that of the sparse network. The benefits of the latter, thus, derive from both the diversity of information and the lower costs of accessing it. Jacobs (1965) and Granovetter (1973) have made similar arguments, identifying the role of "hop-and-skip" links and "loose ties" in information diffusion through communities. This aspect of diversity is very important, because it is well established that significant progress in the creation of intellectual capital often occurs by bringing together knowledge from disparate sources and disciplines. Networks and network structures, thus, represent facets of social capital that influence the range of information that may be accessed (A3 in Figure 6.1) and that becomes available for combination. As such, these structures constitute a valuable resource as channels or conduits for knowledge diffusion and transfer.

However, there are important limitations to the conduit model, in which meaning is viewed as unproblematic and in which the primary concern is with issues of information transfer. For example, Hansen (1996) has found that weak ties facilitate search but impede transfer, especially when knowledge is not codified. Thus, whereas networks having little redundancy may be both effective and efficient for the transfer of information whose meaning is relatively unproblematic, much richer patterns of relationship and interaction are important where the meaning of information is uncertain and ambiguous or where parties to an exchange differ in their prior knowledge. For example, Cohen and Levinthal (1990) have shown that some redundancy is necessary for the development of cross-functional absorptive capacity. Nonetheless, the general point remains that the configuration of the network is an important influence on the accessibility of information resources (A3 in Figure 6.1), although the appropriate level of redundancy is contingent on the degree to which the parties to knowledge exchange share a common knowledge base.

Appropriable Organization

Social capital developed in one context, such as ties, norms, and trust, can often (but not always) be transferred from one social setting to another, thus influencing patterns of social exchange. Examples include the transfer of trust from family and religious affiliations into work situations (Fukuyama, 1995), the development of personal relationships into business exchanges (Coleman, 1990), and the aggregation of the social capital of individuals into that of organizations (Burt, 1992). This suggests that organizations created for one purpose may provide a source of valuable resources for other, different purposes (Nohria, 1992; Putnam, 1993, 1995). Such appropriable social organization can provide a potential network of access to people and their resources, including information and knowledge (A4 in Figure 6.1), and, through its relational and cognitive dimensions, may ensure motivation and capability for exchange and combination (see below). However, such organization also may inhibit such processes; indeed, research demonstrates how organizational routines may separate rather than coordinate groups within organizations, constraining rather than enabling learning and the creation of intellectual capital (Dougherty, 1996; Hedberg, 1981).

Exchange, Combination, and the Cognitive Dimension of Social Capital

Earlier in this article, we defined intellectual capital as the knowledge and knowing capability of a social collectivity. This reflects our belief that, fundamentally, intellectual capital is a social artifact and that knowledge and meaning are always embedded in a social context—both created and sustained through ongoing relationships in such collectivities. Although scholars widely recognize that innovation generally occurs through combining different knowledge and experience and that diversity of opinion is a way of expanding knowledge, meaningful communication—an essential part of social exchange and combination processes—requires at least some sharing of context between the parties to such exchange (Boisot, 1995; Boland & Tenkasi, 1995; Campbell, 1969). We suggest that this sharing may come about in two main ways: (1) through the existence of shared language and vocabulary and (2) through the sharing of collective narratives. Further, we suggest that these two elements constitute facets of shared cognition that facilitate the creation of intellectual capital especially through their impact on combination capability. In each case they do so by acting as both a medium and a product of social interaction.

Shared Language and Codes

There are several ways in which a shared language influences the conditions for combination and exchange. First, language has a direct and important function in social relations, for it is the means by which people discuss and exchange information, ask questions, and conduct business in society. To the extent that people share a common language, this facilitates their ability to gain access to people and their information. To the extent that their language and codes are different, this keeps people apart and restricts their access (B1 in Figure 6.1).

Second, language influences our perception (Berger & Luckman, 1966; Pondy & Mitroff, 1979). Codes organize sensory data into perceptual categories and provide a frame of reference for observing and interpreting our environment. Thus, language filters out of awareness those events for which terms do not exist in the language and filters in those activities for which terms do exist. Shared language, therefore, may provide a common conceptual apparatus for evaluating the likely benefits of exchange and combination (B2 in Figure 6.1).

Third, a shared language enhances combination capability (B3 in Figure 6.1). Knowledge advances through developing new concepts and narrative forms (Nonaka & Takeuchi, 1995). However, as we noted previously, in order to develop such concepts and to combine the information gained through social exchange, the different parties must have some overlap in knowledge. Boland and Tenkasi (1995) identify the importance of both perspective taking and perspective making in knowledge creation, and they demonstrate how the existence of a shared vocabulary enables the combining of information. We suggest it is for all these reasons that researchers increasingly recognize group-specific communication codes as a valuable asset within firms (Arrow, 1974; Kogut & Zander, 1992; Monteverde, 1995; Prescott & Visscher, 1980).

Shared Narratives

Beyond the existence of shared language and codes, researchers have suggested that myths, stories, and metaphors also provide powerful means in communities for creating, exchanging, and preserving rich sets of meanings—a view long held by some social anthropologists (Clark, 1972; Nisbet, 1969). Recently, Bruner (1990) proposed that there are two different modes of cognition: (1) the information or paradigmatic mode and (2) the narrative mode. The former suggests a process of knowledge creation rooted in rational analysis and good arguments; the latter is represented in synthetic narratives, such as fairy tales, myths and legends, good stories, and metaphors. According to Bateson (1972), metaphors cut across different contexts, thus enabling the combining of both imaginative and literal observations and cognitions. Orr (1990) demonstrates how narrative in the form of stories, full of seemingly insignificant details, facilitates the exchanging of practice and tacit experience between technicians, thereby enabling the discovery and development of improved practice. The emergence of shared narratives within a community thus enables the creation and transfer of new interpretations of events, doing so in a way that facilitates the combination of different forms of knowledge, including those largely tacit (B4 in Figure 6.1).

Exchange, Combination, and the Relational Dimension of Social Capital

Much of the evidence for the relationship between social capital and intellectual capital highlights the significance of the relational dimension of social capital. Szulanski (1996) has found that one of the important barriers to the transfer of best practice within organizations is the existence of arduous relations between the source and the recipient. Whereas we have argued that the structural dimension has its primary direct impact on the condition of accessibility, and the cognitive dimension through its influence on accessibility and combination capability, research suggests that the relational dimension of social capital influences three of the conditions for exchange and combination in many ways. These are access to parties for exchange, anticipation of value through exchange and combination, and the motivation of parties to engage in knowledge creation through exchange and combination.

Trust

Misztal defines trust as the belief that the "results of somebody's intended action will be appropriate from our point of view" (1996: 9–10). A substantial body of research now exists (Fukuyama, 1995; Gambetta, 1988; Putnam, 1993, 1995; Ring & Van de Ven, 1992, 1994; Tyler & Kramer, 1996) that demonstrates where relationships are high in trust, people are more willing to engage in social exchange in general, and cooperative interaction in particular (C1 in Figure 6.1). Mishira (1996) argues that trust is multidimensional and indicates a willingness to be vulnerable to another party—a willingness arising from confidence in four aspects: (1) belief in the good intent and concern of exchange partners (Ouchi, 1981; Pascale, 1990; Ring & Van de Ven, 1994), (2) belief in their competence and capability (Sako, 1992; Szulanski, 1996), (3) belief in their reliability (Giddens, 1990; Ouchi, 1981), and (4) belief in their perceived openness (Ouchi, 1981).

Misztal observes that "trust, by keeping our mind open to all evidence, secures communication and dialogue" (1996: 10), suggesting thereby that trust may both open up access to people for the exchange of intellectual capital (C3 in Figure 6.1) and increase anticipation of value through such exchanges (C2 in Figure 6.1). One can find support for this view in research demonstrating that where there are high levels of trust, people are more willing to take risks in such exchange (Nahapiet, 1996; Ring & Van de Ven, 1992). This may represent an increased willingness to experiment with combining different sorts of information. For example, Luhmann (1979) has shown trust to increase the potential of a system for coping with complexity and, thus, diversity—factors known to be important in the development of new intellectual capital. Trust may also indicate greater openness to the potential for value creation through exchange and combination (C2 in Figure 6.1). Boisot highlights the importance of interpersonal trust for knowledge creation in contexts of high ambiguity and uncertainty: "[W]hen the message is uncodified, trust has to reside in the quality of the personal relationships that bind the parties through shared values and expectations rather than the intrinsic plausibility of the message" (1995: 153).

As we noted earlier, there is a two-way interaction between trust and cooperation: trust lubricates cooperation, and cooperation itself breeds trust. This may lead to the development, over time, of generalized norms of cooperation, which increase yet further the willingness to engage in social exchange (Putnam, 1993). In this respect, collective trust may become a potent form of "expectational asset" (Knez & Camerer, 1994) that group members can rely on more generally to help solve problems of cooperation and coordination (Kramer, Brewer, & Hanna, 1996).

Norms

According to Coleman (1990), a norm exists when the socially defined right to control an action is held not by the actor but by others. Thus, it represents a degree of consensus in the social system. Coleman suggests that "where a norm exists and is effective, it constitutes a powerful though sometimes fragile form of social capital" (1988: S104). Norms of cooperation can establish a strong foundation for the creation of intellectual capital. Becoming, in effect, "expectations that bind" (Kramer & Goldman, 1995), such norms may be a significant influence on exchange processes, opening up access to parties for the exchange of knowledge (C4 in Figure 6.1) and ensuring the motivation to engage in such exchange (C5 in Figure 6.1; Putnam, 1993).

For example, Starbuck (1992) notes the importance of social norms of openness and teamwork as key features of knowledge-intensive firms; he highlights the significance of the emphasis on cooperation rather than competition, on open disclosure of information, and on building loyalty to the firm as significant underpinnings of the success of the American law firm Wachtell, Lipton, Rosen and Katz, which specializes in advice on nonroutine, challenging cases. Other norms of interaction that have been shown to be important in the creation of intellectual capital include a willingness to value and respond to diversity, an openness to criticism, and a tolerance of failure (Leonard-Barton, 1995). Such norms may offset the tendency to "groupthink" that may emerge in strong, convergent groups and that represents the way in which high levels of social capital may be a real inhibitor for the development of intellectual capital (Janis, 1982). At the same time, as Leonard-Barton (1995) has shown, norms also may have a dark side; those capabilities and values initially seen as a benefit may become, in time, a pathological rigidity.

Obligations and Expectations

Obligations represent a commitment or duty to undertake some activity in the future. Coleman (1990) distinguishes obligations from generalized norms, viewing the former as expectations developed within particular personal relationships. He suggests that obligations operate as a "credit slip" held by A to be redeemed by some performance by B—a view reminiscent of Bourdieu's (1986) concept of credential we referred to earlier in this article. In the context of the creation of intellectual capital, we suggest that such obligations and expectations are likely to influence both access to parties for exchanging and combining knowledge (C6 in Figure 6.1) and the motivation to combine and exchange such knowledge (C7 in Figure 6.1). The notion that "there is no such thing as a free lunch" represents a commonly held view that exchange brings with it expectations about future obligations—a view explicated in detail by Mauss (1954), Bourdieu (1977), and Cheal (1988). Fairtlough (1994) ascribes considerable importance to the formal, professional, and personal obligations that develop between those involved in cooperative research and development projects between different organizations:

> People in the two companies could rely on each other. . . . This was cooperation which certainly went beyond contractual obligations. It might also have gone beyond enlightened self interest, and beyond good professional behaviour, because the scientists liked working together, felt committed to the overall project and felt a personal obligation to help the others involved (1994: 119).

Identification

Identification is the process whereby individuals see themselves as one with another person or group of people. This may result from their membership in that group or through the group's operation as a reference group, "in which the individual takes the values or standards of other individuals or groups as a comparative frame of reference" (Merton, 1968: 288; see also Tajfel, 1982). Kramer et al. (1996) have found that identification with a group or collective enhances concern for collective processes and outcomes, thus increasing the chances that the opportunity for exchange will be recognized. Identification, therefore, acts as a resource influencing both the anticipation of value to be achieved through combination and exchange (C8 in Figure 6.1) and the motivation to combine and exchange knowledge (C9 in Figure 6.1). We find support for this in the research of Lewicki and Bunker (1996), whose evidence suggests that salient group identification may not only increase the perceived opportunities for exchange but also may enhance the actual frequency of cooperation. In contrast, where groups have distinct and contradictory identities, these may constitute significant barriers to information sharing, learning, and knowledge creation (Child & Rodrigues, 1996; Pettigrew, 1973; Simon & Davies, 1996).

Thus far, we have argued that social capital theory provides a powerful basis for understanding the creation of intellectual capital in general. The various specific links we have proposed are summarized in Figure 6.1. In the next section we suggest that the theory also provides a basis for understanding the nature of organizational advantage since firms, as institutions, are likely to be relatively well endowed with social capital.

SOCIAL CAPITAL, INTELLECTUAL CAPITAL, AND THE ORGANIZATIONAL ADVANTAGE

The last 20 years have witnessed a substantial resurgence of interest in the theory of the firm. During this period, those espousing transaction cost approaches became increasingly influential, positing, at their simplest, that the existence of firms can be explained in terms of market failure and the greater ability of firms, through hierarchy, to reduce the costs of transactions in particular (and relatively restricted) circumstances (Williamson, 1975, 1981, 1985). The transaction cost theory of the firm has proved robust and has been applied across a wide range of issues, but it has also become subject to growing criticism for a range of definitional, methodological, and substantive reasons (see, for example, Conner & Prahalad, 1996, and Pitelis, 1993). More fundamentally, as we noted at the outset of this article, researchers now are seeking to develop a theory of the firm that is expressed in positive terms (Kogut & Zander, 1996; Masten, Meehan, & Snyder, 1991; Simon, 1991b)—away from a market-failure framework to one grounded in the concept of organizational advantage (Moran & Ghoshal, 1996).

Increasingly, the special capabilities of organizations for creating and transferring knowledge are being identified as a central element of organizational advantage. We suggest that social capital theory provides a sound basis for explaining why this should be the case. First, organizations as institutional settings are characterized by many of the factors known to be conducive to the development of high levels of social capital. Second, it is the coevolution of social and intellectual capital that underpins organizational advantage.

Organizations as Institutional Settings Are Conducive to the Development of Social Capital

Social capital is owned jointly by the parties to a relationship, with no exclusive ownership rights for individuals. Thus, it is fundamentally concerned with resources located within structures and processes of social exchange; as such, the development of social capital is significantly affected by those factors shaping the evolution of social relationships. We discuss four such conditions here: time, interaction, interdependence, and closure. We argue that all four are more characteristic of internal organization than of market organization as represented in neoclassical theory and that, as a result, organizations as institutional settings are conducive to the development of high levels of social capital relative to markets. However, as we subsequently note, in practice these conditions may also occur in some forms of interorganizational networks, thereby enabling such networks to become relatively well endowed with social capital.

Time and the Development of Social Capital

Like other forms of capital, social capital constitutes a form of accumulated history—here reflecting investments in social relations and social organization through time (Bourdieu, 1986; Granovetter, 1992). Time is important for the development of social capital, since all forms of social capital depend on stability and continuity of the social structure. The concept of embedding fundamentally means the binding of social relations in contexts of time and space (Giddens, 1990). Coleman highlights the importance of continuity in social relationships:

> One way in which the transactions that make up social action differ from those of the classical model of a perfect market lie in the role of time. In a model of a perfect market, transactions are both costless and instantaneous. But in the real world, transactions are consummated over a period of time (1990: 91).

For example, since it takes time to build trust, relationship stability and durability are key network features associated with high levels of trust and norms of cooperation (Axelrod, 1984; Granovetter, 1985; Putnam, 1993; Ring & Van de Ven, 1992). The duration and stability of social relations also influence the clarity and visibility of mutual obligations (Misztal, 1996).

Although, in the main, social capital is created as a by-product of activities engaged in for other purposes, intentional or constructed organization represents a direct, purposeful investment in social capital (Coleman, 1990, 1993). "These organizations ordinarily take the form of authority structures composed of positions connected by obligations and expectations and occupied by persons" (Coleman 1990: 313). In contrast to the short-term transactions characterizing the markets of neoclassical theory, intentional or constructed organization represents the creation and maintenance of an explicit and enduring structure of ties constituting, through organizational design, a configuration of relationships and resources usable for a variety of purposes—both formal and informal. Moreover, this commitment to continuity facilitates the other processes known to be influential in the development of social capital: interdependence, interaction, and closure.

Interdependence and the Development of Social Capital

Coleman (1990) states that social capital is eroded by factors that make people less dependent upon each other. This appears especially so for the relational dimension of social capital. For example, expectations and obligations are less significant where people have alternative sources of support. Indeed, Misztal (1996) has suggested that the recent resurgence of interest in trust can be explained by the increasingly transitional character of our present condition and the erosion of social interdependence and solidarity. Yet, most authors agree that high levels of social capital usually are developed in contexts characterized by high levels of mutual interdependence.

Whereas markets as institutional arrangements are rooted in the concept of autonomy (and institutional economists largely neglect interdependence between exchange parties; Zajac & Olsen, 1993), firms fundamentally are institutions designed around the concepts and practices of specialization and interdependence and differentiation and integration (Lawrence & Lorsch, 1967; Smith, 1986; Thompson, 1967). Interdependence—and the coordination it implies—

long has been recognized as perhaps the key attribute of business organization (Barnard, 1938). Follet goes so far as to suggest that

> the fair test of business administration, of industrial organization, is whether you have a business with all its parts so co-ordinated, so moving together in their closely knit and adjusting activities, so linking, interlocking and interrelating, that they make a working unit, not a congerie of separate pieces (1949: 61).

Such interdependence provides the stimulus for developing many organizationally embedded forms of social capital. For example, through providing the opportunity to create contexts characterized by the condition of interdependent viability—that is, the requirement that exchanges are positive in outcome for the system overall rather than for each individual member of the system—organizations considerably extend the circle of exchange that takes place among their members (Coleman, 1993; Moran & Ghoshal, 1996), thereby increasing social identification and encouraging norms of cooperation and risk taking.

Interaction and the Development of Social Capital

Social relationships generally, though not always, are strengthened through interaction but die out if not maintained. Unlike many other forms of capital, social capital increases rather than decreases with use. Interaction, thus, is a precondition for the development and maintenance of dense social capital (Bourdieu, 1986). In particular, as we noted already, scholars have shown that the cognitive and relational dimensions of social capital accumulate in network structures where linkages are strong, multidimensional, and reciprocal—features that characterize many firms but that rarely surface in pure market forms of organization. Discussing the development of language, Boland and Tenkasi note that it is "through action within communities of knowing that we make and remake both our language and our knowledge" (1995: 353). According to these authors, such communities must have space for conversation, action, and interaction in order for the codes and language to develop that facilitate the creation of new intellectual capital.

In a different context Boissevain (1974) shows how multiplex relations are more intimate than single-stranded relationships, therefore providing more accessibility and more response to pressure than single-stranded relations. Such relations typically are imbued with higher levels of obligation between network members, as well as trust-based norms (Coleman, 1990). Further, Powell (1996) argues that norm-based conceptions of trust miss the extent to which cooperation is buttressed by sustained contact, regular dialogue, and constant monitoring. He adds that, without mechanisms and institutions to sustain such conversations, trust does not ensue (see also Coleman, 1990). This echoes Bourdieu's earlier emphasis on the fundamental need for "an unceasing effort of sociability" (1986: 250) for the reproduction of social capital in its many forms.

In neoclassical theory, markets as institutional settings are epitomized by impersonal, arm's length, spot transactions. Firms, in contrast, provide many opportunities for sustained interaction, conversations, and sociability—both by design and by accident. Formal organizations explicitly are designed to bring members together in order to undertake their primary task, to supervise activities, and to coordinate their activities, particularly in contexts requiring mutual adjustment (Mintzberg, 1979; Thompson, 1967), change, and innovation (Burns & Stalker, 1961; Galbraith, 1973). Through copresence (Giddens, 1984), colocation (Fairtlough, 1994), and the creation of such processes as routine choice opportunities (March & Olsen, 1976), organizations also create a myriad of contexts and occasions for the more-or-less planned coming together of people and their ideas. Finally, the literature is replete with evidence that organizational life is characterized by a substantial amount of conversation: in meetings, conferences, and social events that fill the everyday life of workers and managers (Mintzberg, 1973; Prescott & Visscher, 1980; Roy, 1960). Together, these can be viewed as collective investment strategies for the institutional creation and maintenance of dense networks of social relationships and for the resources embedded within, available through, and derived from such networks of relationships. Alternatively, these meetings and social events provide the unplanned and unstructured opportunities for the accidental coming together of ideas that may lead to the serendipitous development of new intellectual capital.

Closure and the Development of Social Capital

Finally, there is much evidence that closure is a feature of social relationships that is conducive to the development of high levels of relational and cognitive social capital. Strong communities—the epitome of systems of dense social capital—have "identities that separate and a sense of sociological boundary that distinguishes members from nonmembers" (Etzioni, 1996: 9; see also Bourdieu, 1986). The development of norms, identity, and trust has been shown to be facilitated by network closure (Coleman, 1990; Ibarra, 1992), and the development of unique codes and language is assisted by the existence of community separation (Boland & Tenkasi, 1995). Formal organizations, by definition, imply a measure of closure through the creation of explicit legal, financial, and social boundaries (Kogut & Zander, 1996). Markets, in contrast, represent open networks that benefit from the freedom offered to individual agents but that have less access to the relational and cognitive facets of social capital.

The Coevolution of Social and Intellectual Capital Underpins Organizational Advantage

Our main argument thus far has been that social capital is influential in the development of new intellectual capital and that organizations are institutional settings conducive to the development of social capital. We have noted the significant and growing body of work that indicates organizations have some particular capabilities for creating and sharing knowledge, giving them their distinctive advantage over other institutional arrangements, such as markets. We now pull the strands of our analysis together by proposing that it is the interaction between social and intellectual capital that underpins organizational advantage.

Although our primary aim has been to suggest that social capital influences the development of intellectual capital, we recognize that the pattern of influence may be in the other direction. The view that shared knowledge forms the basis from which social order and interaction flow is a central theme in sociology, exemplified in the work of Berger and Luckman (1966) and Schutz (1970). Within organizational analysis, authors long have suggested that the firm's particular knowledge about how activities are to be coordinated underpins its capability to develop and operate as a social system (Kogut & Zander, 1992, 1996; March & Simon, 1958; Penrose, 1959; Thompson, 1967). We represent the influence of intellectual capital on social capital as a feedback relationship in Figure 6.1. More important, however, we believe that it is the coevolution of social and intellectual capital that is of particular significance in explaining the source of organizational advantage.

Earlier in the article we noted the dialectical process by which social capital is both created and sustained through exchange and, in turn, enables such exchange to take place. As Berger and Luckman observe,

> The relationship between man, the producer, and the social world, his product, is and remains a dialectical one. That is, man (not, of course, in isolation but in his collectivities) and his social world interact with each other. The product acts back upon the producer (1966: 78; see also Bourdieu, 1977).

Giddens, too, examines the self-reproducing quality of social practices, noting that social activities are recursive—that is, "continually recreated by actors via the very means by which they express themselves as actors" (1984: 2). For Giddens this implies a concept of human knowledgeability that underpins all social practice.

The discussion of knowledgeability that ensues suggests the reciprocal quality of the relationship between social and intellectual capital and is consistent with our emphasis on the social embeddedness of both forms of capital. Since both social and intellectual capital develop within and derive their significance from the social activities and social relationships within which they are located, their evolutionary paths are likely to be highly interrelated.

Consideration of the reciprocal relationship between knowledge and its social context permeates the sociology of science (Zuckerman, 1988). Mullins (1973), for example, describes the joint evolution of social interaction, communication networks, and the elaboration of scientific ideas and notes that cognitive development is facilitated by the thickening of communication networks, which then leads to their further elaboration. Research within organizations offers many parallel examples (Burns & Stalker, 1961; Leonard-Barton, 1995; Weick,

1995; Zucker et al., 1996). For instance, in a study of change in health administration, Nahapiet (1988) describes, in detail, how a new accounting calculus both shaped and was, in turn, shaped by the social context in which it was embedded.

Discussing Orr's (1990) influential ethnography of service technicians, Brown and Duguid (1991) provide further insight into this coevolution of knowledge and relationships. Specifically, they describe how technicians achieve two distinct forms of social construction. First, through their work, and "through cultivating connections throughout the corporation" (Brown & Duguid, 1991: 67), technicians engage in the ongoing creation and negotiation of shared understanding—an understanding that represents their view of the world, that is their collective knowledge. The second form of social construction, which, according to Brown and Duguid, is also important but less evident, is the creation of a shared identity. "In telling these stories an individual rep contributes to the construction and development of his or her own identity as a rep and reciprocally to the construction and development of the community of reps in which he or she works" (Brown & Duguid, 1991: 68). In an analysis reminiscent of Weick and Roberts' (1993) discussion of collective mind—itself located in processes of interrelating—these authors highlight the mutually dependent and interactive ways in which social and intellectual capital coevolve.

We suggest that this emphasis on the coevolution of the two forms of capital provides a dynamic perspective on the development of organizational advantage. Spender (1996) argues that it is the collective forms of knowledge that are strategically important, and many authors claim that it is these forms of shared tacit knowledge that underpin what we have termed the "organizational advantage." It is these collective forms of knowledge, we believe, that are particularly tightly interconnected with the relational and cognitive forms of social capital with which, we have argued, organizations are relatively well endowed. Organizations, thus, build and retain their advantage through the dynamic and complex interrelationships between social and intellectual capital.

DISCUSSION AND IMPLICATIONS

The view of organizational advantage we present here is fundamentally a social one. We see the roots of intellectual capital deeply embedded in social relations and in the structure of these relations. Such a view contrasts strongly with the relatively individualistic and acontextual perspectives that characterize more transactional approaches for explaining the existence and contribution of firms. Although we have identified several ways in which facets of social capital may, indeed, reduce transaction costs by economizing on information and coordination costs, we believe that our theoretical propositions go much farther in identifying those factors underpinning dynamic efficiency and growth.

In so doing, we note that our arguments are consistent with resource-based theory in so far as that theory highlights the competitive advantage of firms as based in their unique constellation of resources: physical, human, and organizational (Barney, 1991). Those resources found to be especially valuable are those that are rare, durable, imperfectly imitable, and nontradable (Barney, 1991; Dierickx & Cool, 1989). Among the factors making a resource nonimitable are tacitness (Reed & DeFillippi, 1990), causal ambiguity (Lippman & Rumelt, 1992), time compression diseconomies, and interconnectedness (Dierickx & Cool, 1989), as well as path dependence and social complexity (Barney, 1991; Reed & DeFillippi, 1990). All of these are features integral to the facets of social capital and to its interrelationships with intellectual capital. Thus, we suggest that differences between firms, including differences in performance, may represent differences in their ability to create and exploit social capital. Moreover, at least regarding the development of intellectual capital, those firms developing particular configurations of social capital are likely to be more successful. Evidence for this suggestion is found in studies of knowledge-intensive firms that have been shown to invest heavily in resources, including physical facilities, to encourage the development of strong personal and team relationships, high levels of personal trust, norm-based control, and strong connections across porous boundaries (Alvesson, 1991, 1992; Starbuck, 1992, 1994; Van Maanen & Kunda, 1989). The framework developed here will provide a useful basis for further testing these propositions about firm differences.

In developing our thesis, we have noted several limitations in our approach. First, regarding social capital, our analysis has concentrated primarily, although not exclusively, on how social capital assists the creation of new intellectual capital. However, we recognize that social capital also may have significant negative consequences. For example, certain norms may be antagonistic rather than supportive of cooperation, exchange, and change. Moreover, organizations high in social capital may become ossified through their relatively restricted access to diverse sources of ideas and information. But the general point underpinning our analysis is that institutions facilitate some forms of exchange and combination but limit their scope (Ghoshal & Moran, 1996); thus, effective organization requires a constant balancing of potentially opposing forces (Boland & Tenkasi, 1995; Etzioni, 1996; Leonard-Barton, 1995).

Furthermore, the creation and maintenance of some forms of social capital, particularly the relational and cognitive dimensions, are costly. The development of social capital thus represents a significant investment—conscious or unconscious—and, like all such investments, requires an understanding of the relative costs and benefits likely to be derived from such investment. These are likely to be influenced by the size and complexity of the social structure in which social capital is embedded, since the costs of maintaining linkages usually increase exponentially as a social network increases in size. Although technology may make it possible to stretch the conventional limits of networks of social capital, our arguments about the significance of interdependence, interaction, and closure suggest that there still remain important upper limits. Indeed, adding people to the network may serve to reduce certain forms of social capital, such as personal obligations or high status.

Finally, although we have responded to Putnam's challenge to progress our understanding of the various dimensions and facets of social capital, in our analysis we largely have considered these dimensions separately. Of great interest is the interrelationships among the three dimensions and, indeed, among the various facets within each dimension. We regard this as an important focus for future research.

Second, regarding intellectual capital, we have concentrated on just one aspect: its creation, rather than its diffusion and exploitation. A fuller understanding of knowledge as the source of organizational advantage will require an examination of the ways in which social capital may influence these important and complementary processes. We believe that the framework we develop here provides a sound basis for such examination. Also, we have focused very much on the types and processes of intellectual capital rather than its content—that is, the know-how rather than the know-what. Clearly, the specific knowledge content, including its quality, are important factors to be considered when attempting to gain an understanding of the effective creation of intellectual capital.

Third, our exploration of organizational advantage began with the proposition that knowledge and knowledge processes are major foundations of such advantage. However, our discussion of the coevolution of social and intellectual capital potentially enriches this understanding of organizational advantage in important ways. For instance, our analysis elucidates resource creation within networks, concentrating particularly on the interrelated development of social and intellectual capital as key resources. As such, it is suggestive of the processes whereby organizational networks create value and that, perhaps, underpin their advantage. More generally, we believe that a detailed understanding of social capital itself may be an important element in extending our understanding of the significant, but as yet inadequately understood, concept of organizational advantage. However, we could not explore such issues in this article, and we recognize that much work still needs to be done to elaborate both the concept of organizational advantage and the significance of social capital therein.

Fourth and finally, we have developed our thesis about the relationships between social and intellectual capital in the context of exploring and explaining the source of organizational advantage—that is, we have made the argument regarding these interrelationships within one type of boundary: the firm. It is our view that structures of social capital fundamentally are relatively bounded, and these boundaries typically come from some external physical or social basis for grouping, such as a geographic community (Jacobs, 1965; Putnam, 1993), the family (Coleman, 1988; Loury, 1977), religion (Coleman, 1990), or class (Bourdieu, 1977). As we noted earlier, social capital is typically a by-product of other activities; thus, its development requires a "focus": an entity around which joint activities are organized (Nohria, 1992) and which forms the basis for a level of network closure.

However, our analysis of the conditions conducive to the development of social capital suggests that wherever institutions operate in contexts characterized by enduring relationships—with relatively high levels of interdependence, interaction, and closure—we would expect to see these institutions emerge with relatively dense configurations of social capital. We have argued that these conditions typically occur more within organizations than in neoclassical markets, but they may also be found in particular forms of interorganizational relationship (Baker, 1990; Hakansson & Snehota, 1995; Larson, 1992; Powell, 1996; Ring & Van de Ven, 1992, 1994). Therefore, we see the potential to extend our fundamental analysis to other institutional settings, including those existing between organizations.

Bourdieu (1993) argues that, by making the concept of social capital explicit, it is possible to focus rigorously on the intuitively important concept of "connections" and to establish the basis for research designed to identify the processes for social capital's creation, accumulation, dissipation, and consequence. The concept also provides a theoretical justification for the study of many social practices, such as the "social round," popularly recognized as important but frequently ignored in formal research. In particular, for Bourdieu, systematic analysis of the volume and structure of social capital enables examination of the relationships between social and other forms of capital.

In identifying the interrelationship between social and intellectual capital, we have made a similar argument. That is, by defining the concepts and developing clear propositions about their interrelationships, we have established an agenda for future research that both complements and extends existing knowledge-based theories of the firm. Moreover, we suggest that the model outlined here also provides the foundation of a viable framework to guide the investments—individual or collective—of practitioners seeking to build or extend their network of connections and, therefore, their stocks of social capital. As Bourdieu observes, "[T]he existence of connections is not a natural given, or even a social given . . . it is the product of an endless effort at institution" (1986: 249).

REFERENCES

Alvesson, M. 1991. Corporate culture and corporatism at the company level: A case study. *Economic and Industrial Democracy*, 12: 347–367.

Alvesson, M. 1992. Leadership as a social integrative action. A study of a computer consultancy company. *Organization Studies*, 13: 185–209.

Anderson, J. R. 1981. *Cognitive skills and their acquisition.* Hillsdale, NJ: Lawrence Erlbaum Associates.

Argyris, C., & Schon, D. 1978. *Organizational learning: A theory of action perspective.* Reading, MA: Addison Wesley.

Arrow, K. 1974. *The limits of organization.* New York: Norton.

Ashforth, B. E., & Mael, F. A. 1995. *Organizational identity and strategy as a context for the individual.* Paper presented at the Conference on the Embeddedness of Strategy, University of Michigan, Ann Arbor.

Axelrod, R. 1984. *The evolution of co-operation.* New York: Basic Books.

Baker, W. 1990. Market networks and corporate behavior. *American Journal of Sociology*, 96: 589–625.

Barnard, C. I. 1938. *The functions of the executive*. Cambridge, MA: Harvard University Press.

Barney, J. 1991. Firm resources and sustained competitive advantage. *Journal of Management*, 17: 99–120.

Bateson, G. 1972. *Steps to an ecology of mind*. New York: Ballantine Books.

Berger, P. L., & Luckman, T. 1966. *The social construction of reality*. London: Penguin Press.

Boisot, M. 1995. *Information space: A framework for learning in organizations, institutions and culture*. London: Routledge.

Boissevain, J. 1974. *Friends of friends*. Oxford: Basil Blackwell.

Boland, R. J., & Tenkasi, R. V. 1995. Perspective making and perspective taking in communities of knowing. *Organization Science*, 6: 350–372.

Bourdieu, P. 1977. *Outline of a theory of practice*. Cambridge, England: Cambridge University Press.

Bourdieu, P. 1986. The forms of capital. In J. G. Richardson (Ed.), *Handbook of theory and research for the sociology of education*: 241–258. New York: Greenwood.

Bourdieu, P. 1993. *Sociology in question*. London: Sage.

Brown, J. S., & Duguid, P. 1991. Organizational learning and communities-of-practice: Toward a unified view of working, learning and innovation. *Organization Science*, 2: 40–57.

Burns, T., & Stalker, G. 1961. *The management of innovation*. London: Tavistock.

Bruner, J. S. 1990. *Acts of meaning*. Cambridge, MA: Harvard University Press.

Burt, R. S. 1992. *Structural holes: The social structure of competition*. Cambridge, MA: Harvard University Press.

Campbell, D. T. 1969. Ethnocentricisrm of disciplines and the fish-scale model of omniscience. In M. Sherif & C. Sherif (Eds.), *Interdisciplinary relationships in the social sciences*: 328–348. Chicago: Aldine.

Cheal, D. 1988. *The gift economy*. London: Routledge.

Child, J., & Rodrigues, S. 1996. The role of social identity in the international transfer of knowledge through joint ventures. In S. R. Clegg & G. Palmer (Eds.), *The politics of management knowledge*: 46–68. London: Sage.

Cicourel, A. V. 1973. *Cognitive sociology*. Harmondsworth, England: Penguin Books.

Clark, B. R. 1972. The occupational saga in higher education. *Administrative Science Quarterly*, 17: 178–184.

Cohen, W. M., & Levinthal, D. A. 1990. Absorptive capacity: A new perspective on learning and innovation. *Administrative Science Quarterly*, 35: 128–152.

Coleman, J. S. 1988. Social capital in the creation of human capital. *American Journal of Sociology*, 94: S95–S120.

Coleman, J. S. 1990. *Foundations of social theory*. Cambridge, MA: Belknap Press of Harvard University Press.

Coleman, J. S. 1993. Properties of rational organizations. In S. M. Lindenberg & H. Schreuder (Eds.), *Interdisciplinary perspectives on organization studies*: 79–90. Oxford, England: Pergamon Press.

Conner, K. R., & Prahalad, C. K. 1996. A resource-based theory of the firm: Knowledge versus opportunism. *Organization Science,* 7: 477–501.

Cooke, S. D. N., & Yanow, D. 1993. Culture and organizational learning. *Journal of Management Inquiry,* 2: 373–390.

Crane, D. 1972. *Invisible colleges: Diffusion of knowledge in scientific communities.* Chicago: University of Chicago Press.

D'Aveni, R. A., & Kesner, I. 1993. Top managerial prestige, power and tender offer response: A study of elite social networks and target firm cooperation during takeovers. *Organization Science,* 4: 123–151.

Dierickx, I., & Cool, K. 1989. Asset stock accumulation and sustainability of competitive advantage. *Management Science,* 35: 1504–1511.

Dougherty, D. 1996. Interpretive barriers to successful product innovation in large firms. In J. R. Meindl, C. Stubbart, & J. F. Porac (Eds.), *Cognition within and between organizations:* 307–340. Thousand Oaks, CA: Sage.

Durkheim, E. 1951. (First published in 1897.) *Suicide: A study in sociology.* New York: Free Press.

Etzioni, A. 1996. The responsive community: A communitarian perspective. *American Sociological Review,* 61:1–11.

Fairtlough, G. 1994. *Creative compartments: A design for future organization,* London: Adamantine Press.

Follet, M. P. 1949. Coordination. In L. Urwick (Ed.), *Freedom and co-ordination: Lectures in business organization:* 61–76. London: Management Publications Trust.

Fukuyama, F. 1995. *Trust: Social virtues and the creation of prosperity.* London: Hamish Hamilton.

Galbraith, J. 1973. *Designing complex organizations.* Reading, MA: Addison-Wesley.

Gambetta, D. (Ed.). 1988. *Trust: Making and breaking cooperative relations.* Oxford, England: Basil Blackwell.

Ghoshal, S., & Moran, P. 1996. Bad for practice: A critique of the transaction cost theory. *Academy of Management Review,* 21: 13–47.

Giddens, A. 1984. *The constitution of society: Outline of a theory of structuration.* Cambridge, England: Polity Press.

Giddens, A. 1990. *The consequences of modernity.* Cambridge, England: Polity Press.

Giddens, A., & Turner, J. (Eds.). 1987. *Social theory today.* Cambridge, England: Polity Press.

Gowler, D., & Legge, K. 1982. The integration of disciplinary perspectives and levels of analysis in problem-oriented research. In N. Nicholson & T. Wall (Eds.), *The theory and practice of organizational psychology:* 69–101. London: Academic Press.

Granovetter, M. S. 1973. The strength of weak ties. *American Journal of Sociology,* 78: 1360–1380.

Granovetter, M. S. 1985. Economic action and social structure: The problem of embeddedness. *American Journal of Sociology,* 91: 481–510.

Granovetter, M. S. 1992. Problems of explanation in economic sociology. In N. Nohria & R. Eccles (Eds.), *Networks and organizations: Structure, form and action:* 25–56. Boston: Harvard Business School Press.

Grant, R. M. 1996. Knowledge, strategy and the theory of the firm. *Strategic Management Journal*, 17(S2): 109–122.

Hakansson, H., & Snehota, I. 1995. *Developing relationships in business networks*. London: Routledge.

Hamel, G. 1991. Competition for competence in inter-partner learning within international strategic alliances. *Strategic Management Journal*, 12: 83–103.

Hansen, M. 1996. *Using the wisdom of others: Searching for and transferring knowledge*. Presentation at the London Business School.

Hedberg, B. 1981. How organizations learn and unlearn. In P. C. Nystrom & W. H. Starbuck (Eds.), *Handbook of organizational design*, vol. 1: 3–27. Oxford, England: Oxford University Press.

Ibarra, H. 1992. Structural alignments, individual strategies, and managerial action: Elements toward a network theory of getting things done. In N. Nohria & R. G. Eccles (Eds.), *Networks and organizations: Structure, form and action*: 165–188. Boston: Harvard Business School Press.

Jacobs, J. 1965. *The death and life of great American cities*. London: Penguin Books.

James, W. 1950. *The principles of psychology*, vols. I and II. New York: Dover Publications.

Janis, I. L. 1982. *Groupthink: Psychological studies of policy decisions and fiascos*. Boston: Houghton Mifflin.

Knez, M., & Camerer, C. 1994. Creating expectational assets in the laboratory: Coordination in "weakest link" games. *Strategic Management Journal*, 15: 101–119.

Kogut, B., & Zander, U. 1992. Knowledge of the firm, combinative capabilities and the replication of technology. *Organization Science*, 3: 383–397.

Kogut, B., & Zander, U. 1993. Knowledge of the firm and the evolutionary theory of the multinational corporation. *Journal of International Business Studies*, 24: 625–645.

Kogut, B., & Zander, U. 1995. Knowledge, market failure and the multinational enterprise: A reply. *Journal of International Business Studies*, 26: 417–426.

Kogut, B., & Zander, U. 1996. What do firms do? Coordination, identity and learning. *Organization Science*, 7: 502–518.

Krackhardt, D. 1989. *Graph theoretical dimensions of informal organization*. Paper presented at the annual meeting of the Academy of Management, Washington, DC.

Krackhardt, D. 1992. The strength of strong ties. In N. Nohria & R. G. Eccles (Eds.), *Networks and organizations: Structure, form and action*: 216–239. Boston: Harvard Business School Press.

Kramer, R. M., Brewer, M. B., & Hanna, B. A. 1996. Collective trust and collective action: The decision to trust as a social decision. In R. M. Kramer & T. R. Tyler (Eds.), *Trust in organizations. Frontiers of theory and research*: 357–389. Thousand Oaks, CA: Sage.

Kramer, R. M., & Goldman, L. 1995. Helping the group or helping yourself? Social motives and group identity in resource dilemmas. In D. A. Schroeder (Ed.), *Social dilemmas*: 49–68. New York: Praeger.

Kuhn, T. S. 1970. *The structure of scientific revolutions* (2nd ed.). Chicago: University of Chicago Press.

Larson, A. 1992. Network dyads in entrepreneurial settings: A study of the governance of exchange relations. *Administrative Science Quarterly*, 37: 76–104.

Lawler, E. J., & Yoon, J. 1996. Commitment in exchange relations: Test of a theory of relational cohesion. *American Sociological Review*, 61:89–108.

Lawrence, P. R., & Lorsch, J. W. 1967. *Organization and environment: Managing differentiation and integration*. Boston: Division of Research, Graduate School of Business Administration, Harvard University.

Leonard-Barton, D. 1995. *Wellsprings of knowledge: Building and sustaining the sources of innovation*. Boston: Harvard Business School Press.

Lewicki, R. J., & Bunker, B. B. 1996. Developing and maintaining trust in work relationships. In R. M. Kramer & T. M. Tyler (Eds.), *Trust in organizations: Frontiers of theory and research*: 114–139. Thousand Oaks, CA: Sage.

Lindenberg, S. 1996. Constitutionalism versus relationalism: Two views of rational choice sociology. In J. Clark (Ed.), *James S. Coleman*: 229–311. London: Falmer Press.

Lippman, S. A., & Rumelt, R. P. 1982. Uncertain imitability: An analysis of interfirm differences in efficiency under competition. *Bell Journal of Economics*, 13: 418–438.

Loasby, B. 1991. *Equilibrium and evolution: An exploration of connecting principles in economics*. Manchester, England: Manchester University Press.

Loury, G. C. 1977. A dynamic theory of racial income differences. In P. A. Wallace & A. M. LaMonde (Eds.), *Women, minorities and employment discrimination*: 153–186. Lexington, MA: Lexington Books.

Loury, G. 1987. Why should we care about group inequality? *Social Philosophy, & Policy*, 5: 249–271.

Luhmann, N. 1979. *Trust and power*. Chichester, England: Wiley.

March, J. G., & Olsen, J. P. 1976. *Ambiguity and choice in organizations*. Bergen: Universitetsforlaget.

March, J. G., & Simon, H. A. 1958. *Organizations*. New York: Wiley.

Marshall, A. 1965. *Principles of economics*. London: Macmillan.

Masten, S. E., Meehan, J. W., & Snyder, E. A. 1991. The costs of organization. *Journal of Law Economics and Organization*, 7: 1–25.

Mauss, M. 1954. *The gift*. New York: Free Press.

Merton, R. K. 1968. (First published in 1948.) *Social theory and social structure*. New York: Free Press.

Mintzberg, H. 1973. *The nature of managerial work*. New York: Harper & Row.

Mintzberg, H. 1979. *The structuring of organizations*. Englewood Cliffs, NJ: Prentice-Hall.

Mishira, A. K. 1996. Organizational responses to crisis. The centrality of trust. In R. M. Kramer & T. M. Tyler (Eds.), *Trust in organizations*: 261–287. Thousand Oaks, CA: Sage.

Misztal, B. 1996. *Trust in modern societies*. Cambridge, England: Polity Press.

Monteverde, K. 1995. *Applying resource-based strategic analysis: Making the model more accessible to practitioners*. Working Paper No. 95–1, Department of Management and Information Systems, St. Joseph's University, Philadelphia.

Moran, P., & Ghoshal, S. 1996. Value creation by firms. In J. B. Keys & L. N. Dosier (Eds.), *Academy of Management Best Paper Proceedings*: 41–45.

Mullins, N. 1973. *Theories and theory groups in contemporary American sociology.* New York: Harper & Row.

Nahapiet, J. E. 1988. The rhetoric and reality of an accounting change: A study of resource allocation in the NHS. *Accounting, Organizations and Society,* 13: 333–358.

Nahapiet, J. E. 1996. *Managing relationships with global clients: Value creation through cross-border networks.* Paper presented at the 16th Annual Conference of the Strategic Management Society, Phoenix, AZ.

Nelson, R. R., & Winter, S. G. 1982. *An evolutionary theory of economic change.* Boston: Belknap Press of Harvard University Press.

Nisbet, R. A. 1969. *Social change and history: Aspects of the western theory of development.* London: Oxford University Press.

Nohria, N. 1992. Information and search in the creation of new business ventures. In N. Nohria & R. G. Eccles (Eds.), *Networks and organizations: Structure, form and action:* 240–261. Boston: Harvard Business School Press.

Nohria, N., & Eccles, R. G. 1992. Face-to-face: Making network organizations work. In N. Nohria and R. G. Eccles (Eds.), *Networks and organizations: Structure, form and action.* Boston: 288–308. Harvard Business School Press.

Nonaka, I., & Takeuchi, H. 1995. *The knowledge creating company.* New York: Oxford University Press.

North, D. C. 1990. *Institutions, institutional change and economic performance.* Cambridge, England: Cambridge University Press.

Orr, J. 1990. Sharing knowledge, celebrating identity: Community memory in a service culture. In D. Middleton & D. Edwards (Eds.), *Collective remembering:* 169–189. London: Sage.

Ouchi, W. G. 1981. *Theory Z: How American business can meet the Japanese challenge.* Reading, MA: Addison-Wesley.

Pascale, R. 1990. *Managing on the edge: How the smartest companies use conflict to stay ahead.* New York: Simon and Schuster.

Penrose, E. 1959. *The theory of the growth of the firm.* Oxford, England: Basil Blackwell.

Perrow, C. 1984. *Normal accidents.* New York: Basic Books.

Pettigrew, A. M. 1973. *The politics of organizational decision making.* London: Tavistock.

Pitelis, C. 1993. Transaction costs, markets and hierarchies: The issues. In C. Pitelis (Ed.), *Transaction costs, markets and hierarchies:* 7–19. Oxford, England: Basil Blackwell.

Polanyi, M. 1962. (First published in 1958.) *Personal knowledge: Towards a post-critical philosophy.* London: Routledge and Kegan Paul.

Polanyi, M. 1967. (First published in 1966.) *The tacit dimension.* London: Routledge and Kegan Paul.

Pondy, L. R., & Mitroff, I. I. 1979. Beyond open systems models of organizations. In B. M. Staw (Ed.), *Research in Organization Behavior,* vol. 1: 3–39. Greenwich, CT: JAI Press.

Powell, W. W. 1996. Trust based form of governance. In R. M. Kramer & T. R. Tyler (Eds.), *Trust in organizations: Frontiers of theory and research:* 51–67. Thousand Oaks, CA: Sage.

Prahalad, C. K., & Hamel, G. 1990. *The core competence of the organization.* Harvard Business Review, 68: 79–91.

Prescott, E. C., & Visscher, M. 1980. *Organization capital. Journal of Political Economy,* 88: 446–461.

Putnam, R. D. 1993. The prosperous community: Social capital and public life. *American Prospect,* 13: 35–42.

Putnam, R. D. 1995. Bowling alone: America's declining social capital. *Journal of Democracy,* 6: 65–78.

Quinn, J. B. 1992. *Intelligent enterprise.* New York: Free Press.

Quinn, J. B., Anderson, P., & Finkelstein, S. 1996. Leveraging intellect. *Academy of Management Executive,* 10: 7–27.

Reed, R., & DeFillippi, R. J. 1990. Causal ambiguity, barriers to imitation and sustainable competitive advantage. *Academy of Management Review,* 15: 88–102.

Ring, P. S., & Van de Ven, A. H. 1992. Structuring cooperative relationships between organizations. *Strategic Management Journal,* 13: 483–498.

Ring, P. S., & Van de Ven, A. H. 1994. Developmental processes of cooperative interorganizational relationships. *Academy of Management Review,* 19: 90–118.

Roy, D. F. 1960. Banana time: Job satisfaction and informal interaction. *Human Organization,* 18: 156–168.

Ryle, G. 1949. *The concept of mind.* London: Hutchinson.

Sako, M. 1992. *Prices, quality and trust: Inter-firm relations in Britain and Japan.* New York: Cambridge University Press.

Schumpeter, J. A. 1934. (Reprinted in 1962.) *The theory of economic development: An inquiry into profits, capital, credit, interest and the business cycle.* Cambridge, MA: Harvard University Press.

Schutz, A. 1970. *On phenomenology and social relations.* Chicago: University of Chicago Press.

Scott, J. 1991. *Social network analysis: A handbook.* London: Sage.

Simon, H. A. 1991a. Bounded rationality and organizational learning. *Organization Science,* 2: 125–134.

Simon, H. A. 1991b. Organizations and markets. *Journal of Economic Perspectives,* 5(2): 25–44.

Simon, L., & Davies, G. 1996. A contextual approach to management learning. *Organization Studies,* 17: 269–289.

Slocum, K. R. 1994. Foreword. In G. von Krogh & J. Roos (Eds.), *Organizational epistemology*: ix. Basingstoke, England: Macmillan.

Smith, A. 1986. (First published in 1776.) *The wealth of nations,* books I–III. London: Penguin Books.

Spender, J-C. 1994. Knowing, managing and learning: A dynamic managerial epistemology. *Management Learning,* 25: 387–412.

Spender, J-C. 1996. Making knowledge the basis of a dynamic theory of the firm. *Strategic Management Journal,* 17(S2): 45–62.

Starbuck, W. H. 1992. Learning by knowledge intensive firms. *Journal of Management Studies,* 29: 713–740.

Starbuck, W. H. 1994. Keeping a butterfly and elephant in a house of cards: The elements of exceptional success. *Journal of Management Studies*, 30: 885–922.

Szulanski, G. 1996. Exploring internal stickiness: Impediments to the transfer of best practice within the firm. *Strategic Management Journal*, 17(S2): 27–44.

Tajfel, H. (Ed.). 1982. *Social relations and intergroup relations*. Cambridge, MA: Cambridge University Press.

Teece, D. J. 1988. Technological change and the nature of the firm. In G. Dosi, C. Freeman, R. Nelson, G. Silverberg, & L. Soete (Eds.), *Technical change and economic theory*: 256–281. New York: Pinter.

Thompson, J. D. 1967. *Organizations in action*. New York: McGraw-Hill.

Tichy, N. M., Tushman, M. L., & Fombrun, C. 1979. Social network analysis for organizations. *Academy of Management Review*, 4: 507–519.

Turner, B. A. 1976. The organizational and interorganizational development of disasters. *Administrative Science Quarterly*, 21: 378–397.

Tyler, T. R., & Kramer, R. M. 1996. Whither trust? In R. M. Kramer & T. R. Tyler (Eds.), *Trust in organizations: Frontiers of theory and research*: 1–15. Thousand Oaks, CA: Sage.

Van Maanen, J., & Kunda, G. 1989. Real feelings: Emotional expression and organizational culture. *Research in organizational behavior*, vol. 11: 43–103. Greenwich, CT: JAI Press.

Walsh, J. P. 1995. Managerial and organizational cognition: Notes from a trip down memory lane. *Organization Science*, 6: 280–321.

Wasserman, S., & Faust, K. 1994. *Social network analysis: Methods and applications*. Cambridge, England: Cambridge University Press.

Weick, K. E. 1995. *Sensemaking in organizations*. London: Sage.

Weick, K. E., & Roberts, K. H. 1993. Collective mind in organizations: Heedful interrelating on flight decks. *Administrative Science Quarterly*, 38: 357–381.

Williamson, O. E. 1975. *Markets and hierarchies: Analysis and antitrust implications*. New York: Free Press.

Williamson, O. E. 1981. The economics of organization: The transaction cost approach. *American Journal of Sociology*, 87: 548–577.

Williamson, O. E. 1985. *The economic institutions of capitalism*. New York: Free Press.

Winter, S. G. 1987. Knowledge and competence as strategic assets. In D. J. Teece (Ed.), *The competitive challenge: Strategy for industrial innovation and renewal*: 159–184. New York: Harper & Row.

Zajac, E. J., & Olsen, C. P. 1993. From transaction cost to transactional value analysis: Implications for the study of interorganizational strategies. *Journal of Management Studies*, 30: 131–146.

Zander, U., & Kogut, B. 1995. Knowledge and the speed of transfer and imitation of organizational capabilities: An empirical test. *Organization Science*, 6: 76–92.

Zucker, L. G., Darby, M. R., Brewer, M. B., & Peng, Y. 1996. Collaboration structures and information dilemmas in biotechnology: Organization boundaries as trust production. In R. M. Kramer & T. R. Tyler (Eds.), *Trust in organizations: Frontiers of theory and research*: 90–113. Thousand Oaks, CA: Sage.

Zuckerman, H. 1988. The sociology of science. In N. J. Smelser (Ed.), *Handbook of sociology*: 511–574. Beverly Hills, CA: Sage.

Janine Nahapiet is a fellow of strategic management at Templeton College, Oxford University, and Director of the Oxford Institute of Strategic and International Management. Her current research focuses on the links between strategy and organization in global firms and on value creation through networks. She has a postgraduate diploma in management from the London School of Economics and a first degree in psychology and sociology from the University of Sheffield, England.

Sumantra Ghoshal received his Ph.D. in international management from MIT's Sloan School of Management and a DBA in business policy from the Harvard Business School. He holds the Robert P. Bauman Chair in Strategic Leadership at the London Business School and is on leave from INSEAD in Fontainebleau, France. His current research focuses on the roles and tasks of managers in large corporations.

Chapter 7

Virtual Communities and Social Capital[*]

Anita Blanchard and Tom Horan[**]
Claremont Graduate University

Putnam has developed a theory of social capital to explain the effect of decreasing community participation and civic engagement on declining institutional performance. Subsequently, there has been much speculation as to whether emerging virtual communities can counteract this trend. The authors apply the findings of computer-mediated communication and virtual communities to the networks, norms, and trust of social capital and also examine the possible effects of virtual communities on the privatization of leisure time. They conclude that social capital and civic engagement will increase when virtual communities develop around physically based communities and when these virtual communities foster additional communities of interest. Through a preliminary analysis, the authors identify potential communities of interest including education, exchange of general community information, and opportunities for government and political participation. They conclude with a discussion of current trends and research needs.

The lack of citizen participation in the community has come under scrutiny recently. Although this trend might have started at least a century ago (Wellman & Gulia, in press), it is only lately that the implications of this decline in

[*] Reprinted with permission of *Social Science Review* Vol. 16 No. 3, Fall 1998, 293–307 © 1998 Sage Publications, Inc.
[**] AUTHORS' NOTE: The data for this article were collected as part of an ongoing project on digital communities conducted by the Claremont Graduate University Research Institute in conjunction with the Center for Politics and Economics at the Claremont Graduate University. The authors gratefully acknowledge the assistance of Elizabeth Bergman and William Marelich for their help in this process. Correspondence can be directed to Anita Blanchard at anita.blanchard@cgu.edu or Tom Horan at tom.horan@cgu.edu at the Claremont Graduate University Research Institute.

community participation have been more fully explored. Besides negatively affecting a person's affiliation with his or her own neighborhood, this lack of community has been cited as a major reason for the decline in civic involvement that helps communities operate (Putnam, 1993). Putnam has developed a theory of social capital that attempts to explain the relationship between citizen engagement in the community and the performance of the government and other social institutions. Although Putnam's theory is by no means unchallenged (Greeley, 1996), it has focused attention on understanding the processes that lead to increasing community involvement.

Concurrently, researchers and community activists have observed that communities, or what appear to be communities, are developing over computer-mediated communication (CMC) such as electronic mail (e-mail), interactive chat rooms, computer conferences, and bulletin boards (Baym, 1995; Rheingold, 1993b; Schuler, 1996; Wellman & Gulia, in press). One potential outcome of these emerging virtual communities that might increase social capital is that they may augment face-to-face (FtF) communities and perhaps lessen the problems associated with decreasing FtF community participation. However, at least two other possible outcomes have been proposed. These possibilities are that (a) these emerging virtual communities could detract from FtF communities and worsen the community participation problems or that (b) participation in the two types of communities might not even be related. Therefore, there is much interest in determining the relationship between virtual and FtF communities, especially how community participation could affect social capital.

This article examines the question of how virtual communities will affect social capital. In particular, we identify which forms of virtual community may increase (or decrease) social capital and civic engagement and through what mechanisms. First, Putnam's theory of social capital is briefly outlined. Then the findings on virtual communities are examined, with particular attention paid to the factors that may affect social capital. We then present preliminary data on a particular physically based community that is in the process of going "on-line." A discussion of these findings and future trends follows.

SOCIAL CAPITAL

Putnam (1995a) describes social capital as the "features of social organization such as networks, norms, and social trust that facilitate coordination and cooperation for mutual benefit" (p. 66). Social capital can take many forms, although Putnam has more intensely examined those forms that serve civic ends such as civic engagement. Civic engagement refers to "people's connections with the life of their community" (Putnam, 1995b, p. 665) and includes things such as membership in neighborhood associations, choral societies, or sports clubs. Putnam (1993, 1995b) found convincing evidence that civic engagement is strongly and positively related to performance of the government and other social institutions. He also shows that civic engagement and, consequently, social capital have declined in the United States in the past 20 years.[1]

Networks, norms, and trust are interrelated and essential parts of the theory of social capital (Putnam, 1995b). Trust eases cooperation, and the more that people trust others and the more they feel that others trust them, the greater the likelihood of cooperation among these people. According to Putnam, this social trust arises from two related sources: norms of reciprocity and networks of civic engagement. Although there are several norms of behavior that compose social capital, the norm of reciprocity is the most important. With this norm, there is a belief that "good acts" or pro-social behavior will be reciprocated at a later point.

Networks of civic engagement also are key in the process of social capital. An individual can learn about the trustworthiness of another individual through personal interactions. However, information about a person's trustworthiness also travels through his or her social network of relationships. Dense networks of social interactions also contribute to social capital by increasing the potential costs to a defector in any individual transaction, fostering robust norms of reciprocity and sustaining information about past collaborative successes.

Putnam cites two other characteristics of networks that are important. First, flatter or more horizontal networks add to social capital, whereas vertical or more hierarchical networks detract from it. Second, weak ties in the network such as ties among acquaintances or colleagues in a civic organization contribute more to social capital than do strong ties among kin and intimates. Weak network ties provide the mechanism through which information about an individual's trustworthiness travels to a wide variety of groups. The more complicated a community of groups, the more reliance there is on networks for information about a person's trustworthiness.

In summary, Putnam's theory of social capital involves the norms of reciprocity and networks of civic engagement that encourage social trust and cooperation. The decreasing level of community participation and, hence, social capital in the United States is troubling to many social scientists and community activists. Putnam (1995a, 1995b) cites television and its effect on privatizing Americans' leisure time as a primary cause of this decline. Without the opportunity to interact with others outside of one's home, weak social network ties are lost, which adversely affects norms of reciprocity and social trust. This process is self-reinforcing and cumulative, and eventually it leads to decreased institutional performance.

Many researchers and community activists are interested in whether the virtual communities that are facilitated by CMC can counteract this negative

---

[1] Putnam's theory of social capital is not without its detractors. Greeley (1996), Ladd (1996) and Pettinico (1996) provide an overview of these criticisms that mainly question how much civic engagement has declined (or not). Although this scholarly debate continues, it has not yet affected the form of Putnam's theory of social capital, nor does it negate the importance of CMC and virtual communities in community participation.

effect of television. Can an increase in participation in virtual communities compensate for the decrease in social capital caused by decreased participation in FtF communities? Before we can answer this question, we must examine how virtual communities may affect the three basic components of social capital: networks, norms, and trusts. Then we can examine the nature of civic engagement in the age of CMC and how it may decrease the privatization of leisure time.

VIRTUAL COMMUNITIES

What are virtual communities?[2] Some researchers argue that virtual communities actually are pseudo-communities (Harasim, 1993) or should only be considered as metaphors for communities (McLaughlin, Osborne, & Smith, 1995). Although there are most likely differences between virtual and FtF communities, in this article we assume that virtual communities are "real" communities because the participants believe that they are communities (Rheingold, 1993b).

Within virtual communities, it is important to distinguish between two different types of communities. The first involves the more traditional sense of a physically based community that adds electronic resources for its citizens' use. For example, a town or city that puts information about its city hall, schools, and community organizations on-line and that provides electronic access to government employees as well as other forms of e-mail, electronic bulletin boards, and the Internet would be a *physically based virtual community*.[3] The second type of virtual community is geographically dispersed with members participating due to their shared interests in a topic and not their shared locations. These *virtual communities of interest* can occur through bulletin boards on Usenet, through a national Internet provider such as America Online, or through e-mail via listserv programs.[4] The members of these communities might never meet each other, and their interactions might be limited to just that topic or community of interest.

---

[2] Communities that form through (CMC are known by a variety of terms including electronic, on-line, and virtual communities. In this article, we primarily use the term virtual communities.

[3] A community does not need to put all of these resources on-line to become a physically based virtual community. However, we show later that certain technologies and resources such as those that foster communication between community members are more important than others in increasing social capital in this community.

[4] Electronic bulletin boards consist of a list of electronic messages centered around a particular topic. Users can pick and choose which messages to read and respond to. One feature about bulletin boards is that users must maneuver around their systems to get to the bulletin boards. A listserv is essentially similar to the bulletin board system except that all the messages are sent directly to users through e-mail. Thus, users do not have to "go" anywhere to receive these messages; the messages are automatically sent to their regular e-mail addresses.

The distinction between these two types of electronic communities is not often made, although we feel that it is important. First, little is known about the relationship between these two types of virtual communities. They may be in competition with each other (Michaelson, 1996). Markus (1994) found that e-mail users were likely to interrupt FtF conversations to read and respond to their e-mail messages. Also, people can maintain only a certain number of community ties (Wellman et al., 1995), and if they increase their ties to dispersed virtual communities of interest, then how will this affect their ties to their physically based communities? Second, it is not clear which type of virtual community may be stronger in its sense of itself as a community. Much of on-line contact currently is between people who see each other and who live locally (Wellman & Guilt, in press). Thus, virtual communities may be stronger where there can be both computer-mediated and FtF communication. On the other hand, there has been much speculation that people may have stronger ties with their virtual communities of interest than with their own physically based communities because the former are based on shared interests and not just shared location (Michaelson, 1996; Wellman & Gulia, in press). However, it may be easier to disrupt communities that exist only on-line and do not have FtF interactions (Wellman & Gulia, in press).

A third reason to distinguish between the two types of communities is that researchers and community activists might incorrectly assume that virtual communities will strengthen FtF geographical communities or might even replace them with corresponding pro-social communities (Kling, 1996). It is possible that this strengthening may be more likely for physically based virtual communities and less likely for dispersed ones. Finally, there might be different effects of member participation in these two types of communities in regard to social capital and civic engagement. Both dispersed virtual communities and physically based communities may have the potential to increase social capital, but physically based communities might be more likely to increase civic engagement (especially membership in an FtF group) because this community already is associated with a civic center, so to speak. Thus, it will be useful to consider both types of virtual communities in this analysis.

VIRTUAL COMMUNITIES AND SOCIAL CAPITAL

The question to be addressed here is how virtual communities may affect the networks, norms, and trust that comprise social capital. This section examines the findings related to each of these issues and then examines how CMC may affect the privatization of leisure time as well as civic engagement.

Networks

Networks are generally defined as specific types of relations linking defined sets of people, objects, or events (Knoke & Kuklinski, 1982). Putnam (1993) focuses on people's networks of civic engagement in a community. Therefore, we examine the networks of civic engagement in virtual communities. However, the question immediately arises as to how one defines virtual civic engagement. As discussed previously, Putnam (1993) defines civic engagement as participation in organized groups such as choral societies or bowling leagues. The corresponding example in CMC is participation in groups organized around certain topics such as parenting groups, exercise groups, or a variety of other informational or social topics. A major difference between Putnam's examples of civic engagement and these virtual examples is the lack of a unifying physical activity (e.g., singing, bowling) in virtual groups. However, one may argue that it might be the exchange of information or social support within these groups that is the essential contributor to social capital and that this exchange is present in both FtF and virtual groups.

Considering these types of virtual civic engagement, how might they affect a person's networks? The most dramatic effects occur when considering CMC through the Internet. The Internet often is described as a series of networks connected to other networks that comprise a very large network (Baym, 1995; McLaughlin et al., 1995). Thus, anyone (and everyone) across the globe who also has an Internet connection can join many groups with which they share interests. It appears that this will create a type of global village in which everyone is communicating with everyone else to create a tight-knit but large community. However, people can maintain only a limited number of ties, so unlimited relationships and communication with the rest of the world is unlikely (Wellman & Gulia, in press). In addition, Wellman and Gulia (in press) point out that instead of a global village, it is more likely that one's village will span the globe; that is, one's personal community could be scattered around the world and might not necessarily overlap with anyone else's community. Parks and Floyd's (1996) research supports this scenario. They found that overlap in social networks among people involved in friendships in a geographically dispersed virtual community was quite low as compared to FtF friendships.

Putnam's (1993) theory of social capital would argue that this dispersal of social networks would decrease social capital because it is dense social networks that facilitate the norms of reciprocity and social trust. However, the dispersion of one's network is more likely to occur when an individual primarily participates in geographically dispersed virtual communities of interest and not physically based ones. Physically based virtual communities would increase the chances of overlapping with FtF communities.

A second important feature of virtual communities is the ability to search for others who share specific interests and, thus, form communities of interest. Wellman and Gulia (in press) term this "boutique shopping" in that the person "shops around" for a wide variety of social and informational resources to meet his or her needs. One community of interest that has attracted much attention in the media is the parenting support groups (Ryan, 1996). Formally and informally organized groups such as Parent Soup, Parents Helping Parents, and the Fathering Homepage provide social support and information to any parent who has access to the Internet. One advantage that often is cited in these groups is the ability to connect with like-minded others at any time of the day or night to obtain specific information or help.

Implicit in the discussions of these communities of interest is the idea that these relationships are developing among people who are geographically dispersed. Certainly, people are more likely to find others who share highly specialized interests when they can search a broader population. However, it also is possible that people can find others who share their specialized interests in their physically based virtual communities (Michaelson, 1996). For example, parenting groups also can form on physically based community networks (Schuler, 1996), although there has not been as much research on or media attention paid to these local communities. This lack of attention is unfortunate given that these physically based communities of interest may contribute to denser networks as the number of overlapping relationships among community members increases.

Other observations about CMC and virtual communities that may increase social capital is that they foster equality of status and participation among members (Hiltz & Turoff, 1993), facilitate weak ties (Pickering & King, 1995), and encourage multiple partial relationships (Wellman & Gulia in press). An interesting finding from Parks and Floyd (1996) is that personal relationships among members of a virtual community are common and that these relationships are likely to move off-line and include the telephone, postal service, and FtF communication. This movement off-line is striking considering that their study examined only geographically dispersed virtual communities.

With this information, how might networks in virtual communities affect social capital? First, a person's social network may expand and include previously unknown others, but the number of significant relationships in the network might not change. In geographically dispersed virtual communities, social networks may spread out and become less dense. Subsequently, the network might not be able to facilitate norms of reciprocity and trust and could weaken social capital. In physically based virtual communities where the likelihood of FtF network overlap is greater, social capital may increase as networks increase in density. Second, although weak ties are important in social capital in spreading information about an individual's trustworthiness, weak ties might not serve the same purpose in virtual communities. Information about group members will travel through relevant social networks only if some subset of members are participating in multiple electronic groups together. This overlap is more likely to occur in groups that form in physically based virtual communities than in geographically dispersed communities of interest. The physically based virtual communities can tap into their FtF social networks for information about others' trustworthiness as well. Therefore, virtual communities will have the most positive effect on social capital when they can increase network density and facilitate the spread of information. This increase is more likely to occur with physically based communities than with dispersed virtual communities.

Norms

Norms of behavior in electronic groups have been addressed in some detail. Although this focus often is on general norms of polite behavior such as "netiquette" or network etiquette, there has been growing attention paid to norms of reciprocity that directly relates to Putnam's theory of social capital. In FtF communities, reciprocity occurs when one community member helps another member and eventually is helped in return. Although these acts of helping often are not defined, it is assumed that they refer to physical acts of help as well as to information and social exchange. In virtual communities, information is the primary "act" of help that is exchanged (Rheingold, 1993a; Schuler, 1996). Participants pose a question, and other members answer it directly through personal e-mail or provide information to the whole group. Occasionally, people will offer unsolicited information to the whole group that they feel may be useful (Nickerson, 1994). Group members also exchange social support with other members (Baym, 1995; Jones, 1995) and occasionally provide physical benefits (e.g., financial support) (Rheingold, 1993b). Reciprocal support is a vital part of virtual communities, and the evidence that it occurs is substantial (Wellman & Gulia, in press). In addition, because the costs of helping are so low, people can easily obtain assistance from others when the group is large.

An interesting phenomenon that occurs in virtual communities and not FtF communities is that a single act of helping can be more easily viewed by the entire group (Wellman & Gulia, in press). In the aggregate, small individual acts of helping can sustain a large virtual community because the act is seen by the entire group. Thus, a few group members' helpful actions will reinforce the group's concept of itself as being helpful to its members.[5]

Finally, lurking presents an interesting unresolved norm of behavior. Lurking occurs when members of the electronic group read the messages but do not participate in the discussions. Although some active group members do not consider lurkers as "real" group members, others do (McLaughlin et al., 1995). These lurking virtual community members might be breaking norms of reciprocity by following discussions but not actively contributing to them (Kollock & Smith, 1994). Thus, they might perceive the group as having a strong norm of

[5] There is an interesting observation to be made about how typical these early virtual communities have been so far as their propensity to help is concerned. As more people go on-line, will they follow the patterns of behavior set up by these early adopters? For example, the WELL, an early virtual community, has the reputation for being an active and helpful community (Rheingold, 1993b). Is this the result of the ease of assistance, or is it due to the special nature of the people who have been early participants? This issue remains to be answered as additional people go on-line.

reciprocity even though they do not feel the pressure to contribute. Because it is so difficult to detect lurking, very little is known about people who lurk on virtual communities.

How do the norms that have emerged in virtual communities affect social capital? The most interesting and direct relationship involves the norms of reciprocity. First, reciprocal acts of help and support occur in, and are an important part of, virtual communities. Second, small acts of helping might create the perception of a strong norm of reciprocity within a virtual community. This leads to a final observation about whether an individual needs to directly participate in the exchange of help for social capital to be affected. This answer may be no. If one of the main functions of the norm of reciprocity is to increase trust among members, then simply observing a helpful act might be sufficient.

Trust

Trust is a vital part of social capital and a very interesting concept in virtual communities. One significant feature of CMC is the lack of physical, social, and other nonverbal information exchanged among group members. Although at one point it was believed that this would prevent the development of social relationships through CMC, it has not (Walther, 1992). This lack of social cues, and even the outright anonymity provided by some systems, has been somewhat beneficial. Individuals can improve their first (and subsequent) impressions by thoughtfully composing and editing their comments (Rheingold, 1993a; Walther, 1996). Disenfranchised groups such as women, minorities, those with disabilities, and the homeless can participate in group discussions without having to encounter stereotypes based on their physical characteristics (Rheingold, 1993b; Schuler, 1996).

Another interesting phenomenon is reported by Walther (1996). Under some circumstances, members of electronic groups inflate their perceptions of their partners. This inflation is likely to occur as an interaction between the strength of a person's identity with the electronic group and the absence of other group members. Stronger group identity leads to attributions of greater similarity when members are physically distant. Group members will even report that their partners are more attractive over CMC (where they receive no physical cues) than they are in FtF or telephone interactions.

Although this inflated perception of group partners does not directly address trust, it might be related to it. The more a person identifies with a group and perceives similarity with the group members, the more likely he or she may be to trust others in that group. Because it is assumed that little information comes through the person's social networks about other group members (especially in geographically dispersed communities of interest), highly active members of virtual communities might be more trusting of other group members than is observed in FtF communities.

There are other behaviors observed in CMC that may decrease trust in virtual communities. Flaming may negatively affect social trust (Kling, 1996). Flaming consists of generally intense and hostile communication toward one person or a group of people. It usually is considered a breach of netiquette (Kollock & Smith, 1994), although in milder forms it sometimes is used to reinforce behavioral norms (McLaughlin et al., 1995).

Deception is another feature of CMC that may decrease trust. Because social and physical cues are unavailable through CMC, participants generally reveal personal information about themselves slowly as they are building relationships (Walther, 1996). However, establishing the authenticity of this information is difficult (Harasim, 1993). Some people might alter small portions of their person information (e.g., weight, income), whereas others might change their identities altogether. Turkle (1995) found that people sometimes will change their gender or a major personality trait when they go on-line. Although this behavior might be more common in role-playing computer conferences and such games, it also is possible in more "serious" virtual communities. One example is the story of a male psychiatrist who posed as "Joan," a handicapped female neuropsychologist who entered into a support group for women with disabilities, seduced other women into trying lesbian cybersex, faked "her" own death, and was caught (Van Gelder, 1991). Obviously, this type of example and less extreme ones should negatively affect trust.

To prevent the possibility of deceptions, some virtual communities do not allow anonymous communications and try to keep participants honest about their identities (Harasim, 1993; Rheingold, 1993b). Certainly, examples of extreme dishonesty such as the "Joan" case may be less likely in physically based virtual communities, where the chances of being caught are higher due to information flowing through FtF communication networks.[6] Also, the purpose of the virtual group and the norms associated with this group may influence the likelihood of being honest.

PRIVATIZATION OF LEISURE TIME

The privatization of leisure time caused by television viewing habits is cited by Putnam (1995b) as being one of the primary causes of the decreases in networks, norms, and trust of social capital. There has been much speculation about whether personal computers and the Internet can counteract that trend. Computer use might overcome the passivity of watching television, as pointed out by Meyrowitz (1985), but might not replace it with more public interaction. Computer use might even "hyperprivatize" leisure time as family members no longer watch television together but rather play or explore their own computers alone. Thus, Putnam (1995a) might say that computer use will continue the negative

---

[6] This is partially how "Joan" was caught (Van Gelder, 1991).

effect on the privatization of leisure time as people stay at home playing interactive computer games and exploring World Wide Web pages for information.

Other researchers, however, might disagree with this assessment, but only if the time on the computer is spent communicating with other people and not simply (or always) playing games or browsing for information. Kling (1996) states that the ways in which people communicate via computer networks destabilizes the traditional distinction between what is public and what is private. Obviously, the person who is communicating over the computer at home is in a private space, but when the person is communicating with others in a virtual community, is that occurring in a private or public area?

One key feature of CMC is that people see that activity as social (Harasim, 1993; McLaughlin et al., 1995), and social activities generally take place with other people. Harasim (1993) is one of the first researchers to note that the computer communication networks "have come to be experienced as *places* where we network" (p. 15, emphasis in original). These social places have become places that people "go to" or "drop in," even though they do not move from in front of their computer screens. McLaughlin and her colleagues (1995) point out that activity takes place in conceptual rather than perceptual space, although people talk about it as if it were a "real" place. Therefore, when people are communicating with multiple others in some type of electronic forum, is it public communication from a private space or does it remain private communication in a private space? If this communication can positively affect social capital, then its interpretation as a new form of public communication from a private space is better supported.

In addition, it might be useful to consider whether an individual is communicating with others in physically based or dispersed communities. Although the mechanics of conversing through CMC in either type of community are the same, their effect on the person's public life might be different. If communication or relationships that develop through CMC can affect one's FtF relationships or social networks, then it seems more reasonable to consider this a public activity. Geographically dispersed virtual communities might have a much more limited effect on one's public life in this sense compared to physically based ones.

SUMMARY OF SOCIAL CAPITAL AND VIRTUAL COMMUNITIES

The current findings relating to CMC and virtual communities have been applied to social capital. Table 7.1 summarizes the potential effects of virtual communities on networks, norms, trust, and privatization of leisure time. From this review, we believe that virtual communities can increase social capital in the following conditions. First, from the table, it is clear that physically based virtual communities are more likely to increase social capital than are geographically

TABLE 7.1 Summary of Effects of Virtual Communities on Networks, Norms, Trust, and Privatization of Leisure Time

Virtual Community	Networks	Norms	Trust	Decreasing Privatization of Leisure Time
Geographically dispersed	Should ease access to previously unknown others who share interests (+)	Information is primary help exchanged; social support also is exchanged	Members may report inflated perceptions of other CMC group members (+)	Game playing and information retrieval will not increase "public" leisure time (−)
	Should create less dense networks as they expand across greater areas (−)	Small acts of helping create perception of strong norms of reciprocity (+)	Flaming may occur (−)	Communication with others from a private space may increase "public" time (+)
			Deception may occur at a variety of levels (e.g., changing income or weight, changing gender) (−)	
Physically based	Should ease access to previously unknown others who share interests (+)	Information is primary help exchanged; social support also is exchanged	Members may report inflated perceptions of other CMC group members (+)	Game playing and information retrieval will not increase "public" leisure time (−)
	Should create denser networks through overlap with FtF networks (+)	Small acts of helping create perception of strong norms of reciprocity (+)	Flaming may occur (−)	Communication with public others from a private space may increase "public" time, especially as this affects FtF relationships (+)
	More likely to tap into FtF networks to		Deception may occur, but extreme	

TABLE 7.1 *Continued*

provide infor- mation about other commu- nity members (+)	examples are less likely because of probability of being "caught" through informa- tion passed in FtF networks (+)

Note: CMC = computer-mediated communication; FtF = face-to-face; plus sign (+) indicates a potential positive impact; minus sign (–) indicates a potential negative impact.

dispersed ones. Although both types of virtual communities may cause a general increase in trusting and norms of reciprocity, the effect on social capital will be stronger when virtual networks overlap FtF networks and facilitate network density and the flow of information.

Second, social capital should increase when opportunities for civic engagement are facilitated by physically based virtual communities. As discussed previously, virtual civic engagement occurs through membership and participation in virtual communities of interest. This means that physically based virtual communities must do more than just provide information about town hall meetings, phone numbers, and office hours of relevant community organizations. In addition, e-mail to government employees and city council members may provide individual community members with information, but it probably will not be as effective in establishing community ties as is communication with other community members. Therefore, physically based virtual communities must provide forums that enable community members to establish ongoing connections with other community members.

A caveat to the process of increasing social capital through virtual communities needs to be stated. We have proposed that if a physically based virtual community with forums to foster communication among members exists, then over time, networks, norms, and trust will be strengthened and social capital in this community will increase. However, connectivity does not ensure community (Jones, 1995; Schuler, 1996). Simply providing electronic access to communities and even setting up these forums does not mean that community members will participate in them. Wellman and his colleagues (1995) point out that membership in virtual communities is voluntary, and although we might assume that people will naturally affiliate when given the opportunity in a social environment (Walther, 1992), we know very little about the process by which virtual communities are created and maintained. Therefore, we might have identified the factors by which virtual communities increase social capital, but we do not know how to encourage the development of active virtual communities of interest.

Nevertheless, a key issue that still can be addressed is what communities of interest will increase the likelihood of members participating; that is, if communication forums correspond to community members' interests, then the probability of members starting and maintaining a community based on these interests increases. As a first step in understanding the effects of virtual communities on social capital, identifying these interests is essential.

PRELIMINARY IDENTIFICATION OF COMMUNITIES OF INTEREST

An exploratory analysis was conducted to identify which communities of interest would be attractive to members of a physically based community at the beginning of their process of going on-line. A total of 342 community members of a mid-sized southern California city were surveyed about their interests in on-line services along with their current computer experience and current civic engagement.

Participants were the first available adults, age 18 years or older, in the households and had a mean age of 46 years (SD = 14.61). Approximately 56% of the participants were female, 84% were White or European American, and more than 80% had at least some college or vocational education. In general, this sample is better educated, is more politically conservative, and has higher reported income as compared to the average American, although it is representative of the community from which the sample was taken. In addition, this distribution is typical of Internet users (Wellman et al., 1995) except for the percentage of females in this sample, which is higher than what usually is reported for Internet users.

Communities of Interest

Table 7.2 lists the percentages of participants interested in the different possible services that could be offered in this physical community's developing virtual community. Participants' interests were determined by asking whether they would use the service in the new virtual community. Although the question

TABLE 7.2 Interest in Services in Developing Virtual Community

Area	Percentage Interested
Self or child's education	78.7
Community, bulletin boards, etc.	76.3
Communicating with friends or relatives	69.6
Participating in government or politics	62.2
Telecommuting	58.5
Home shopping	35.7

wording relates more strongly to potential services than to topics of interest, we feel that this information still provides useful information about areas in which community members express an interest. More than three quarters of the participants expressed an interest in using the virtual community for educational and community information including bulletin board services. Participants expressed the least interest in using the virtual community system for home shopping.

We also examined whether there were differences in interests based on computer experience and civic engagement by conducting a series of exploratory analyses. Computer experience was measured in two ways: (a) the participants' overall computer use measured by the average number of hours of computer use at home and work and (b) frequency of home e-mail use on a scale of 0 (*never*) to 3 (*always*). For level of civic engagement, a sum was created of all civic organizations (e.g., Parent-Teacher Associations, church groups, sports groups) to which the participants reported belonging. Participants reported a mean computer use of nearly 6 hours per week (*SD* = 3.3), a mean frequency of e-mail use of 0.77 (*SD* = 1.1), and a mean level of civic engagement of 2.3 groups (*SD* = 1.9).

These measures of computer use, e-mail use, and civic engagement were then correlated with the participants' interest in the various services using point-biserial correlations. To control for inflated alpha errors that might occur during exploratory analyses, a more conservative *p* level was calculated using the Bonferroni split-alpha test. We determined that $p < 0.005$ was the appropriate level to obtain statistical significance.[7]

Table 7.3 presents the results of these analyses. Computer experience was significantly related to interest in using the virtual community for participating in

TABLE 7.3 Correlations of Interest in Services in Virtual Community, by Level of Experience with Computers, E-Mail, and Civic Involvement

Area of interest	Computer Experience	E-Mail Experience	Level of Civic Engagement
Self or child's education	0.09	0.10	0.14
Community, bulletin boards, etc.	0.15[*]	0.16[*]	0.12
Communicating with friends or relatives	0.14	0.20[**]	0.05
Participating in government or politics	0.20[**]	0.18[**]	0.19[**]
Telecommuting	0.19[**]	0.19[**]	0.00
Home shopping	0.11	0.19[**]	−0.03

[*]$p < 0.001.$ [**]$p < 0.005.$

[7] Each of the three experience levels (computer experience, e-mail experience, and civic engagement) was correlated separately with the six areas of interest. To control for inflated alpha errors, we adjusted the alpha using the Bonferroni method with 0.05 / 6 = 0.008, which we conservatively rounded down to 0.005. Therefore, we can be better assured that the rate of alpha error for any one set of analyses is less than 0.05 (Hays, 1988).

government or political activities as well as for telecommuting. E-mail experience was significantly related to interest in using the system for communicating with friends, participating in government or politics, telecommuting, and home shopping. Level of civic engagement was significantly related only to using the system for participating in government and politics.

From these results, several observations can be made about community members' interests in the new virtual community. First, more than three quarters of the residents of this community expressed an interest in services related to the education of themselves or their children as well as in the exchange of general community information. Therefore, interest groups related to educational issues and general community information might be popular. In addition, interest in both of these services is not related to community members' computer experience or to their level of civic engagement; that is, *everyone* appears to be interested in the educational aspects and community potential of the virtual community.

Residents also expressed an interest in communicating with friends and relatives. However, those people with more e-mail experience were more interested in using the system to communicate with others than were those with less experience. This might be because the former already have had experience with computer communications and are interested in continuing their communications in the new virtual community. Those with less e-mail experience might see less of a need for using the virtual community for communicating. This lower interest might present a challenge to encourage those with little or no e-mail experience to use the virtual community for communicating privately with other members.

Community members also expressed an interest in using the new virtual community to participate in government. Although this possible use is popular among residents, it is significantly related to the residents' computer and e-mail experience as well as to their current level of civic engagement. Thus, people who use their computers and e-mail more and those who are more involved in the community are more interested in using the new system for government involvement. What is interesting here is that this is the only service to which level of civic engagement is related. The more people are already engaged in civic activity, the more interested they are in using the new system to become involved in government and politics.

Finally, telecommuting and home shopping were the least preferred uses of the proposed virtual community, with the number of residents interested in home shopping drastically lower than the number interested in other services. One interesting, and perhaps alarming, observation about both of these services is that they would contribute to the privatization of work and leisure time. Community members, especially those using e-mail, might want to work and shop from home. Again, this is only interest and not behavior, but it is interesting that computer use and e-mail use are related to these interests.

This preliminary analysis was conducted to determine the possible uses that residents might have for their physically based virtual community. Specifically, what communities of interest could be fostered for a specific community going on-line? From this analysis, we can conclude that for this community, focus should be given to facilitating educational groups and promoting the exchange of community information. Included under the auspices of education, electronic interest groups relating to children's education and perhaps even to more general parenting issues might be popular enough to create active communities of interest; parenting groups have been quite popular in a variety of virtual community forums (cf. Ryan 1996). Information about, and the ability to participate in discussions about, the community and other relevant local government and political issues also should be made available.

CURRENT TRENDS AND RESEARCH NEEDS

In this article, we have applied the research on CMC and virtual communities to Putnam's (1993) theory of social capital. We argued that physically based virtual communities of interest can increase social capital. Physically based virtual communities of interest occur when virtual communities of interest (e.g., educational groups, parenting groups, general community information) intersect with actual physical communities. One key component of this argument, we believe, is linking the physical and virtual communities to create a new type of community form, that is, a new "space" or "place" where people can interact with their physical (and virtual) neighbors. We conclude with a brief examination of this space or place, highlighting some of the key issues and trends related to the link between the virtual and physical communities and perhaps society in general.

First, as we discussed previously, the new sense of place emerging in virtual communities can create a new public space, even though the person might be communicating from a private space (e.g., home). Virtual communities might, therefore, decrease the trend of the privatization of leisure time caused in part by television (Meyrowitz, 1985; Putnam, 1995b). By linking virtual communities of interest to physical communities, new public spaces are created, and opportunities for interaction among members are increased. However, very little is known about this new form of virtual community space. In addition, although several authors have remarked about the "sense of physical place" (cf. Hiss, 1990; Hubbard, 1995), much less is known about how it interacts with the new virtual space.

Second, we still are only beginning to understand what effects participating in the virtual community has on the people. Gergen (1991) argues that the various social (e.g., work, home, personal) and mediated (e.g., computer, telephone, television) environments in which we interact are eroding our sense of self and destroying community attachment and moral development. However, Gergen does not consider mediated communications that overlap with a person's corresponding physical community; he focuses on environments and communications that are dispersed over great distances. Thus, people's sense of connectedness in a community and their functioning as moral individuals within a linked physical and virtual community is open for further study.

Finally, a key question is why the knowledge about virtual communities of interest that are linked to physical communities lags so far behind that about unlinked virtual communities of interest. One potential reason is that virtual community activists and researchers are unaware of the importance of setting up and fostering these types of communities when their communities go on-line. In addition, most of the virtual community research has focused on unlinked virtual community interest groups and their members. To properly understand how virtual communities affect physical communities and the people within them, we must examine virtual communities of interest within physical communities. Then we will be able to better understand how virtual communities can increase social capital and foster more engaged communities.

REFERENCES

Baym N. (1995). The emergence of community in computer mediated communication. In S. G. Jones (Ed.), Cybersociety: Computer mediated communication and community (pp. 138–163). Thousand Oaks, CA: Sage.

Gergen, K. J. (1991). *The saturated self: Dilemmas of identity in contemporary life*. New York: Basic Books.

Greeley, A. (1996). The strange reappearance of civic America: Religion and volunteering. (Available on-line: http://www.agreeley.com/civic.html)

Harasim, L. (1993). Networlds: Networks as social space. In L. M. Harasim (Ed.), *Global networks: Computers and international communication* (pp. 3–14). Cambridge, MA: MIT Press.

Hays, W. L. (1988). *Statistics* (4th ed.). New York: Holt, Rinehart & Winston.

Hiltz, S. R., & Turoff, M. (1993). *The network nation: Human communication via computer* (rev. ed.). Cambridge, MA: MIT Press.

Hiss, T. (1990). *The experience of place*. New York: Vintage Books.

Hubbard, B. (1995). *A theory for practice: Architecture in three discourses*. Cambridge, MA: MIT Press.

Jones, S. G. (1995). Understanding community in the information age. In S. G. Jones (Ed.), *Cybersociety: Computer mediated communication and community* (pp. 10–35). Thousand Oaks, CA: Sage.

Kling, R. (1996). Synergies and competition between life in cyberspace and face-to-face communities. *Social Science Computer Review*, 14, 50–54.

Knoke, D., & Kuklinski, J. H. (1982). *Network analysis*. Newbury Park, CA: Sage.

Kollock, P., & Smith, M. (1994). *Managing the virtual commons: Cooperation and conflict in computer communities*. (Available on-line: http://www.sscnet.ucla.edu/soc/csoc/vcommons.htm)

Ladd, E. C. (1996, June-July). The data just don't show erosion of America's "social capital." *The Public Perspective*, pp. 1–6.

Markus, M. L. (1994). Finding a happy medium: Explaining the negative effects of electronic communication on social life at work. *ACM Transactions on Information Systems*, 12, 119–149.

McLaughlin, M. L., Osborne, K. K., & Smith, C. B. (1995). Standards of conduct on Usenet. In S. G. Jones (Ed.), *Cybersociety: Computer mediated communication and community* (pp. 90–111). Thousand Oaks, CA: Sage.

Meyrowitz, J. (1985). *No sense of place.* New York: Oxford University Press.

Michaelson, K. L. (1996). Information, community and access. *Social Science Computer Review,* 14, 57–59.

Nickerson, R. S. (1994). Electronic bulletin boards: A case study of computer mediated communication. *Interacting With Computer,* 6, 117–134.

Parks, M. R., & Floyd, K. (1996). Making friends in cyberspace. *Journal of Computer Mediated Communication,* 1(4). (Available on-line: http://cwis.usc.edu/dept/annenberg/voll/issue4/parks.html)

Pettinnico, G. (1996, June-July). Civic participation is alive and well in today's enviromental movement. *The Public Perspective,* pp. 27–30.

Pickering, J. M., & King, J. L. (1995). Hardwiring weak ties: Interorganizational computer mediated communication, occupational communities and organizational change. *Organization Science,* 6, 479–504.

Putnam, R. D. (1993). *Making democracy work: Civic traditions in modern Italy.* Princeton, NJ: Princeton University Press.

Putnam, R. D. (1995a). Bowling alone: America's declining social capital. *Journal of Democracy,* 6, 65–78.

Putnam, R. D. (1995b). Tuning in, tuning out: The strange disappearance of social capital in America. *Political Science and Politics,* 28, 664–683.

Rheingold, H. (1993a). A slice of life in my virtual community. In L. M. Harasim (Ed.), *Global networks: Computers and international communication* (pp. 57–80).Cambridge, MA: MIT Press.

Rheingold, H. (1993b). *The virtual community: Homesteading on the electronic frontier.* New York: Harper Perennial

Ryan, K. O. (1996, June 16). United in cyberspace. *Los Angeles Times,* p. E3.

Schuler, D. (1996). *New community networks: Wired for change.* New York: ACM.

Turkle, S. (1995). *Life on the screen: Identity in the age of the Internet.* New York: Simon & Schuster.

Van Gelder, L. (1991). The strange case of the electronic lover. In C. Dunlap & R. Kling (Eds.), *Computerization and controversy: Value conflicts and social choices* (pp. 364–378). San Diego: Academic Press.

Walther, J. B. (1992). Interpersonal effects in computer-mediated interaction: A relational perspective. *Communication Research.* 19, 52–90.

Walther, J. B. (1996). Computer mediated communication: Impersonal, interpersonal and hyperpersonal interaction. *Communication Research,* 23, 3–43.

Wellman, B., & Gulia, M. (in press). Net suffers don't ride alone: Virtual communities as communities. In P. Kollock & M. Smith (Eds.), Communities in cyberspace. New York: Routledge.

Wellman, B., Salaff, J., Dimitrova, D., Garton, L., Gulia, M., & Haythornwaite, C. (1995, September). *Computer networks as social networks: Collaborative work, telework, and virtual community.* Paper presented at the annual conference of the American Sociological Association, Washington, DC.

Anita Blanchard is a doctoral candidate at the Claremont Graduate University in the School of Behavioral and Organizational Sciences. She is interested in virtual communities in both organizational and social contexts. She currently is finishing her dissertation examining the social and virtual components of the enviroments in virtual communities.

Tom Horan, Ph.D., is executive director of the Claremont Graduate University Research Institute. His research interests include the changing sense of place caused by the interrelationship between virtual and face-to-face communities. Current projects include a book (with William J. Mitchell), *Recombinant Urban Designs: Building the City of Bits*.

Chapter 8

Social Capital and Capital Gains in Silicon Valley[*]

Stephen S. Cohen and Gary Fields

It is difficult to imagine an example of regional economic development that is more successful, or more famous, than California's Silicon Valley. Investors from all over the world arrive with suitcases of money to place in what they hope will be the Valley's next success story. Ambitious, educated people—mostly young—from dozens of nations come to the Valley to take their chances in start-ups fueled by stock options. Regional development theorists study Silicon Valley to identify the underlying characteristics that have enabled this area to become one of the most innovative and prosperous regional economies in the world. Policy makers visit seeking to determine whether the characteristics identified by the theorists and journalists—and the stories they are told during their visit—can somehow be transferred to develop innovation-based economic development in their own regions.

Riding the newest wave of regional development theory is the notion of social capital popularized by Robert Putnam in his influential book, *Making Democracy Work*.[1] Putnam's idea refers to the complex of local institutions and relationships of trust among economic actors that evolve from unique, historically conditioned local cultures. Such institutions and social relationships, built upon the experiences of a shared deep history, become embedded within a localized economy. They form what Putnam describes as *networks of civic engagement* that facilitate the activities of politics, production, and exchange. In these locales of tight civic engagement, people know one another and one another's families. They meet frequently in non-work related organizations and activities. They constitute a dense and rich social *community*. Business relationships are embedded in community and family structures. Those structures reinforce trust by sanctioning against, in powerful and multidimensional ways, the breaking of

---

[1] Robert D. Putnam, *Making Democracy Work: Civic Traditions in Modern Italy* (Princeton, N J: Princeton University Press, 1993).

trust. In Putnam's model, cooperation based on trust propels development. It is rooted in complex and deep social ties and is an inherited historical characteristic.

Does the wave of regional development theory represented by Putnam's model of social capital apply to Silicon Valley? The answer is no, because Putnam's particular concept of social capital, whatever its power as an explanation of local prosperity elsewhere, does not fit the experience of Silicon Valley. Worse yet, it obscures the specific nature of the social capital on which Silicon Valley was built and through which it continues to construct itself.

The sources of technological dynamism in Silicon Valley can be described in many ways, but there is little truth in the idea of Silicon Valley as a community of dense civic engagement. Silicon Valley is notoriously a world of strangers; nobody knows anybody else's mother there. There is no deep history, little in the way of complex familial ties, and little structured community. It is a world of independent—even isolated—newcomers. With its spatially isolated and spread-out residential patterns, its shopping strips and malls, its auto gridlock, its rapid demographic turnover, and the rampant individualism among its most talented workers, Silicon Valley would be hard-pressed to present the image of a close-knit civil society that, according to the social capital theorists, is the pre-condition for economic prosperity.

Silicon Valley is, however, an economic space built on social capital, but it is a vastly different kind of social capital than that popularized by the civic engagement theorists. In Silicon Valley, social capital can be understood in terms of the collaborative partnerships that emerged in the region, owing to the pursuit by economic and institutional actors of objectives related specifically to innovation and competitiveness. It is the networks resulting from these collaborations that form the threads of social capital as it exists in Silicon Valley. What these networks of innovation in Silicon Valley share with the networks of civic engagement is simply and only a common network-like structure. There is virtually nothing in the history of Silicon Valley to connect its networks of innovation to a dense civil society.

The network environment in Silicon Valley is the outcome of historically conditioned, specifically chosen collaborations between individual entrepreneurs, firms, and institutions focused on the pursuit of innovation and its commercialization. Its foundations can be traced in part to ideas proposed by Alfred Marshall and Thorsten Veblen that have influenced social capital theory. These collaborations also result from what some theorists refer to as "historical accident," as well as broader, nationally based, institutionally driven trajectories of development and competitive choice.[2] They are buttressed by the nature of the

[2]   Paul David, "Historical Economics in the Long Run: Some Implications of Path-Dependence," in Graeme Donald Snooks, eds., *Historical Analysis in Economics* (London: Routledge, 1993). pp. 29–40; W. Brian Arthur, "Competing Technologies, Increasing Returns, and Lock-in by Historical Small Events," *The Economic Journal*, 99 (1989): 116–131.

Silicon Valley markets for labor and capital, by the internal dynamic of successive innovation, and by the simple momentum of economic success. From the convergence of local historical chance, national historical currents, and choice emerged the collaborations at the foundation of Silicon Valley's technological dynamism.

SOCIAL CAPITAL NETWORKS IN SILICON VALLEY

Silicon Valley is traditionally defined as an area beginning about 35 miles south of San Francisco, California, and extending through San Jose. It encompasses some 1,500 sq. miles, with a population of 2.3 million, and 1.2 million jobs (although "the Valley" has been rapidly extending beyond these borders). About one-fourth of the residents are foreign born. The area has added about 200,000 jobs since 1992, with about 53,000 added in 1997. Average annual wages are $46,000 (versus the $29,000 U.S. average).[3] In 1997, venture capital invested into Silicon Valley amounted to $2.7 billion, constituting about 21% of the national total.[4] About 3,575 new firms were incorporated in the Valley in 1997.[5]

The Silicon Valley economy is dominated by rapid innovation and commercialization in an expanding set of new technologies. Microelectronics, semiconductors (e.g., Intel, AMD, National Semiconductor), and later computers (e.g., Apple, Sun Microsystems, Hewlett-Packard) put the Valley on the world map and continue to be major activities. Computer networking, both hardware and software (e.g., Cisco, Netscape, Yahoo, Broadvision), has recently exploded as a shaping activity. Biotechnology along with medical devices and drug delivery systems constitutes the third major new technology in which the Valley is a national center, perhaps the world center. Along with these core industries, venture finance and intellectual property law have become significant activities in their own right. The Valley is an enormously prosperous region. Standard income data, which rely on wages and salaries (more than 150% of the national average), miss the critical turbocharger: capital gains from stock options which add hugely to the valley's wealth accumulation—not just at the very peak of the income distribution, but quite a way down into the engineering, professional, and managerial ranks (and occasionally even lower). The constraint on this growth is classic Ricardo's law of rent: real estate prices, rising wages (average wages in software, semiconductors, and semiconductor equipment firms hit $85,500 in 1996) and congestion (average delays in auto traffic keep rising) create a constant spin-off of new plants and facilities into other, lower-cost regions. Silicon Valley firms no longer manufacture many semiconductors in the Valley.

---

[3] Joint Venture: Silicon Valley Network, *1998 Index*. See http://www.jointventure.org/resources/1998index/index.html

[4] PricewaterhouseCoopers, *Venture Capital Survey*, 1998.

[5] Joint Venture: Silicon Valley Network, *1998 Index*.

The main networks of social capital in Silicon Valley are not dense networks of civic engagement, but focused, productive interactions among the following social institutions, instruments, and entities:

- *The Great Research Universities*—Stanford, U.C. Berkeley, and U.C. San Francisco (U.C. Medical School) have an innovative approach that creates tight relationships to outside actors who commercialize applications of their research and researchers. They also recruit faculty and graduate students from all over the world, not just locally or nationally. For a non-trivial example, about one-third of the graduate students at Berkeley in electrical engineering and computer science are foreign nationals; a similar proportion of the faculty is foreign born.[6]
- *U.S. Government Policy*—In the early phases of microelectronics and computer networking, it served both as a sponsor of University research and, critically, as the lead user.
- *Venture Capital Firms*—These firms have served not only as a homegrown source of early stage capital, but also as a locus of high-tech investment expertise and Godfather services to start-up companies (such as the provision of experienced executives at critical moments of a firm's development, strategic and operational advice, and links and leads to potential customers and partners).
- *Law Firms*—Law firms provide another source for locating key personnel, finance contacts, and corporate and intellectual property legal services. They often take payment in stock rather than cash.
- *Business Networks*—The leading figures in university engineering departments, venture firms, law firms, and operating firms in the valley know one another (through frequent business and professional contact). The density of lawyers in this community (about one lawyer per ten engineers)[7] provides an operational definition of the limited role of informal, familial, and communitarian trust. The opposite of trust is "accountability" and the arbiters of accountability are accountants and auditors (in Silicon Valley they outnumber the lawyers).[8] In sum, there is one lawyer or accountant per five engineers.
- *Stock Options*—Employees (not counting a firm's "founders" and CEO) often hold options and shares easily amounting to 10 to 15% (or more at the early stages) of a firm's capital value. These reward success with giant payoffs and also serve to extend the loyalty and employment tenure of key employees for the several years of the option-holding period. The amounts are non-trivial. For example, an extremely successful Valley firm, Cisco Systems, now has a capital value that exceeds that of the Ford Motor Company.
- *Labor Market*—The Valley labor market has several important characteristics that define the Valley's particular brand of social capital.

  - First, there is no stigma in leaving a large and very successful company such as Hewlett-Packard or Sun Microsystems to launch a start-up. A few years ago, this was not the case in many leading companies in Europe—not to mention

[6] Graduate Division, University of California at Berkeley, *Department of Electrical Engineering and Computer Science Statistics*, December 1997.
[7] Employment Development Department, Labor Market Information Division, *Occupational Projections*, June 1997. See http://www.calmis.cahwnet.gov/htmlfile/msa.htm
[8] Ibid.

Japan. What also continues to differentiate the Valley is that even if such a start-up should fail, there are ample jobs awaiting entrepreneurs at large Valley firms as well as venture capitalists and head hunters looking for executive leadership for other new companies.

- Second is rapid turnover. People (at all levels) shift from company to company. This has many consequences, one of which is technology diffusion. In Silicon Valley, technology and know-how have legs.
- Third is recruitment of talent—especially scarce technical and entrepreneurial talent—from literally the entire world. To meet the needs of their clients, Silicon Valley law firms have developed a substantial capability—sometimes in-house, sometimes networked—in immigration law.

- *The Nature of the Industry*—Industries differ. The industry that defines a region's specialization also defines its social structure and institutions more than any other single factor. Coal and steel districts in Wales, Wallonia, Asturias, and Pennsylvania had similar social structures. Industries define their regions in two ways.

  - First by the speed of their growth and transformation. The semiconductor industry, the initial shaper of Silicon Valley, has grown by about 3,000 per cent over the past twenty years.[9] Such growth makes small companies into big companies at amazing speed and accumulates capital into world historical piles.
  - Second, locally dominant industries shape their societies by valuing some kinds of social structures compared to others (e.g., unions and friendly societies in coal and steel communities, intellectual property and employment contract law in Silicon Valley). Automobile districts, regardless of where they are, differ more from footwear districts or software districts than from one another. In much of the recent literature that focuses on the social characteristics of specialized industrial districts and how those social structures propel or retard growth and transformation, too little attention has been paid to how substantively different kinds of industrial activities favor different industrial and social structures. This is true even when the industries are quite similar. For example, comparisons between Boston's high-tech industrial district and Silicon Valley vastly neglect the important differentiating characteristics of defense electronic systems and mini-computers (the defining activities on the Boston side) as compared with microelectronics and computer networking (the defining activities in Silicon Valley). Similarly, research universities, abundant engineering talent, and venture capital play only a limited role, if that, in Milan's dynamic high-fashion district, or in the Italian tile-making district, or in Detroit's (and now Kentucky's) auto districts, or in Georgia's carpet and towel belt. Ultimately, what you do shapes how you do it—all the way back up the value chain, and all the way out into forms of social organization. It would be an ill-advised policy that strives to make electronics innovation into the new industrial standard bearer in the same social milieu as footwear, underwear, axles, or carpeting.

It is the cooperative—and competitive—interaction of these critical elements that defines Silicon Valley as a system of social capital. All the rest (such as

---

[9] www.semichips.org/stats/

informal conversations in bars or bowling alleys) is, relative to other places, somewhat underdeveloped and ancillary. Unlike Putnam's vague, but radically deterministic concept of the historic formation of civic culture and social capital, these key elements of social capital both accurately define the reality of the Silicon Valley's experience and are far more amenable to shaping by well-informed policy.[10]

THE LINEAGE OF SOCIAL CAPITAL AND ITS CRITIQUE

In his engaging account of the divergent economic fortunes manifested by different Italian regions. Robert Putnam insists that there is a connection between the degree of social capital accumulated within a region and its economic performance. The vexing question for Putnam, along with others sympathetic to his approach, is what constitutes this elusive concept of "social capital."

According to Putnam, social capital is akin to a "moral resource."[11] It refers to the features of social organization that facilitate coordination and cooperation for mutual benefit.[12] Social capital is embodied in what Putnam calls "networks of civic engagement" that evolve over time owing to the historical traditions of citizen involvement in a broad range of social, economic, and political activities. Where there is a vibrant civil society, there are bonds of trust and reciprocity. These bonds facilitate the networks of civic life at the core of social capital. The relative strength or weakness of these networks within a region will have a paramount impact on the character of the region's economic life.

Despite the somewhat mysterious nature of how these networks actually get created, Putnam is very clear on the link between social capital and economic development as well as the policy implications of this link. Communities, he argues, did not forge networks of civic engagement because of their prosperity. On the contrary, communities in Putnam's view become prosperous because they are civic.[13] "The social capital embodied in networks of civic engagement seems to be a precondition for economic development."[14] According to Putnam, there is an obvious policy lesson to be learned from the connection between social capital and economic prosperity, and he implores policymakers to take note of the way that "civics matters." The policy lesson to be drawn from Putnam's thesis is

---

[10] On how Putnam sets the development trajectory of his regions as fixed by the late middle ages, and more generally on the deterministic character of Putnam's concept, see Jonah Levy, *Tocqueville's Revenge* (Boston, MA: Harvard University Press, 1998): S. Tarrow in *American Political Science Review*, 90/2 (1996): 389ff.

[11] Robert D. Putnam, "The Prosperous Community: Social Capital and Public Life," *The American Prospect* (Spring 1993b), p. 37.

[12] Ibid., pp. 35–36: Putnam (1993a), op. cit., p. 167.

[13] Putnam (1993a), op. cit., pp. 152–162.

[14] Putnam (1993b), op, cit., p. 37.

that if communities create networks of social capital, prosperity is likely to follow.

Two distinct theoretical lineages converge in Putnam's work on the relationship between social capital and localized economic performance. One tradition derives from Alfred Marshall and his notion of economic vibrancy within localized industrial districts. The other tradition, perhaps less commonly associated with social capital, is traceable to the writings of Thorstein Veblen on how institutions create competitive trajectories of growth and technological innovation.

While the emphasis of Marshall's monumental work is the power of supply and demand to generate equilibrium prices in markets, he nevertheless established a unique framework for understanding the dynamism within certain localized regions through his concept of external scale economies.[15] According to Marshall, economies of scale are not restricted to the internal operations of the individual firm. The concentration of firms in an industry in one location can also provide benefits to individual firms owing to the effects of proximity to one another. Such firms that are clustered together can take advantage of access to specialized suppliers, skilled labor, and an environment enabling the spillover of technological knowledge from one firm to another. For Marshall, these external economies operated much like internal economies by lowering costs and they helped explain the phenomenon behind the agglomerations of firms from the same industry that he termed "industrial districts." In his celebrated metaphor describing the concentration of the cutlery industry in the area of Sheffield, England, Marshall writes that in such a district where firms from the same industry are concentrated: "The mysteries of the trade become no mysteries, but are as it were in the air."[16] Thus, from Marshall and his notion of external scale economies emerges a picture of localized economic vibrancy, nurtured by the cost savings of resource sharing and information exchange that occurs within a localized industrial environment. However, Marshall's magisterial work provides more of an understanding of an "industrial district"—that is, a successful specialized local economy—than any special insight into the nature of social capital.

In contrast to Marshall, Thorstein Veblen rejected the neoclassical notion of equilibrium in markets and embraced metaphors from evolutionary biology in arguing that the key to economic development resided in the capacity of institutions to adapt to ever-changing market conditions.[17] Veblen likened the economy to an evolutionary phenomenon of disequilibrium in which competition and natural selection prevailed.[18] In this evolutionary process, industrial structures and

---

[15] Alfred Marshall, *Principles of Economics*, two volumes (London: Macmillan and Company, 1961 [1890]), pp. 267–277, 314–320.
[16] Ibid., p. 271.
[17] Thorstein Veblen, "Why is Economics Not an Evolutionary Science?" *The Quarterly Journal of Economics*, 12 (1898): 373–97.
[18] Thorstein Veblen, *The Theory of the Leisure Class: An Economic Study of Institutions.* (New York, NY: B.W. Heubsch, 1924 [1899]). p. 188.

institutions develop in an interlocking embrace. Once established within the context of this interactive evolution, institutions play a fundamental role in shaping the market process by assuming one of two basic tendencies. Institutions either remain static and rigid (thereby giving rise to a type of "friction" between an existing industrial structure and the institutional arrangements that have emerged around it)[19] or institutions may adapt to changing market forces (enabling industrial structures and economic development to assume a dynamic and more technologically advanced character). What Veblen was intent upon uncovering were those factors promoting or precluding institutional adaptation that enabled the process of technological innovation to occur for economic advance.

What eventually caused the insights of Marshall and Veblen to resurface in the social capital literature were the debates initiated in the late 1970s on the differences distinguishing regional economies. These debates rekindled interest in the phenomenon of industrial districts. Providing the catalyst for these debates was a dramatic reversal in economic development trends beginning in the 1970s. These trends included:

- the tendency of certain regional economies with heavy concentrations of small and medium-sized firms to outperform other economies owing to their capacity for innovation;[20]
- the apparently disproportionate contribution to economic growth and development made by smaller firms in the context of this crisis;[21] and
- the competitive difficulties experienced by large firms beginning in the late 1970s and their seeming inability to evolve and adapt to a transforming world marketplace.[22]

In our view, the starting-point observations about the relative weaknesses of giant firms, especially the ill-conceived assumption about their inability to adapt and evolve, constitute a major weakness at the very heart of this literature.

---

[19] Thorstein Veblen, *Imperial Germany and the Industrial Revolution* (New York, NY: Macmillan, 1915); Geoffrey M. Hodgson, "Precursors of Modern Evolutionary Economics: Marx, Marshall, Veblen, and Schumpeter," in Richard W. England, ed., *Modern Institutional Economics* (Ann Arbor, MI: University of Michigan Press, 1994), p. 25.

[20] Sebastian Brusco, "The Emilian Model: Productive Decentralization and Social Integration," *Cambridge Journal of Economics*, 6 (1982): 167–184.

[21] David L. Birch, *The Job Generation Process* (Cambridge, MA: MIT Program on Neighborhood and Regional Change, 1979), p. 31; Michael B. Teitz, Amy Glasmeier, and Douglas Svensson, "Small Business and Employment Growth in California," Working Paper No. 348, Institute of Urban and Regional Development, Berkeley, CA, 1981.

[22] Michael J. Piori and Charles F. Sabel. *The Second Industrial Divide* (New York, NY: Basic Books, 1984), Linda Weiss, *Creating Capitalism: The State and Small Business since 1945* (Oxford: Blackwell, 1988); Sengenberger et al., eds., *The Reemergence of Small Enterprises.* (Geneva: International Labor Institute, 1990). For an opposing view that reviews some of this literature, see Bennet Harrison, *Lean and Mean: The Changing Landscape of Corporate Power in the Age of Flexibility* (New York, NY: Basic Books, 1994).

As in its emphasis on local culture and regional development, it was a bit blind to sector-specific effects and a bit too quick to generalize from a small set of overlapping case studies. In most sectors in most of the industrialized world, established industrial giants—such as GE, Boeing, Coca-Cola, Hewlett Packard, Nestlé, Merck, Monsanto, Unilever, ATT (now Lucent), Ford, Volkswagen, Merrill Lynch, Citicorp, United Parcel Service, and even IBM (not to mention the Japanese majors such as Toyota, Sony, and Toshiba)—have grown, adapted, and evolved quite handsomely. Big firms proved to be quite flexible and adaptable—perhaps more so than most specialized districts.

James Coleman, another social capital theorist, provides a romantic, and telling, analysis of New York's diamond district. There, trust is total. Sacks of diamonds worth thousands are taken without signatures or serious control. This highly functioning trust is built on the deepest of civic engagements and hugged by the sinews of a totally closed society. However, Coleman never extends his admiring analysis upstream to mention the name De Beers, the giant multinational that completely controls the diamond industry.[23] It is likely that many of the "deep trust" industrial districts exist in relation to major multinational corporations the way the New York diamond district lives in relation to De Beers: total dependency with ties of civic engagement serving to exclude outsiders and thereby both improve efficiency and capture rents that would ordinarily be competed away. Silicon Valley is the exact opposite. The society is open and so is the market. Silicon Valley is not an ecology of small and dependent companies holding on to a small rent in a larger revenue stream. Valley companies sell to a broad universe of clients, and sometimes grow to be very large indeed. The small companies harbor big ambitions and see themselves as young, not permanently small.

Nonetheless, theorists working within this particular approach began to reassess what drives the process of economic development within regions. They began to contemplate how the factors driving development could be reproduced, through policy choices, from place to place. The result was the "rediscovery of the region" by contemporary regional development theorists and a search for the factors underlying the "resurgence of regional economies."[24]

Perhaps the defining moment in this reappraisal of the region and search for what made certain regional economies technologically dynamic, was the celebrated work by Michael Piore and Charles Sabel, *The Second Industrial Divide* (1984). For Piore and Sabel, the second industrial divide marked a profound historical separation between the formerly dominant system of mass production

---

[23] James S. Coleman, "Social Capital in the Creation of Human Capital." *American Journal of Sociology*, 94 [supplement S95–S190] (1988): pp. S98–99. See also, for the same analysis and omissions, Lisa Bernstein, "Opting Out of the Legal System: Extralegal Contractual Relations in the Diamond Industry." *Journal of Legal Studies*, 21/1 (1992): 115–157.

[24] Michael Storper, "The Resurgence of Regional Economies, Ten Years Later: The Region as a Nexus of Untraded Interdependencies." *European Urban and Regional Studies*, 2/3 (1995): 191–221.

and a newly emerging paradigm of flexibly specialized production. In this divide was a very real phenomenon—the late twentieth-century industrial district—that was the economic and geographical manifestation of the future. In the midst of the difficulties experienced by large firms and the districts dependent upon them, certain industrial districts had continued to prosper (most notably in Italy, but also in Germany, Japan, and even the U.S.). Firms within these enclaves had become more innovative owing to their small size and their resultant capacity to overcome the constraints of mass production. According to Piore and Sabel, such districts, based upon small and flexibly specialized companies, had their origins in the craft production of the late nineteenth century.

This contemplation of the future in terms of the past by Piore and Sabel garnered further support in the research of historians such as Herbert Kisch (1989), Sidney Pollard (1973, 1981), and more recently Gary Herrigel (1996). Kisch, Pollard, and Herrigel all supplied potent historical justifications for the phenomenon of industrial districts in Europe, arguing that such regional industrial economies, based upon smaller specialized firms, had far-reaching historical roots in the period of so-called "proto-industrialization" of the eighteenth century. These historical accounts provided additional evidence that the (re)discovery of localized industrial systems by Piore and Sabel was not something ephemeral or limited in scope. Economic development within vibrant regionally based industrial districts had a strong historical basis.

Inspired by the historically based thesis of Piore and Sabel, scholars searched for the secrets of what made these localized regional economies technologically dynamic and successful. In this search, the aim of theorists was not only to link the economic performance of successful regional economies to flexible networks of resource- and information-sharing among firms and adaptive local institutions. Instead, the research agenda of regional theorists focused on uncovering what was at the foundation of local networks and adaptive institutions. What was added to the framework (established by Marshall and Veblen) by theorists was a critically important, albeit elusive concept—the concept of trust. It is this notion of trust that ultimately resurfaces as a key element in Putnam's theory of social capital and economic prosperity.[25]

Trust lies at the foundation of relationships between firms and individuals, whose collective activity in competing and cooperating within a regional setting is a key aspect of innovative local economies. A broad literature has emerged dealing with this concept and how the presence or absence of an environment of trust among economic actors within a place helps explain regional economic performance and regional differentiation. According to Charles Sabel, trust refers to the mutual confidence that no party involved in an exchange transaction in the

---

[25] On trust, see D. Gambetta, ed., *Trust* (Oxford: Basil Blackwell, 1988), p. 32; R. Mayntz, "Modernisation and the Logic of InterOrganizational Networks." *Knowledge and Policy*, 6 (Spring 1993): pp. 3–16.

market will exploit the others' vulnerability.[26] For Sabel, such trust requires time to evolve. Where it does evolve, it makes possible an environment of cooperation existing alongside competition that becomes a source of mutual benefit for firms and individuals. This helps explain how regional economies engendering such trust are able to prosper.[27] According to Sabel, the creation of trust in certain localities is actually a process of learning—a process of determining how to create forms of consensus building among economic actors with both competing and mutual interests. The associations of mutual confidence that emerge from this learning process result in what Sabel terms "studied trust."[28] For Sabel, the fact that trust is learned provides cautious optimism that policy-makers can actually play a role in promoting the creation of trust as a strategy for economic   revitalization.[29]

Much of the debate about trust and cooperation among economic actors has focused on whether social networks (social and personal ties—or more formal, institutional hierarchies are the carriers of this learning process. In a much-cited contribution to this literature, Mark Granovetter accepts the premise (outside the assumptions of neoclassical economics) that trust is a necessary pre-condition in successful market relations but argues that formal institutions, as enforcers of rules and norms, are insufficient to explain why firms and individuals cooperate in the process of market exchange.[30] He insists instead that trust is "embedded in networks of interpersonal relations which avoids the extremes of both under-socialized [market-oriented, rational choice] and over-socialized [legal institutional] views of human action"—a definition that makes disagreement difficult.[31] For Granovetter, social relations developing in both work and non-work settings, and the process by which relationships become embedded over time, form the bonds through which human beings learn to cooperate. What results is the reciprocity that facilitates both idea sharing and market exchange, the keys to growth and prosperity.

Granovetter's view of human action attempts to construct the missing link in Putnam's concept of social capital. Absent trust and the social interactions upon which trust is built, it is difficult to conceive how networks of civic engagement can be created. Without networks of civic engagement (the foundations of social capital) there is, for Putnam, little chance of economic prosperity since social capital is the precondition for economic prosperity, not the other way around.

---

[26] Charles F. Sabel, "Studied Trust: Building New Forms of Cooperation in Volatile Economy." in Richard Swedberg, ed., *Explorations in Economic Sociology* (New York, NY: Russell Sage Foundation, 1993), p. 104.
[27] Ibid., p. 105.
[28] Ibid., p. 130.
[29] Ibid., pp. 131, 141.
[30] Mark Granovetter, "Economic Action and Social Structure: The Problem of Embeddedness," *American Journal of Sociology*, 91/ 3 (1985): 481–510.
[31] Ibid., p. 504.

There is a problem, however, in assigning a causal link between this particular kind of social capital and economic prosperity and in using such a connection to build a policy program for regional economic development. This problem stems from the way that Putnam specifies how networks of civic engagement—built upon trust, reciprocity, and social interaction—are created historically and how these elements interact to produce the phenomenon of social capital. Putnam *insists* that those regions in Italy endowed with social capital have been built upon traditions of civic involvement with roots in the Middle Ages. He traces the origins of social capital networks on the Italian Peninsula to the medieval communes of the eleventh century. Does this mean that absent such historical experience and the exceedingly long period of gestation required for networks of civic engagement to flourish, social capital networks cannot take root? If the phenomenon of social capital, as Putnam suggests, is contingent upon a particular historical experience, how then in a policy sense, short of altering history, can social capital networks be created? Such questions raise the disquieting possibility that the connections between social capital and economic outcomes, if such connections even exist, are in some way historically predetermined. Putnam is well aware of this dilemma, but his argument that uncivic regions can "learn by doing" amplifies, rather than resolves, the paradox of his historical approach.[32] If, in effect, it is the past that establishes a certain pathway for the creation of social capital networks, and if, by definition, the past is basically fixed, how then can social capital networks be created? The result of this historical puzzle is that while the concept of social capital provides an imaginative insight for explaining economic outcomes, it is limited as a concept for framing policy choices.[33]

One effort to resolve this dilemma appears in the work of AnnaLee Saxenian, who borrows aspects of Putnam's thesis on social capital and economic life

---

[32] Putnam (1993a). op. cit., pp. 183–184.

[33] Henri Pirenne's celebrated thesis of an eleventh-century trade revival, when placed alongside Putnam's account of social capital's eleventh-century origins, raises several engaging questions about whether prosperity follows or acts as the catalyst for a vibrant civil society. According to Pirenne, the eleventh-century commercial revolution, occurring in Flanders and Italy, ignited the process of European urbanization leading to "a new era in the internal history of Western Europe." Henri Pirenne. *Medieval Cities: Their Origins and the Revival of Trade.* (Princeton, NJ: Princeton University Press, 1969 [1925]), p. 213. From Pirenne's story, supported by numerous other historical accounts, there is a suggestion that the origins of the communes themselves lie in an economic phenomenon as centers of trade and market activity. Presumably, from these economic origins, civic life in Italy began to flourish, paving the way for the traditions that are of paramount interest to Putnam. Nevertheless, if the origins of the communes are to be found in the prosperity associated with the rise of commerce, and if, as Putnam suggests, the origins of the civic networks in Italy are to be found in the communes, then it seems difficult to conclude, as Putnam concludes, that civics is a precondition for prosperity. Instead, the history of the Italian medieval communes suggests that civic engagement is not the cause, but the outcome of economic advance.

but uses Putnam in connection with ideas from Marshall and Veblen to develop a much broader explanation for regional economic competitiveness. In her account of the Silicon Valley economy, Saxenian develops the concept of a localized "industrial system" (adapted from Gary Herrigel's notion of "industrial order") to account for the region's competitive advantages. According to Saxenian, industrial systems vary from one locality to another and consist of three primary characteristics: local institutions; a local industry structure based upon relationships among firms; and a dominant organizational structure within firms. What differentiates regional economies such as the Silicon Valley and helps explain why some regions are able to prosper is the capacity of regional industrial systems for adaptation and change—the capacity to become what Saxenian calls, "Protean Places."[34] Where Saxenian borrows from social capital theorists is in her effort to account for the differences within regional industrial systems. Aspects of social capital such as trust may help explain what makes industrial systems flexible or rigid. Saxenian's work, however, aims not at any definitive link of social capital to economic prosperity. Instead, she is interested in revealing how—but not how much—actual social capital networks, verifiable in an ethnographic sense, contribute to the formation of institutions and industrial structures that are taken to account for competitive performance.

The Berkeley Roundtable on the International Economy (BRIE)—a research group at the University of California, Berkeley, that has deep roots in Silicon Valley—developed the concept of competitiveness and has used it to formulate an approach to economic development policy that is substantively different from that derived from civic engagement.[35] The BRIE approach begins from the premise that competitiveness is not necessarily a function of natural endowments but is instead something that can be created over time. Underlying this view are three important arguments. One argument insists upon the idea that markets and the market process are products of politics and institutions. At the core of the second argument is the idea that institutions and institutional frameworks play a key role in the performance of economies. In the third argument, institutions can be transformed through policy choices in order to affect market outcomes. These three arguments, embedded in a substantial literature, create the basis for a theory of economic development that more accurately depicts how the networks of innovation in Silicon Valley emerged and how policy can be used to affect economic outcomes in other regions.[36]

In a classic exposition of the first argument, Karl Polanyi shows how political authorities throughout history have shaped the formation of markets by creating the institutions and the rules that govern the process of market

---

[34] Annalee Saxenian. *Regional Advantage: Culture and Competition in Silicon Valley and Route 128* (Cambridge, MA: Harvard University Press, 1996), p. 161.
[35] See Report of the President's Commission on Competitiveness, Vol. III. Washington, D.C., 1984.
[36] See http://brie.berkeley.edu/BRIE/

accumulation.[37] By comparing the formation of markets during periods of feudalism, mercantilism, and industrial capitalism, and by uncovering a common political and institutional theme in this story, Polanyi's work shows clearly that markets—not the markets of economists but those in the real world—do not exist independently or operate spontaneously as in neoclassical models of rational choice. They are the products of institutional, political, and legal frameworks that structure how buying and selling and the very organization of production takes place.

From this historical observation of the role played by institutions and politics in the creation of markets, it is but a small step to the idea in the second argument, namely, that "institutional frameworks are the key to the relative success of economies."[38] This idea, elaborated during the last quarter century by North and adherents of the new institutionalism, actually derives from Veblen and his contention that economic development is a function of institutional adaptation. In addition to influencing North's institutionalist economic history, insights from Veblen have resurfaced as part of a literature known as "late development" to explain how nations in a condition of relative backwardness have successfully industrialized.[39] Recent contributions to the literature in this lineage on the ascendancy of postwar Japan (and later Korea) have provided compelling examples of how economic performance (current difficulties notwithstanding) is linked to unique institutional settings.[40]

When Polanyi's observation of institutional embeddedness in markets is added to Veblen's notion of institutional adaptation and economic development, the result is a powerful policy prescription for creating competitive advantage. In this framework, competitiveness is a function of the way politics and institutions imbue markets with certain attributes. These attributes are the result of the choices made by economic and political actors to shape institutions for the purpose of achieving desired economic outcomes. If one economy is more competitive than another, it is due to the capacity of institutions to shape the market process in a way that generates risk-taking, innovation-creating behavior by economic actors, and the capacity of economic and political actors to frame policies that shape the structure of institutions. From this perspective, competitiveness is a function of policy choices in which institutions can be adapted to achieve economic outcomes.

In this view, Silicon Valley is built of social capital, but it is the interaction of the economic and institutional actors in pursuit of explicitly competitive aims,

[37] Karl Polanyi, *The Great Transformation* (Boston, MA: Beacon Press, 1957).

[38] Douglass C. North, *Institutions, Institutional Change and Economic Performance* (Cambridge: Cambridge University Press, 1990), p. 69.

[39] Alexander Gerschenkron, *Economic Backwardness in Historical Perspective* (Cambridge: Harvard University Press, 1962).

[40] Chalmers Johnson. *MITI and the Japanese Miracle* (Stanford, CA: Stanford University Press, 1982); Alice Amsden, *Asia's Next Giant: South Korea and Late Industrialization* (Oxford: Oxford University Press, 1989).

not dense networks of civic engagement, that structures the region's innovation networks. The choices that configured and continuously reconfigure these networks are shaped by a specific environment of local and national history in which institutional decisions, policy programs, and industrial trajectories play leading roles. The fact that government policy and decisions by major institutions play such a critical role provides encouragement for efforts to create innovative milieux elsewhere. This is very different from Putnam's vague, but radically deterministic concept of historically framed civic cultures—a concept that seems so inaccessible to development policy initiatives.

While the broad outlines of this story are well known, they are worth recounting in order to identify how the region's networks of innovation have emerged from specific historical and institutional settings.[41]

THERE IS NO GEMÜTLICHKEIT IN SILICON VALLEY

The story of the Silicon Valley economy is dominated by a single overriding theme: innovation/commercialization. While the folklore of innovation in Silicon Valley tends to elevate the role of the individual inventor or entrepreneur (and there are indeed numerous examples of how such individuals have affected technological outcomes in the region), the history of the region reveals innovation to be the result of a collaborative process. This collaborative process generates and refines what is essentially the intangible raw material of technological change—ideas. The pathway from ideas to innovation occurs in Silicon Valley along networks of communication through which the region's economic and institutional actors engage in relationships to solve problems.

It is these innovation networks that constitute the region's resource base of social capital. Despite the case made by social capital theorists on the link between a vibrant civil society and an innovative local economy, it would be difficult to establish such a connection in the case of Silicon Valley. Instead, the puzzle posed by the Silicon Valley is how these networks emerged instead from a combination of local historical chance, national historical trends, specialized locally based "borderless" institutions, and competitive choices.

One of the most important historical attributes of the Silicon Valley, in comparison to other regional economies in the United States, is its status as a

[41] Michael Borrus, *Competing for Control: America's Stake in Microelectronics* (Cambridge, MA: Ballinger Publishing Co., 1988); M. Malone, *The Big Score* (Garden City, NY: Doubleday, 1985). Some easy to read books include: E. Rogers and J. Larsen, *Silicon Valley Fever* (New York, NY: Basic Books, 1984); Tim J. Sturgeon, *The Origins of Silicon Valley: The Development of the Electronics Industry in the San Francisco Bay Area*, MA Thesis Paper in Geography, University of California at Berkeley, 1988; Saxenian, op. cit.; M. Wilson, *The Difference between God and Larry Ellison* (New York, NY, 1997): also see *San Francisco Chronicle*, "Networking Industry and Reshaping the Valley." March 26, 1996.

"latecomer." As an industrial economy, the Valley has no 18th century or 19th century or even early 20th century beginnings. This characteristic, while posing a challenge for industrial development, actually conferred certain advantages upon the region. In the absence of an existing industrial structure and unencumbered by an established local business culture tied to a specific set of institutions or industrial practices, economic actors in Silicon Valley were able to create an economic environment more conducive to risk taking, innovation, and growth. From the favorable conditions offered by this environment emerged the partnerships between individuals, firms, and institutions that would evolve into the networks of innovation at the foundation of the Silicon Valley.

These networks' origins are to be found in the relationship between Stanford University and a small group of entrepreneurs during the late 1930s. From this emerged the region's first high-technology companies. The most famous firm spawned from this relationship was the Hewlett-Packard Company (founded in 1937). Fredrick Termain, an electrical engineering professor who moved to Stanford from MIT, encouraged and financially supported his two graduate students William Hewlett and David Packard to commercialize an invention known as an audio oscillator. After the initial prototype development, Termin helped arrange additional financing with a Palo Alto Bank that enabled them to begin commercial production of the invention. During this same period, Stanford also helped support Charles Litton as well as Sigurd and Russell Varian whose efforts would result in the founding of Litton Industries and Varian Associates. This early activity demonstrated how major research institutions and farsighted individuals within such institutions could provide the catalyst for entrepreneurship. The role played by Stanford in the formation of these firms blurred the boundaries between individual entrepreneurialism and large institutions and provided the initial threads of Silicon Valley's networks of innovation. Forged on the basis of linkages, these networks of innovation lie at the foundation of the region's broader social structure of economic development. Relationships between the Valley and Stanford, U.C. Berkeley, and U.C.S.F remain at the heart of the Valley's continuing success.

An equally important catalyst for the region occurred in the form of military contracts during the Second World War and the Cold War. The fortunes of Hewlett-Packard, for example, increased roughly twentyfold from 1941–1945, with sales expanding from $37,000 to over $750,000 as a result of military contracts for the company's electronic measuring devices and receivers. The klystron microwave tube, invented by the Varians with the support of Stanford, was an integral component in radar systems used during the war, resulting in big benefits to both the company and the university. Military funding also helped support other start-ups in the Silicon Valley during their formative years. Nevertheless, it is important to recognize that while the Valley's fledgling companies benefited from the War, East Coast high-technology companies (huge firms such as RCA, Philco, GE, and Westinghouse) profited from the wartime situation to a much greater extent than their tiny brethren in Northern California. However, they have all since failed in advanced electronics.

More research and development for the war effort took place in universities on the East Coast and even Termin himself left Stanford for the Defense Department's major effort at Harvard during the war years. Owing to this disparity, it became the goal of the high-technology community in Silicon Valley to strengthen the Valley's attractiveness as a research center and to identify ways that Silicon Valley firms could secure a greater share of government contracts. After the war, Termin returned to Stanford to become the Dean of the Engineering School and dedicated himself to strengthening Stanford as a center for research that would support a technologically advanced industrial base in the region. His idea was to use the engineering program at Stanford to build a "community of technical scholars." This community would be the foundation for the networks of innovation upon which the regional economy of Silicon Valley would develop and thrive.

Three institutional innovations initiated by Stanford reflect the relationships between research institutions, entrepreneurs, and firms in the region. The first innovation was the creation of the Stanford Research Institute (SRI) to conduct government-supported research and to assist West Coast high-technology firms in securing government contracts. Initially dedicated to military-related research, SRI for a while became an important conduit for solidifying the relationships between private sector high-technology firms, government, and university research establishments. Second, Stanford opened its engineering classrooms to local companies through its Honors Cooperative Program so that employees could enroll in graduate courses. This program had no parallels elsewhere. Third, Stanford promoted the creation of the Stanford Industrial Park, one of the first in the country, which reinforced the emerging pattern of cooperation between the University and electronics firms in the area to the long-term prosperity of both. In effect, these institutional arrangements encouraged the types of public/private partnerships and collaborations between universities, government, and firms that made possible the networks of innovation in Silicon Valley.

This model of collaboration between a university research institution and high-technology firms spread beyond Stanford to nearby Berkeley and later to the University of California Medical School in San Francisco. During the 1960s, owing to the example of Stanford, the University of California at Berkeley rapidly expanded its programs in electrical engineering and encouraged the outreach of its university environment to firms in the Silicon Valley. By the mid-1970s, Berkeley was training more engineers than Stanford and had become a premier research center in its own right for firms in Silicon Valley. Programs for technology transfer and professorships endowed by Silicon Valley firms were the hallmarks of this growing partnership between Berkeley and the Silicon Valley. In addition, the University of California at San Francisco was, and continues to be, one of the nation's preeminent medical research establishments with vital links to another emerging high-technology industry in which the Bay Area is the world's leading center, namely, the biotech industry (with about 168 biotech firms).[42] In effect, the presence of three world-class scientific, medical, and engineering research institutions that were actively involved in Silicon Valley industry created the most formidable university-industry partnerships in the world, its only rival being MIT.

Owing to these innovations and collaborations, the cluster of electronics firms in Silicon Valley grew rapidly during the 1960s and 1970s. This growth involved not only new start-ups, but also older established firms interested in taking advantage of the collaboration between Stanford and the high-technology community. Lockheed Aerospace, for example, set up a research lab for its Missiles and Space Division in the Stanford Industrial Park in 1956. Stanford agreed to train Lockheed employees while Lockheed in turn would help rebuild Stanford's aeronautical engineering department. Westinghouse, Ford Aerospace, Sylvania, Raytheon, ITT, and IBM would follow. Perhaps the most celebrated example of an older established firm coming to the Stanford/Silicon Valley research complex is Xerox, which in 1970 setup its storied Palo Alto Research Center (PARC). From Xerox PARC emerged such technologies as the computer operating system that was first successfully used by Apple and then even more successfully by Windows, laser printing, the computer mouse, and computer networking. Most of these technologies served to enrich neighboring companies rather than Xerox headquarters back East, which was preoccupied by "its core business."

By 1975, the region's high-technology enterprises employed over 100,000 workers. This growth, in turn, compelled similar types of partnerships to develop between Silicon Valley firms and the local community colleges and a nearby state university. By the 1970s, the region's six community colleges offered specialized technical programs oriented specifically to the needs of the area's firms, while San Jose State University was actually training as many engineers as either Stanford or Berkeley. Following the familiar and successful model, the community colleges made contracts with local companies to teach their employees while the companies provided the colleges with part-time teachers and consultants to help develop curricula. Firms also donated equipment to area schools. After Tandem Computers donated more than $1 million in computer equipment to Foothill College, for example, the school was able to triple (to over 5,000) the number of students in its computer course.

While firms and supporting institutions in Silicon Valley expanded together, the region also grew as a result of an entirely new industry, the semi-conductor industry. This fundamentally transformed the economic landscape and provided the region with its name (after the silicon strata on which both semiconductors and the Valley were built).

The semiconductor industry took root in the area when Shockley Transistor located in Palo Alto in 1955. Founded by William Shockley (a Stanford

---

[42] President's Industry-University Cooperative Research Initiative, *The BioSTAR Project: Critical Linkages Project*, 1998.

graduate and one of the inventors of the transistor at Bell Labs in Pennsylvania), the firm was the first in a line of spin-offs and competing ventures that led first to Fairchild Semiconductor and eventually to Intel, AMD, and National Semiconductor (among others).[43] Between 1966–1976, a total of thirty-six semiconductor firms were founded in the United States. Of these thirty-six firms, thirty-one were located in the Silicon Valley.[44] The semiconductor industry and the Silicon Valley had effectively become synonymous.

The impetus for the early growth of this industry came almost exclusively from the military. Virtually no other customers existed for semiconductors when they were initially developed. In 1962, the government was the sole market for semiconductor devices.[45] However, as the computer industry itself gradually expanded, the government accounted for a diminishing share of the semiconductor business. By 1978, the government accounted for only a 10% market share for semiconductors.[46] While this diffusion is impressive, the Department of Defense and NASA nevertheless played a crucial role as "creative first users" of the new technology.[47] A key element in the formative years of Silicon Valley's industrial structure and business culture was the Defense Department's insistence on "dual sourcing." It diffused technology and helped to proliferate competing—and cooperating—firms.

By the early 1970s, venture capital (specifically, venture capital limited partnerships) came to replace the military as the lead source of financing for Silicon Valley start-ups. The explosive growth of venture capitalists in the region paralleled the growth of the local semiconductor industry itself. By 1974, over 150 venture capital firms operated in Silicon Valley, with Stanford University investing a portion of its own endowment in venture activities. By 1988, Silicon Valley was attracting 40% of the national total of venture capital investment.[48]

What distinguished this industry from venture capital in other parts of the country was the fact that venture capitalists in Silicon Valley invariably had prior careers with technology firms in the region. As a result, Silicon Valley venture capitalists understood the technical dimensions of the business far better than their East Coast counterparts. Perhaps more importantly, the personal connections of Silicon Valley venture capitalists to colleagues in local firms forged the personal knowledge and shared business and technological outlook upon which relationships between entrepreneurialism, innovation, and financial backing

---

[43] Sturgeon, op. cit.

[44] Michael Borrus, James Millstein, and John Zysman. *U.S.-Japanese Competition in the Semiconductor Industry* (Berkeley, CA: Institute of International Studies, 1982), pp. 26–27.

[45] Ibid., p. 18.

[46] Ibid., p. 18.

[47] Ibid., p. 17.

[48] Richard Florida and Martin Kenney, *The Breakthrough Illusion: Corporate America's Failure to Move from Innovation to Mass Production* (New York, NY: Basic Books, 1990), p. 68.

flourished. Venture capitalists in the Valley are "hands-on" investors heavily involved in the strategic and managerial decisions of the companies they back.[49] As a result of this unique relationship, Silicon Valley venture firms are embedded within the broader fabric of high-technology development and are an integral part of the social structures that facilitate the process of innovation. In effect, venture capitalists in Silicon Valley created a new and different kind of financial institution. They became central actors in the establishment of networks in the region, incorporating finance, entrepreneurship, innovation, customer and partner identification, and troubleshooting.

Alongside the venture capitalists, local law firms function as important actors within the region's networks of entrepreneurship and innovation. The Valley's leading law firms have grown to specialize in intellectual property rights, technology licensing, encryption law, and immigration. The lawyers know the venture capitalists; and both of these groups know large numbers of experienced technology executives who can be called in to help deal with an organizational or strategic problem or opportunity. They sit on boards of companies that can be key customers or partners for new firms. The networks of overlapping board memberships could be considered another element of social capital, but cannot be considered deep civic engagement (except, of course, the boards of non-profit institutions, where many of the same players are to be found).

A defining element of the networks of innovation of Silicon Valley is the character of the labor market. One word perhaps best distinguishes how this labor market functions: mobility. From the early 1970s, Silicon Valley has been differentiated from other regional economies by the unusually high number of employees moving from one job to another, from one company to another. The geographic proximity of so many firms within the same industry undoubtedly contributes to this fluidity. Two other explanations, each quite different in tone, lie at the core of how the extremely mobile job market in Silicon Valley operates.

The first explanation focuses on how Valley employees' loyalty is greater to the craft of innovation than to any particular company.[50] The result of such commitment is a rapid turnover of employees. As individuals move from one project and one firm to another, their paths overlap and create networks of information sharing that accelerate the diffusion of technological capabilities and know-how. It is in these pathways of labor mobility that networks of innovation get created.

The second explanation depicts a much darker image of this mobility process. Employees in Silicon Valley work under exceedingly high levels of pressure to produce the types of technological breakthroughs characteristic of the region. With pay linked to performance and management techniques that push workers to the limit, employees put in superhuman work hours.[51] Owing to the strain, they eventually "burn out" and consequently move to other firms, enticed

[49] Ibid., p 69.
[50] Saxenian, op. cit., p. 36.
[51] Florida and Kenney, op. cit., p. 44.

by the recruitment efforts of competitors. Nevertheless, while this picture is of a much more Hobbesian world, the end result of labor mobility is still the same—networks that support and fuel innovation and its rapid commercialization.

Labor turnover and the competition for workers has created a market niche for another entity that participates in the creation of innovation networks: headhunter companies. Like the venture capital and legal firms, headhunters supply high-technology companies with its most essential resource. Without the highly skilled "think" workers provided by headhunters, high-tech companies would be without the source of ideas lying at the foundation of the innovation process in Silicon Valley.

Perhaps the most striking consequence of labor mobility and the efforts of headhunter firms is the truly international character of the high-technology community. Aspiring entrepreneurs and ambitious engineers from all over the world come to Silicon Valley. Many of these overseas individuals remain in the area after attending one of the local universities. Others come from abroad, attracted by the open hiring gates of both established firms and start-ups. The openness of the labor market to foreigners is one of the region's most valuable assets.

The value of this diversity is not limited to the Silicon Valley community. It is a key, enabling asset for other regions with aspirations to high-tech specialization. There are, for example, perhaps as many as 10,000 French in the Valley, at least twice as many Taiwanese, growing thousands of Indians, and a few thousand Israelis.[52] The data is inherently imprecise. People come and go. Some pass through quickly, but many work for years and years. Many become citizens and return "home" much later. They are a vital transmission belt, diffusing technology and market knowledge, sometimes establishing offshore facilities that seed new districts and serve as connectors into the Valley. They have been a key factor in developing successful (sometimes very successful) high-tech districts "back home." As a development policy, few investments have paid off so well for the "brain drain" nations.

CONCLUSIONS

A particular industry defines a region's specialization and industries differ in growth potential, in their capacity to generate new activities and new industries, and in the kinds of social structures they breed. High-fashion districts, coal and steel districts, and mass production textile districts typically resemble one another independent of nation or ethnicity. The recent literature, especially the profuse literature stemming from Sabel's work on Italian districts, pays too much attention to the social characteristics of specialized industrial districts and

---

[52] Estimates from consulate officials. Census data is out of date (from 1990) and it misses dual passport holders. For more information and a visit to these communities see: http://www.tie.org/ (India), or www.dree.org/usa/default.htm (France), http://sf.roc-taiwan.org/ (Taiwan).

consequently too little to the relatively more technical issues surrounding the specific nature of the industries. For example, comparisons between the Boston high-tech industrial district and Silicon Valley overstate the weight of "Boston Brahmin" culture. However, Brahmin culture never defined or even penetrated MIT, the fountainhead of Boston high-tech. A more useful comparison would focus on the structural differences between Boston's dominant activities (defense electronics systems and then mini-computers) and Silicon Valley's (semiconductors and then micro-computers and computer networking). Similarly, Silicon Valley is not to be distinguished by the mild California climate or the absence of neckties. Southern California's massive aerospace industry in no way resembles Northern California's electronics cluster—not in industrial structure, not in forms of payment, not in rates of new company formation, not in the proliferation of intermediating *metiers*, and not, ultimately, in flexibility. Research universities play a limited role, if that, in Milan's dynamic "Marshallian district" of high fashion. Venture firms, laws firms, and graduate students occupy little space in the much studied Italian tile district, or in Antwerp's diamond center, or in Detroit's (and now Kentucky's) auto districts, or in Georgia's carpet and towel belt. Ultimately, what you do shapes how you do it—all the way back up the value chain, all the way out into forms of social organization.

Of course, there is trust in Silicon Valley; there is no such thing as a productive milieu, or even a functioning society, where there is no trust. At issue is the specific nature of that trust. What kind is it? What does it do and not do? Where does it originate—that is, where are its social foundations? Frequent, commercially focused contacts generate judgement: "He's reliable, he's straight, you can count on him to fulfill his end and do it well, reliably, on time." This is the stuff of reputation, of commercially valuable trust. Such specific, performance generated trust is the building block of Silicon Valley's particular brand of social capital. The sequence runs from performance to trust, not from community. Perhaps policy would be well advised to aim for that trajectory, even if it entails loosening some deep and exclusionary civic engagements. All the rest (such as informal conversations in bars or bowling alleys) is, relative to many other places, somewhat underdeveloped and ancillary. It exists, it matters, but it is second in sequence and importance. It is not the defining or distinguishing element.

The performance-focused trust in Silicon Valley is different in kind from the trust engendered by deep civic engagement that makes for economic success in some regions. It is more than just an easily assembled substitute. It might be a superior form. It is open to outsiders. Trust can be extended, rather quickly, to people from other places and other cultures, and even to people with different ideas.

Chapter 9

Social Capital, Violations of Trust and the Vulnerability of Isolates: The Social Organization of Law Practice and Professional Self-regulation[*]

Bruce L. Arnold[**]
Department of Sociology, University of Calgary

Fiona M. Kay
Department of Anthropology and Sociology, University of British Columbia, Canada

INTRODUCTION

Escalating changes in the social organization of the legal profession have created increased ethical dilemmas for lawyers and law societies. Research has addressed issues surrounding professionalism and ethics (Elkins 1985; Smith & Carroll 1991; Robb 1992) and, in particular, the relationship between pressures for financial success and unethical conduct (McDowell 1991). In response to transformations in legal practice, law schools instruct law students about

[*] Reprinted from the *International Journal of the Sociology of Law* 1995, 23, 321–346, Bruce L. Arnold and Fiona M. Kay "Social Capital, Violations of Trust and the Vulnerability of Isolates: The Social Organization of Law Practice and Professional Self-Regulation" © 1995, by permission of the publisher Academic Press.
[**] Author to whom correspondence should be addressed at: Department of Sociology, 2500 University Drive N.W., University of Calgary, Calgary, Alberta, Canada, T2N 1N4.

contemporary ethical hazards and law societies continue to develop ethical standards, disciplinary procedures, committees and penalties. Notwithstanding these efforts, the self-regulatory powers of the legal profession are increasingly questioned regarding their ability to effectively control the unethical behaviour of lawyers. For instance, some scholars have drawn attention to the amoral ethical role of lawyers (Pepper 1986) in relation to professionalism and self-regulation (Moore 1987). In contrast, other researchers maintain that granting professional bodies self-regulatory powers is the most efficient way to regulate the activities of lawyers (Usprich 1975; Ostry 1976; Reiter 1978; Bierig 1983; Sibenik 1988).

In part, questions surrounding the principles and effectiveness of self-regulation remain unresolved because of the tendency of research to focus either on professional training and informal socialization processes, or to query professional associations' mandate to control the market for legal services. After outlining some of the major tenets of these two approaches, we introduce a social capital framework (see Coleman 1990) which emphasizes the importance of networks of social relations in establishing and enforcing both norms of conduct as well as access to lucrative markets for legal services. This approach identifies differential levels of social-structural resources that characterize the stratification of contemporary law practice. We argue that lawyers are embedded within social networks that act as a form of 'social capital' and that the accumulation of social capital is directly related to firm size. These associations are connected to both the probability of engaging in professional misconduct and the risk of official complaints and apprehension for these violations. We maintain that social resources structure both pressures to violate codes of conduct and buffers which shield against detection by law society disciplinary bodies. Our analysis details the accumulation of social capital (Coleman 1990), social organization of trust (Shapiro 1987, 1990) and ethical vulnerabilities inherent to law practice (Gilson & Mnookin 1985) in relation to the structure of law practice.

We provide a preliminary investigation of these relationships using detailed records systematically collected from the archives of a Canadian law society. These data were collected using two sampling frames to investigate the two-stage processing of misconduct by the Law Society: decisions to prosecute and sanction. The first involved complaints of misconduct against lawyers referred to the Law Society Disciplinary Committee for prosecution between 1 January 1979 and 31 December 1986 ($n = 634$). A second random sample of approximately equal size ($n = 640$) was selected from written complaints of misconduct that were initially received by the Law Society but which did not result in prosecution. Data gathered for each lawyer in the sample included complaint characteristics, complaint histories, professional position, gender and the outcome of complaint cases. In addition, more in-depth qualitative materials were collected and transcribed from Law Society video-taped interviews with some of the disbarred lawyers. The interviews provide a more detailed understanding of the process by which lawyers enter into unethical activities and the personal consequences of being disbarred for professional misconduct. We begin with a brief overview of the background to the professional regulation of lawyers in the United States and Canada.

FORMAL PROFESSIONAL REGULATION THROUGH LAW SOCIETIES

During the 1970s the U.S. bar associations came under severe attack for their inability to uncover and respond to unethical conduct among lawyers. During this period, bar associations' responsibility for disciplining professional misconduct was reduced and transferred to the criminal justice system (Powell 1985:281; Powell 1986:34; Wilkins 1992:802). Barber notes that in the late 1970s throughout the United States, the legal profession was "criticized for their selfishness, their public irresponsibility, and their lack of effective self-control" (1978:599). As Powell observes:

> A watershed in this rather sudden reversal of fortunes of the professions was the 1975 United States Supreme Court decision overturning on antitrust grounds the minimum fee schedules maintained by bar associations (Goldfarb vs. Virginia State Bar). The decision had manifold consequences for the professions. The floodgates were opened and the professions faced with numerous challenges to their self-regulatory prerogatives. (1985:282).

Thus, the American lawyer-discipline systems underwent substantial reorganization in the majority of American states during the 1970s, with responsibility for their operation being transferred from the bar associations to agencies of the state supreme courts (Powell 1986:31). The structure of lawyer discipline designed by the bar associations, including ethical codes to govern lawyers' conduct, grievance and inquiry committees to investigate complaints and conduct hearings, and general counsel to prosecute lawyers, had remained unchallenged for close to a century (Powell 1986:34). Yet, by 1983, responsibility for the operation of lawyer discipline was vested in commissions or committees of state supreme courts in a majority of states (see Powell 1985, 1986). In sharp contrast, Canada's legal profession continues to have a system of formal self-regulation.

Our understanding of professional self-regulatory authority remains clouded by the changing nature of professional control. Empirical investigations of self-regulation require systematic examinations of historically specific professional control mechanisms. Professional regulation can occur informally through the law firm and/or through formal professional (bar) associations sanctioned by the state. However, insights into self-regulation may be gained through an examination of regulatory powers specific to professional associations. The Canadian law societies provide a unique opportunity for such inquiry. Each provincial law society represents the province's lawyers; membership is mandatory. The Law Society is a large complex organization with considerable autonomous regulatory power over most aspects of professional practice, including the power to govern admission to the bar, set educational qualifications, prescribe ethical codes of conduct, and discipline unethical practitioners (Powell 1985:281; Halliday et al. 1993:518).[1]

APPROACHES TO PROFESSIONAL SELF-REGULATION

Two general and contradictory perspectives characterize the nature of professional self-regulatory authority. Functionalist approaches focus upon the role of professional training which, through informal socialization processes, advances principles of competence, altruism and community service, and seeks to ensure that lawyers comply with ethical standards rather than fall prey to forms

---

[1] Misconduct can be considered either 'professional misconduct' or 'conduct unbecoming'. However, the Law Society Act does not provide definitions for these categories. Instead, offenses are determined by the Discipline Department and Committees who process and hear complaints against lawyers. Professional misconduct is generally considered as occurring during the discharging of professional duties and includes the following categories:
   (i) Dishonest and criminal conduct including fraud and misappropriation in the nature of theft;
   (ii) Other willful unethical conduct which evidences breach of duty of clients, colleagues and the courts, including conflict of interest and borrowing from clients, misleading courts, other lawyers and clients, failure to protect clients and the Law Society from consequences of potential negligence, failing to meet financial obligations arising out of practice, and failing to defend civil actions or pay judgements arising out of practice;
   (iii) 'Bookkeeping offences' including misapplication of funds, and failure to maintain appropriate books and records;
   (iv) 'Ungovernability' in terms of failure or refusal to cooperate with the Society in its investigation of complaints and refusal to be governed by the Society's rules and regulations including failure to cooperate with the Society, and practicing while under suspension;
   (v) Gross negligence, failure or inability to serve clients in a competent and efficient manner and other conduct which is detrimental to clients or the profession.
Conduct unbecoming involves a member's activities that do not occur during professional undertakings but which bring the legal profession into disrepute. These include:
   (i) Criminal and quasi-criminal conduct which does not involve the member's practice of law, whether or not the member has been charged criminally or has been convicted;
   (ii) Criminal convictions involving moral turpitude, whether arising out of the member's practice or not;
   (iii) Conviction under the Income Tax Act, or other statutes with penal consequences;
   (iv) Other conduct which tends to bring the legal profession or the administration of justice into disrepute, including:
      (a) contempt of court;
      (b) public statements or conduct calculated to subject the courts or other lawyers to ridicule;
      (c) gross financial irresponsibility.

of avarice more commonly associated with the business community (Parsons 1939). Proponents of this perspective maintain that self-regulation is in fact the quintessential form of social control.[2] The state's granting of professional self-government is justified as a necessary safeguard to the public interest by reinforcing ethical values and standards (Usprich 1975; Ostry 1976; Sibenik 1988). The legal profession is seen as the best protector of this interest as lawyers alone must formulate their own standards of conduct since they possess the specialized knowledge for such a task. The public is ill-equipped to "understand fully what professionals do and [therefore it] cannot evaluate the judgements professionals must make" (Bierig 1993:617). Other arguments assert that self-regulation is also a more efficient and less costly remedy to misconduct than government regulation or regulation through criminal or civil proceedings (Usprich 1975; Brockman & McEwen 1990). In addition, law societies claim that they scrutinize a wide array of behaviour and thereby ensure higher standards of conduct than if the public had to depend upon government regulation. That is, the profession claims to 'funnel in' misconduct for observation, investigation and sanctions which might otherwise not be subject to such careful monitoring by government controls (Brockman & McEwen 1990:3).

In contrast, critics of the functionalist approach question the role and purpose of self-regulatory claims to professional socialization and ethical compliance. For instance, they argue that the preoccupation with codification of rules of professional misconduct and attempts to socialize law students through ethical instruction in law school and Bar admission courses assume that the rules will be internalized and therefore become self-enforcing. Research suggests that this assumption is not justified in practice. Abel (1986:403) argues:

> One source of dissonance is control over the disciplinary process; there is something inherently suspect in the claim by an occupational category that its members will punish each other for infractions that all find tempting and many commit. (see also, Carlin 1966; Steele & Nimmer 1976).

As a result, proponents of this approach address the occupational power advantages associated with professional self-regulation. They argue that professional associations are not primarily designed to ensure adequate services to clients and the community. Rather, professional powers are used to maintain market monopoly while reinforcing the profession's relative autonomy from state legal controls (Larson 1977; Reasons & Chappell 1985:49). These scholars argue that self-regulating organizations cannot effectively serve both their members and the best interests of the public. In effect, self-regulation creates a risk of conflict of interest (Gellhorn 1976; Rhode 1981; Weber 1987; Abel 1989). Professional associations have been accused of discouraging complaints against

---

[2] Durkheim maintained that occupational activities are best regulated by their own members who are intimate with its functions (Durkheim 1933:1–10; Giddens 1972: 183–188).

practitioners and of reacting leniently when misconduct is established (Macaulay 1986; Abel 1989). From this perspective, organizations established to discipline their own members are seen as an exercise in public relations rather than effective mechanisms for the control of professional misconduct (see Brockman & McEwen 1990: 3–4). As such, self-regulating organizations serve to protect their members from coming into contact with the criminal justice system, thereby protecting them from state legal sanctions (Coleman 1985:153).[3]

Functionalist and critical perspectives posit two apparently paradoxical components of self-regulation with the former advocating socialization, altruism and ethical compliance, while the latter draws attention to issues of economic power that underlay law practice. However, concentration upon these competing paradigms detracts from a more thorough analysis of how professional associations attempt to both ensure the production of competent and ethical practitioners as well as controlling the market for their services (Abel 1989). Integrating research questions regarding compliance with ethical standards and competition for financial rewards must be located in the context of how law practice is organized within the different strata of the legal profession. Therefore, a conceptual framework addressing opportunities for unethical behaviour, the effects of intraoccupational controls, and disciplinary processes is required. We propose a social capital perspective to investigate issues of ethical compliance in relation to socialization processes, disciplinary actions by law societies, and the power differences that characterize contemporary law practice.[4]

SOCIAL CAPITAL AND LAW PRACTICE

The social capital perspective identifies the importance of concrete personal relations and networks of relations in generating trust, in establishing expectations and in creating and enforcing norms. Granovetter (1985) terms this the 'embeddedness' of economic transactions in social relations. Building on Granovetter's work, Coleman (1990) conceives of these social-structural resources as a capital asset for the individual, that is, as 'social capital'. Coleman observes that "unlike other forms of capital, social capital inheres in the structure of

---

[3] Bar associations receive a wide range of complaints, including charges of lawyers' delays, discourtesy, neglect, irresponsibility, and excessive fees (Steele & Nimmer 1976:956–966; Curran 1977:224–231). This tension in combination with the fact that the disciplinary process is entirely reactive, discourages clients from raising all but an insignificant fraction of their complaints (Steele & Nimmer 1976:962–963; Abel 1986:403).

[4] Embeddedness in our model is measured through intra-professional position. We view contemporary occupational differentiation as synonymous with relations of power and labour within occupations (see Wright 1985). Positions of intra-professional power involve their structural location in the social organization of work (Hagan & Parker 1985). These are professional status (i.e. partner, sole practitioner, associate and employee) and size of law firm.

relations between persons and among persons. It is lodged neither in individuals nor in physical implements of production" (Coleman 1990:302).[5] Moreover:

> Social capital is defined by its function. It is not a single entity but a variety of different entities, with two elements in common: they all consist of some aspect of social structures, and they facilitate certain actions of actors— whether persons or corporate actors—with the structure. Like other forms of capital, social capital is productive, making possible the achievement of certain ends that in its absence would not be possible. (Coleman 1988:S98).

Forms of social capital include both individual and collective economically relevant expectations which structure behaviour, opportunities and sanctions. One example of collective action is a business firm created by owners of financial capital for the purpose of earning income. Coleman argues that these organizations take the form of authority structures composed of positions connected by obligations and expectations, and occupied by persons.[6] Like other forms of capital, social capital requires an investment in the design of the structure of obligations and expectations, responsibility and authority, and norms (or rules) and sanctions which will ensure an effectively functioning organization (Coleman 1990:313). Therefore, compliance to specific behaviours creates opportunities for accumulating social capital as well as avoiding sanctions for failing to adhere to these collective expectations. Expectations include avoiding behaviour based on greed, fulfilling expectations of reciprocity, and subordinating present desires to longer term organizational expectations (Portes & Sensenbrenner 1993).

Accumulating social capital, while avoiding sanctions for failed expectations, can be particularly problematic for legal practitioners considering the potential conflict between occupational demands to provide professional services and the pressure to exploit markets. Moreover, the risk of unethical conduct and possible professional penalties is not evenly distributed within the legal profession but can vary depending upon the nature of the social organization of law practice. For example, potential offenders can only benefit given suitable opportunities.[7] These opportunities are related to the way in which a law practice is organized, to levels of supervision, and to the level of trust which exists in the relationship between lawyers and clients (Croall 1992:60). These relationships constitute what is described as the social organization of trust (Coleman 1987:432; Shapiro 1990). So, certain lawyers may occupy positions that are

---

[5]   Coleman maintains that social capital exists in several forms: as obligations and expectations, information potential, norms, authority relations and social organization (1990:312).

[6]   Coleman (1990:313) notes that "In creating such an organization, an entrepreneur or capitalist transforms financial capital into physical capital in the form of buildings and tools, social capital in the form of the organization of positions, and human capital in the form of persons occupying positions."

[7]   Obviously, lawyers can only profit economically if they have access to money, goods or other assets which can readily be misappropriated (Croall 1992:60).

inherently vulnerable to criminogenic activities due to freedoms associated with their positions of trust (see Hagan 1994:111–112).

Law is a distinctively stratified profession (Erlanger 1980; Heinz & Laumann 1982; Powell 1985; Hagan et al. 1988). There are apparent divisions of labour, clientele and rewards (Arthurs et al. 1987:500; Abel 1989:101). The structure of power, social organization and therefore control of the marketplace for legal services, has changed dramatically with the expansion of large firms. During the last 20 years, contractual relations between lawyers and clients have shifted from a mode of legal production organized largely around the activities of sole practitioners, to a mode of production more often organized around law firms, characterized by a small number of partners and multiple-tiered levels of lawyer associates and employees. The transition from self-employment, the sole practitioner and small firm organization, to larger firms has been documented extensively in the literature (Heinz & Laumann 1982; Galanter 1983; Nelson 1983; Curran et al. 1985; Curran 1986; Abel 1989). Galanter (1983:153) describes this transformation in the market for legal services as a trend toward 'mega-lawyering'. The dominance of large law firms has segmented the profession into two hemispheres, in which major corporations and wealthy individuals are usually represented by large firms, while small businesses and individuals of modest incomes usually seek representation by small firms or sole practitioners (Heinz & Laumann 1982; Nelson 1983). The transformation of legal practice toward law firms, and increasingly larger law firms, is salient to our understanding of the social organization of legal practice and the context in which opportunities for misconduct exist. As we discuss below, larger law firms are better equipped than sole practitioners or small firm lawyers to generate and maintain the social capital necessary for strict adherence to ethical standards and competence which is essential for maintaining control over access to a more financially lucrative practice.

The large law firm offers a unique environment for the accumulation and reproduction of social capital. The law firm involves the entrance of a number of lawyers into cooperative associations (i.e. firms) based on an exchange of human capital for labour. Galanter & Palay (1991) argue that lawyers gradually combine labour with capital they acquire over time. The lawyer's capital derives primarily from four types of human assets: education, experience, reputation and clients. Perhaps more importantly, lawyers invest in their professional reputations. By reputation, a lawyer disseminates information to clients and other lawyers about "his[/her] qualifications, skills, temperament, legal philosophy, honesty, and integrity" (Galanter & Palay 1991:14). Many lawyers acquire a surplus of reputational capital, in the sense that they can no longer satisfy client demands for services. When this occurs, senior lawyers may choose to enter associations with more junior lawyers, lending their capital (reputational and clientele) and increasing its productive value. The resulting law firm provides internal organization, a marketplace for the sharing of capital (Hagan et al. 1991). Herein lies the essence of social capital. As Coleman remarks, "If physical capital is wholly tangible, being embodied in observable material form, and human capital is less tangible, being embodied in the skills and knowledge acquired by an individual, social capital is less tangible yet, for it exists in the relations among persons" (1988:S100–101).[8]

The key to the formation and growth of firms is that social capital grows faster than human capital. That is, individual lawyers often develop excess capital, in particular, reputational and relational capital, which leads to engaging the labour of other lawyers as associates. The sharing of these capital assets requires more than simply a marketplace for the exchange of labour and capital; but rather, it requires protection from opportunistic conduct through the organization of *trust relations* (see Macaulay 1963:55–67). Norms within law firms constitute a powerful form of social capital. For example, a prescriptive norm within an organization that represents an especially important form of social capital is the norm that one should forgo self-interest and act in the interests of the collectivity (Coleman 1988:S104–105). Thus, the firm operates as a "mutual monitoring device" (Gilson & Mnookin 1985:313).

Gilson & Mnookin (1985) point to three sources of vulnerability lawyers and firms confront when engaging the labour of other lawyers: their propensity to shirk responsibilities, grab assets and/or leave the firm. Coleman argues that two elements are critical to social capital: "the level of trustworthiness of the social environment, which means that obligations will be repaid, and the actual extent of obligations held. Social structures differ in both of these dimensions, and actors within a particular structure differ in the second" (Coleman 1990:306). The primary incentive in this monitoring process is the prospect of partnership. Galanter & Palay describe the promotional ladder within law firms as a tournament in which associates of a particular entering 'class' compete for the reward of partnership (1991:100). Firms are organized into partner-associate tiers that use subordinating and monitoring mechanisms to protect the cultural and social capitals of the firm and its partners while simultaneously extracting a profit from the labour of employed lawyers (Hagan et al. 1991:242).

A further vulnerability law practice must confront is the risk that a member of the firm will engage in unethical or criminal behaviour, marring the distinguished yet fragile reputation of the firm and hence the client base of the firm. Bourdieu (1977:182) highlights the fragility of reputation when he observes that similar to families, professions such as law share a "hypersensitivity to the slightest slur or innuendo" and that such institutions develop a "multiplicity of strategies designed to belie or avert them". Furthermore, social capital, in terms of social networks of clients as well as coordination of lawyers within the firm,

---

[8]   Bourdieu also describes social capital as the sharing of resources through networks of social relations. For Bourdieu, social capital is "the aggregate of the actual or potential resources which are linked to possession of a durable network or more or less institutionalized relationships of mutual acquaintance and recognition—in other works, to membership in a group—which provides each of its members with the backing of the collectivity-owned capital, a 'credential' which entitles them to credit, in the various senses of the word" (Bourdieu 1986:248–249).

represents a form of capital which depreciates over time if it is not renewed. Coleman notes that "social relationships die out if not maintained; expectations and obligations whither over time; and norms depend on regular communication" (1990:321). It is the cultural and social forms of legal capital (reputational and client relational forms) that generate the hyper-, but rational, sensitivity to potential devaluation. This capital is vulnerable in ways that other forms of capital are not (see Hagan et al. 1991:242). Hagan et al. (1991:243) document how firms shared "a constant concern with monitoring growth, assuring that new associates and partners were responsible, trustworthy, working hard" and ultimately focusing on whether prospective partners can generate sufficient new capital, by way of clients and reputation, to sustain the growth.

Therefore, social capital consists of social obligations or 'connections'.[9] The social relations within the firm structure, through relations among lawyers, represents a process of ongoing socialization, by way of mentoring and supervision. Fundamental ethical views about professional work are developed during these early years of law practice, under the influence of colleagues and superiors, rather than in law school (Carlin 1966). The larger the firm, the more intense the socialization process (Zemans & Rosenblum 1981:173–187). Therefore, the firm structure represents an important system of informal and formal controls: informally, the firm is crucial to the development of internal controls attained through the lengthy and rigorous process of recruitment and socialization of new associates; more formally, the firm represents the structure that exercises considerable authority over the ethical conduct and legal services of its junior members (see Abel 1986:394). This notion of social control through the structure of the law firm is rooted in ideas of social capital.

In contrast, the social contexts of the work of sole practitioners and small firm lawyers, especially the patterns of opportunity and pressure to which they are exposed to in their practice, leaves these lawyers at a disadvantage to produce superior social capital and to compete effectively in the legal marketplace (see Carlin 1966, 1994). Law school is often criticized for failing to endow the fledgling lawyer with necessary business and management skills (Zeman & Rosenblum 1981:135–140; Abel 1986:395). Yet, the larger law firm provides new recruits with an arena for ongoing socialization, legal training and a large network of expertise resources. By contrast, the sole practitioner and small firm lawyer lack such extensive resources and social support. The ongoing process of

---

[9]   Two criteria determine the volume of the social capital an individual has at his or her disposal: the size of the network of connections that the agent can effectively mobilize and the volume of capital possessed by each of those to whom the agent is connected (Bourdieu 1986:249). In other words, "the network of relationships is the product of investment strategies, individual or collective, consciously aimed at establishing or reproducing social relationships that are directly usable in the short or long term . . ." (Bourdieu 1986:249).

socialization and resources characteristic of the large law firm appear to serve as a powerful source of social control.[10]

Small firms and sole practitioners also operate within economic constraints which may contribute to patterns of offending (Croall 1989:169). For example, sole practitioners are typically employed by lower-status clients, with a disproportionate number of individual proprietors, small businesses and middle to low income individuals. In contrast, large law firms tend to serve corporations and wealthy individuals (Heinz & Laumann 1982). The lower the status of the lawyer's clientele, the more precarious and insecure the practice. Lower status clientele tend to be more unstable, with higher rates of turnover. The weak and intermittent demand for legal services from lower-status clients results in an instability of practice, with greater temptation, if not pressure, to violate ethical norms (Carlin 1966:66–68). Understandably, these practice settings are also likely to be more adversely affected by economic conditions and are less likely to be able to cushion their effects (Croall 1992:74). If economic uncertainty creates a situation in which legitimate means of profit-making are blocked or threatened, pursuing profits by illegitimate means becomes a rational choice (Croall 1992:70). Smaller firms, and sole practitioners in particular, may be 'victims of circumstance', whose marginality may leave them preoccupied with a 'struggle for survival' (Sutton & Wild 1985). In sum, there appears to be a relationship between the amount of social capital and informal controls, such as ongoing ethical socialization and access to the market of clients. We would then expect that lawyers with little social capital, especially sole practitioners, to be more likely to receive complaints of misconduct and to be accused of more serious ethical violations.

Table 9.1 illustrates a statistically significant relationship between professional embeddedness and the number and seriousness of complaints received by the Law Society. Sole practitioners, who generally possess the least social capital,

---

[10] For example, an extensive study of self-regulation of the Canadian legal profession (Reiter 1978), examining the competence-related complaints between 1975 and 1977 found the most likely candidate for a complaint is a busy sole practitioner who has been complained about on several occasions in the past, has largely individuals as clients, and whose practice is centered in the real estate, litigation or estates fields (Reiter 1978:88). Reiter (1978) notes that the matters that were formally considered by the discipline committee tended to come from individual clients complaining about sole or small firm practitioners. A survey of business clients suggests that they "express their displeasure by means other than reporting the lawyer to the Law Society" (Reiter 1978:105; see also, Reasons & Chappell 1985:40). For example, most dissatisfied clients of large firms speak directly to their lawyer, or to his or her partners, and then take their business elsewhere to another firm if this strategy did not resolve a concern about ethics or competency—rather than report their complaint to the Law Society (Yale 1982). Since sole practitioners and small firm lawyers lack these additional layers of response and accountability, clients are more apt to pursue formal control and sanctioning mechanisms through the Law Society, a strategy which is generally considered only as a last step by large firm clientele.

TABLE 9.1 Professional Embeddedness and Complaint Seriousness

	Professional position					
Complaint seriousness	Employees (firm or government employee)	Sole practitioner	Semi-auto-nomous lawyer	Small firm partner	Medium-sized firm partner	Large firm partner
High	4	128	8	14	0	1
	3.9%	16.2%	10.5%	5.2%	0%	5.9%
Medium	40	322	28	100	6	4
	38.8%	40.8%	36.8%	37.5%	33.3%	23.5%
Low	59	339	40	153	12	12
	57.3%	43.0%	52.6%	57.3%	66.7%	70.6%
Number of cases	103	789	76	267	18	17
Column total(%)	8.1%	62.0%	6.0%	21.0%	1.4%	1.3%

$n = 1270$ $P<0.001$

appear to receive the majority of complaints of professional misconduct (62%). Small law firm partners, who also have limited social capital receive the second largest number of complaints (21%). In contrast, partners of medium and large law firms receive only 1.4% and 1.3% of all complaints. There also appears to be a similar relationship between the seriousness of complaints and social capital. In particular, complaints against sole practitioners appear to be more serious than those against other lawyers. Of the 789 complaints against sole practitioners, 16% are in the most serious category and 41% in the second most serious category. Similarly, semi-autonomous lawyers, who also have little social capital receive a relatively high proportion of complaints. This sharply contrasts with the smaller proportions of serious complaints against lawyers in other professional positions that are characterized by increased social capital resources. The process by which lawyers with complaints of professional misconduct tumble from grace is explained by two disbarred lawyers. These comments lend insight into the often subtle and escalating nature of the transition to deviance that is more common in solo practice where early warning signs of misconduct cannot be identified by coworkers.

> I remember cancelling a court appearance. Basically, I was unprepared. I hadn't done my work and I wasn't prepared for court. Things like this can snowball, get out of hand. The ball keeps rolling and you're not conscious of all this going down hill . . . and this is the scary part. And the final stage was being reported to the Law Society.
>   . . . you know that you're travelling downhill and you don't know you're heading for a crash and you can't stop . . . you all of a sudden know that you've gone too far and you're crashing into the wall [charged with professional misconduct].

SOCIAL CAPITAL AND TRUST VIOLATIONS

We mentioned earlier that accumulating social capital is associated with the nature of the relations, between lawyers and clients, which constitute the social organization of trust. Shapiro explains that 'trustees' or 'agents' (providers of services, such as lawyers) are entrusted to carry out functions by 'principals' (clients, that is)—who are unable to supervise trustees or who may lack the appropriate expertise to judge their performance. Opportunities for trust violation derive from these basic arrangements. In particular, the structure of these relationships is profoundly unbalanced. First, in providing access and expertise, lawyers hold monopolies of information that cannot readily be verified or assessed by their clients. These information asymmetries, notes Shapiro, are of two kinds: (1) hidden information unavailable to the lawyer on which his or her actions are based (termed 'adverse selection' by economists); and (2) hidden action of the lawyer in discharging his or her obligations (what economists call 'moral hazard') (Shapiro 1990:348; see also Moe 1984; Arrow 1985:38). Shapiro argues further that agents are delegated power, property, collective assets, responsibility and discretion. Thus, agents have custody and control over other people's property, and with this power they hold "the capacity to create wealth, and discretion over the distribution of opportunity" (Shapiro 1987:629). Finally, these "acting-for" roles are structurally ambivalent; they institutionalize conflict between fidelity to client interests and lawyer self-interest (Shapiro 1990:348).

Ironically, the very factors that encourage individuals to seek legal expertise impede the exercise of control against professional misconduct. First, lawyers provide expertise to those who do not have it and who are, therefore, unable to specify or evaluate the performance of their lawyer. Coleman highlights the ignorance of clients about what kind of services they need and the strong emphasis on mutual trust in the professional-client relationship that leads many clients to an unquestioning acceptance of the lawyer's judgement (1987:434). Trust articulates general procedural norms that seek to check the inherent opportunities and temptations for abuse. These norms reflect the fundamental structural imbalances of these agency relationships:

> asymmetries of information; usage of rights to resources, delegated power, custody, and discretion; and expertise (Shapiro 1990:350).

As a result of these information asymmetries between lawyers and clients, sole practitioners appear most likely to engage in trust violations, the sort of 'moral hazard' that Shapiro (1987, 1990) identifies with 'agents' free of norms that check opportunities and temptation for abuse. Recall that the notion of social capital emphasizes the importance of social obligations and the organization of trust relations within the law firm (Macaulay 1963). The structure of the law firm, through the dynamics of social capital, activates informal controls against trust violations. These forms of social control and ongoing intense

TABLE 9.2 Professional Embeddedness and Trust Violations

Levels of trust	Professional position					
	Employee (firm or government employee)	Sole practitioner	Semi-auto-nomous lawyer	Small firm partner	Medium-sized firm partner	Large firm partner
High	36	432	35	135	4	6
	35.0%	54.8%	46.1%	50.4%	22.2%	35.3%
Low	67	357	41	133	14	11
	65.0%	45.2%	53.9%	49.6%	77.8%	64.7%
Number of cases	103	789	76	268	18	17
Column total (%)	8.1%	62.1%	6.0%	21.1%	1.4%	1.3%
$n = 1271$ $P < 0.001$						

socialization processes are more effective in the larger law firms (see Zemans & Rosenblum 1981:173–187). As previously discussed, sole practitioners possess lower levels of social capital which, in part, is the result of fewer informal controls and market accessability. We would therefore expect them to be more prone to formal complaints of unethical conduct involving trust violations than lawyers in other sectors of the legal profession.

Table 9.2 reveals that sole practitioners are indeed more likely than lawyers engaged in other private practice settings to participate in violations involving high levels of trust. It appears that 62% of all offenses involving trust violations were committed by sole practitioners. Furthermore, nearly 55% of sole practitioners, against whom complaints were registered with the Law Society, engaged in high trust violations. The next most prominent professional position is that of small firm partners. These lawyers represented 21% of all those against whom complaints of trust violations were filed with the Law Society. Fifty percent of these violations by small firm partners involved high levels of trust. In contrast, lawyers whose professional positions are associated with high levels of accumulated social capital appear to receive few complaints of trust violations. For example, only 1.3% and 1.4% of trust violation complaints received by the Law Society were against partners of large and medium law firms and, compared to lawyers in other professional positions, most of these complaints were of a minor nature.

Further insight into social capital and lawyers' initial flirtation with unethical conduct and subsequent patterning of trust violations is offered through the comments of a sole practitioner disbarred by the Law Society. This lawyer discussed his experience of professional misconduct and escalating trust violations. His account illustrates the difficulties associated with the financial aspects of establishing a solo law practice. He also informs us of the unethical dangers underlying poor business decisions and how they can quickly slip away from good intentions to ongoing trust violation when law practice suffers from weak professional organizational ties.

> I was an innocent lamb when I graduated from the Bar Admission course. In hindsight, when I opened my practice I really don't think that I had the right to open an office as a solo practitioner being so ill-prepared from the point of view of business in terms that 50% of your time is doing business things. It was a struggle juggling the business aspect and the practice of law and that continuing tension ultimately led to my misappropriation and being disbarred.

> When I came out of the Bar Admission I really didn't know my [trust account] obligations to clients and the Law Society. We had a friendly bank manager and we didn't really know how much we owed. We owed a lot. We had all the bells and whistles: cars, computers. It was our first mistake, not knowing how to keep on top of all of this.

> I had made a commitment to a client even though he had run out of funds so I was the only one prepared with the case and knew the facts. I couldn't just walk away, so I said I would continue. From a business point of view it was a poor decision. When the account was eventually settled I paid the whole shot to the bank and still didn't have enough to cover other expenses. I virtually had no practice.

> I don't know many sole practitioners or small firms that, after a real estate transaction, who don't transfer all of the funds into a trust and look after it for four to six weeks. But, it's easy to fall into a pattern of doing that. You transfer money without an account which you shouldn't be doing to start with. That's step number one. Step number two would be having money in trust and say you figure you have two thousand dollars of work into the file and the money is sitting in trust and your money in the general account is tight. So you've started this pattern with real estate transactions and it's easy to move to the next step and you figure you've earned the money so you borrow from the account. In a lot of ways you have earned it, but you don't fulfill your obligation of rendering an account which is taxable and maybe have a client complaint about the bill. You figure in the future you just include the two thousand dollars in a future bill which will smooth things over. The next step then is your current account is short. Then you say, hey listen, I have this money sitting in the trust account and I know that I will have some money coming in next week, so if I transfer the money today I'll satisfy my creditors and I'll pay it back next week. And at the end of this step you invariably have more than you can replace. And, the more you do this the more easy it becomes to transfer money to pay bills.

RESPONSES TO COMPLAINTS OF MISCONDUCT: THE APPLICATION OF FORMAL SANCTIONS

Self-regulatory disciplinary processes have often been criticized as excessively lenient. Abel (1986:403) points out that at each successive stage most of the unresolved grievances are disposed of with little or no punishment; only a trivial number of serious sanctions (lengthy suspension or disbarment) are ever imposed (see also Carlin 1966; Tisher et al. 1977; Reiter 1978). In the United States, Klein (1984:90) notes a pattern of minimal discipline of lawyers in the cases reported; and when sanctions do occur, punishment is likely to be lax. In Canada, a study by Reasons & Chappell (1985:51–52) finds that over 90% of complaints, on average, do not result in a formal citation or negative sanction, and of those cases resulting in formal citation, an even smaller percentage receive public sanctions (i.e. disbarment, suspension or limitation of practice imposed).

We have argued that issues of trust relations and embeddedness in the social organization of law practice influence decision-making to engage in misconduct. We now posit that these same issues can also influence regulatory decision-making. For instance, Shapiro argues that structural properties of trust relationships do not merely facilitate misconduct; but rather, "[t]hey confound systems of social control, impeding the discovery and investigation of misdeeds and complicating efforts to deter or punish offenders" (1990:353). Lawyers may also bridge physical and social distance in social exchange and are often further separated from their clients "by a pyramid of indirect ties" with intervening agents, such as numerous associate lawyers working on a single case (Shapiro 1990:249; see also, Heimer 1988:12). As Shapiro notes, ". . . it is not only for the privacy protections that organisations prove impervious to outside scrutiny. Structural features of organisations and inter-organisational networks that collectively offer fiduciary services—hierarchy, specialisation, internal diversification, task segregation and the like—mask illicit acts, create pockets of secrecy, and block the flow of information not only from outsiders, but from the potentially watchful eyes of insiders as well" (Shapiro, 1990:354). These features suggest that the 'powerful' have greater immunity from prosecution, as the characteristics of disciplined lawyers may reflect enforcement decisions rather than 'true' rates of misconduct. In this vein, Reasons & Chappell argue:

> Therefore, given their low status and power within the profession and increasingly marginal economic existence with increased mega-lawyering, certain types of lawyers are more likely to be publicly sanctioned, while others may be less likely to be discovered and sanctioned for similar behaviour. (1985:52).

We might therefore expect lawyers with reduced amounts of social capital to be more likely to be sanctioned by law societies.

The findings in Table 9.3 indicate a statistically significant relationship between professional embeddedness and sanctioning. For example, a relatively small proportion of cases against sole practitioners (48%), compared to small-firm (76%) and medium-sized (78%) partners, are resolved without being prosecuted. However, these findings are not conclusive evidence of the relationship between professional embeddedness and sanctioning because of the unexpected proportion of cases involving large-firm partners (24%) that were sanctioned.

TABLE 9.3 Professional Embeddedness and Disposition

	Professional position					
Disposition	Employee (firm or government employee)	Sole practitioner	Semi-auto-nomous lawyer	Small firm partner	Medium-sized firm partner	Large firm partner
Sanctioned	14	322	19	45	2	4
	13.6%	40.9%	25.0%	16.8%	11.1%	23.5%
Prosecuted	16	87	6	19	2	1
	15.5%	11.1%	7.9%	7.1%	11.1%	5.9%
Early resolution	73	378	51	204	14	12
	70.9%	48.0%	67.1%	76.1%	77.8%	70.6%
Number of cases	103	787	76	267	18	17
Column total (%)	8.1%	62.0%	6.0%	21.1%	1.4%	1.3%
$n = 1269$ $P<0.001$						

Only 406 of the sample cases resulted in sanctioning by the Law Society. However, there appears to be a distinct disparity between professional embeddedness and sanctioning suggesting that leniency is not invariant but rather related to the accumulation of social capital. For instance, partners from small-sized firms (17%) and medium-sized firms (11%) are less likely to be disciplined than semi-autonomous lawyers (25%) and, most noticeably, sole practitioners (41%). A sole practitioner describes some of his experiences resulting from disbarment. His comments suggest that without supportive organizational ties, sole practitioners receive a professional and personal setback that is long-lasting and certainly cannot be characterized as lenient treatment by the Law Society.

> . . . it [disbarment] crushes you to a pulp. You read the employment statistics in the newspaper and it doesn't do anything for you, but when you are not practicing and you are looking for a job it has a real impact on you. I've found a job, just a job, and it's hurt me tremendously, both in my pocketbook and personally. It's been devastating. The style of living that you're used to has disintegrated.
> The consequence for me in terms of the public reaction is that you have become a pariah in every sense of the word. You've gone from being well known and involved in many boards and groups . . . and at this stage you are like the person who voted for Richard Nixon. You go from knowing everyone, from the Mayor on down, to being virtually friendless due to the stigma of being a lawyer and having committed a serious offense. The reaction of the public is much more severe, though the legal community is very severe.

CONCLUSIONS

We have argued for the utility of reconceptualizing professional self-regulation and ethical behaviour in terms of the accumulation of social capital. Previously, professional conduct among lawyers has been approached from one of two perspectives. Traditional functionalist approaches emphasize the ability of law schools and the legal community to socialize practitioners to adhere to ethical standards and to dispense their expertise thereby balancing the individual's desire for monetary gain with ensuring clients' interests and advantage. From this perspective, professional associations are presumed to play a major role in formally establishing and monitoring ethical standards in all domains of legal practice. In contrast, critical perspectives view self-regulatory powers as a buffer against state controls and a strategy to enhance financial accumulation through the regulation of markets for legal services. Proponents of this perspective maintain that professional self-regulatory powers are ineffective for serving the interests of their members and the public and result in the lenient treatment of complaints of misconduct. Functionalist and critical perspectives illustrate two apparently paradoxical components of self-regulation: community service and the advancement of professional power through market control. Arguments perpetuating this conceptual anomaly mask rather than examine the underlying duality of professional powers and obligations (Abel 1989).

We maintain that the social capital approach provides a useful conceptual tool for reconsidering issues of self-regulatory controls underlying functionalist and critical perspectives. A social capital framework highlights the importance of the networks of social relations in communicating and enforcing norms of conduct and access to markets for legal services. Granovetter's (1985) concept of 'embeddedness', which is central to theories of social capital, provides new avenues for insights into structural aspects of professional misconduct and sanctioning. Lawyers are embedded within networks of social relations that provide ethical obligations, expectations (which are dependent upon trust relations), information channels and social norms (Coleman 1988). We have argued that the increased accumulation of social capital is more pronounced among larger law firms. As a result, sole practitioners, who have accumulated the least amount of social capital, are at greater risk of receiving complaints of misconduct and being prosecuted and punished by the Law Society.

Our overview of the social organization of law practice demonstrates that large law firms are better equipped than either sole practitioners or small firm lawyers to create and reproduce the forms of social capital essential for developing and maintaining lawyers' compliance with ethical standards. Larger firms offer an ongoing process of control through the 'embeddedness' of junior lawyers in networks of expectations and obligations. Firm lawyers, specifically junior associates, experience fewer opportunities for violations of trust, through the division of responsibility and the multiple layers of supervision, as well as through greater monitoring of their conduct via the 'partnership tournament' and their daily interactions with colleagues and superiors. Meanwhile, sole practitioners and small firm lawyers are not afforded embeddedness in such rich networks of social relations (in terms of status of clientele and sharing of vast expertise within the firm); they accumulate reduced social capital (i.e. reputation and clientele relations), and therefore endure greater exposure to opportunities for trust violations. Lacking the various internal control mechanisms that large firms employ to monitor and deal effectively with ethical violations, small firm lawyers and sole practitioners are more likely to be subject to direct control from the governing body of the profession, the Law Society. It is important to note that the characteristics of professional deviance may reflect equally on the process of social control as on the actual behaviour of lawyers. This suggests that, rather than directing research exclusively at the characteristics of complaints and recipients of complaints, we should attempt to understand individual offending within the broader context of the social organization of the legal profession (see Reasons & Chappell 1985:41). Therefore, we have examined the contemporary legal profession—reconsidering the self-regulation debate by exploring the social organization of the profession. Functionalist and critical theories suggest complimentary as well as competing predictions about the activities of self-regulating organizations. A social capital perspective is helpful in bringing these predictions together and in developing their implications for the changing stratification of legal practice and the profession's ability to regulate misconduct.

ACKNOWLEDGEMENTS

The authors thank John Hagan for comments on an earlier draft. Authors are listed alphabetically and do not reflect seniority. This research was partly facilitated by a University of British Columbia Humanities and Social Sciences research grant, and by the Socio-legal Research Unit, Faculty of Social Sciences, University of Calgary, Canada.

REFERENCES

Abel, R. L. (1986) Lawyers. In *Law and the Social Sciences* (Lipson, L. & Wheeler, S., Eds). Russell Sage Foundation: New York, pp. 369–444.

Abel, R. L. (1989) *American Lawyers*. Oxford University Press: New York.

Arrow, K. (1985) The economics of agency. In *Principals and Agents: The Structure of Business* (Pratt, J. W. & Zeckhauser, R. J., Eds). Harvard Business School Press: Boston.

Arthurs, H. W., Weisman, R. & Zemans, F. H. (1987) The Canadian legal profession. *American Bar Foundation Research Journal* 447–532.

Barber, B. (1978) Control and responsibility in the powerful professions. *Political Science Quarterly* 93, 599.

Bierig, J. R. (1983) Whatever happened to professional self-regulation? *American Bar Association Journal* 69, 616–619.

Brockman, J. & McEwen, C. (1990) Self-regulation in the legal profession: funnel in, funnel out, or funnel away, *Canadian Journal of Law and Society* 5, 1–46.

Bourdieu, P. (1977) *Outline of a Theory of Practice.* Cambridge University Press: Cambridge.

Bourdieu, P. (1986) The forms of capital. (R. Nice, Transl.). In *Handbook of Theory and Research of Education* (Richardson, J. C., Ed.). Greenwood Press: New York, pp. 241–258.

Carlin, J. E. (1966) *Lawyers' Ethics: A Survey of the New York City Bar.* Russell Sage Foundation: New York.

Carlin, J. E. (1994) *Lawyers on their Own: The Solo Practitioner in an Urban Setting.* Austin and Winfield Publishers, Inc: San Francisco.

Coleman, J. S. (1990) *Foundations of Social Theory.* Belknap Press of Harvard University Press: Cambridge.

Coleman, J. W. (1987) Toward an integrated theory of white-collar crime. *American Journal of Sociology* 93, 406–439.

Coleman, J. W. (1985) *The Criminal Elite: The Sociology of White Collar Crime.* St. Martin's Press: New York.

Coleman, J. S. (1988) Social capital in the creation of human capital. *American Journal of Sociology* 94 (suppl.), S95–S120.

Coleman, J. W. (1992) The theory of white-collar crime: from Sutherland to the 1990s. In *White-Collar Crimes Reconsidered* (Schlegel, K. & Weisburd, D., Eds). North Eastern University Press: Boston.

Croall, H. (1989) Who is the white-collar criminal. *British Journal of Criminology* 29, 157–174.

Croall, H. (1992) *White Collar Crime: Criminal Justice and Criminology.* Open University Press: Buckingham.

Curran, B. A. (1986) American lawyers in the 1980s: a profession in transition. *Law and Society Review* 20, 19–51.

Curran, B. A., Rosich, K. J., Carson, C. N. & Puccetti, M. C. (1985) *The Lawyer Statistical Report: A Statistical Profile of the U.S. Legal Profession in the 1980s.* American Bar Foundation: Chicago.

Curran, B. A. (1977) *The Legal Needs of the Public: The Final Report of a National Survey.* American Bar Foundation: Chicago.

Durkheim, E. (1933) *The Division of Labour.* Free Press: New York.

Elkins, J. R. (1985) Ethics: professionalism, craft, and failure. *Kentucky Law Journal* 73, 937–965.

Erlanger, H. (1980) The allocation of status within occupations: the case of the legal profession. *Social Forces* 58, 883–903.

Galanter, M. (1983) Larger than life: mega-law and mega-lawyering in the contemporary United States. In *The Professions: Lawyers, Doctors and Others* (Dingwall, R. & Lewis, P., Eds). Macmillan: London.

Galanter, M. & Palay, T. (1991) *Tournament of Lawyers: The Transformation of the Big Law Firm.* University of Chicago Press: Chicago.

Gellhorn, W. (1976) The abuse of occupational licensing. *University of Chicago Law Review* 44, 6–27.

Giddens, A. (1972) *Durkheim*. Fontana/Collins: Glasgow.

Gilson, R. J. & Mnookin, R. H. (1985) Sharing among the human capitalists: an economic inquiry into the corporate law firm and how partners split profits. *Stanford Law Review* 37, 313–392.

Granovetter, M. S. (1974) *Getting a Job: A Study of Contacts and Careers*. Harvard University Press: Cambridge.

Granovetter, M. S. (1985) Economic action and social structure: the problem of embeddedness. *American Journal of Sociology* 91, 481–510.

Hagan, J. (1994) *Crime and Disrepute*. Pine Forge Press: Thousand Oaks.

Hagan, J. & Parker, P. (1985) White-collar crime and punishment: the class structure and legal sanctioning of securities violations. *American Sociological Review* 50, 302–316.

Hagan, J., Huxter, M. & Parker, P. (1988) Class structure and legal practice: inequality and mobility among Toronto lawyers. *Law and Society Review* 22, 9–56.

Hagan, J., Zatz, M., Arnold, B. L. & Kay, F. (1991) Cultural capital, gender and the structural transformation of legal practice. *Law and Society Review* 25, 239–262.

Halliday, T. C., Powell, M. J. & Granfors, M. (1993) After minimalism: transformation of state bar associations, 1918–1950. *American Sociological Review* 58, 515–535.

Heimer, C. A. (1988) Dimensions of the agency relationship. Paper presented at the Public Choice meetings, San Francisco.

Heinz, J. P. & Laumann, E. O. (1982) *Chicago Lawyers: The Social Structure of the Bar*. Russell Sage Foundation: New York.

Klein, M. S. G. (1984) *Law, Courts, and Policy*. Prentice-Hall, Inc: Englewood Cliffs, NJ.

Larson, M. S. (1977) *The Rise of Professionalism: A Sociological Analysis*. University of California Press: Berkeley.

Macaulay, S. (1986) Private government. In *Law and the Social Sciences* (Lipson, L. & Wheeler, S., Eds). Russell Sage: New York, pp. 445–518.

Macaulay, S. (1963) Non-contractual relations in business: a preliminary study. *American Sociological Review* 28, 55.

McDowell, B. (1991) *Ethical Conduct and Professional's Dilemma*. Quorium Books: New York.

Moore, N. J. (1987) Review essay: professionalism reconsidered. *American Bar Foundation Research Journal* 4, 773–789.

Moe, T. M. (1984) The new economics of organization. *American Journal of Political Science* 28, 739–777.

Nelson, R. L. (1983) The changing structure of opportunity: recruitment and careers in large law firms. *American Bar Foundation Research Journal* 109–142.

Ostry, S. (1976) Competition policy and the self-regulating professions. In *The Professions and Public Policy* (Slayton, P. & Trebilcock, M. J., Eds). University of Toronto Press: Toronto, pp. 17–29.

Parsons, T. (1939) The Professions and Social Structure. *Social Forces* 17, 457–466.

Pepper, S. L. (1986) The lawyer's amoral ethical role: a defence, a problem, and some possibilities. *American Bar Foundation Research Journal* 4, 613–635.

Portes, A. & Sensenbrenner, J. (1993) Embeddedness and immigration: notes on social determinants of economic action. *American Journal of Sociology* 98, 1320–1350.

Powell, M. J. (1985) Developments in the regulation of lawyers: competing segments and market, client, and government controls. *Social Forces* 64, 281–305.

Powell, M. J. (1986) Professional divestiture: the cession of responsibility for lawyer discipline. *American Bar Foundation Research Journal* 1, 31–54.

Reasons, C. E. & Chappell, D. (1985) Continental capitalism and crooked lawyering. *Crime and Social Justice* 26, 38–59.

Reiter, B. J. (1978) *Discipline as a Means of Assuring Continuing Competence in the Professions and Tables of Discipline Activities by Profession: A Study of the Disciplinary Processes in the Professions of Accounting, Architecture, Engineering, and Law in Ontario*. Working Paper Number 11. Professional Organizations Committee: Toronto.

Rhode, D. L. (1981) Policing the professional monopoly: a constitutional and empirical analysis of unauthorized practice prohibitions. *Stanford Law Review* 34, 1–112.

Robb, G. (1992) *White Collar Crime in Modern England: Financial Fraud and Business Morality, 1845–1929*. Cambridge University Press: Cambridge.

Shapiro, S. P. (1990) Collaring the crime, not the criminal: reconsidering white-collar crime. *American Sociological Review* 55, 346–365.

Shapiro, S. P. (1987) The social control of impersonal trust. *American Journal of Sociology* 93, 623–658.

Sibenik, P. M. (1988) The black sheep: the disciplining of territorial and Alberta lawyers, 1885–1929. *Canadian Journal of Law and Society* 3, 109–139.

Smith, H. R. & Carroll, A. B. (1991) Organizational ethics: a stacked deck. In *Business Ethics in Canada* (2nd Edition) (Deborah, C. P. & Waluchow, W. J., Eds). Prentice-Hall Canada: Scarborough, pp. 130–135.

Steele, E. H. & Nimmer, R. T. (1976) Lawyers, clients, and professional regulation. *American Bar Foundation Research Journal* 917–1019.

Sutton, A. & Wild, R. (1985) Small business: white-collar villains or victims? *International Journal of the Sociology of Law* 13, 247–259.

Tisher, S., Bernabei, L. & Green, M. (1977). *Bringing the Bar to Justice: A Comparative Study of Six Bar Associations*. Public Citizen: Washington, D.C.

Usprich, S. J. (1975) *The Theory and Practice of Self-Regulation*. Communications and Justice, Canada. Privacy and Computers Task Force.

Weber, D. O. (1987) Still in good standing: the crisis in attorney discipline. *American Bar Association Journal* 73, 58–63.

Wilkins, D. B. (1992) Who should regulate lawyers? *Harvard Law Review* 105, pp. 801–887.

Wright, E. O. (1985) *Classes*. Verso: Thetford.

Xie, Y. & Manski, C. F. (1989) The logit model and response-based samples. *Sociological Methods and Research* 17, 283–302.

Yale, J. (1982) Public attitudes towards lawyers: an information perspective. In *Lawyers and the Consumer Interest: Regulating the Market for Legal Services* (Evans, R. G. & Trebilcock, M. J., Eds). Butterworths and Co., Ltd: Toronto.

Zemans, F. K. & Rosenblum, V. G. (1981) *The Making of a Public Profession*. American Bar Foundation: Chicago.

PART III

Empirical Works

Chapter 10

Social Capital, Structural Holes and the Formation of an Industry Network[*]

Gordon Walker, Bruce Kogut and Weijian Shan

Cox School of Business, Southern Methodist University, Dallas, Texas 75275, The Wharton School, University of Pennsylvania, Philadelphia, Pennsylvania 19104, J.P. Morgan, Hong Kong

This paper is of interest because of its comparison of social capital theory and structural hole theory in explaining network formation. The paper demonstrates, in the case of biotechnology start-ups, that network formation and industry growth are significantly influenced by the development and nurturing of social capital. The paper raises several important implications: structural hole theory may apply more to networks of market transactions than to networks of cooperative relationships, and that the study of the structure of interfirm collaborations over time requires an analysis of the network as a whole.

—Arie Y. Lewin

Abstract—*The formation of a network is determined by the opposition of two forces. The first is the reproduction of network structure as a general social resource for network members. The second is the alteration of network structure by entrepreneurs for their own benefit. The idea of reproduction is a conventional one in organizational sociology but has taken on increased importance due to the work of Bourdieu and Coleman. In contrast, Burt stresses the entrepreneurship of individual agents in exploiting structural holes that lie between constrained positions. Though complementary, the theories of social capital and*

[*] Reprinted by permission, the Institute for Operations Research and the Management Sciences (INFORMS), 901 Elkridge Landing Road, Suite 400, Linthicum, Maryland 21090–2909, USA.

structural holes have fundamentally different implications for network formation.

This paper investigates these theories by examining empirically the formation of the interorganizational network among biotechnology firms. We propose that network structure determines the frequency with which a new biotechnology firm (or startup) establishes new relationships. Network structure indicates both where social capital is distributed in the industry and where opportunities for entrepreneurial action are located. The reproduction of network structure depends on how startups value social capital compared to these opportunities. The critical test is, consequently, whether new relationships reproduce or alter the inherited network structure. We find strong support for the power of social capital in reproducing the network over time.

(Social Network; Social Capital; Structural Holes; Network Formation; Biotechnology)

INTRODUCTION

There is a fundamental conflict in the formation of a network. On the one hand, there are powerful forces toward the reproduction of dense regions of relationships. Reproduction is powerful because it is based upon the accumulation of social capital that requires the maintenance of and reinvestment in the structure of prevailing relationships. Yet, it is exactly this principle of conservation that generates the opportunities for entrepreneurial actors to bridge these regions and alter the structure of the network.

The formation of interfirm networks is a critical point of contention between otherwise complementary views of network structure. For Pierre Bourdieu (1980) and James Coleman (1990a), a network tends toward the reproduction of an inherited pattern of relationships due to the value *to the individual* in preserving social capital. The notion of social capital implies a strategy of maintaining the structure of existing relationships. To Bourdieu, "social capital is the sum of the resources, actual or virtual, that accrue to an individual or a group by virtue of possessing a durable network of more or less institutionalized relationships of mutual acquaintance and recognition" (Bourdieu and Wacquant 1992, p. 119). Similarly, Coleman notes that an advantage of modern society is that organizations provide stability, even if people are mobile. "The social invention of organizations," he notes, "having positions rather than persons as elements of the structure has provided one form of social capital that can maintain stability in the face of instability of individuals" (Coleman 1990b, p. 320). Similarly, firms may tend toward the reproduction of existing interfirm relationships to maintain the value of their inherited social capital.

Ronald Burt (1992) has a different view of the conservative tendency of networks toward reproduction. To him, the emphasis should be placed on the opportunities for entrepreneurs to exploit the "structural holes" between dense pockets of relationships in the network. It is exactly the structural constraints on what people know and can control, created by the inheritance of past relationships, that presents the opportunities for brokers. These brokers seek out partners with whom they can form unique, or "nonredundant," relationships that bring new information and the possibility of negotiating between competing groups. Through forming these new and unique relationships, entrepreneurs transform network structure.

The theories of social capital and structural holes have important implications for understanding the formation of relational networks in high growth, technology-intensive industries. In these industries, the extensive innovative activities of small firms (Bound et al. 1984, Acs and Audretsch 1989) push out industry boundaries into new subfields and increase the level of competition in traditional markets. However, opportunities for cooperation are created by unintended spillovers and intended agreements. Organizations are also related through their members' professional connections, joint suppliers and customers, and industry associations. These commonalities may be sources of information about competitor behavior, new technological developments, and other industry trends. However, formal agreements are the most salient and reliable indicator of resource and information sharing between firms and the origin of information regarding a firm's cooperative strategy. This information is critical for future decisions regarding cooperation for product development and commercialization.

The emergence of the network of formal cooperative agreements influences the course of industry growth and innovation. A swelling network of cooperative agreements may provide a positive externality to which potential investors respond (Hagedoorn and Schakenraad 1992). Also, since poorly positioned firms may have access to less than adequate resources to achieve their economic goals, the network may act as a selection mechanism, culling out some firms on the basis of their partners' weakness.

Early in the history of an industry, social capital among firms is low, and yet it is critical for the identification and acquisition of new relationships. Rapid industry growth aggravates this problem of acquiring valid information on other firms. In this early period, firms enter relationships according to their differences in need and capability, and these relationships initialize the network (Kogut et al. 1994). In biotechnology, for example, small startups have extensive expertise in technological innovation but lack resources in marketing and distribution possessed by large incumbents. Cooperation between a startup and incumbent gives each access to a resource necessary for product commercialization. Variation in firm-level attributes, especially the effective management of interfirm cooperation, contributes to network growth. But this contribution is partial. As an unintended outcome of their cooperative strategies, firms build the network that serves as a map for future association.

Network formation occurs as new relationships by incumbent firms or startups exploit the opportunities inherent in the network, reinforcing the existing network structure or reshaping it (Galaskiewicz and Wasserman 1981, Marsden

1985, Kogut et al. 1994). Two types of opportunity drive the process of network formation. First, network structure is a vehicle for inducing cooperation through the development of social capital. Firms draw upon network structure as a system-level resource to facilitate the governance of their relationships. Second, however, gaps in the pattern of information flows reflect potentially profitable opportunities for establishing connections between unlinked firms (Burt 1992). These opportunities stimulate entrepreneurial action to broker different segments of the industry.

The relative advantages and risks of inducing cooperation and exploiting brokering opportunities have an important implication for network formation. The structural conditions inducing cooperation free resources for the establishment of new relationships that in turn strengthen the structure as a useful system for controlling noncooperative behavior. If the structure is reinforced by new relationships, early patterns of cooperation should persist, resulting in a path dependence analogous to the imprinting effect on an industry of the era in which it was formed (Stinchcombe 1965). However, if some firms have specific capabilities for information arbitrage, they may choose to broker relationships between organizations in different regions of the network. In this case, the existing structure is not strengthened but repeatedly reshaped. The early pattern of relationships is blurred as more organizations are linked together.

To address these issues, we examine network formation in terms of its structural development, positing network structure as a social fact interacting with firm-level behavior over time. Our theory below follows most closely recent developments in structural sociology, especially the ideas of Coleman (1990) and Burt (1992). The tests of our propositions on data from the biotechnology industry show strong support for this approach to analyzing the process of network formation.

THEORY

Social Capital

Social capital is a means of enforcing norms of behavior among of individual or corporate actors and thus acts as a constraint, as well as a resource. Successful cooperation cannot be achieved in interorganizational relationships without constraints on the partners to perform according to each other's expectations. These constraints allow firms to risk greater investment with a partner in a relationship that would otherwise be hindered by the threat of opportunism. Lower levels of constraint are associated with difficulties in finding information about current or potential partners and therefore impede effective cooperation. Because cooperation is less frequent, network and consequently industry growth are hindered.

The network serves an important function in the development of social constraint directing information flows in the building and maintaining of social capital. Consider two extreme examples of network structure. If all firms in an industry had relationships with each other, interfirm information flows would lead quickly to established norms of cooperation. In such a dense network, information on deviant behavior would be readily disseminated and the behavior sanctioned. Firms in this industry would benefit equally from the network as a reputation building mechanism. Coleman (1992; see also Loury 1977, Bourdieu 1980) characterizes the extreme case of a fully connected network as "closed." Members of closed networks are connected to each other. In a closed network, firms as institutional actors have access to *social capital*, a resource that helps the development of norms for acceptable behavior and the diffusion of information about behavior. As the predictability of behavior is increased in a system that is already connected, self-seeking opportunism is constrained and cooperation enabled.

At the other extreme is an "open" network. Firms in open networks have no social capital on which to rely. If firms are not connected to each other extensively, norms regarding cooperation are more difficult to achieve, and information on behavior in relationships diffuses more slowly. Without relationships that determine behavior and carry information, firms are less able to identify or control opportunism. In support of this conjecture, Raub and Weesie (1990) use a Prisoner's Dilemma framework to show that a firm embedded in a closed network is constrained to be more cooperative than a comparable firm embedded in an open network. Similarly, Granovetter (1985) argues, through extensive examples, that embeddedness in dense networks leads to effective interfirm cooperation.

However, a common result of research on interfirm network structure is that it is neither uniformly dense nor sparse (Knoke and Rogers 1978, Van de Ven et al. 1979, Nohria and Garcia-Pont 1991). The structure is uneven, composed of regions that are more or less filled with relationships. The positions firms occupy in the network are embedded in these regions. Some firms occupy positions that are embedded in regions filled with relationships, indicating a high level of available social capital, but other positions are located in regions with few relationships, suggesting a low social capital. In such a complex network, the degree of social capital available to a firm is thus determined by its position in the network structure.

A central premise of the present paper is that social capital influences how the network forms. Network formation proceeds through the establishment of new relationships, building on the base of existing interfirm ties. Managing these ties requires ongoing attention and resources, of which organizations have only limited amounts. Social capital is thus a valuable additional asset for managing interorganizational relationships since it constrains a firm's partners to be more cooperative. Firms with less social capital are more vulnerable to opportunistic behavior and less able to build an enduring history of effective cooperative behavior with their partners over time. They, therefore, are required to expend greater time and effort monitoring the relationship. In contrast, the more social capital available to a firm, the fewer resources it needs to manage existing relationships and the more resources it can use to establish new ones. Coleman explains:

> Social capital is defined by its function. It is not a single entity but a variety of different entities, with two elements in common: they all consist of some aspect of social structures, and they facilitate certain actions of actors—whether persons or corporate actors—within the structure (Coleman 1988, p. S98).

In the present study, the social structure is the interorganizational network. The amount of social capital depends on the firm's position in the network structure. The action facilitated by this structure is the formation of new relationships. These arguments lead to the central proposition that firms in network positions with higher social capital are likely to have more relationships with new partners in the following time period.

An important question follows: how do a firm's new cooperative relationships affect the social capital available to it? If social capital improves cooperation, then it seems likely that firms would seek partners that are more rather than less constrained by network structure. That is, firms should try to increase the social capital available to them through the new relationships they establish. Thus, the value of social capital motivates firms to reproduce the existing network structure, building the social capital available to them.

The amount of social capital that can be increased by new relationships should be related to the base amount. Mayhew and Levinger (1976) show that network density tends to attenuate as the network grows larger. Thus, firms that begin a year with high social capital cannot improve their network positions as much as those firms that are structurally less advantaged. Therefore, the more social capital available to a firm, the less the firm can increase it through forming new relationships.

Structural Holes

Burt (1992) presents an alternative to the social capital argument. Emphasizing the importance of open rather than closed networks, he argues that the network positions associated with the highest economic return lie *between* not *within* dense regions of relationships. He calls these sparse regions *structural holes*. Structural holes present opportunities for brokering information flows among firms. These opportunities have greater economic payoffs because the broker's information advantage creates the potential for arbitrage in markets for goods and services.

Burt assumes that partner selection, more than social capital, determines effective cooperation between firms (Burt 1992, p. 16). Burt's argument subtly weaves between normative implications and positive theory. He places more emphasis than Bourdieu or Coleman on the strategic action of entrepreneurs. In Burt's view, the benefits of increasing social constraint from establishing relationships in closed regions of the network are offset by a reduction in independence. Firms with relationships in open networks have greater latitude in their cooperative strategies. These firms have higher economic gains because they are most able to parlay their superior, i.e., less redundant, information into increasing their control. Burt (1992, p. 37) argues:

> The higher the proportion of relationships enhanced by structural holes, the more likely and able the entrepreneurial player, and so the more likely it is that the player's investments are in high-yield relationships. The result is a higher aggregate rate of return on investments.

Structural hole theory therefore raises the problem of free-riding on the public good of social capital. Over time, firms will seek to exploit the holes between the islands of social capital in which relationships are embedded. As a result, the social capital available to an entrepreneur should decrease as the firm forms new relationships.

In each year, new relationships change network structure. Firms are much more likely to experience these changes as they happen, rather than all at once at the end of each year. If structural constraint represents social capital, the change in structure should determine the resources available to a firm to form new relationships. From Coleman and Bourdieu's perspective, increasing social capital in a period should enable more relationships. Alternatively, if, as Burt asserts, trust is determined only by careful partner selection, increases in social capital should have no effect on the number of new relationships. The arguments regarding network formation from both the social capital and structural hole perspectives are set out as propositions in Figure 10.1.

Control Variables

We test these propositions against the view that only organizational attributes determine interfirm cooperation. Since firms with similar attributes may occupy the same network position (Burt 1992, chapter 5), controlling for these attributes makes the analysis of network formation more robust. We identify five control variables: firm size, firm experience in cooperating with other firms, public offering of the firm's equity, the concentration of the firm's partners across global regions, and the average number of relationships of the firm's partners. The last two of these variables might be viewed more properly as partner characteristics. However, since they are aggregated by firm, they are included as firm-level controls.

Firm size is a measure of a firm's capacity to cooperate and a measure of its capacity to do without cooperation. Whereas Shan (1990) found a negative relationship between size and cooperation, Boyles (1969) and Powell and Brantley (1991) found that the frequency of cooperative relationships more than

Social Capital Perspective	Tests of Propositions
1. Firms with higher social capital are likely to have more relationships with new partners in the following time period.	Regression of new relationships on social capital (for incumbent and entering partners), see Table 10.6.
2. The more relationships a firm forms, the more likely its social capital will increase.	Regression of change in social capital on new relationships (for incumbents and entering partners), see Table 10.7.
3. The more social capital at the beginning of a time period, the lower the increase in social capital in the next time period.	Regression of change in social capital on level of social capital in the previous time period, see Table 10.7.
4. The more a firm's social capital increases over a time period, the more relationships it should have during this time period.	Regression of new relationships (for incumbent and entering partners) on change in social capital, see Table 10.6.
Structural Hole Perspective	
5. The more relationships a firm forms in a year, the more its social capital should decrease.	Regression of change in social capital on new relationships (for incumbents and entering partners), see Table 10.7.
6. Lack of empirical support for Proposition 4 above would be consistent with the Structural Hole Perspective.	Regression of new relationships (for incumbent and entering partners) on change in social capital, see Table 10.6.

FIGURE 10.1 List of Propositions Developed in the Theory Section and Their Tests

proportionally rises with size. Whether this difference rises from a nonlinearity in the association between size and the frequency of cooperation is partly addressed below.

Firm experience with cooperation, represented as the number of relationships it has established, presents a similar set of issues. The more relationships a firm has, the more it should know about how to manage them and so the less costly it should be to form new relationships. On the other hand, the lower incremental learning from new relationships may attenuate their formation. Again, we address this potential nonlinearity in our analysis.

The effect of issuing public equity on interfirm cooperation also has an ambiguous interpretation. First, a public offering is one form of getting resources. As a publicly held corporation, an entrepreneurial startup can probably go to the capital markets to finance projects, thereby decreasing the need to cooperate for this purpose. However, going public may also be an indicator of the legitimacy of the firm and signal a strong position in the network. Firms with higher legitimacy are likely to attract more partners for cooperative ventures.

Regional concentration represents how a firm's partners are distributed across three major global regions: United States, Europe, and Japan. As Hofstede et al. (1990) have shown, national cultures have a significant impact on work behavior. Managing partners across different regions should therefore be a more complex and difficult task than managing partners from the same region. The higher the concentration, the more partners from a single region are represented in the firm's organization set and the less difficult its task of managing them.

The experience of an organization's partners in interfirm agreements may influence its tendency to cooperate. The more agreements a firm's partners currently have, the more likely they are to be embedded in closed regions of the network and therefore to be constrained from acting opportunistically (see Baker 1991). However, partners with more relationships may also be less dependent on the firm for its information, goods and services, releasing normative pressures for equitable behavior. Partner experience may therefore either heighten or dampen the firm's tendency to cooperate.

Finally, in studying the reproduction of network structure, it is important to differentiate between relationships with partners entering the network and relationships with partners already in the network. The first are called entering partners and the second incumbent partners. Splitting partners in this way provides a robust test of the social capital argument. In the broadest sense, social capital releases resources to firms for further cooperation whether the firm engages partners that are new to the network or already network members. A narrower view of social capital suggests that social capital theory applies to network formation only for relationships with network incumbents. If this is the case, future research must consider network incumbency as a moderator of social capital's effect.

Data

We test these hypotheses by examining network formation in the biotechnology industry.[1] As most earlier studies have shown, the frequency of interfirm relationships in this industry is quite high, primarily between large established firms in a variety of businesses (pharmaceuticals, chemicals, agricultural products, food products) and small, entrepreneurial startup firms (Barley et al. 1992, Powell and Brantley 1992, Kogut et al. 1995). These relationships have been shown to increase the capabilities of startup firms, indicating a motivation for continuing cooperation (Shan et al. 1994). The incidence of these relationships has been explained both by network (Kogut et al. 1992) and firm-level variables (Shan 1990, Pisano 1990).

---

[1] Biotechnology includes all techniques for manipulating microorganisms. In 1973 Cohen and Boyer perfected genetic engineering methods, an advance that enabled the reproduction of a gene in bacteria. In 1975, Cesar Millstein and Georges Kohler produced monoclonal antibodies using hybridoma technology; and in 1976 DNA sequencing was discovered and the first working synthetic gene developed. These discoveries laid the technological base for the "new biotechnology."

Biotechnology is typical of industries with high rates of innovation and a significant entrepreneurial sector. The motivation for interfirm cooperation in these industries is quite strong, based on the complementarity of large and small firm capabilities. Because of the tremendous potential market for new biotechnology products, established companies have sought access to this new technology both by starting up biotechnology operations in-house and by forming cooperative agreements with startup firms, typically begun by scientists. Startup firms, in turn, have been willing to enter into cooperative agreements to provide established firms with new technologies and products in exchange for funding and to breach the barriers to entry in marketing, distribution, and government certification (Shan 1987). As firms become connected through these agreements, a broad network, typically global in scope, is formed.

To analyze network formation in biotechnology, we examine new relationships by startups rather than those by established firms, for several reasons.[2] Kogut et al. (1994) showed that startups have a much greater propensity to cooperate than established firms over time and correspondingly have more relationships. Network growth is therefore determined more by the expansion of startup organization sets than by the organization sets of their established firm partners. Startups also have much higher variability than established firms in number of relationships over time and are more central in the network (Barley et al. 1992).

Although startups have relationships with each other, their relationships with established firms are far more prevalent. Only six percent of relationships existing in 1988 were between startups. A description of the timing of foundings of startups and the pattern of their relationships with established firms is given in Tables 10.1 to 10.4. (See Appendix A for a description of data sources and the characteristics of our sample.) The distribution of cooperative relationships is shown in Tables 10.1 and 10.2. Startup foundings (shown in Table 10.1) lead the formation of these relationships by three to five years (shown in Table 10.2). Startup foundings peak in 1981, while the number of relationships with partners peaks in 1984 with a second mode in 1986. This second (1986) mode can be partly attributed to the entry into the network of established firms (see Table 10.3). The modal year for all relationships, by both new and incumbent startups, is also 1986 (see Table 10.4).

Since the process of developing, testing, and commercializing biotechnology products takes many years, cooperative relationships endure for a long time.

---

[2] Our definition of interfirm cooperative relationships is inclusive. For our purposes a cooperative relationship may be organized as equity or nonequity joint ventures, licensing, marketing or distribution agreements, or research and development limited partnerships (see Appendix A). Further, we define a relationship between firms rather than between projects so that new relationships entail new partners rather than old partners attached to new projects. This definition coincides with our focus on network formation, rather than the evolution of a single interfirm relationship.

TABLE 10.1 Number of Sampling Startups Founded in Each Year

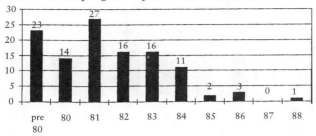

TABLE 10.2 Number of Sample Startups Entering Network in Each Year

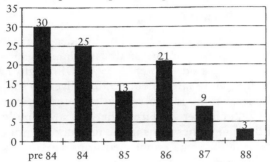

TABLE 10.3 Number of Established Firms Entering Network in Each Year

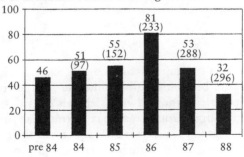

In this table, the number of established firms in 1988 does not include 24 which left the network between 1986 and 1988.

Only 18 percent of the relationships in the industry from its beginning until 1988 had a fixed duration (that is, their termination date was formally specified when they were initiated); and only 31 percent of fixed duration relationships ended before 1988. Furthermore, only 11 percent of the relationships with unfixed durations were terminated before 1988. Thus, in 1988 some 85 percent of all the agreements that had ever been formed were still in effect.

TABLE 10.4 Number of Cooperative Relationships Formed in Each Year

METHOD

Measuring Social Capital

Our measure of social capital is based on the idea of structural equivalence, which has been frequently used in the analysis of interorganizational networks (Knoke and Rogers 1978, Van de Ven et al. 1979, DiMaggio 1986, Schrum and Withnow 1988, Nohria and Garcia-Pont 1990, Oliver 1990). Determining the structural equivalence of firms is also central to network analysis in structural hole theory (Burt 1992, chapter 2). Firms that are structurally equivalent have relationships with the same other firms in the network. In principle, structurally equivalent startups have the same established firms as partners and structurally equivalent established firms have the same startups as partners. The emergence of this type of structure therefore depends on the pattern of partner sharing.[3] An idealized example of this type of network structure is shown in Figure 10.2. Rows represent startups and columns their established firm partners. An "X" indicates a relationship and a "O" the absence of a relationship. Note that the intersections of row and column groups are either dense with relationships or sparse.

A network where all groups of firms are densely related to each other is rare, since such it would be almost fully connected. Therefore, measuring structural equivalence in practice almost always depends on an assessment of relative partner overlap. While some groups may have firms that share almost all their partners, firms in other groups may share hardly any of their partners.

One way of measuring how much firms in a group share partners is to examine the dispersion of intergroup densities around the network average. A group of firms that share partners extensively should have dense relationships with some partner groups and sparse or no relationships with other partner

---

[3]   We do not observe the actual communication of information regarding partner behavior among startups. However, conversations with board members of startup firms confirm that such communication is quite common (Hamilton 1992).

groups. This pattern is found for all the groups, both row and column, in Figure 10.2. An equation that calculates density dispersion is:

$$G_i = n_i \sum_j m_j (d_{ij} - d^*)^2. \tag{1}$$

In this equation, G_i is the measure of the dispersion of intergroup densities for the ith group in the network, n_i is the number of firms in the ith group, m_j is the number of partners in the jth partner group, d_{ij} is the density of the intersection of the ith and jth groups, and d^* is the overall density of the network.[4] A higher value of G_i indicates greater dispersion of a group's densities and therefore more partner sharing by the firms in group i. Note that this measure penalizes small groups of firms with small partner groups.

To show how the structure of the biotechnology network differs from the idealized network of Figure 10.2, we use a method that builds on G_i to analyze the biotechnology network of relationships formed before 1984. Since G_i reflects the deviation of intergroup relationships from the average network density, summing G_i over all groups produces a measure of network structure:[5]

$$G = \sum_i \sum_j n_i m_j (d_{ij} - d^*)^2.$$

The details of the methodology are presented in Appendix B, which shows how the pre-1984 network was analyzed.

Figure 10.3a shows the partitioned raw data. There are four startup groups and six partner groups. Group I has the largest number of firms, which have relationships predominantly with partner groups A, B, and C. Because the number of relationships Group I has with each of the partner groups is much smaller than the number of possible relationships, the densities of these intergroup relationships are quite low (see Figure 10.3b). Unlike Group I, Groups II, III and IV are densely related to their partner groups. Group II contains only one firm, the only startup to have agreements with Group E. Furthermore, this firm has only one other relationship in the network, with a partner in Group F. Finally, both Groups III and IV are composed of several startups that have established relationships with Groups D and F, respectively.

---

[4] Density is defined as: k/mn, where k is the number of actual relationships a group of n structurally equivalent startups and a group of m structurally equivalent partners. The densities of each intersection can be calculated to form a density matrix. This matrix is the basis for the construction of a blockmodel, a binary matrix representing relations among groups of structurally equivalent firms in the network (White et al. 1976, Arabie et al. 1978). Blockmodels typically are constructed only for symmetric networks—i.e., networks that are formed by relationships between only one type of firm, say, startups. Consequently, we do not develop a conventional block-model for our data.

[5] This function has been used to analyze sparse networks in a number of studies (Boorman and Levitt 1983, Walker 1985, 1988) which found it to have strong construct and predictive validity.

Partners

Startups		Group 1	Group 2	Group 3	Group 4
	Group 1	xxxooxxx xxxxooxx oxxxxoxx	oooooooooooo ooooooooooo oooooooooooo	oooooooooooo oooooooooooo ooooooooo	oooooooooooo oooooooooooo oooooo
	Group 2	oooooooooooo oooooooooooo ooooooooo	xxxxxxooox xxxoxxxxox xxoxxxoxxx	oooooooooooo oooooooooooo ooooooooo	xxxxxxxoox xoxxoxxxox xxxxxoxxox
	Group 3	oooooooooooo oooooooooooo ooooooooo	oooooooooooo oooooooooooo ooooooooo	ooxxxxxxxxx xxxxoxxxxo xoxoxxoxxxx	oooooooooooo oooooooooooo oooooo
	Group 4	oooooooooooo oooooooooooo ooooooooo	oooooooooooo oooooooooooo ooooooooo	oooooooooooo oooooooooooo ooooooooo	xxxxxoxoox xxoxxoxxxo oxxxxoxxox

FIGURE 10.2 An Idealized Network Structure Based on Structural Equivalence

Only a few firms contribute significantly to the structure of biotechnology network. To demonstrate this, we divide Equation (1) by Equation (2) to get a measure of each group's percentage contribution to network structure. This variable, bounded by zero and one, represents the dispersion of startup group densities normalized by a measure of how structured the network is in a time period.

Startup groups in the network occupy distinct positions which vary in their social capital. A group's contribution to network structure in a time period indicates how tightly packed are its relationships with partners. Higher density means greater partner sharing within a startup group, creating a stronger focal point for conversation.[6] Startups in groups with higher contributions have greater social capital available to them.[7] If a group's contribution to network structure increases with new relationships, we assume that startups have chosen partners so that social capital is increased. However, increased social capital also means increased social constraint. Following Burt's argument (Burt 1982, p. 57), if startups are searching for lower social constraint, the startup group's contribution to network structure should decline over time.

Testing the Propositions

Although structurally equivalent startups that occupy the same position will have the same amount of social capital, they will differ in the number of

---

[6] See endnote 3.

[7] This measure of social capital is structural, consistent with Coleman's (1990) usage and arguments. Alternative measures based on attributes of specific interfirm relationships may be useful when global network data are not available (see Baker 1990).

relationships they establish in each year and in the control variables. We therefore designed the empirical tests at the firm level, consistent with the way they are stated, over each pair of years from 1984 to 1988. The data are pooled cross-sections of year pairs from 1984 to 1988; e.g., 1984–1985. Dummy variables for each year pair are included to correct for time-period effects.

We use several regression techniques: negative binomial, two-stage least squares and generalized least squares regression. Like Poisson regression, the negative binomial model treats the dependent variable as a count variable but allows for a direct measure of heterogeneity (see Cameron and Trivedi 1986). Estimating heterogeneity not only relaxes the stringent Poisson assumption of equal mean and variance in the error term but also accounts for omitted variable bias.

However, the negative binomial model does not correct for the potential bias due to the simultaneity of new relationships and change in social capital over time. To make this correction, we assume that the dependent variable

```
                                    Partner Groups

                        A             B   C       D       E         F
           OOOOOOOOOOOOOOOOOOOOO •OO •OOXOO •OOOOO •OOOOOO•OOOOOOOOO
           OXOOOOOOOOOOOOOOOOOOO •OO •OOOOO •OOOOO •OOOOOO•OOOOOOOOO
           OOOOOXOOOOOOOOOOOOOOO •OO •XOOOO •OOOOO •OOOOOO•OOOOOOOOO
           OOOOOOOOOOOOOOOOOOXO  •OO •OOOOO •OOOOO •OOOOOO•OOOOOOOOO
           OOOOOOOOOOOOOOOOOOX   •OO •OOOOO •OOOOO •OOOOOO•OOOOOOOOO
           OOOXOOOOOOOOOOOOOOOO  •OO •OOOXX •OOOOO •OOOOOO•OOOOOOOOO
           OOOOOOXXOOOOOOOOOOOO  •OX •OOOOO •OOOOO •OOOOOO•OOOOOOOOO
           OOOOOOOOXOOOOOOOOOOO  •OO •OOOOO •OOOOO •OOOOOO•OOOOOOOOO
           OOOXOOOOOOOOOOOOOOOO  •OO •OOOOO •OOOOO •OOOOOO•OOOOOOOOO
      I    OOOOOOOOOOOOOOOOOOOO  •OO •OOOOO •OOOOO •OOOOOO•OOOOOXOOO
           OOOOOOOOOOOOOOOOOOOO  •XO •OOOOO •OOOOO •OOOOOO•OOOOOOOOO
           OOOOOOOOOOXOOOOOOOOO  •OO •OOOOO •OOOOO •OOOOOO•OOOOOOOOO
 Startup   XOOOOOOOOOOOOOOOOOOO  •OO •OOOOO •OOOOO •OOOOOO•OOOOOOOOO
 Groups    OOOOOOOOOOOOOOOOOOOO  •OX •OOOOO •OOOOO •OOOOOO•OOOOOOOOO
           OOXOOOOOOOOOOOOOOOOO  •OO •OOOOO •OOOOO •OOOOOO•OOOOOXOOO
           OOOOOOOOOOOXOOXOOO    •OO •OXOOO •OOOOO •OOOOOO•OOOOOOOOO
           OOOOOOOOOXOOOOOOOOO   •OO •OOOOO •OOOOO •OOOOOO•OOOOOOOOO
           OOOOOOOOOOOXOOOOOO    •OO •OOOOO •OOOOO •OOOOOO•OOOOOOOOO
           OOOOOOOOOOOOOOOOOO    •XO •OOOOO •OOOOO •OOOOOO•OOOOOOOOO
           OOOOOOOOOOOOOOOXOO    •OO •OOOOO •OOOOO •OOOOOO•OOOOOOOOO
           OOOOOOOOOOOXOOOOOO    •OO •OOOOO •OOOOO •OOOOOO•OOOOOOOOO
           OOOOOOOOOOOOXOOOO     •OO •OOOOO •OOOOO •OOOOOO•OOOOOOOOO
     ----------------------------------------------------------------
      II   OOOOOOOOOOOOOOOOOOOO  •OO •OOOOO •OOOOO •XXXXX•XOOOOOOO
     ----------------------------------------------------------------
           OOOOOOOOOOOOOOOOOOOO  •OO •OOOOO •OXXXO •OOOOOO•OOOOOOOOO
     III   OOOOOOOOOOOOOOOOOOOO  •OO •OOOOO •XXOOX •OOOOOO•OOOOOOOOO
     ----------------------------------------------------------------
     IV    OOOOOOOOOOOOOOOOOOOO  •OO •OOOOO •OOOOO •OOOOOO•XOXOXOOOO
           OOOOOOOOOOOOOOOOOOOO  •OO •OOOOO •OOOOO •OOOOOO•XXOOOXXOO
           OOOOOOOOOOOOOOOOOOOO  •OO •OOOOO •OOOOO •OOOOOO•XOOOXOOOO
           OOOOOOOOOOOOOOOOOOOO  •OO •OOOOO •OOOOO •OOOOOO•OOOXOXOOX
           OOOOOOOOOOOOOOOOOOOO  •OO •OOOOO •OOOOO •OOOOOO•OOOXOXOXO
```

FIGURE 10.3A Partitioned Raw Data for 1983 Network

	A	B	C	D	E	F
I	0.05	0.09	0.05	0	0	0.01
II	0	0	0	0	1	0.11
III	0	0	0	0.6	0	0
IV	0	0	0	0	0	0.33

FIGURE 10.3B Density Matrix of 1983 Network

is not a count but continuous and use two-stage least squares. Generalized least squares permits corrections for serial correlation in the error term and unobserved firm-level effects. Figure 10.1 shows how these regressions test the propositions based on the theories of social capital and structural holes.

RESULTS

Table 10.5 shows the means, standard deviations and correlations among the variables, and Table 10.6 presents the findings for the regressions. Five of the explanatory variables have consistent results: the social capital and change in social capital, startup experience, partner experience, and public offering (IPO). Both network variables explain the frequency of new relationships strongly, as social capital theory predicts. Interestingly, neither startup nor partner experience has an effect on new relationships, controlling for the network variables.[8] This finding shows that new relationships are not explained by how many relationships a startup or its partner has, but how the relationships are distributed across partner groups. Public offering has a positive, significant effect on establishing relationships with entering partners but no influence on relationships with incumbents.

The results for startup size and regional concentration are not as clear. Neither has an effect for incumbent partners. However, for entering partners, the results for the two techniques differ in significance but not in sign.

Table 10.7 reports the results of testing whether social capital and the number of new startup relationships influence change in social capital. Included in the model are dummy variables for each year and a variable indicating the number of firms in a startup's group. Controlling for this variable is necessary since G (in Equation (1)) is linearly related to it. The two-stage least squares regression shows that more new relationships increase social capital. Also, the increase in social capital is lower when a startup has more social capital in the beginning period.

---

[8]   To test whether the effect of startup experience on new startup relationships might be quadratic, we included experience^2 in the equation, without significant results. We made the same test for startup size, also without significant results.

TABLE 10.5 Means, Standard Deviations and Correlations

Variables	MN	STD				Correlations					
1. Social Capital	0.039	0.036	1.00								
2. Change in Social Capital	−0.001	0.027	−0.52	1.00							
3. Number of Relationships with Entering Partners in Each Period	0.73	1.16	0.25	0.17	1.00						
4. Number of Relationships with Incumbent Partners in Each Period	0.52	0.95	0.17	0.14	0.27	1.00					
5. Size	170.08	245.99	0.38	0.01	0.27	0.07	1.00				
6. IPO	0.74	0.44	0.12	0.01	0.19	0.12	0.16	1.00			
7. Regional Concentration	1.79	0.61	0.03	−0.001	0.04	0.03	0.41	0.10	1.00		
8. Startup Experience	3.94	4.64	0.55	−0.08	0.14	0.18	0.41	0.26	0.05	1.00	
9. Partner Experience	2.45	1.52	−0.09	0.04	−0.14	−0.11	−0.12	0.12	0.06	0.03	1.00
10. Number of Startups in Group	40.16	28.09	−0.65	0.37	−0.19	−0.13	−0.20	−0.06	−0.07	−0.32	0.14	1.00

Startup propensities to cooperate may vary to some extent. There may be unobserved firm-level factors that influence how frequently cooperation occurs. The *a* term in the negative binomial regression captures these unobserved variables to a degree.

To explore this problem further, we regressed the frequency of new startup relationships on the explanatory variables including firm-specific dummy variables to account for unobservable effects. Since our sample draws from a larger population of startup firms, a random effects specification is appropriate. The hypotheses are therefore tested, without simultaneity, using Generalized Least Squares. The results of this GLS regression are stronger than those of the negative binomial and two-stage least squares regressions.[9] Consequently, we can be reasonably confident that unobserved firm-level variation in the propensity to cooperate does not confound our findings.

---

[9] The GLS results are not shown and are available from the authors on request.

TABLE 10.6A Results for Regression Explaining New Startup Relationships

Explanatory Variables:	Entering Partners		Incumbent Partners	
	Negative Binomial	2SLS[1]	Negative Binomial	2SLS
Constant	-1.35^{***}	-0.15	-1.97^{***}	-0.13
	$(0.42)^2$	(0.28)	(0.67)	(0.23)
Social Capital	8.08^*	17.94^{***}	13.08^{**}	11.82^{***}
	(4.27)	(5.39)	(5.32)	(4.26)
Change in Social Capital	13.06^{***}	27.52^{***}	18.84^{***}	16.95^{***}
	(3.12)	(8.26)	(5.74)	(6.28)
Startup Experience	0.002	-0.03	0.023	0.0042
	(0.031)	(0.024)	(0.038)	(0.02)
Partner Experience	-0.057	-0.035	0.089	-0.59
	(0.057)	(0.043)	(0.27)	(0.38)
Size	0.0004	0.0004	-0.001	-0.0004^*
	(0.0003)	(0.0003)	(0.0006)	(0.0003)
IPO	0.79^{***}	0.39^{***}	0.39	0.12
	(0.23)	(0.15)	(0.27)	(0.13)
Regional Concentration	0.09	0.0004	0.089	0.0001
	(0.15)	(0.0001)	(0.27)	(0.0009)
D86	0.52^{**}	0.73^{**}	1.04^{***}	0.64^{***}
	(0.26)	(0.25)	(0.39)	(0.21)
D87	-0.30	-0.056	0.77^*	0.39^{**}
	(0.29)	(0.24)	(0.44)	(0.20)
D88	-0.99^{***}	-0.34	0.26	0.16
	(0.35)	(0.26)	(0.48)	(0.22)
α	0.081		0.59^*	
	(0.13)		(0.32)	
F-value		12.49		5.27
df		$10,262$		$10,261$
R^2		0.32		0.16
Adj. R^2		0.29		0.13

[1] 2SLS coefficients are adjusted for serial correlation in the error term.
R^2 terms pertain to unadjusted estimates.
[2] Standard errors are reported in parentheses.
 $^*p < 0.10$
 $^{**}p < 0.05$
$^{***}p < 0.01$

TABLE 10.6B

Explanatory Variables:	Entering Partners		Incumbent Partners	
	Negative Binomial	OLS[1]	Negative Binomial	OLS
Constant	−1.08***	0.51***	−1.50**	−0.32*
	(0.40)[2]	(0.19)	(0.69)	(0.17)
Social Capital				
Change in Social Capital				
Startup Experience	0.029	0.026*	0.056	0.042***
	(0.020)	(0.016)	(0.037)	(0.014)
Partner Experience	−0.057	−0.037	−0.12	−0.057
	(0.066)	(0.044)	(0.084)	(0.039)
Size	0.0008***	0.0009***	−0.0002	−0.0001
	(0.0003)	(0.0003)	(0.0006)	(0.0003)
IPO	0.87***	0.47***	0.47*	0.16
	(0.24)	(0.15)	(0.27)	(0.13)
Regional Concentration	0.17	0.0004	0. 18	0.0003
	(0.16)	(0.001)	(0.28)	(0.0009)
D86	0.15	0.26	0.63	0.35*
	(0.23)	(0.19)	(0.42)	(0.18)
D87	−0.67***	−0.45**	0.31	0.13
	(0.26)	(0.19)	(0.42)	(0.17)
D88	−1.43***	−0.79***	−0.26	−0.14
	(0.29)	(0.19)	(0.48)	(0.18)
α	−0.27		0.99**	
	(0.17)		(0.40)	
F-value		9.94		3.15
df		8,263		8,263
R^2		0.22		0.087
Adj. R^2		0.19		0.059

[1] The OLS regression results reported are adjusted for autocorrelated error. The F-statistic reported is not adjusted for this error.

DISCUSSION

We have posed two theories to explain the incidence of new relationships. One theory emphasizes the positive effect of social capital, as structural constraint, on new cooperation. The other argues that highly constrained cooperation has lower rewards and is therefore avoided. Our analysis of biotechnology startups shows that social capital theory is the better predictor of

TABLE 10.6C

Explanatory Variables:	Entering Partners		Incumbent Partners	
	Negative Binomial	$2SLS^1$	Negative Binomial	2SLS
Constant	-0.94^{***}	0.15	-1.87^{***}	-0.13
	(0.26)	(0.18)	(0.39)	(0.16)
Social Capital	11.91^{***}	14.75^{***}	12.17^{***}	9.62^{***}
	(2.34)	(1.97)	(3.73)	(1.77)
Change in Social Capital	17.22^{***}	21.14^{***}	18.16^{***}	13.09^{***}
	(3.41)	(2.66)	(5.003)	(2.38)
D86	0.72^{***}	0.69^{***}	1.12^{***}	0.60^{***}
	(0.25)	(0.19)	(0.38)	(0.17)
D87	-0.1	-0.095	0.75^{*}	0.36^{**}
	(0.28)	(0.19)	(0.38)	(0.17)
D88	-0.80^{**}	-0.42^{**}	0.27	0.10
	(0.32)	(0.19)	(0.41)	(0.17)
α	-0.24		0.75^{**}	
	(0.16)		(0.34)	
F-value		22.93		9.82
df		5,266		5,266
R^2		0.30		0.16
Adj. R^2		0.29		0.14

[1] The 2SLS regression results reported are adjusted for autocorrelated error. The F-statistic reported is not adjusted for this error.

cooperation over time. More constrained firms cooperate with partners that can be firmly embedded in the historical network structure. The network is thus increasingly structured over time. Network formation, and industry growth, are therefore significantly influenced by the development and maintenance of social capital.

Why have biotechnology startups chosen to increase social capital rather than exploit structural holes? First, relationships in the biotechnology network last a long time. Long durations entail extensive, ongoing interaction over a broad range of technical and commercial problems. Were partners to behave in a self-interested way during the course of such a long relationship, a substantial investment in time and effort would be jeopardized. Structural stability is therefore desirable. In a network where relationships are of shorter duration, the structure would undoubtedly be less stable and less available as a resource for action. Enduring interfirm ties sustain the structure that facilitates new cooperation. Second, structural hole theory may apply more to networks of market transactions than to networks of cooperative relationships. Lacking the

TABLE 10.7 Results of Two-stage Least Squares Regression on Change in Social Capital

Explanatory Variables:	*Dependent Variable: Change in Social Capital*	
Constant	0.0043	0.0049
	(0.0054)	(0.0077)
Number of Startup Relationships with Entering Partners	0.018^{***}	
	(0.0038)	
Number of Startup Relationships with Incumbent Partners		0.036^{***}
		(0.017)
Existing Social Capital	-0.44^{***}	-0.41^{***}
	(0.056)	(0.086)
Number of Startups in Group	0.0001^{*}	0.0003^{**}
	(0.00007)	(0.0001)
D86	-0.025^{***}	-0.037^{***}
	(0.0054)	(0.010)
D87	-0.0047	-0.023^{***}
	(0.0051)	(0.009)
D88	0.0018	-0.014^{*}
	(0.0054)	(0.0075)

$^{*}p < 0.10$
$^{**}p < 0.05$
$^{***}p < 0.01$

requirement to cooperate over time, firms may not experience structural constraint in their relationships. Third, interfirm relationships in biotechnology are based on a kind of mutual dependence that may prevent either startups or established firms from gaining control over the other. Biotechnology startups and their established firm partners have complementary resources that are jointly necessary for product development and commercialization.

Such mutuality may not be present to such an extent in other technology-intensive industries. For example, Kogut et al. (1992) argue that cooperative agreements between startups and established firms in the semiconductor industry are based on the technical standards which large firms own. Large firms dominate the network structure of the semiconductor industry as they compete for technological dominance through their alliances with startups. In such a structure, embeddedness clearly has a different meaning than in the biotechnology network (compare, e.g., Marsden 1983).

Our results lead to the conclusion that some firms continuously improve their already strong social endowments, although at a decreasing rate, while other firms have less social capital to draw upon in forming new relationships.

This conclusion holds for relationships with both incumbent and newly-entering partners, indicating that the effect of network structure on forming new relationships is not moderated by partner incumbency. Although the results for network formation are similar for both incumbent and entering partners, these partner types differ in two important ways. First, entering partners tend to establish relationships with startups whose equity is publicly traded while the choice of incumbents does not depend on the characteristics of individual startups. *IPO* (Initial Public Offering) appears to signal organizational legitimacy to entering firms rather than represent a source of potential startup capital substituting for a partner's financial resources. A second difference between incumbent and entering partners is in the time trends. For relationships with entering firms, the signs on the year dummy variables turn from negative to positive to negative over the four years. Relationships with entering partners decline in the later years simply because there are fewer firms coming into the network. But, as shown in Table 10.4, the trend for incumbent partners remains positive, though declining in the later years. When there are fewer entrants, incumbent partners attract more attention.

Path Dependence in Network Formation

The firms in the industry recreate a stable network structure whose foundation was laid at an early point in the industry's history. Firms' early partner choices thus have a significant impact on the course of future cooperation. To examine this conjecture, we analyze and compare the network structures from 1984 to 1988. Examining structural equivalence over time indicates how much network structure is altered by network growth through entry and new relationships among incumbents.

Table 10.8 presents cross-tabulations showing whether pairs of firms remained structurally equivalent or nonequivalent from one year to the next. Entries on the main diagonal in each table indicate persistence. To assess whether these entries are larger than the off-diagonal entries, we calculated the cross-product ratio for each table. The cross-product ratio is a commonly used statistic for estimating the degree of association between two variables (see Agresti 1984, p. 15). A cross-product ratio of zero indicates no association between the variables, and values of the ratio greater than one imply a positive relationship. Because the logarithm of the cross-product ratio is less skewed than the ratio itself, we use the log of the ratio to test for structural persistence (Wickens 1989, pp. 218–222). These log ratios are all positive and strongly significantly different from zero for both startups and partners. Except for the 1983–1984 period, the tables show that once a pair of startups are structurally equivalent, the odds are significant that they will continue to be so. Furthermore, the reverse is also generally true: if a pair of startups are not structurally equivalent, they are likely to remain this way.

TABLE 10.8 Structural Equivalence of Organizations over Time

1. Startups

1984	Str. eq.	Not. Str. eq.		1985	Str. eq.	Not. Str. eq.		1986	Str. eq.	Not. Str. eq.
Str. eq. 1983	52*	190		Str. eq. 1984	189	99		Str. eq. 1985	917	528
Not. Str. eq.	4	189		Not. Str. eq.	605	592		Not. Str. eq.	270	631

Log cross product ratio = 2.56, Std. error = 0.53

Log cross product ratio = 0.62, Std. error = 0.14

Log cross product ratio = 1.40, Std. error = 0.09

1987	Str. eq.	Not. Str. eq.		1988	Str. eq.	Not. Str. eq.
Str. eq. 1986	1162	1067		Str. eq. 1987	1609	519
Not. Str. eq.	426	1261		Not. Str. eq.	903	1722

Log cross product ratio = 1.17, Std. error = 0.07

Log cross product ratio = 1.78, Std. error = 0.07

2. Established Firms

1984	Str. eq.	Not. Str. eq.		1985	Str. eq.	Not. Str. eq.		1986	Str. eq.	Not. Str. eq.
Str. eq. 1983	56	187		Str. eq. 1984	141	270		Str. eq. 1985	257	651
Not. Str. eq.	15	777		Not. Str. eq.	187	4058		Not. Str. eq.	377	10190

Log cross product ratio = 2.74, Std. error = 0.03

Log cross product ratio = 2.43, Std. error = 0.13

Log cross product ratio = 2.47, Std. error = 0.09

1987	Str. eq.	Not. Str. eq.		1988	Str. eq.	Not. Str. eq.
Str. eq. 1986	339	1097		Str. eq. 1987	368	1561
Not. Str. eq.	784	24808		Not. Str. eq.	971	37855

Log cross product ratio = 2.28, Std. error = 0.03

Log cross product ratio = 2.22, Std. error = 0.07

*Entries in cells are pairs of organizations

Predicting partner groups over time depends mostly on the persistence of structural dissimilarity, however. Between 1987 and 1988, for example, the odds that a pair of partners will continue to be structurally equivalent are roughly one to five (368/1561), while the odds that they will remain structurally nonequivalent are roughly forty to one (37855/971). The reason for this pattern is the large number of entering partners relative to partners already in the network.

The structural development of the industry, based on the building and reinforcement of social capital, offers a simple insight into the rigidity of organizational forms. Since an organization depends on the resources available in its network, organizational inertia may be less an inherent property of organizations than a product of the organization's position in a rigid network. The persistence of these positions, as shown in Table 10.8, suggests that a startup's characteristics may endure because of structural conditions (see Shan et al. 1994).

CONCLUSION

Social capital, as outlined by Coleman and Bourdieu, is a powerful concept for understanding how interfirm networks in emerging industries are formed. It is important to note that network formation need not lead towards an optimal structure for innovation or product commercialization.[10] Although there is evidence that interfirm cooperation and startup patent activity are related (Shan et al. 1994), the local benefits of partner sharing may not be distributed so that the most productive and useful technological advances are commercialized successfully.

The importance of network formation for interfirm cooperation has important consequences for organization theory. Taking the transaction as the unit of analysis is inadequate to capture the structural effects we have identified. The study of interfirm cooperative agreements over time requires an analysis of the network as a whole.

The persistence of network structure has subtle implications for entrepreneurial behavior. Structural persistence does not imply that firms are equally situated to exploit profitable opportunities for cooperation. Because the structure is relatively inert, brokering positions are established early in the history of the network. In fact, if structure did not persist, all firms would be potential brokers but with few enduring opportunities. Given the relative fixity of brokering positions, the kind of entrepreneurship Burt proposes, as the exploitation of structural holes, should be especially profitable. An intriguing hypothesis is that the pursuit of these rewards explains the current wave of mergers and acquisitions among biotechnology firms.

The persistence of the past is welcomed if alternative futures look less promising, especially scenarios with free-rider or prisoner-dilemma problems. But social capital can also be associated with encumbering commitments that impede competition and change. If biotechnology firms could rewrite their histories of cooperation, few would be surprised that an alternative path of network formation would emerge. It is this gap between the desired and the actual that expresses most clearly the idea that structure both enables and constrains entrepreneurial ambitions.

ACKNOWLEDGMENT

This research was supported through a grant from AT & T administered under the auspices of the Reginald H. Jones Center. We would like to acknowledge the helpful comments of Arthur Stinchcombe.

---

[10] For different perspectives on this topic see Baker (1987) and Delany (1988).

APPENDIX A

Data Sources

The primary source of data is BIOSCAN (1988, 1989), a commercial directory of biotechnology firms, published and updated quarterly by ORYX Press, Inc. Because it has generally been considered the most comprehensive compendium of information on relationships in the industry, any relationship listed in BIOSCAN is included in our sample. However, because BIOSCAN may have omitted some relationships terminated before 1988, we collected data from the three other sources: (1) a proprietary database obtained from a leading biotechnology firm (called the "black volumes") in 1986: (2) a database developed by the North Carolina Biotechnology Center, based on published announcements of cooperative agreements; and (3) a direct mail survey of and telephone interviews with startups.

Because these latter three sources had neither BIOSCAN's history of direct contact with startups and their partners nor its depth of information about agreements, we relied less on their data. We added an agreement if it appeared in at least two of these sources. We found 46 relationships in this category. As they do not appear in the 1988 BIOSCAN directory, we assumed that these relationships had been terminated before 1988; the network analysis for 1988 therefore excluded them.

All startups in the final sample were independent businesses specializing in the commercialization of biotechnology products. Their portfolio of products must include diagnostic or therapeutic pharmaceuticals. The agreements consisted of joint ventures, licensing, and long term contracts between startups and their partners. Powell and Brantley (1992) found that different types of relationships—e.g., licensing, joint venture, research and development limited partnership—were not statistically related to how much firms engaged in cooperative agreements. Consequently, the network we analyze contains these types of relationship together. Since only firms that have engaged in at least one agreement can contribute to network structure, startups without relationships are excluded from the sample.

Application of these criteria produced a sample of 114 startups that had cooperative agreements before 1989. These startups differed in their time of entry into the network, as Table 10.2 shows. Thirteen have agreements only with universities, government agencies and research institutes. (Many of these relationships represent licenses of the original patents stemming from university research.) We dropped these startups from the sample in order to retain a group of partners whose interests were clearly commercial. Whereas university ties are important for the initial licensing and subsequent consulting services, our focus is on the structuring of relationships among commercial partners.[11]

---

[11] See Barley et al. (1992) on the sparseness of the university/NBF density matrix, as well as a breakdown of agreements by type (e.g., licensing, joint venture).

APPENDIX B

Operationalization of Measures of Network Structure

We analyzed the asymmetric matrix of cooperative relationships with CONCOR, a network analysis algorithm (Breiger et al. 1975) that has been used frequently in interorganizational research (Knoke and Rogers 1978, Van de Ven et al. 1979, DiMaggio 1986, Schrum and Withnow 1988). The usual practice of applying CONCOR (see Arabie et al. 1978) is to dichotomize the full set of network members; then to split these two groups separately; then to split these results; and so on until either (1) a desired number of groups are obtained or (2) groups are obtained with a specific number of members. We used the following rules for applying CONCOR to both startups and their partners: (1) groups with fewer than 10 members were not split; and (2) when splitting a group produced a singleton subgroup, the group was kept whole. We followed this practice separately for both the startups (rows) and their partners (columns) of the matrix of relationships. The purpose of these rules is to avoid groups with small sizes that are inappropriate relative to the size of the network (see Walker 1985).

Although CONCOR's results at the two-group level have been benchmarked against an optimality criterion (Noma and Smith 1985), the results of subsequent splitting have not been evaluated. Because of potential variation in decision rules for subsequent splits of the data, different results may be achieved for the same data set. To address this problem, we applied a second algorithm to the partition of network members produced by CONCOR. This algorithm, called CALCOPT, reallocates network members from group to group in the partition if the shift in group membership improves a target function consistent with Lorrain and White's (1971) original definition of structural equivalence. This target function is Equation (2). Thus CALCOPT reallocates network members from one group to another if the move increases the dispersion of densities in the density matrix. CALCOPT evaluates the CONCOR row partition and then the column partition iteratively until no reassignment improves the target function.

CONCOR and CALCOPT were applied to each year of data from 1984 to 1988. The data for each year are all cooperative relationships that were established between the startups and their partners up to that year minus any relationships that were terminated during that year. For example, the 1985 network includes the 1984 network plus all agreements begun between 1984 and 1985 minus terminated relationships. Thus five separate networks, one for each year, were analyzed to identify (1) groups of structurally equivalent startups and groups of structurally equivalent partners and (2) the pattern of intergroup densities used to measure social capital.

REFERENCES

Acs, Z. and D. B. Audretsch (1989), "Entrepreneurial Strategy and the Presence of Small Firms," *Small Business Economics*, 1, 3, 193–213.

Agresti, A. (1984), *Analysis of Categorical Data*, New York: John Wiley.

Arabie, P., S. A. Boorman, and P. R. Levitt (1978), "Constructing Blockmodels: How and Why," *Journal of Mathematical Psychology*, 17, 21–63.

BIOSCAN (1988, 1989), Phoenix, AZ: Oryx Press.

Baker, W. (1984), "The Social Structure of a National Securities Market," *American Journal of Sociology*, 89, 775–811.

—— (1990), "Market Networks and Corporate Behavior," *American Journal of Sociology*, 96, 589–625.

Barley, S. R., J. Freeman, and R. C. Hybels (1992), "Strategic Alliances in Commercial Biotechnology," in N. Nohria and R. G. Eccles (Eds.), *Networks and Organization*, Cambridge, MA: Harvard Business School Press.

Boorman, S. A. and P. R. Levitt (1983), "Blockmodelling Complex Statutes: Mapping Techniques Based on Combinatorial Optimization for Analyzing Economic Legislation and Its Stress Points over Time," *Economic Letters*, 13–19.

Bound, J., C. Cummins, Z. Griliches, B. H. Hall, and A. Jaffe (1984), "Who Does R & D and Who Patents?," in Z. Griliches (Ed.), *R & D, Patents, and Productivity*, 21–54, Chicago, IL: University of Chicago Press.

Bourdieu, P. (1980), "Le Capital Sociale: Notes Provisaires," *Actes de la Recherche en Sciences Sociales*, 3, 2–3.

—— and L. Wacquant (1992), *An Invitation to Reflexive Sociology*, Chicago, IL: University of Chicago Press.

Boyles, S. E. (1968), "Estimate of the Number and Size Distribution of Domestic Joint Subsidiaries." *Antitrust Law and Economics Review*, 1, 81–92.

Breiger, R. L., S. A. Boorman, and P. Arabie (1975), "An Algorithm for Clustering Relational Data, with Applications to Social Network Analysis and Comparison with Multidimensional Scaling," *Journal of Mathematical Psychology*, 12, 326–383.

Burt, R. L. (1980), "Models of Network Structure," *Annual Review of Sociology*, 6, 79–141.

—— (1987), "Social Contagion and Innovation, Cohesion versus Structural Equivalence," *American Journal of Sociology*, 92, 1287–1335.

—— (1992), *Structural Holes*, Cambridge, MA: Harvard University Press.

Calhoun, C. (1993), *Bourdieu: Critical Perspectives*, C. Calhoun, E. Lipuma, and M. M. Postone (Eds.), Cambridge, UK: Polity Press.

Cameron, A. and P. Trivedi (1986), "Econometric Models Based on Count Data: Comparisons and Applications of Some Estimators," *Journal of Applied Econometrics*, 1.

Clark. K., W. B. Chew, and T. Fujimoto (1987), "Product Development in the World Auto Industry," *Brookings Papers on Economic Activity*, 3, 729–782.

Coleman, J. (1990a), "Social Capital in the Creation of Human Capital," *American Journal of Sociology*, 94, S95–S120.

—— (1990b), *Foundations of Social Theory*, Cambridge, MA: Harvard University Press.

Delany, J. (1988), "Social Networks and Efficient Resource Allocation: Computer Models of Job Vacancy Allocation through Contacts," in B. Wellman and S. Berkowitz (Eds.), *Social Structure: A Network Approach*, Cambridge, UK: Cambridge University Press.

DiMaggio, P. and W. W. Powell (1983), "The Iron Cage Revisited: Institutional Isomorphism and Collective Rationality in Organization Fields," *American Sociological Review*, 43, 147–160.

DiMaggio, Paul (1986), "Structural Analysis of Organizational Fields: A Blockmodel Approach," *Research in Organizational Behavior*, 8, 335–370.

Doz, Y. (1988), "Technology Partnerships Between Larger and Smaller Firms: Some Critical Issues," in F. Contractor and P. Lorange (Eds.), *Cooperative Strategies in International Business*, 317–338, Lexington, MA: Lexington Books.

Evan, W. M. (1972), "An Organization-set Model of Interorganizational Relations," in M. Tuite, R. Chisolm and M. Radnor (Eds.), *Interorganizational Decision-Making*, 181–200, Chicago, IL: Aldine.

Fruen, M. (1989), "Cooperative Structure and Competitive Strategies: The Japanese Enterprise System," Unpublished Manuscript, INSEAD.

Galaskiewicz, J. and S. Wasserman (1981), "A Dynamic Study of Change in a Regional Corporate Network," *American Sociological Review*, 46, 475–484.

Grabher, G. (1988), *De-Industrialisierung oder Neo-Industrialisierung?*, Berlin, Germany: Wissenschaftszentrum Berlin fur Sozialforschung.

Granovetter, M. (1985), "Economic Action and Social Structure: The Problem of Embeddedness," *American Journal of Sociology*, 78, 1360–1380.

Hagedoorn, J. and J. Schakenraad (1992), "Leading Companies and Networks of Strategic Alliances in Information Technologies," *Research Policy*, 21, 163–190.

Herrigel G. (1991), "The Politics of Large Firm Relations with Industrial Districts: A Collision of Organizational Fields in Baden Wurtemberg," in *County Competitiveness*, B. Kogut (Ed.), London, UK: MacMillan.

Hofstede, G., B. Neujien, D. Daval Ohayv, and G. Sanders (1990), "Measuring Organizational Culture: A Qualitative and Quantitative Study Across Twenty Cases," *Administrative Science Quarterly*, 3, 286–316.

Judge, G., W. E. Griffiths, R. C. Carter, H. Lutkepohl, and T.-C. Lee (1985), *The Theory and Practice of Econometrics*, New York: Wiley.

Knoke, D. and D. L. Rogers (1978), "A Blockmodel Analysis of Interorganizational Networks," *Social Science Research*, 64, 28–52.

Kogut, B. (1991), "Joint Ventures and the Option to Expand and Acquire," *Management Science*, 37, 19–33.

———, W. Shan and G. Walker (1994). "Knowledge in the Network and the Network as Knowledge," in G. Grabher (Ed.), *The Embedded Firm*, London, UK: Routledge.

———, G. Walker and D.-J. Kim (1995), "Cooperation and Entry Induction as a Function of Technological Rivalry," *Research Policy*.

———, ———, W. Shan, and D.-J. Kim (1995), "Platform Technologies and National Industrial Networks," in J. Hagedoorn (Ed.), *The Internationalization of Corporate Technology Strategies*.

Lorrain, F. and H. C. White (1971), "Structural Equivalence of Individuals in Social Networks," *Journal of Mathematical Sociology*, 1, 49–80.

Loury, G. (1977), "A Dynamic Theory of Racial Income Differences," in P. A. Wallace and A. Le Mund (Eds.), *Women, Minorities, and Employment Discrimination*, Lexington, MA: Lexington Books.

Mansfield, E. (1988), "The Speed and Cost of Industrial Innovation in Japan and the U.S.: External vs. Internal Technology," *Management Science*, 34, 10, 1157–1168.

Marsden, P. V. (1983), "Restricted Access in Networks and Models of Power," *American Journal of Sociology*, 88, 4, 686–717.

Mayhew, B. H. and R. L. Levinger (1976), "Size and the Density of Interaction in Human Aggregates," *American Journal of Sociology*, 82, 86–110.

Meyer, J. W. and B. Rowan (1977), "Institutionalized Organizations: Formal Structure as Myth and Ceremony," *American Journal of Sociology*, 83, 340–363.

Nohria, N. and C. Garcia-Pont (1991), "Global Strategic Linkages and Industry Structure," *Strategic Management Journal*, 12, 105–124.

Noma, E. and D. R. Smith (1985), "Benchmarks for the Blocking of Sociometric Data," *Psychological Bulletin*, 97, 583–591.

Office of Technology Assessment (1984), *Commercial Biotechnology, An International Analysis*, U.S. Congress.

Oliver, C. (1988). "The Collective Strategy Framework: An Application to Competing Predictions of Isomorphism," *Administrative Science Quarterly*, 24, 405–424.

Pisano, G. (1990), "The R & D Boundaries of the Firm: An Empirical Analysis," *Administrative Science Quarterly*, 35, 153–176.

——— (1991), "The Governance of Innovation: Vertical Integration and Collaborative Arrangements in the Biotechnology Industry," *Research Policy*, 20, 237–250.

Powell, W. W. and P. Brantley (1992), "Competitive Cooperation in Biotechnology: Learning through Networks?," in N. Nohria and R. G. Eccles (Eds.), *Networks and Organization*, Cambridge, MA: Harvard Business School Press.

Raub, W. and J. Weesie (1990), "Reputation and Efficiency in Social Institutions: An Example of Network Effects," *American Journal of Sociology*, 96, 626–654.

Scherer, F. M. (1986). *Innovation and Growth: Schumpeterian Perspectives*, Cambridge, MA: MIT Press.

Schrum, W. and R. Withnow (1988). "Reputational Status of Organizations in Technical Systems," *American Journal of Sociology*, 93, 882–912.

Schumpeter, J. A. (1934), *The Theory of Economic Development*, Cambridge: MA: Harvard University Press.

Shan, W. (1987), "Technological Change and Strategic Cooperation: Evidence from Commercialization of Biotechnology," Ph.D. Dissertation, University of California, Berkeley.

——— (1990), "An Empirical Analysis of Organizational Strategies by Entrepreneurial High-technology Firms," *Strategic Management Journal*, 11, 129–139.

———, G. Walker, and B. Kogut (1994), "Interfirm Cooperation and Startup Innovation in the Biotechnology Industry," *Strategic Management Journal*, 15, 5, 387–394.

Stinchcombe, A. L. (1965), "Social Structure and Organizations," in J. G. March (Ed.), *Handbook of Organizations*, 142–193, Chicago, IL: Rand McNally.

Teece, D. (1988), "Capturing Value from Technological Innovation: Integration, Strategic Partnering and Licensing Decisions," *Interfaces*, 18, 46–61.

Van de Ven, A., G. Walker, and J. Liston (1979), "Coordination Patterns within an Inter-organizational Network," *Human Relations*, 32, 19–36.

Walker, G. (1985), "Network Position and Cognition in a Computer Software Firm," *Administration Science Quarterly*, 30, 103–130.

—— (1988), "Network Analysis for Interorganizational Cooperative Relationships," in F. Contractor and P. Lorange (Eds.), *Cooperative Strategies in International Business*, Lexington, MA: Lexington Books.

White, H., S. A. Boorman, and R. Breiger (1976), "Social Structure from Multiple Networks, I, Blockmodels of Roles and Positions," *American Journal of Sociology*, 81, 730–780.

Wickens, T. D. (1989), *Multiway Contingency Tables Analysis for the Social Sciences*, Hillsdale, NJ: Lawrence Erlbaum.

Chapter 11

The Contingent Value of Social Capital[*]

Ronald S. Burt
University of Chicago

I present argument and evidence for a structural ecology of social capital that describes how the value of social capital to an individual is contingent on the number of people doing the same work. The information and control benefits of bridging the structural holes—or, disconnections between nonredundant contacts in a network—that constitute social capital are especially valuable to managers with few peers. Such managers do not have the guiding frame of reference for behavior provided by numerous competitors, and the work they do does not have the legitimacy provided by numerous people doing the same kind of work. I use network and performance data on a probability sample of senior managers to show how the value of social capital, high on average for the managers, varies as a power function of the number of people doing the same work.

I benefited from exchange with audiences to whom portions of this material have been presented: the 1993 meetings of the Society for the Advancement of Socio-Economics; a 1993 seminar at INSEAD; a 1993 Department of Sociology colloquium at the University of Illinois, Chicago; a 1993 social organization workshop and 1994 labor economics workshop at the University of Chicago; a 1993 SCOR workshop at Stanford University; a 1994 workshop at Carnegie-Mellon University; a 1994 workshop at the Harvard Business School; a 1995 NBER behavioral labor economics workshop sponsored by a Russell Sage Foundation grant to Robert Shiller and Richard Thaler; the 1995 annual meetings of the Academy of Management; the 1995 annual meetings of

[*] Approval of request to reprint courtesy of *Administrative Science Quarterly* © 1997
42: 339–365
© 1997 by Cornell University. 0001–8392/4202–0339/$1.00.

the American Sociological Association; and the 1996 Social Science &
Statistics Conference in honor of Clifford C. Clogg at Pennsylvania State
University. The contingency function metaphor emerged in a graduate
seminar on network and ecological models applied to human resource
management. I give credit to the seminar participants who argued the
ecological perspective (Ray Reagans and Beth Rosenthal) and network
perspective (Susan Carroll, Greg Janicik, Beth Rosenthal, and Susan
Wittry), especially those who challenged me to find a productive appli-
cation (Sheila Goins and Justin Townsley). My primary debt is to Linda
Johanson's tenacious editing and the ASQ review process, which pro-
vided some of the most productive comments I have received on a draft
manuscript.

Some people enjoy higher incomes than others. Some are promoted faster. Some are leaders on more important projects. The human capital explanation is that inequality results from differences in individual ability. The usual evidence is on general populations, as is Becker's (1975) pioneering analysis of income returns to education, but the argument is widely applied by senior managers to explain who gets to the top of corporate America—managers who make it to the top are smarter or better educated or more experienced. But, while human capital is surely necessary to success, it is useless without the social capital of opportunities in which to apply it.

Social capital can be distinguished in its etiology and consequences from human capital (e.g., Coleman, 1990; Bourdieu and Wacquant, 1992; Burt, 1992; Putnam, 1993; Lin, 1998). With respect to etiology, social capital is a quality created between people, whereas human capital is a quality of individuals. Investments that create social capital are therefore different in fundamental ways from the investments that create human capital (Coleman, 1988, 1990). I focus in this paper on consequences, a focus in network analysis for many years (Breiger, 1995). With respect to consequences, social capital is the contextual complement to human capital. Social capital predicts that returns to intelligence, education, and seniority depend in some part on a person's location in the social structure of a market or hierarchy. While human capital refers to individual ability, social capital refers to opportunity. Some portion of the value a manager adds to a firm is his or her ability to coordinate other people: identifying opportunities to add value within an organization and getting the right people together to develop the opportunities. Knowing who, when, and how to coordinate is a function of the manager's network of contacts within and beyond the firm. Certain network forms deemed social capital can enhance the manager's ability to identify and develop opportunities. Managers with more social capital get higher returns to their human capital because they are positioned to identify and develop more rewarding opportunities.

I begin with an introduction to the network structure of social capital and evidence of social capital's effect on manager success. Given baseline evidence of social capital's value to the average manager, I turn to the issue of how its value to individual managers is contingent on the number of people doing the same work.

THE NETWORK STRUCTURE OF SOCIAL CAPITAL

Structural hole theory gives concrete meaning to the concept of social capital. The theory describes how social capital is a function of brokerage opportunities in a network. The following is a brief synopsis sufficient to set the stage for arguing contingency (see Burt, 1992, for detailed discussion). The structural hole argument draws on several lines of network theorizing that emerged in sociology during the 1970s, most notably, Granovetter (1973) on the strength of weak ties, Freeman (1977) on betweenness centrality, Cook and Emerson (1978) on the power of having exclusive exchange partners, and Burt (1980) on the structural autonomy created by network complexity. More generally, sociological ideas elaborated by Simmel (1955) and Merton (1968), on the autonomy generated by conflicting affiliations, are mixed in the structural hole argument with traditional economic ideas of monopoly power and oligopoly to produce network models of competitive advantage. In a perfect market, one price clears the market. In an imperfect market, there can be multiple prices because disconnections between individuals, holes in the structure of the market, leave some people unaware of the benefits they could offer one another. Certain people are connected to certain others, trusting certain others, obligated to support certain others, dependent on exchange with certain others. Assets get locked into suboptimal exchanges. An individual's position in the structure of these exchanges can be an asset in its own right. That asset is social capital, in essence, a story about location effects in differentiated markets. The structural hole argument defines social capital in terms of the information and control advantages of being the broker in relations between people otherwise disconnected in social structure. The disconnected people stand on opposite sides of a hole in social structure. The structural hole is an opportunity to broker the flow of information between people and control the form of projects that bring together people from opposite sides of the hole.

Information Benefits

The information benefits are access, timing, and referrals. A manager's network provides access to information well beyond what he or she could process alone. It provides that information early, which is an advantage to the manager acting on the information. The network that filters information coming to a manager also directs, concentrates, and legitimates information received by others about the manager. Through referrals, the manager's interests are represented in a positive light, at the right time, and in the right places.

The structure of a network indicates the redundancy of its information benefits. There are two network indicators of redundancy. The first is cohesion. Cohesive contacts—contacts strongly connected to each other—are likely to have similar information and therefore provide redundant information benefits. Structural equivalence is the second indicator. Equivalent contacts—contacts who link a manager to the same third parties—have the same sources of information and therefore provide redundant information benefits.

Nonredundant contacts offer information benefits that are additive rather than redundant. Structural holes are the gaps between nonredundant contacts (see Burt, 1992: 25–30, on how Granovetter's, 1973, weak ties generalize to structural holes). The hole is a buffer, like an insulator in an electric circuit. A structural hole between two clusters in a network need not mean that people in the two clusters are unaware of one another. It simply means that they are so focused on their own activities that they have little time to attend to the activities of people in the other cluster. A structural hole indicates that the people on either side of the hole circulate in different flows of information. A manager who spans the structural hole, by having strong relations with contacts on both sides of the hole, has access to both information flows. The more holes spanned, the richer the information benefits of the network.

Figure 11.1 provides an example. James had a network that spanned one structural hole. The hole is the relatively weak connection between the cluster reached through contacts 1, 2, and 3 and the cluster reached through contacts 4 and 5. Robert took over James's job and expanded the social capital associated with the job. He preserved connection with both clusters in James's network but expanded the network to a more diverse set of contacts. Robert's network, with the addition of three new clusters of people, spans ten structural holes.

Information benefits in this example are enhanced in several ways. The volume is higher in Robert's network simply because he reaches more people indirectly. Also, the diversity of his contacts means that the quality of his information benefits is higher. Each cluster of contacts is a single source of information because people connected to one another tend to know the same things at about the same time. Nonredundant clusters provide Robert with a broader information screen and, therefore, greater assurance that he will be informed of opportunities and impending disasters (access benefits). Further, since Robert's contacts are only linked through him at the center of the network, he is the first to see new opportunities created by needs in one group that could be served by skills in other groups (timing benefits). He stands at the crossroads of social organization. He has the option of bringing together otherwise disconnected individuals in the network when it would be rewarding. And because Robert's contacts are more diverse, he is more likely to be a candidate for inclusion in new opportunities (referral benefits). These benefits are compounded by the fact that having a network that yields such benefits makes Robert more attractive to other people as a contact in their own networks.

(a)

(b)

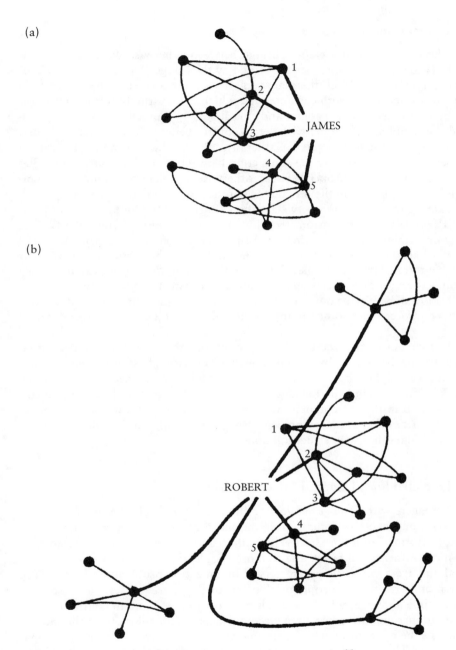

FIGURE 11.1(a) and **11.1(b)** Illustrative Managers' Networks[**]

[**] Thick lines represent a managers' direct contacts.

Control Benefits

The manager who creates a bridge between otherwise disconnected contacts has a say in whose interests are served by the bridge. The disconnected contacts communicate through the manager, giving the manager an opportunity to adjust his or her image with each contact, which is the structural foundation for managerial robust action (Padgett and Ansell, 1993). Simmel and Merton introduced the sociology of people who derive control benefits from structural holes: The ideal type is the *tertius gaudens* (literally, "the third who benefits"), a person who benefits from brokering the connection between others (see Burt, 1992: 30–32, for review). As the broker between otherwise disconnected contacts, a manager is an entrepreneur in the literal sense of the word—a person who adds value by brokering the connection between others (Burt, 1992: 34–36; see also Martinelli, 1994). There is a tension here, but not the hostility of combatants. It is merely uncertainty. In the swirling mix of preferences characteristic of social networks, where no demands have absolute authority, the *tertius* negotiates for favorable terms. Structural holes are the setting for *tertius strategies*, and information is the substance. Accurate, ambiguous, or distorted information is strategically moved between contacts by the *tertius*. The information and control benefits reinforce one another at any moment in time and cumulate together over time.

Networks rich in structural holes present opportunities for entrepreneurial behavior. The behaviors by which managers develop these opportunities are many and varied, but the opportunity itself is at all times defined by a hole in the social structure around the manager. In terms of the structural hole argument, networks rich in the entrepreneurial opportunities of structural holes are entrepreneurial networks, and entrepreneurs are people skilled in building the interpersonal bridges that span structural holes.

Predicted Social Capital Effect

Managers with contact networks rich in structural holes know about, have a hand in, and exercise control over the more rewarding opportunities. They monitor information more effectively than it can be monitored bureaucratically. They move information faster, and to more people, than memos. These entrepreneurial managers know the parameters of organization problems early. They are highly mobile relative to people working through a bureaucracy, easily shifting network time and energy from one solution to another. More in control of their immediate surroundings, entrepreneurial managers tailor solutions to the specific individuals being coordinated, replacing the boiler-plate solutions of formal bureaucracy. There is also the issue of costs: entrepreneurial managers offer inexpensive coordination relative to the bureaucratic alternative. Managers with networks rich in structural holes operate somewhere between the force of corporate authority and the dexterity of markets, building bridges between disconnected parts of the firm where it is valuable to do so. They have more opportunity to add value, are expected to do so, and are accordingly expected to enjoy higher returns to their human capital. The prediction is that in comparisons between otherwise similar people like James and Robert in Figure 11.1, it is people like Robert who should be more successful.[1]

Evidence of the Predicted Effect

Three lines of empirical evidence emerged in sociology during the 1970s to support the prediction. First, laboratory experiments have been used to show that resources distributed through a small-group exchange network accumulate in people with exclusive exchange relations to otherwise disconnected partners (e.g., Cook and Emerson, 1978; Cook et al., 1983; Markovsky, Willer, and Patton, 1988). Second, census data have been used to describe how producer profit margins increase with structural holes in the producer network of transactions with suppliers and customers. Burt (1983) described the association in 1967 with profits in American manufacturing markets, defined at broad and detailed levels of aggregation, and extended the results into nonmanufacturing through the 1960s and 1970s (Burt, 1988, 1992). Burt, Yasuda, and Guilarte (1996) extended the results through the 1980s. Using profit and network data on markets in other countries, similar results have been found in Germany during the 1970s and 1980s (Ziegler, 1982; Burt and Freeman, 1994), Israel during the 1970s (Talmud, 1994), Japan in the 1980s (Yasuda, 1993), and Korea in the 1980s (Jang, 1997).

Third, and most relevant to the evidence to be presented here, survey data have been used to describe the career advantages of having a contact network rich in structural holes. The earliest and most widely known study is Granovetter's (1973, 1995) demonstration that white-collar workers find better jobs faster through weak ties that bridge otherwise disconnected social groups. Lin worked with several colleagues to present evidence of the importance of ties to distant contacts for obtaining more desirable jobs (e.g., Lin, Ensel, and Vaughn, 1981; Lin and Dumin, 1986; Lin, 1998).

Similar empirical results appear in Campbell, Marsden, and Hurlbert (1986), Marsden and Hurlbert (1988), and Flap and De Graaf (1989). Moving to the top of organizations, Burt (1992) and Podolny and Baron (1997) presented survey evidence from probability samples of managers showing that senior managers with networks richer in structural holes are more likely to get promoted early. Working with more limited data, Gabbay (1996) showed how

---

[1] I focus on rewards to the individual manager (Brass, 1992. Lazega, 1994; Breiger, 1995, review related works). I assume that managers with intrepreneurial contact networks add value to their firm and therefore receive from the firm compensation, in one form or another, that is above average. The more general argument describes how the firm is shaped by managers searching for early information to resolve corporate and market uncertainties (see Stinchcombe. 1990).

promotions occur more quickly for salespeople with strong-tie access to structural holes (cf. Meyerson, 1994; Pennings, Lee, and Witteloostuijn, 1997), and Sparrowe and Popielarz (1995) innovatively reconstructed past networks around managers to estimate an event-history model of how structural holes in yesterday's network affect the likelihood of promotion today. The benefits that accrue to individuals aggregate to the management teams on which they serve. Studying quality management teams in several midwestern manufacturing plants, Rosenthal (1996) showed that the teams composed of employees with more entrepreneurial networks were significantly more likely to be recognized for their success in improving the quality of plant operations (cf. Krackhardt and Stern, 1988, on higher group performance with cross-group friendships between students, and Fernandez and Gould, 1994, on organizations in broker positions within the national health policy arena being perceived as more influential).[2]

There is a process element missing in the above studies that can be seen in other styles of analysis. Gargiulo and Benassi (1993) directly measured what they termed "coordination failure" as the extent to which the people with whom a manager consults are not the people relevant for the manager's assigned projects. With data on managers in a research consulting unit of a large Italian firm, they showed that coordination failures are significantly more likely for managers with small, dense, hierarchical networks. For rich detail on the brokerage process, historical accounts of individual entrepreneurs offer a glimpse of the process by which brokers have built bridges across structural holes (e.g., DiMaggio, 1992: 129–130; Padgett and Ansell, 1993). Direct observation offers the richest detail. Kotter's (1982) cases illustrate the information and control advantages of an entrepreneurial network in performing the two tasks of the successful general manager: reading the organization for needed business policy and knowing which people to bring together to implement the policy. Mintzberg (1973) is similarly rich in case material on the central importance to managers of getting their information live, through personal discussions rather than through official channels. Sutton and Hargadon (1996) and Hargadon and Sutton (1997) describe a firm, IDEO, that relies on brainstorming to create product designs. The firm's employees work for clients in diverse industries. In the brainstorming sessions,

---

[2]   These results are consistent with Coleman's (1988, 1990) use of a network metaphor to motivate his social capital explanation of why certain children perform better in school. Children perform better if they have a constrained network in which friends, teachers, and parents are all strongly connected to one another so as to eliminate entrepreneurial opportunities for the child to play contacts against one another. The imagery is the same as in structural hole theory: a small network of interlocked relations constrains action. Constraint from parents and teachers has positive long-term consequences for children, forcing them to focus on their education (cf. Hirschi, 1972, on the negative consequences of network constraint from delinquent friends). At some point on the way to adulthood, however, the child shaped by the environment takes responsibility for shaping the environment. Constraint, positive for the child, is detrimental to adults, particularly adults charged with managerial tasks at the top of their firm (see Portes and Landolt, 1996, for more diverse examples).

technological solutions from one industry are taken to solve client issues in other industries where the solutions are rare or unknown. The firm profits from brokering the flow of technology between industries (cf. Allen and Cohen, 1969, on gatekeepers). Sutton and Hargadon's evidence on IDEO offers process detail that corroborates the more authoritative but static survey evidence of the social capital value of structural holes.

Contingent Value

The argument explaining why structural holes are valuable as social capital implicitly defines when and where they are valuable. The key context variable is number of peers. A number of people can do the same work as any given manager in an organization. These are the manager's peers. The manager could have a large number of peers, a few, or none, if he or she is the only person doing a particular kind of work.

Number of peers and the value of social capital are connected through competition and legitimacy (Belliveau, O'Reilly, and Wade, 1996, on the significance of relative social capital among peers). Having many peers affects the manager's freedom to define his or her job and the firm's response to the manager's definition. First, the many peers create a competitive frame of reference. Their aggregate behavior indicates how the manager should perform, and peer competition keeps the manager tuned to peers' job performance. Beyond informal pressures to conform, the firm is likely to provide guidelines for jobs held by a large number of employees. Second, legitimacy is established by many people doing the same work. The way in which the job is performed is legitimate because many people perform it that way (e.g., economists in a business school).

The two conditions are reversed for a manager who has few peers: First, there is no competitive frame of reference. It would be inefficient for the firm to define how a job peculiar to a few employees should be performed, and there are no peers for informal guidance. The manager has to figure out for him- or herself how best to perform the job (see Kohn and Schooler, 1983, on occupational self-direction). Second, legitimacy does not come with the job; it has to be established. With few people doing the work, establishing the legitimacy of a manager's job performance depends on getting others to accept his or her definition of the job (e.g., sociologists in a business school).

Social capital is more valuable to the manager with few peers. The information and control benefits of structural holes position managers better to read the diverse interests in their organization to define needed policy and to know who can be brought together productively to implement policy. The ability to identify and develop opportunities is essential to the manager evaluating how best to fulfill his or her job responsibilities in a way valued by the firm and the market. That has little value to a manager whose work is defined by corporate convention or the boss. In short, the value of social capital to a manager should be contingent on the number of the manager's peers.

The contingency argument is both structural end ecological. Structural holes among people who are similar allow outsiders to play the people against one another, which erodes the value of whatever social capital they hold (Burt, 1992: 44–45). A manager's ability to develop entrepreneurial opportunities is constrained by the presence of one or more peers in a position to undercut or denigrate the manager's proposals. The contingency argument is also analogous to ecological arguments describing the competition and legitimacy consequences of an increasing number of organizations in a market (Hannan and Freeman, 1989: 131–141; Burt, 1992: 215ff.; Han, 1993, 1994). I focus on the network implications of numbers here, but the competition and legitimacy mechanisms are familiar from research in organization demography (e.g., Pfeffer, 1983; Haveman and Cohen, 1994). I study the contingency effect within an ecological framework because the framework provides a concrete measure of constraint—number of peers—but remain mindful of the structural argument. Number of peers per se does not affect the value of social capital. The causal variables are competition and legitimacy, which are correlated with number of peers. The contingency prediction is that peers erode the value of social capital to the extent that disorganization among peers intensifies competition between the peers and elicits behavioral guidelines from higher authority. Ceteris paribus, number of peers should be an acceptable indicator.

METHOD

I use two kinds of evidence to make my case for the contingent value of social capital. First, I use network and performance data on a probability sample of managers drawn from the senior ranks of a large electronics firm. The partial correlation between performance and a network measure of social capital, holding background variables constant, establishes a baseline average value of social capital. The stronger the correlation, the higher the value of social capital for the average manager in the study population. In the baseline results below, I show associations between social capital and early promotion in manufacturing, and then I use a different date set on bank officers to show a similar association with large bonuses. Second, I use data on the manufacturing managers to compare managers with different numbers of peers to show how the value of social capital varies with number of peers. If the contingency argument is correct, then the value of social capital should be lower for managers with more peers.

Data

I collected network, background, and performance data on 170 men in senior positions at the end of 1989 with one of the largest American firms in electronic components and computing equipment. The firm employed more than 100,000 people at the time. The 170 men analyzed here are a probability sample of the 2,500 men in the three ranks just below the rank of vice president (women are a minority at 12 percent of this study population and are analyzed elsewhere, in Burt, 1997b). Although the managers are all employed in the same firm, they are a heterogeneous sample in the sense that they are scattered across the country, with zero to 30 years in the firm's diverse corporate functions. The data come from company personnel records and a short network survey. The company personnel records provided each manager's rank (three levels defined by the firm), when he was promoted to his current rank, when he entered the firm, the function in which he works (defined by the firm as sales, service, manufacturing, information systems, engineering, marketing, finance, and human resources), and the usual personnel-file variables such as gender, family, income, and so on. The sampling and network survey items are described in detail elsewhere (Burt, 1992: 118–131). On the survey, each manager described his network of key contacts within and beyond the firm: Contacts were identified with nine name-generator questions on diverse kinds of relations, such as informal discussion and socializing, political support, critical sources of buy-in for projects, authority relations with supervisor and promising subordinates, and so on (see Burt, 1997a, on content distinctions between the kinds of relations; cf. Podolny and Baron, 1997). Network size varied from a minimum of 7 contacts to a maximum of 22, with an average of 12.6 contacts. Relations with and between contacts were scaled to vary from 0 to 1 with emotional closeness (Burt, 1992: 287–288). Some managers had sparse networks of disconnected contacts (minimum density is 0.07). Others had dense networks of interconnected contacts (.82 maximum density). On average, the networks were as dense as observed in other studies (e.g., 0.47 average density for the 170 managers, versus 0.42 average density for Americans with more than a high school education in the 1985 General Social Survey).

Social Capital Measured by Network Constraint

I measured social capital in terms of network constraint. The network around a manager constrains entrepreneurial action to the extent that the network is directly or indirectly concentrated in a single contact. More constraint means fewer structural holes and, so, less social capital. The network constraint index C varies with three network conditions (see Burt, 1992: 50ff., 1995, 1997b, for details): network size (larger networks are less constraining), density (networks of more strongly interconnected contacts are more constraining), and hierarchy (networks in which all contacts are exclusively tied to a single dominant contact are more constraining). The index begins with a measure of the extent to which all of manager i's network is directly or indirectly invested in his or her relationship with contact j: $C_{ij} = (p_{ij} + \Sigma_q p_{iq} p_{qj})^2$ for $q \neq i,j$, where p_{ij} is the proportion of i's relations invested in contact j. The sum $\Sigma_q p_{iq} p_{qj}$ is the portion of i's relations invested in contacts q who are in turn invested in contact j. The total in parentheses is the proportion of i's relations that are directly or indirectly invested in the connection with contact j. The sum of squared proportions, $\Sigma_j C_{ij}$, is the network constraint index C. I multiply constraint scores by 100 so that I can discuss social capital effects per point of constraint. The range of scores to be discussed is illustrated by the difference between Robert and James in Figure 11.1. Network constraint is 20.0 for Robert's network, 53.6 for James's.

BASELINE EVIDENCE

The test for social capital effects begins with a human capital model: $R = \beta\ (T, S)$. The rewards, R, that managers receive for their work are a function of assigned tasks (T, typically rank and function variables) and human capital skills they bring to the tasks (S, typically education and experience). Social capital adds covariates to the human capital model: $R = \beta\ (T, S) + [\gamma + \lambda\ (T, S)](C)$, where C is network constraint. The social capital effect γ is negative to the extent that the information and control benefits of structural holes are valuable. Effect adjustments, λ, measure the extent to which the value of social capital is contingent, such that value γ is higher for certain kinds of people doing certain kinds of work.

Early Promotion

Figure 11.2 contains baseline evidence for the analysis of contingent value. On the vertical axis of Figure 11.2 is early promotion, the performance variable in this study. Because income in the study population is too closely tied to job rank to measure the relative success of individual managers, time to rank is a better performance variable (Burt, 1992: 196–197). Whether promoted internally or hired from the outside, people promoted to senior rank in large organizations have several years of experience preceding their promotion. A period of time is expected to pass before people are ready for promotion to senior rank (see Merton, 1984, on socially expected durations). How much time is an empirical question, the answer to which differs with individual managers. Some managers are promoted earlier than others. Early promotion is the difference between when a manager was promoted to his current rank and a human capital baseline model predicting the age at which similar managers are promoted to the same rank to do the same work: $E(age) - age$. Expected age at promotion, $E(age)$, is the average age at which managers with specific personal backgrounds (education, race, gender, and seniority) are promoted to a specific rank within a specific function (rank, function, and plant location). For example, a score of −5.5 indicates a manager was promoted five and a half years behind similar managers promoted to the same job. Twelve percent of the variance in promotion age is predicted by the baseline model, and residuals are distributed in a bell curve around expected promotion age (Burt, 1992: 126–131; 1995).

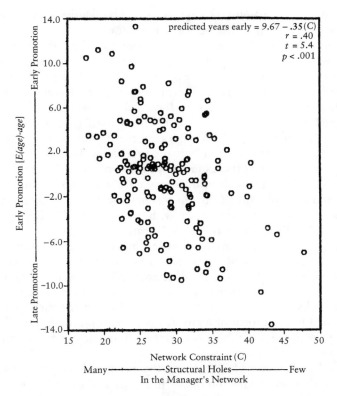

FIGURE 11.2 Social Capital Matters: Negative Association between Network Constraint and Early Promotion

The negative association between early promotion and network constraint in Figure 11.2 shows that early promotions go to managers with more social capital. Managers promoted early tend to have low-constraint networks (left side of the graph). Managers promoted late tend to have high-constraint networks (right side of the graph). The -0.35 estimate of the slope γ means that each point of additional constraint is associated with an average promotion delay of four months (-5.4 t-test, $p < 0.001$).

Large Bonus: Corroborating Other Evidence with Clear Causal Order

The structural hole argument gives a causal role to social structure. Consistent with the argument, I assume the primacy of social structure for theoretical and heuristic purposes. I am limited to assuming the primacy of social structure because the data I collected in the manufacturing firm are cross-sectional and so offer no evidence of causation (see Burt, 1992: 173–180, for discussion). It is difficult to gather survey network data, wait for the relative success of managers to emerge over time, then gather performance data.

I therefore use other data here to corroborate the baseline social capital effect displayed in Figure 11.2. The other data describe all senior men in the investment banking division of a large American financial organization. The data were obtained as part of a consulting project on the firm's compensation system. All of the data and data categories, including the network data, are from company personnel records. These data provide more than a replication of the social capital effect shown in Figure 11.2 because there is a clear time order of six months between the network and performance data. The organization gathers network data on its senior officers in one year in preparation for the distribution of bonuses the next year. Each year, officers are asked to identify people with whom they had substantial or frequent business dealings during the year and to indicate how productive it was to work with each person. The firm uses the average of these peer evaluations in bonus deliberations, but there is a network structure implicit in the evaluations that, according to structural hole theory, has implications for an officer's performance, which in turn is a key determinant of his bonus (see Eccles and Crane, 1988: chap. 8). To analyze these data, I identified the people cited as productive contacts by each senior man, then looked at the evaluations by each of his contacts to see how each contact evaluated the other contacts. I use the form of analysis I used for Figure 11.2 to communicate the evidence in these data without getting into details that might violate confidentiality.

Figures 11.3(a) and 11.3(b) show the predicted social capital effect on bonuses. The criterion variable on the vertical axis at the top of Figure 11.3 measures relative success in terms of bonus compensation, adjusted for human capital variables. I use bonus compensation rather than salary because salary is almost entirely determined by the human capital variables. Of many human capital variables I tested for association with compensation (including all of the variables used to define early promotion in the manufacturing sample of managers), rank and seniority (officer rank, years with the firm, and years in current job) accounted for 73 percent of the variance in bonus compensation (versus 95 percent of variance in salary compensation). An individual officer's bonus can be higher or lower than the bonus predicted by his rank and seniority. To measure relative bonus, I regressed dollars of bonus across seniority within each rank, then computed the z-score of the residual. An officer with a z-score of 1.0 on the vertical axis at the top of Figures 11.3(a) and 11.3(b) received a bonus one standard deviation larger than the average officer at his rank with his seniority.

Social capital is again linked with higher returns. The regression results at the top of Figures 11.3(a) and 11.3(b) show a significant negative association with network constraint (-6.5 t-test for γ). I get the same result if I hold human capital constant by using the ratio of bonus to salary compensation as a criterion variable (-4.2 t-test). The dollar metric for the effect at the top of Figures 11.3(a) and 11.3(b) is that the average bonus of the most-senior officers decreases by

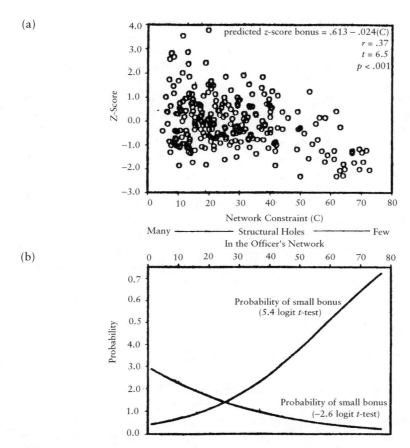

FIGURE 11.3(a) and **(b)** Social Capital Matters: Negative Association between Network Constraint and Bank Officers' Bonuses

seven thousand dollars per point of network constraint (the standard deviation of residual bonuses for the most-senior officers is $291 thousand). The high-constraint officers at the right in Figure 11.3 have only a few contacts, who tend to cite one another as contacts. The low-constraint officers on the left in Figures 11.3(a) and 11.3(b) have many contacts disconnected from one another, contacts who rarely cite one another as substantial or frequent business contacts. In other words, the officers on the left in Figures 11.3(a) and 11.3(b) have entrepreneurial networks, like Robert in Figure 11.1, with strong relations to contacts in otherwise disconnected parts of the firm.

The logit results at the bottom of Figures 11.3(a) and 11.3(b) show that the social capital effect is even stronger than implied by the data in the top panel of the figure. The top panel shows a triangular pattern in the data. On the right side of the graph, officers with the most constrained networks receive low bonuses.

On the left, officers receiving larger bonuses than their peers tend to have entrepreneurial networks, but many officers with equally entrepreneurial networks receive small bonuses. I attribute this to annual data. Entrepreneurial networks provide better access to rewarding opportunities, but that is no guarantee of exceptional gains every year. There is a 0.47 partial correlation between bonus in the current year and bonus in the previous year (after rank and seniority are held constant). Even the most productive officers sometimes see a lucrative year followed by a year of routine business. So, the logit results at the bottom of Figure 11.3 more accurately describe the social capital effect in these data. I divided the officers into three bonus categories: large (bonus more than a standard deviation larger than expected from rank and seniority), medium, and small (bonus more than a standard deviation less than expected from rank and seniority). Network constraint in the current year significantly decreases the probability of receiving a large bonus the next year (-2.6 t-test), but the stronger effect is the increased probability of receiving a low bonus next year (5.4 t-test).

Figures 11.2 and 11.3 offer baseline evidence of the average value of social capital. I now return to the probability sample of manufacturing managers described in Figure 11.2 to present evidence for the second part of my contingency argument, that the value of social capital decreases with the number of a manager's peers.

EVIDENCE OF CONTINGENT VALUE

The first issue is defining each manager's peers. The theoretical criterion is people who are substitutable in a structural equivalence sense of having similar relations with the same kinds of contacts (Burt, 1992: 208–215; Burt and Talmud, 1992; cf. Anheier, Gerhards, and Romo, 1995, on equivalence distinctions between forms of capital). Since I do not have network data sufficient to define peers by the theoretical criterion, however, I used the organization chart to define peers. I defined a manager's peers to be all of the people employed by the firm at his rank (senior, more senior, or most senior) in the same business function, broadly distinguishing field functions (sales and service), production functions (engineering and manufacturing), and corporate functions (human resources, finance, management information systems, and marketing).

Company records give the total number (N) of managers employed by the firm at each rank in each function. Adding this covariate to the regression model displayed in Figure 11.2 yields the following results (t-tests in parentheses):

$$predicted\ years\ early = 9.5476 - 0.3492\ C + 0.0008\ N + 0.0012\ C * N,$$
$$(-5.4) \qquad (0.7) \qquad (2.6)$$

which can be rewritten as:

$$predicted\ years\ early = (9.5476 + 0.0008\ N) - (0.3492 - 0.0012\ N)\ C.$$

To preserve the zero-point in the regression in Figure 11.2, N is measured as the deviation from its average across the 170 managers ($N = N$ – mean N). The regression results show three things. First, the social capital effect here is almost identical to the effect in Figure 11.2 (.3492 here versus 0.35 in Figure 11.2). In other words, the average value of social capital is not changed for these managers by adding the number of peers as a covariate. Second, the number of peers has no direct effect on early promotion (0.7 t-test). This is not surprising, because rank and function (and thus some variation in number of peers defined by rank and function) were held constant to define early promotion. A promotion is early relative to peers at the same rank within the same function. Third, the predicted effect of peers is significant (2.6 t-test, $p < 0.01$). For every additional person hired to do the same work, the value of social capital decreases by 0.001 for the work. If another 291 people were to be hired for the average job in this study population, social capital could be expected to have no value to managers in the job

$$(-0.3492 + 0.0012*291 = 0).$$

Confounding Effects

The value of social capital varies with several features of managerial work. I want to determine the unique effect of number of peers. Sixteen categories of managers are distinguished in Figure 11.4. The horizontal axis is the number of study population managers in each category (peers). The vertical axis is the correlation between network constraint and early promotion for sample managers from each category. The higher a category is in the graph, that is, the more negative the correlation between network constraint and early promotion, the more valuable social capital is for that category of managers. The value of social capital varies from a low among senior managers in jobs at the core of the firm ($r = -0.20$) to a high among the most-senior managers in sales and service ($r = -0.90$).

The first confounding factor is managerial rank. Social capital is more valuable to men in more-senior ranks. This is to be expected because there are fewer people at the top of the organization and they are more the authors of their jobs. The social capital effect on early promotion to senior rank is significant ($\gamma = -0.25$, -3.1 t-test; 98 respondents; circles in Figure 11.4), but stronger for early promotion to the more-senior rank ($\gamma = -0.44$, -3.0 t-test; 44 respondents; hollow triangles in Figure 11.4), and much stronger for early promotion to the most-senior rank ($\gamma = -0.79$, -5.6 t-test; 28 respondents; solid triangles in Figure 11.4; see Burt, Jannotta, and Mahoney, 1997, for similar contingency in social capital's association with annual performance evaluations). In fact, between human and social capital, social capital is the primary factor distinguishing managers promoted early to the highest rank. This can be seen by computing expected promotion age, *E(age)*, from the human-capital baseline model

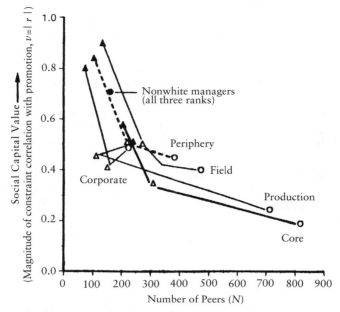

Values of Social Capital Varies with Number of Peers.

▲ Most-senior managers ▲ More -senior managers O Senior managers
*Lines connect ranks in same function or location·

FIGURE 11.4 Values of Social Capital Varies with Number of Peers.*

introduced with Figure 11.2, and regressing age at promotion to current rank over $E(age)$ and network constraint C to estimate β and γ. The standardized estimates of β and γ are 0.22 and 0.18, respectively, for senior managers, 0.02 and 0.26 for more-senior managers, and 0.04 and 0.76 for the most-senior managers. Managers sorted by human capital (β) at lower ranks are sorted by social capital (γ) at higher ranks. This is not to say that networks are richer in structural holes at the top of the firm. Analysis of variance shows no difference between ranks in average network constraint ($F_{2,167} = 0.08$, $p = 0.92$). What changes with managerial rank is the strength of association between network constraint and early promotion, which is stronger toward the top of the firm.

The second confounding factor is the higher value of social capital to managers working across significant boundaries within or around the firm (see Burt, 1992: 131ff.; Raider and Burt, 1996, for discussion). The work of these boundary managers presents issues unique to the situation of each manager. The boundary managers in this firm work in sales or service with specific client firms. They work at remote plant locations. They are newly hired managers. They are the nonwhite managers working in a firm composed primarily of whites. These managers are more visibly dealing with people different from themselves and so have to be more careful about how they craft relationships. The sales and service managers have to monitor interests in client firms. The managers at remote plants have to spend more time keeping in touch with shifting interests at corporate headquarters. Nonwhite and newly hired managers have to monitor colleagues more carefully because the errors of minorities and newcomers are more visible (Kanter, 1977: 206ff.). These tasks are made easier by the information and control benefits of structural holes, so it is not surprising to see a strong association between network constraint and early promotion for the boundary managers (−5.9 *t*-test for these managers versus −1.7 for other managers). There are several categories of boundary managers in Figure 11.4: nonwhites (solid circle), field managers (all three ranks of which are higher in Figure 11.4 than comparable ranks in other functions), and managers in remote plants or recently hired (the periphery managers in Figure 11.4, so called because they are on the periphery of the firm's social system).

These confounding effects notwithstanding, the most conspicuous feature of Figure 11.4 is the tendency for the value of social capital to decrease with the number of managers doing the same work. The value of social capital is higher for managers on the left side of the graph (where there are few peers) than it is for those on the right side of the graph (where there are many peers). The peer effect can be difficult to see because it is so closely associated with job rank. Fewer managers hold higher rank and social capital is more valuable for small N and high rank. The regression results for model II in Table 11.1 summarize the effects in Figure 11.4. Only two variables have a direct association with the value of social capital. The first is peers. Social capital is less valuable to managers with numerous peers (*t*-tests of −4.6 to −7.5). Second, social capital is more valuable to boundary managers (2.2 and 5.5 *t*-tests). Holding these two variables constant, variation by rank and function is negligible ($F_{5,8} = 2.73$, $p = 0.10$).

The Functional Form of Contingent Value

Figure 11.4 is repeated on the left in Figure 11.5 without lines connecting categories of adjacent ranks, displaying the aggregate regression line. The line, defined by regression model I in Table 1, is a social capital contingency function that describes how the value of social capital is contingent on the number of managers doing the same work.

Specifically, value decreases as a power function of peers. The value (v) of social capital to a category of managers doing the same work can be inferred from the magnitude of the negative correlation (r) between network constraint and relative success within the category, holding human capital differences constant: $v = |r|$, and predicted as a power function of the number (N) of managers in the category:

$$v = aN^b,$$

TABLE 11.1 Value of Social Capital Contingent on Number of Peers[*]

Variables	I	II
Intercept	8.44	5.05
Number of peers	−0.53	−0.46
	(−6.0)	(−4.6)
Job on a boundary of the firm	−	0.29
		(2.2)
Job at the most-senior rank		0.18
	−	(1.3)
Job at the more-senior rank	−	−0.13
		(−1.2)
Job in sales or service	−	0.06
		(0.5)
Job in production	−	−0.04
		(−0.3)
Corporate job	−	0.01
		(0.1)
R^2	0.72	0.95

[*]These are ordinary least-squares estimates from the 16 data points in Figure 11.4 predicting the magnitude of the correlation between early promotion and network constraint (value of social capital, v) Standard errors are given in parentheses. To estimate value v as a power function of number of peers N, the estimation equation is the following: $\ln(v) = \ln(a) + b \ln(N) + BX$, where B is a vector of regression coefficients and X contains the dummy variables in the rows. The dummy variable distinguishing boundary managers is one for nonwhites, managers hired during the last four years, managers in remote plants, and field managers.

where a and b are parameters to be estimated, $|r|$ is the absolute value of the correlation between network constraint and relative success, and estimates are available from the log form of the combined equations, $\ln |r| = \ln(a) + b(\ln N)$, though in a study population in which social capital is extremely valuable, r can be close to maximum, so Fisher's z can be a useful criterion variable.[3]

---

[3]   Useful in testing hypotheses about non-zero levels of correlation, Fisher's z is the arc hyperbolic tangent of a correlation its utility as a criterion variable measuring the value of social capital is that it keeps value scores within an upper bound of 1.0. Raw and transformed correlations are nearly identical for magnitudes from zero to about 0.5, then z is increasingly larger than r. The estimation equation with Fisher's z as the criterion variable $|r| = \ln(a) + b(\ln N)$, from which scores for the value of social capital can be recovered; $v = tanh[a(N)^b]$, where $atanh$ is the arc hyperbolic tangent, and $tanh$ is the hyperbolic tangent. Over the range of correlations in Figure 11.5, raw and transformed correlations yield similar predicted values of social capital scores for v predicted with z versus r as the criterion variable are correlated 0.98 for the categories of managers on the left in Figure 11.5, and 0.99 for the subsample data on the right in Figure 11.5.

The graph on the right in Figure 11.5 offers more data on the contingency function. For each manager, I drew a random subsample of similar managers within the total sample. I then computed the average number of peers, N, for managers in the subsample and the correlation, r, between network constraint and early promotion within the subsample.[4] Each of the 170 observations in the graph is a subsample correlation plotted against the corresponding subsample mean number of peers. The graph is like a sampling distribution across the social capital contingency function. The nonlinear contingency function is still evident in these more detailed data. The data fit the function about as well, despite the many more data now displayed (0.66 R^2 versus 0.72), and if I add the boundary and job rank variables from Table 11.1 to the regression equation, there is a strong effect for number of peers (−15.3 t-test for a −0.51 coefficient), a significant tendency for social capital to be more valuable to boundary managers (4.4 t-test), and a negligible association with job rank (1.5 t-test).

Further analysis reveals nothing to contradict the summary description in Figure 11.5. I fit alternative functional forms across the sixteen manager categories (left side of Figure 11.5) and the 170 subsample observations (right side of Figure 11.5). There is little difference between results obtained with the absolute value and square of the correlation r as the criterion variable measuring the value of social capital. Linear functions of N yield consistently weaker results than nonlinear functions. Power, exponential, and log functions yield similar results, but the power function better captures high values of social capital (closer association with Fisher's z) and does about as well as the other nonlinear forms across lower values. Given the simplicity of the power function and no loss of fit in describing contingent value as a power function of N, I limit my discussion to power functions. I also checked for continuity in the contingency function with a surface plot of performance scores averaged across a grid of network constraint on one axis and number of peers on the other. There are no significant bumps, dips, or discontinuities in the contingent value of social capital. The slope of the association between early promotion and network constraint changes systematically from a steep negative association for managers with few peers to a weaker negative association for managers with many peers. Only the slope is changing. Early promotion and network constraint are the same on average, and vary

---

[4]   This is a resampling procedure to test the robustness of the contingency function (e.g., Finifter, 1972). I created a list of managers, first, in order of the population size of categories in Figure 4, then at random within each category. The subsample around each manager i contains managers $i - n$ through $i + n$ on the list. I obtained results for alternative sizes of n. Small subsamples of n less than a handful generate wildly different results from one subsample to another because so few managers are in each subsample. Large subsample of n more than 30 obscure the steep part of the contingency function over few peers. The subsample results in Figure 11.5 are based on n equal to 5 percent of the population size of manager i's category (e.g., n is 8 for the most-senior field managers, of whom there are 150 in the study population).

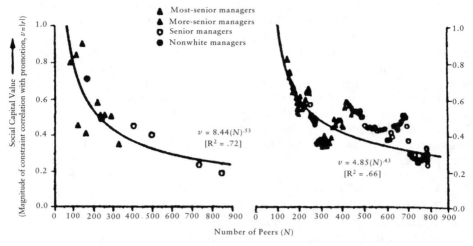

FIGURE 11.5 Contingency Function

similarly, for managers with many peers and managers with few peers. What differs across numbers of peers is the extent to which early promotion is correlated with network constraint—strong for managers with few peers, weak for managers with many peers. The smooth performance surface means that the contingency function in Figure 11.5 represents continuous change in the value of social capital.

DISCUSSION

I have presented argument and evidence for a structural ecology of social capital that describes how the value of social capital is contingent on the number of people doing the same work. Social capital, valuable on average, is especially valuable for managers with few peers because such managers do not have the guiding frame of reference provided by numerous competitors, nor the legitimacy provided by numerous people doing the same kind of work. The contingency function has two characteristics that say two things about the value of social capital: First, the value of social capital decreases with an increasing number of people doing the same work. Second, the rate at which peers erode the value of social capital is steepest where social capital is most valuable. In other words, peers most erode the value of social capital to leaders and other boundary-spanning managers who have few or no peers. Understanding the contingent value of social capital is a useful addition in its own right to organization theory, but the contingency function in particular can be a useful tool for thinking about organizations more generally. I close with three implications for organization research: virtual monopoly, network organizations, and research design.

Virtual Monopoly

Kinds of managerial work are distinguished in Figure 11.6 by the contingent value of social capital for the work. The solid bold line, function A, is the contingency function for the sample managers in Figure 11.5: $v = 4.85(N)^{-0.43}$. The dashed bold line, function A', shows the function for the same data but estimated with Fisher's z as the criterion variable. The two bold lines are parallel across the sample managers, diverging at low numbers of peers, numbers beyond the circumstances observed in the study population. Fisher's z preserves an upper bound of 1.0, which is reasonable, since value is a predicted magnitude of correlation.

Correlations predicted to be stronger than 1.0, however, are an interesting diagnostic of organization behavior. They indicate the number of peers below which managers have a virtual monopoly over their work. A manager for whom N equals 1 has no peers and so has a monopoly over the kind of work he or she does. His or her work is unique, perhaps as the chief executive officer, chairman of the board, or the key broker across an organization boundary. Beyond the human capital requirements of his or her work, the monopoly manager's success depends entirely on coordination with people doing other kinds of work—which means that the information and control benefits of social capital are especially valuable. How valuable is defined by the first parameter in the contingency function model. Given a contingency function estimated for a category of managers, $v = a(N)^b$, parameter a is the expected correlation between network constraint and success for managers with a monopoly on their job. When N equals 1, v equals a.

A near-zero estimate of parameter a means that social capital has no value. For example, function B in Figure 11.6 is estimated for the sample managers to describe the contingent value of social capital defined only by the authority relations. I recomputed network constraint from only the manager's authority relations (subordinates, boss, key sources of buy-in). Function B describes the association between early promotion and constraint in the network of a manager's authority relations. For reasons discussed elsewhere in an analysis of network content (Podolny and Baron, 1997; Burt, 1997a), there is little social capital value in the authority relations. Managers adapt to whatever structure of authority defines their jobs. Function B shows that the expected correlation between early promotion and authority-network constraint is consistently low, regardless of peers. The correlation is only 0.23 even at the extreme of monopoly ($a = 0.23$), implying that there are no circumstances for these senior managers in which the structure of authority relations generates social capital.

An estimate of parameter a larger than 1 means that managers with one or more peers enjoy a virtual monopoly over their work. In a large organization, two managers can do the same work but be isolated from one another such that each has a virtual monopoly over his or her work. These are managers virtually

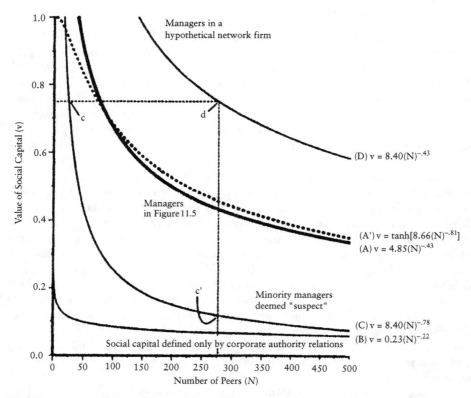

FIGURE 11.6 Work Conditions Distinguished by Social Capital Contingency Functions

free of peers, in terms of competition and legitimacy. Their relative success is completely determined by their relative access to the information and control benefits of social capital for reading the interests of significant other kinds of managers and knowing who can be brought together productively on new projects.

There is no one criterion number of peers that ensures a virtual monopoly. The number below which managers have a virtual monopoly depends on the extent to which managers doing their kind of work are scattered through the organization. The criterion is defined in a general way, however, by the contingency function. Solving the function for N when v equals 1 gives: virtual monopoly $N = (1/a)^{1/b}$. For example, the study population of senior managers in Figure 11.5—managers at the top of a large organization that grants substantial job autonomy to its senior managers—is differentiated such that a manager who is one of less than 40 people doing the same kind of work has a virtual monopoly: $(1/4.85)^{-1/.43} = 39.4$. At N equal to 39.4, the solid bold line in Figure 11.6 crosses the upper boundary of v equal to 1.

Other contingency functions in Figure 11.6 illustrate higher and lower thresholds for virtual monopoly. Virtual monopoly is readily available to managers described by function D, a hypothetical function included here as a heuristic device. I expect functions like D in a highly differentiated organization such as a large consulting firm or law practice containing many partners who are located in many cities and have diverse expertise. A manager has only to be one of less than 143 managers doing the same work in hypothetical function D to enjoy a virtual monopoly: $(1/8.4)^{-1/.43} = 142.6$.

In contrast, function C describes the contingent value of social capital for minority managers deemed "suspect" in the manufacturing firm from which I drew the sample of senior managers. Women and entry-rank men are the suspect senior managers in this firm in the sense that they are treated as outsiders (Burt, 1997b). Function C in Figure 11.6 is estimated for a probability sample of these suspect minority managers in the same way that function A was estimated for the probability sample of senior men. The steep slope of function C shows that women and entry-rank men in only the most unusual job assignments enjoy the benefits of social capital. Relative to senior men, women and entry-rank men are more visible in Kanter's (1977: 206ff.) sense of "tokens" being visible. There are fewer women in the senior ranks (12 percent), so they are visible across broader distances within the firm. Comparisons are more likely between a senior woman in marketing and a senior woman in finance, for example, than between similarly senior men in the two functions, because the two men would not stand out as so obviously different from the typical senior manager. While the senior men in Figure 11.5 have a virtual monopoly if they are one of less than 40 peers, women enjoy a comparable monopoly only if they are one of less than 17 peers: $(1/8.4)^{-1/.76} = 16.5$.

Network Organization

Observers from diverse perspectives see a shift in contemporary organizations away from bureaucracy, with layers of formal control replaced by fewer layers of negotiated informal control. The new form is a network organization. Sociological understandings of this change became articulate with Powell's (1990) discussion of network forms of organization. Powell and Smith-Doerr (1994) offered a stimulating synthesis of work on network organization (especially pp. 379ff. on the firm as a network of treaties, cf. Baker, 1992; Nohria, 1994; Sheppard and Tuchinsky, 1996), and Nohria (1996) has provided evidence of the shift to network forms of organization in even the largest of American corporations.

The shift away from bureaucracy means that managers cannot rely as much on directives from the firm. They are more than ever the authors of their own work. Firms gain by being able to identify, and adapt more readily to, needed production changes and market shifts (e.g., Piore and Sabel, 1984, on flexible specialization). There are new opportunities for managers, but there are also new costs. Coordination costs once borne by the corporate bureaucracy—each person responsible for coordination within a limited domain of responsibility—are now borne by individual managers who have responsibility for coordination across broader domains, with a corresponding increase in uncertainty, stress, and potentially disruptive conflict. In this environment, social capital is important. The shift away from bureaucracy is a shift to social capital as the medium for coordination within the organization.

The shift away from bureaucracy calls for a shift in research strategy for studying organizations. The tradition has been to identify forms of organization by their structure. The shift from a unitary to a multidivisional form of hierarchy is easy to see, for example, as a change in the formal structure of firms. The shift from hierarchy to network organization is more difficult to see in the same way because the change is not structural so much as procedural. The shift is from one coordination mechanism to another: formal coordination via bureaucracy to informal coordination via interpersonal negotiation. There is associated structural change in the form of fewer layers of bureaucracy and more complex interpersonal relations, but the structural change is only attendant to the fundamental change from formal to informal coordination.

Given that formal structure is such an imperfect indicator of network organization, and given the difficulty of observing interpersonal negotiations in any systematic way across the managers in a firm, a network organization needs to be defined and analyzed in terms of consequences. While informal relations are random noise in a traditional bureaucracy, they are the central coordination mechanism in a network organization. A firm can be said to be a network organization to the extent that success in the firm depends on informal relations. In other words, a firm is a network organization to the extent that a manager's success depends on social capital. When coordination is based on negotiated informal control, as in a network organization, more successful managers will be the managers with better access to the information and control benefits of structural holes.

A social capital definition of network organization has three virtues. First, it gives the concept operational meaning for empirical research. A firm is a network organization to the extent that there is a strong correlation within the firm between relative success and network constraint. Second, it makes explicit, through the contingent value of social capital, the fact that network organization is a matter of degree, not an absolute. All firms have network forms toward the top of the organization. Social capital is valuable to the work of managers with few peers, whether the managers are in a traditional hierarchy or a network organization. What makes a network organization different is that social capital is also valuable to the work of managers with more peers. In a traditional hierarchy, the benefits of social capital are only available to managers in unique positions. The slope of the contingency function for a set of managers indicates the rate at which individuals are subject to peer pressure and corporate convention. A steep slope means that the value of social capital plummets as the number of peers increases from virtual monopoly ($\partial v/N = bN^{b-1}$). Competition between peers leaves little room for individuals to develop entrepreneurial opportunities. Emphasis on corporate convention indicates the firm's lack of interest in the efforts of individual managers to develop opportunities.

The point is illustrated by functions C and D in Figure 11.6. Hypothetical function D predicts a correlation of −0.75, for example, between network constraint and relative success for managers who are one of 276 managers doing the same work (point d on the function). That magnitude of correlation is only observed among the sample managers at the highest rank (just below vice president, top of Figure 11.4). Function D describes managers in a network organization. Function C, in contrast, describes managers in a traditional hierarchy in that they are widely denied the benefits of social capital. The function shows that the 0.75 magnitude of correlation occurs among minority managers, but only if they are one of 24 or fewer managers doing the same work (point c on the function). Social capital has no effect on their relative success when there are 276 minority managers doing the same kind of work (v equals 0.12 when N equals 276; point c' on the function).

Third, the social capital definition of a network organization makes explicit, again through the contingent value of social capital, that network organization need not be equally present even for managers doing the same work in the same firm. Two managers can do the same work in the same firm, but one can experience the firm as a traditional hierarchy while the other experiences the firm as a network organization. Function C in Figure 11.6 shows that minority managers experience the study organization as a traditional bureaucracy. Social capital is only valuable when they have very few peers. More peers quickly trigger peer pressure to conform and regulation by corporate convention. The higher average value of social capital implied by function A shows that non-minority managers experience the same firm as more of a network organization.

Designing Research

Contingency functions are a frame of reference for designing research and cumulating results across studies. An average social capital effect estimated from a sample, as in Figure 11.2, depends on the shape of underlying contingency function(s) and where along the function(s) managers were selected for study. The expected magnitude of correlation between social capital and success, $E(v)$, is the sum of where sample managers i exist on function, v_i, and the probability, p_i, with which managers at that point are sampled for study: $E(v) = \Sigma_i p_i v_i$. For example, minority managers are largely denied the benefits of social capital (function C in Figure 11.6), but a sample of minority managers with unique jobs would show evidence of a strong social capital effect (point c on the function).

The most obvious implication for research design is that the richest evidence on social capital lies in data on managers with few peers. Some jobs are held by managers operating in consensus with peers and in accord with the corporate bureaucracy's chain of command. Other jobs are held by managers operating relatively independent of the corporate bureaucracy. The second kind of manager will reveal more evidence of social capital effects. Illustrations in this analysis are managers in the highest ranks of the organization, boundary managers, and, more generally, managers with few peers.

The contingency function is particularly important to research at the other end of the socioeconomic scale: where people are trying to break out of lower classes into a better way of life. It might seem that social capital is irrelevant, since individuals at the bottom of the socioeconomic scale have relatively little control over their lives. Whatever its value on average, however, social capital will be more valuable to those few individuals who try to break away from peers and bureaucratic regulations to find their own route to success. Network entrepreneurs at the bottom of the socioeconomic scale are a promising and important subject for social capital research, as initial results are starting to show (e.g., Portes and Zhou, 1992; Bian, 1994: chap. 5; Borjas, 1995; Sanders and Nee, 1996).

The implication for cumulating research results across studies follows similarly. In the absence of a contingency function, research is aggregated across studies as if each were a replicate test of the same proposition. A naive observer can be expected to summarize a set of studies by stating the proportion of studies that reported a strong social capital effect on performance. But suppose one had data on the employees who respond to telephone complaints and inquiries from customers. These people work in large rooms of peers, and their calls are monitored by a manager who is listening to ensure adherence to the firm's guidelines for the job. These are employees at the boundary of the firm because of their contact with clients, but in their large numbers the firm is not looking for innovation so much as courteous reliability. These are employees on the far right of contingency functions like that in Figure 11.5. There is no reason to expect social capital to be valuable for success in this job, though it might prove useful in escaping to a new job.

Thus, understanding the contingent value of social capital allows for more accurate comparison across research projects, which means faster cumulation. Social capital studies of managers in jobs with large numbers of peers can be put aside as ill-designed. Studies of managers with few peers warrant close scrutiny. Studies reporting different strengths of association between managerial success and social capital can be integrated in terms of the relative extent to which managers in the separate studies work with different numbers of peers. This is precisely the kind of analytical power needed to establish social capital explanations on a par with the human capital explanations on which we were weaned.

REFERENCES

Allen, Thomas J., and Saul Cohen 1969 "Information flow in R&D labs." *Administrative Science Quarterly*, 14: 12–19.

Anheler, Helmut K., Jürgen Gerhards, and Frank P. Romo 1995 "Forms of capital and social structure in cultural fields: Examining Bourdieu's social topography." *American Journal of Sociology*, 100: 859–903.

Blan, Yanjie 1994 *Work and Inequality in Urban China* Albany, NY: State University of New York Press.

Baker, Wayne 1992 "The network organization in theory and practice." In Nitin Nohria and Robert G. Eccles (eds), *Networks and Organizations* 397–429. Boston: Harvard Business School Press.

Becker, Gary 1975 *Human Capital*, 2d ed Chicago: University of Chicago Press.

Belliveau, Maura A., Charles A. O'Reilly, and James B. Wade 1996 "Social capital at the top: Effects of social similarity and status on CEO compensation." *Academy of Management Journal*, 39:1568–1593.

Borjas, George J. 1995 "Ethnicity, neighborhoods, and human-capital externalities." *American Economic Review*, 85:365–390.

Bourdieu, Pierre, end Loïc J. D. Wacquant 1992 *An Invitation to Reflexive Sociology*, Chicago: University of Chicago Press.

Brass, Daniel J. 1992 "Power in organizations: A social network perspective." In Gwen Moore and J. A. Whitt (eds.), *Research in Politics and Society*: 295–323. Greenwich, CT: JAI Press.

Breiger, Ronald L. 1995 "Socioeconomic achievement and social structure." In *Annual Review of Sociology*, 21: 115–136. Palo Alto, CA: Annual Reviews.

Burt, Ronald S. 1980 "Autonomy in a social topology." *American Journal of Sociology*, 85:892–925.

—— 1983 Corporate Profits and Cooptation. New York: Academic Press.

—— 1988 "The stability of American markets." *American Journal of Sociology*, 93 356–395.

—— 1992 *Structural Holes*. Cambridge, MA: Harvard University Press.

—— 1995 "Le capital social, les trous structuraux, et l'entrepreneur." Trans. by Emmanuel Lazega. *Revue Francaise de Sociologie*, 25: 599–628.

—— 1997a "A note on social capital and network content." *Social Networks*, vol. 19 (in press).

—— 1997b "The gender of social capital." *Rationality and Society*, vol. 9 (in press).

Burt, Ronald S., and John H. Freeman 1994 "Market structure constraint in Germany." Working paper, Graduate School of Business, University of Chicago.

Burt, Ronald S., Joseph E. Jannotta, Jr., and James T. Mahoney 1997 "Personality correlates of structural holes." *Social Networks*, vol 19 (in press).

Burt, Ronald S., and Ilan Talmud 1992 "Market niche." *Social Networks*, 14 139–149.

Burt, Ronald S., Yuki Yasuda, and Miguel Guilarte 1996 "Competition, contingency, and the external structure of markets." Paper presented at INSEAD conference, Organizations in Markets, Fontainebleau, France.

Campbell, Karen E., Peter V. Marsden, and Jeanne Hurlbert 1986 "Social resources and socio-economic status." *Social Networks*, 8: 97–117.

Coleman, James S. 1988 "Social capital in the creation of human capital." *American Journal of Sociology*, 94: S95–S120.

—— 1990 *Foundations of Social Theory*. Cambridge, MA: Harvard University Press.

Cook, Karen S., and Richard M. Emerson 1978 "Power, equity and commitment in exchange networks." *American Sociological Review*, 43: 712–739.

Cook, Karen S., Richard M. Emerson, Mary R. Gillmore, and Toshio Yamagishi 1983 "The distribution of power in exchange networks: Theory and experimental results." *American Journal of Sociology*, 89: 275–305.

DiMaggio, Paul 1992 "Nadel's paradox revisited: Relational and cultural aspects of organizational structure." In Nitin Nohria and Robert G. Eccles (eds.) *Networks and Organizations*, 118–142. Boston: Harvard Business School Press.

Eccles, Robert G., and Dwight B. Crane 1988 *Doing Deals*. Boston: Harvard Business School Press.

Fernandez, Roberto M., and Roger V. Gould 1994 "A dilemma of state power: Brokerage and influence in the national health policy domain." *American Journal of Sociology*, 99: 1455–1491.

Finifter, Bernard M. 1972 "The generation of confidence: Evaluating research findings by random subsample replication." In Herbert L. Costner (ed.), *Sociological Methodology*, 1972: 112–175. San Francisco: Jossey-Bass.

Flap, Hendrik D., and Nan D. De Graaf 1989 "Social capital and attained occupational status." *Netherlands Journal of Sociology*, 22: 145–161.

Freeman, Linton C. 1977 "A set of measures of centrality based on betweenness." *Sociometry*, 40: 35–40.

Gabbay, Shaul M. 1996 "Social capital in the creation of financial capital." Unpublished Ph.D. dissertation, Columbia University.

Gargiulo, Martin, and Mario Benassi 1993 "Informal control and managerial flexibility in network organizations." Working paper, INSEAD.

Granovetter, Mark S. 1973 "The strength of weak ties." *American Journal of Sociology*, 78: 1360–1380.

———— 1995 *Getting a Job*. Chicago: University of Chicago Press.

Han, Shin-Kap 1993 "Churning firms in stable markets." *Social Science Research*, 21: 406–418.

———— 1994 "Mimetic isomorphism and its effect on the audit services market." *Social Forces*, 73: 637–664.

Hannan, Michael T., and John H. Freeman 1989 *Organizational Ecology*. Cambridge, MA: Harvard University Press.

Hargadon, Andrew B., and Robert I. Sutton 1997 "Technology brokering and innovation: Evidence from a product design firm." *Administrative Science Quarterly*, vol. 42 (in press).

Heather A., and Lisa E. The ecological dynamics of careers: The impact of organizational founding, dissolution, and merger on job mobility." *American Journal of Sociology*, 100: 104–152.

Hirschi, Travis 1972 *Causes of Delinquency*. Berkeley, CA: University of California Press.

Jang, Ho 1997 "Market structure, performance, and putting-out in the Korean economy" Unpublished Ph. D. dissertation, University of Chicago.

Kanter, Rosabeth M. 1977 *Men and Women of the Corporation*. New York: Harper & Row.

Kohn, Melvin L., and Carmi Schooler 1983 *Work and Personality*. Norwood, NJ: Ablex.

Kotter, John P. 1982 *The General Managers*. New York: Free Press.

Krackhardt, David, and Robert N. Stern 1988 "Informal networks and organizational crisis: An experimental simulation." *Social Psychology Quarterly*, 51: 123–140.

Lazega, Emmanuel 1994 "Analyse de réseaux et sociologie des organizations." *Revue Francaise de Sociologie*, 34: 293–320.

Lin, Nan 1998 *Social Resources and Social Action*. New York: Cambridge University Press (forthcoming).

Lin, Nan, and Mary Dumin 1986 "Access to occupations through social ties." *Social Networks*, 8: 365–385.

Lin, Nan, Walter Ensel, and John Vaughn 1981 "Social resources and strength of ties: Structural factors in occupational status attainment." *American Sociological Review*, 46: 393–405.

Markovsky, Barry, David Willer, and Travis Patton 1988 "Power relations in exchange networks." *American Sociological Review*, 53: 220–236.

Marsden, Peter V., and Jeanne Hurlbert 1988 "Social resources and mobility outcomes: A replication and extension." *Social Forces*, 66: 1038–1059.

Martinelli, Alberto 1994 "Entrepreneurship and management." In Neil J. Smelser and Richard Swedberg (eds.), *The Handbook of Economic Sociology*: 476–503. Princeton, NJ: Princeton University Press.

Merton, Robert K. 1968 "Continuities in the theory of reference group behavior." In Robert K. Merton, *Social Theory and Social Structure*: 335–440. New York: Free Press.

——— 1984 "Socially expected durations: A case study of concept formation in Sociology." In Walter W. Powell and Richard Robbins (eds.), *Conflict and Consensus*: 262–283. New York: Free Press.

Meyerson, Eva M. 1994 "Human capital, social capital and compensation: The relative contribution of social contacts to managers' incomes." *Acta Sociologica*, 37: 383–399.

Mintzberg, Henry 1973 *The Nature of Managerial Work*. New York: Harper and Row.

Nohria, Nitin 1994 "The virtual organization." In Charles Heckscher and Anne Donnellon (eds.), *The Post-Bureaucratic Organization*: 108–128. Thousand Oaks, CA: Sage.

——— 1996 "From the M-form to the N-form: Taking stock of changes in the large industrial corporation." Harvard Business School working paper 96–054.

Padgett, John F., and Christopher K. Ansell 1993 "Robust action and the rise of the Medici, 1400–1434." *American Journal of Sociology*, 98: 1259–1319.

Pennings, Johannes M., Kyung-mook Lee, and Arjen van Witteloostuijn 1997 "Intangible resources and firm mortality: A study of professional services firms." *Academy of Management Journal*, vol. 100 (in press).

Pfeffer, Jeffrey 1983 "Organizational demography." In L. L. Cummings and Barry M. Staw (eds), *Research in Organizational Behavior*, 5: 299–357. Greenwich, CT: JAI Press.

Plore, Michael, and Charles Sabel 1984 *The Second Industrial Divide* New York Basic Books.

Podolny, Joel M., and James N. Baron 1997 "Relationships and resources: Social networks and mobility in the workplace." *American Sociological Review*, vol. 62 (in press).

Portes, Alejandro, and Patricia Landolt 1996 "The downside of social capital." *American Prospect*, 16: 18–21.

Portes, Alejandro, and Min Zhou 1992 "Gaining the upper hand: Economic mobility among immigrant and domestic minorities." *Ethnic and Racial Studies*, 15: 491–522.

Powell, Walter W. 1990 "Neither market nor hierarchy: Network forms of organization." In L. L. Cummings and Barry M. Staw (eds.), *Research in Organizational Behavior*, 12: 295–336. Greenwich, CT: JAI Press.

Powell, Walter W., and Laurel Smith-Doerr 1994 "Networks and economic life." In Neil J. Smelser and Richard Swedberg (eds.). *The Handbook of Economic Sociology*: 368–402. Princeton, NJ: Princeton University Press.

Putnam, Robert D. 1993 *Making Democracy Work: Civic Traditions in Modern Italy*. Princeton, NJ: Princeton University Press.

Raider, Holly J., and Ronald S. Burt 1996 "Boundaryless careers and social capital." In Michael B. Arthur and Denise M. Rousseau (eds.), *The Boundaryless Career*: 187–200. New York: Oxford University Press.

Rosenthal, Elizabeth A. 1996 "Social networks and team performance." Unpublished Ph.D. dissertation, University of Chicago.

Sanders, Jimy M., and Victor Nee 1996 "Immigrant self-employment: The family as social capital and the value of human capital." *American Sociological Review*, 61: 231–249.

Sheppard, Blair H., and Maria Tuchinsky 1996 "Micro-OB and the network organization" In Roderick M. Kramer and Tom R. Tyler (eds.), *Trust in Organizations*: 140–165. Thousand Oaks, CA: Sage.

Simmel, Georg 1955 *Conflict and the Web of Group Affiliations*. Trans. by Kurt H. Wolff and Reinhard Bendix New York: Free Press.

Sparrowe, Raymond T., and Pamela A. Popielarz 1995 "Weak ties and structural holes: The effects of network structure on careers." Working paper, Department of Management, University of Illinois-Chicago.

Stinchcombe, Arthur L. 1990 *Information and Organizations*. Berkeley, CA: University of California Press.

Sutton, Robert I., and Andrew B. Hargadon 1996 "Brainstorming groups in context: Effectiveness in a product design firm." *Administrative Science Quarterly*, 41: 685–718.

Talmud, Ilan 1994 "Relations and profit: The social organization of Israeli industrial competition." *Social Science Research*, 23: 109–135.

Yasuda, Yuki 1993 "A comparative structural analysis of American and Japanese markets" Unpublished Ph.D. dissertation, Columbia University.

Ziegler, Rolf 1982 "Market structure and cooptation" Working paper, Institut für Soziologie, University of Munich.

Chapter 12

Human Capital, Social Capital and Compensation: The Relative Contribution of Social Contacts to Managers' Incomes[*]

Eva M. Meyerson[**]

Industriens Utredningsinstitut, Stockholm, Sweden

In this study the additional effect of social capital over and above the contribution of human capital on the income attainment of managers is explored. A regression analysis of a 1985 sample of 111 executive team members in Swedish public firms shows that social capital is an important influencing factor of managers' incomes. The results also show that firm size increases managers' income levels. Furthermore, it is not, as argued in earlier network research, weak ties that generate these instrumental effects but strong ties.

1. INTRODUCTION

Next to financial and human capital, social capital or social network is an important asset. In the scientific literature social capital has been analyzed less, both theoretically and empirically, than human capital. Given the influence of

---

[*] Reprinted from Eva Meyerson, "Human Capital, Social Capital and Compensation: The Relative Contribution of Social Contacts to Managers Income:, *Acta Sociologica* 1994, vol. 37, pp. 383–399, by permission of Scandinavian University Press, Oslo, Norway.
[**] Eva M. Meyerson Industriens Utredningsinstitut, Box 5501, 114 85 Stockholm, Sweden.

human capital on managers' income attainment the additional effect of social capital is studied. The analysis focuses on private rates of return on social capital.

Results from interface research on stratification and network analysis point to the relative importance of social capital for individual gains such as compensation benefits. Boxman, De Graaf & Flap (1991) report that social capital adds to rather than replaces human capital in managers' income attainment. Human capital produces social capital, but the effect is not very strong. Social capital and human capital interact in the income attainment process but the hypothesis that social capital multiplies the return on human capital is refuted. Contrary to what is often assumed, returns on human capital decrease when managers have access to a large volume of social capital. Based on these findings Boxman, De Graaf & Flap (1991) suggest a duplication of the study in different institutional contexts.

In this article I present some results from an investigation of the relationship between Swedish executive managers' social and human capital and their incomes. In the first section I relate the human capital theory of investment to ideas on social capital effects on individuals' attainment of income. The second section reports some new results on the type of ties that make social capital enhance income attainment.

Finally, I discuss some implications of the results. The main conclusion is that social capital exhibits a strong effect on managers' income and that the social capital that generates high income mainly contains networks based on strong ties. The findings have implications for the recruitment of managerial talent. As earlier research shows managers recruited to top positions have talents determined partly by their social capital. The social capital that generates higher income is not necessarily the social capital that generates talented managers. The results shed some light on the question of how the Swedish society allocates managerial talent.

2. HUMAN CAPITAL AND SOCIAL CAPITAL AS RESOURCES

Nobel prize winner Gary Becker's most famous scientific contribution to date is the theory of human capital investment in which the determinants of the distribution of income are put forth. The theory is formulated as a set of rate of return functions from human capital investment that determines the correlation between income from work and human capital (see Lindbeck 1992; Becker 1992, 1964). Human capital is created when a person's skills and capabilities are augmented. The acquisition of human capital improves the conditions for an individual to act in new ways (Coleman 1992: 304).

Investments in human capital are often measured as years of schooling and workplace experiences. According to Becker's theory, investment in human capital is profitable for an individual if the present value of the expected future rate of return of that investment is greater than the investment costs. Many empirical studies of inequality rely on a human capital analysis like: differences in schooling and training and differences in income profiles and income over time (see Lindbeck 1992 and Kazamaki Ottersten et al. 1994 and Lindbeck 1992 for an overview). Yet, according to Lazear (1993) the empirical support for traditional human capital models is weak and often difficult to interpret.

Becker (1992) claims that the theory of human capital investment relates inequality in earnings to differences not only in talents and bequest but also to family background and other assets (see also Becker & Tomes 1986). Family background, such as the amount of attention a child receives from his parents, is argued by Coleman to be of extreme importance for school performance. Social infrastructure, such as a child's family relationships, is part of the social capital (see Coleman 1965, 1992; Loury 1977, 1987.) The idea of social relationships extending an individual's access to human capital is easy to envisage. For instance, if you do not have the skill to mend your bike you ask a friend, who does it for you. Even though you lack a skill you have access to it through your relationships, although the access is clearly not as straightforward as it would be if it were your own skill. That type of skill is typically not as available as your own. In this case there is at least one type of cost involved; a credit slip is issued. You help me today and I will help you sometime in the future. By adding social capital to a traditional human capital model, new and more easily interpreted results can be generated.

2.1. Social Capital

An important idea within network research is that a person's relationships are resources for instrumental action (Lin 1982; Lin & Dumin 1986).[1] Burt refers to social networks as a form of social capital analogous to human capital. Just as human capital can be defined as the array of valuable skills and knowledge a person has accumulated over time, social capital is the array of valuable

---

[1] There is a great variety of networks research from different perspectives, yet there is no integrated systematic theory of networks to be found. The concept of a network is often used as a metaphor. The problem with metaphors, especially in science, is that the concepts in use become unclear and therefore difficult to interpret (Mitchell 1969). There are, however, suggestions on how to define a network and its body of concepts. A frequently used definition is that a network is a set of direct and indirect social relationships centered around a given person, object or event (see Mitchell 1969). Anderson & Carlos (1979) state that these links are instrumental in the sense that they serve in the attainment of certain ambitions or goals and communicate aspirations and expectations. Links or ties that connect different actors in a network can be expressed as strong or weak, and as positive or negative. Ties are dynamic by nature and likely to change.

relationships a person has accumulated over time (Burt 1991).[2] According to Burt, a network is not only a device to receive resources, but a network is also a device to create resources such as other networks, that in turn create new resources and opportunities, thus the term social capital. '*Your social capital gives you opportunities to turn a profit from the application of your human capital*' (Burt 1992).

The social context of the involved actors is the crucial factor in deciding how an instrumental network should be structured. One type of relational structure may be instrumental in a specific social context where another type may not be.[3] I suggest that the effects of the relational structure, i.e., of the social capital, are contingent on the strategic situation. Social capital can be applied for different purposes given different contexts, and therefore can be structured in different ways (Coleman 1992: 302).

2.2. Social Capital for Mobilizing or for Information Accrual?

What type of social relations turn into instrumental social capital? Granovetter presented the thesis that a specific type of weak tie, the bridge tie, is more instrumental for access to information than strong ties (Granovetter 1973). Granovetter defines a bridge tie as a tie that links two networks with each other that otherwise would not be connected; Burt (1991) names this tie non-redundant. The bridge tie is typically weak, since the process of cognitive balance tends to eliminate unbalanced triads that make all three persons interconnected (Granovetter 1973: 1364–1365).

According to Granovetter the bridge tie is the element that forms the access to new networks, thus increasing the diversity and size of the network. Granovetter (1974) found that it is easier to find jobs through weak ties than through strong ties. It is often suggested that a weak tie increases an individual's reservation wage. The number of weak ties gives him job options and hence increases his bargaining power (see Montgomery 1992). Freidkin's (1980) test of the Granovetter thesis also showed that novel information tends to flow through bridge ties (weak non-redundant ties) and not through strong or weak redundant (overlapping) ties.

---

[2] Burt suggests that research within this stream may be divided into two sections. In the first, a network is seen as something that provides you with specific resources, for example becoming wealthy, or getting a job (Granovetter 1973; Lin 1982; Lin & Dumin 1986). The second line of research suggested by Burt looks at how the structure of your network is a form of capital in its own right (see Burt 1990: 3; 1992).

[3] According to Coleman, '*Social capital is defined by its function. It is not a single entity but a variety of different entities, with two elements in common: they all consist of some aspect of social structures, and they facilitate certain actions by actors, whether persons or corporate actors within the structure. Like other forms of capital, social capital is productive, making possible the achievement of certain ends that in its absence would not be possible*' (1988: S98; 1992: 302).

A strong tie between two individuals increases the likelihood that their other contacts, friends and colleagues will be introduced to one another (see Granovetter 1973). Hence, an individual connected to others mainly through strong ties will have a restricted network made up of ties that are overlapping, i.e., ties connecting to the same set of individuals (Burt calls the overlap of ties redundant ties).

Strong ties are less conducive to carrying novel information than are weak non-redundant ties.[4] On the other hand, strong ties re-enforce cohesion. *Cohesive groups create norms that influence individuals' choice of action, and also their choice to refrain from action* (Merton 1968; Pinard 1968; Granovetter 1973, 1974; Coleman 1988; see also Meyerson 1992: ch. 11 for an extensive discussion). In terms of exerting influence, strong redundant ties are instrumental in mobilizing or restraining others' actions. The existence of strong ties and redundant ties suggests that the individual belongs to a network that has a configuration of a rigid system of norms. Effective norms demand what Coleman labels closure. 'Where there is an interdependence between two or more individuals there is a risk for actor "a" to impose externalities on actor "b" if no efficient norms have emerged to restrict unwanted actions' (Coleman 1988: S105). The interdependence between individuals such as described above, where the actors pay a very high cost to leave the interdependent relationship, is argued to create a cohesive network based on strong ties of business associates with emerging norms.[5]

So far it has been argued that strong ties are crucial for making others do or not do things for you and non-redundant ties instrumental to novel information since non-commitment to consensus prevents susceptibility to novel information. Networks that are made up of strong ties become more mobilization oriented and networks made up of non-redundant ties become more information oriented. My argument is that you cannot have both information-oriented and mobilization-oriented networks in a stable equilibrium. Our next task is to establish the motive for the point that you cannot have it all: both a mobilization-oriented network and an information-oriented network in one group: cohesion restricts novel information accrual.

The literature suggests two ways in which cohesion restricts information accrual. One of the processes is formulated by Granovetter (1973), who claims that what makes a small group cohesive is strong ties. Granovetter suggests that '. . . *the strength of a tie is a (probably linear) combination of the amount of*

---

[4] This does not mean that information flows are not found between individuals with strong connections, as mentioned by Granovetter (1982). However, novel information tends to be less novel where a crowd is highly interconnected.

[5] However, these ties are of course of no use if they do not yield access to valuable resources for the person, such as a Chief Executive Officer. Strong overlapping networks are not instrumental unless they mobilize relevant resources. In this special context our focus is on the structure of professional networks that are assumed to have been established because they are resource contacts.

time, the emotional intensity, the intimacy (mutual confiding), and the reciprocal services which characterize the tie' (1973: 1361). Granovetter claims that more intensive dyadic interaction ultimately leads to the formation of a dense, close-knit network in which most members directly interact with one another while weak dyadic ties produce a loose-knit network in which many of its members do not interact directly with one another. As a result, a highly cohesive network tends to become exclusively self-sufficient and increasingly isolated. The network or the group becomes more or less closed to outsiders and the boundary between members and non-members becomes rigid (Granovetter 1973). Granovetter's point is that individuals in loose-knit networks are more likely to be exposed to information sources that provide novel information.

The reasoning behind Granovetter's idea is twofold. First, building strong ties involves more time commitment (Granovetter 1973). The more cohesive the group becomes, the greater amount of interaction it demands, and vice versa. Ties external to the network will be less entertained. Second, cognitive balance theory postulates that if a and b are connected by strong ties and a and c interact intensively, b and c also will interact (the transitivity argument). However, it in possible to find examples of how a person learns to live with, or even learns to prefer, imbalanced triads, especially in larger structures. While there is no doubt that '. . *structural balance theory has received impressive corroboration in empirical research . . . transitivity is certainly not expected to occur as a matter of course in political networks, in fact imbalance triads are very common in politics'* (Anderson 1979: 455–456). Anderson further states that a friendship relation is in practice often intransitive as well. Meanwhile, research points to the fact that individuals dissimilar to the rest of the team members tend to exit the team (Wagner, Pfeffer & O'Reilly 1984) and groups marked by internal differences are most likely to dissolve (Newcomb 1961; McCain, O'Reilly & Pfeffer 1983).

A second factor likely to limit information accrual in cohesive groups is cognitive dissonance. According to the theory of cognitive dissonance, individuals are more willing to expose themselves to information that is consistent with their beliefs or decisions than they are to information that conflicts with their beliefs or previous decisions. Individuals connected with strong ties tend to develop a commitment to one another and to their group. According to theories of cognitive dissonance, information that disturbs the consensus of the group's basic perception of reality is likely to be rejected. If there is a collision between an individual's values and those of his group the individual will handle the situation and avoid experiencing cognitive dissonance by adjusting his values.

An illustration of cognitive dissonance is given by Gilad, Kaish & Loeb (1987). They found that poorly performing business acquisitions are often not divested until the senior executive responsible for the acquisition leaves the firm. This suggests the biasing effect of strongly held beliefs on the ability to cope with contradictory information, and to arrive at an important decisions such as that to divest. (For further elaboration of cognitive dissonance see Festinger 1957; Frey 1982.)

Hence, the ties that make up network structures efficient in information accrual are precisely the ties that are non-instrumental restraining and mobilizing others for action. If enough ties in the network are made up of strong ties, over time the non-redundant will either be refuted because of time restriction for entertaining them or because they provide information threatening to the consensus, or be incorporated and eventually become strong.

The chief executive officer, the CEO, who wants a team talented in information accrual would thus want to recruit members who can put out tentacles into different spheres of life and who are free to take in novel information. In order to achieve this goal the CEO must avoid creating a cohesive team, and recruit dissimilar members instead. The CEOs choice of strategy influences all levels in the organizational hierarchy and consequently all managers will behave in accordance to this rule if they want to make a career within the organization. As a consequence, the ability of an executive to use his social capital to obtain resources is not always a question of diversity or size of a network.[6]

The recruitment of managers are often based on strong ties (Meyerson 1992). The use of strong ties in the recruitment of executive teams members is prominent in the sample of teams in Swedish public firms. A recruitment procedure where individuals recruit one another produces trust. Established norms can be re-enforced by owners or CEOs when they select what they consider to be loyal and talented people. Hence a mobilization-oriented network can be instrumental for high salaries.

The higher up a position in an organization is located, the stronger the impact an individual has on the performance of the firm. In cases with asymmetric information I suggest that trust becomes a substitute for other selection rules in the recruitment of top executives (see Montgomery 1988; Meyerson 1992). Trust is in this context interpreted in Williamson's terminology as 'calculative' trust—trust justified by expectations of positive reciprocal consequences (economic exchange) however loosely coupled to a specific significant other. Hence,

---

[6] Meyerson (1992) finds support for the thesis that, given the social and economic context of an executive team in a Swedish public firm, different characteristics of social capital were developed. Social capital of an executive team (in this case the external relational structure) is structured in a way to give an integrated team (strong cohesion among the team members) an external network with a mobilizing function, while a differentiated team's (weak cohesion among the members) efficient social capital is more oriented towards information accrual. Furthermore, a mobilizing external network contains strong and redundant ties, whereas the information-accrual network is structured by weak and non-redundant ties. The motive for the choice of different network structure is that the differentiated teams were found in firms where there was an easy access to financial capital while the opposite is the case where a differentiated team is in place.

calculative trust mitigates risk (see Williamson 1992: 38).[7] (See also the discussion on partnership in Meyerson 1992 and in Dasgupta 1990.) In this context, a manager who violates a rule of an implicit or explicit agreement may suffer from a bad reputation among significant others such as other managers. This may in turn reduce the willingness of these managers to use their referral capacity for the violating manager.

The value of trust rises when trust is sought after. I suggest that the scarcity of trustworthy candidates for an executive team segments the market for managers. The more trust is used as a recruitment and selection device, the more the market resembles an implicit cartel. Managers in a segmented labor market increase their bargaining position and hence their reservation wages by building networks on strong redundant ties.[8] An executive manager would then try to build up a cohesive network in order to obtain a high salary and be compensated for his trustworthiness. The following hypothesis is empirically assessed:

> Hypothesis 1. Given a certain level of human capital, strong ties are likely to add to the executive's income.

2.3. Interaction Effects on Income

Scholars like Bordieu (1980), Coleman (1988) and Burt (1992) have put forward the idea that the more social capital one has, the better use one can put this human capital investment to. Coleman (1988) argues that a pupil's access to social capital increases his ability to accumulate human capital. Well-organized and well-educated significant others (parents and the like) are important for a child's ability to assimilate education.

Yet, the exact causal order of social and human capital is not always apparent. Does human capital influence access to social capital? A strategic position with access to important social networks demands a well-educated and experienced individual. It is easy to imagine that human capital investment provides opportunities for an individual to establish and develop social contacts generated from having a good position in the firm at the start of a well-educated

---

[7] Williamson distinguishes between three categories of trust: calculative trust, personal trust, and institutional trust (p. 37). Apart from the calculative trust defined above, personal trust is characterized by the absence of monitoring, favorable or forgiving predilections and discreetness (p. 35). Institutional trust is defined as transaction-specific safeguards (governance) that vary systematically with the institutional environment within which the transactions are located. Williamson describes some contextual features with respect to which transaction-specific governance is crafted. There are six kinds of embeddedness attributes: societal culture, politics, regulation, professionalization, networks and corporate culture (p. 27).

[8] The idea of an implicit cartel segmenting the market for managers is compatible with the Lindbeck & Shower (1988) suggestion that the insiders' profitable bargaining situation increases wage level and prevents the outsider from being employed.

individual's career. The relative high position that a well-educated individual starts from provides a greater lifetime visibility and therefore increases the access to social capital.

I argue that executive managers establish a track record over the course of their careers. Their cumulative skills, education and work experience decrease in signalling importance and therefore diminish in importance as selection criteria. The type and level of human capital may still have an effect on an executive's productivity. (See also Berndt 1992: ch. 5, for a discussion on the non-linear effect of human capital on wage.)

As trustworthiness becomes the more important characteristic in the selection process of managers, the effect of human capital decreases in importance. Given a certain selection bias in schooling in the recruitment of managers, the actual interaction between human capital accumulation and the accumulation of important social ties cannot be assessed in a meaningful way in the present study. However, the little information we have is being used and interaction effects are incorporated in the model.

2.4. Institutional Effects on the Impact of Social Capital

If it is easier for individuals with a certain structure of social capital to attain high incomes, why is it that not all executives develop such a network? The reason is that individuals differ in their opportunities and in their risk behavior.

Certain executives have as their main task the accrual of new information. However, it is not possible to have both a cohesive network and an information-accrual network (Meyerson 1992). Individuals also differ in risk behavior. In Meyerson & Lang (1993) it is shown that CEOs who have a partnership with one of the main owners were more risk prone than CEOs who confront a dispersed ownership situation and are not able to build such a partnership. There is an increased 'threat' of hostile takeovers in the latter situation. It is conjectured that an individual who chooses a 'safe career' with a strong controlling owner makes a tradeoff between a high income today for a more secure employment with a lower income.

If ownership structure sets the opportunities and influences managers' risk behavior and if the distribution of ownership structure is part of the institutional environment, then a duplication of the Dutch study carried out by Boxman, De Graaf & Flap (1991) has to be modified and must consider differences in the institutional setting. Boxman, De Graaf and Flap did not account for ownership structure.

According to claims in the property rights literature, differences in monitoring costs influence managers' discretion (Hedlund et al. 1985). Less monitoring would give managers more discretion to set their wages and the opposite would be the case with strong monitoring. Therefore, one would expect managers in firms with strong shareholders to receive lower salaries than managers in firms with a dispersed ownership.

> Hypothesis 2. Managers in firms with a private concentrated owner have lower pay than managers in firms with dispersed ownership.

Furthermore, Boxman, De Graaf & Flap (1991) suggest that the size of the firm could matter. Efficiency wage theory (Akerlof & Yellon 1986) claims that the higher the pay the higher the productivity. One suggested reason for this is that the assumed chance of getting caught cheating, and the consequent punishment of the cheater discourage cheating. According to Lucas (1988) the more able a manager is, the larger the organization he would lead and, hence, the more he would get paid. These theories suggest that firm size varies with pay and hence has little to do, directly, with managers' choice of social capital.

> Hypothesis 3. The larger the size of the organization, the higher a manager's pay.

2.5. Other Variables to Consider

Statistical control for rival explanatory variables is always wise. Simon & Warner (1992) show that use of informal ties in getting a job increases the initial salary. Yet, they do not include other important factors in their analysis such as personal characteristics, internal labor ladders or the productivity of the individual. Bridges & Villemez showed already in 1986 that the type of ties or ways of searching for a job explained very little of the variance in initial salary. In Meyerson (1992) it was shown that for managers recruited to the executive team, whether it was from outside the firm or inside, strong ties between the manager and the recruiter were prominent.

According to the reasoning above, an individual's starting salary could be expected to even out on the promotion ladder, the reason being the segmented market at the top (segmentation due to the importance of trust). The reward system may not be path-dependent all the way to the top as implied by Lazear (1993). Since our sample only includes individuals at the top executive level, initial salaries are argued to be redundant in the analysis. However, given the dubious empirical results shown above, statistical control is performed for external versus internal recruitment of top executives. Furthermore, managers' reservation wage increases with options for new employments; hence, the number of job changes during their professional career can also influence the level of income. Other typical individual variables to be taken into account would be class background, personality and intelligence. The last two aspects are very difficult to isolate and hence in the present analysis only social background is accounted for.

3. THE EMPIRICAL INVESTIGATION

The main purpose of this study is the empirical support of the suggested relationships between the executives' social capital and income attainment. A path model of the suggested hypotheses is presented in Figure 12.1. The relationships between the variables in the hypotheses H1, H2 and H3 are investigated by regression analysis.

Detailed information on managers' compensation contracts is difficult to gather for obvious reasons. I use a database originally organized for other purposes, containing unique information on managers' compensation contracts. A number of Swedish public firms in existence both in 1980 and in 1985 were ranked by their most negative abnormal return for any month during 1985. The selection criterion 'abnormal return' is defined as the difference between the actual and the expected return on shareholdings. The expected return is linear to the expected return of the general index. The strength of this relation is dependent on the degree of covariation with the market portfolio (see Appendix 1 for an elaborate discussion on the selection criterion). The ranking list contains only those firms with a negative abnormal return greater than one standard deviation from the mean of the sample. From the ranking list the 32 firms with the lowest abnormal return were selected. Four of the 32 firms with the lowest abnormal return refrained from participation, therefore, only 28 firms are analyzed.

The population of publicly traded firms can be characterized by three different dimensions: ownership structure, market size and performance. The first two dimensions are well represented in the sample, i.e., the sample contains both private and institutional, concentrated and dispersed ownership, and large and small firms. The third dimension, however, the performance measured by the abnormal return is not. Hence, there is a selection bias of firms' poor performance in the sample. Consequently, the results can only be generalized to firms experiencing a negative abnormal return.

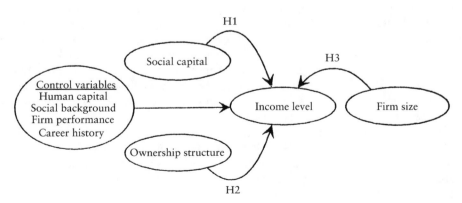

FIGURE 12.1 A Path Model Expressing the Three Hypotheses

Another measurement error concerns the variation in negative abnormal return, the crisis signal, among the sample firms. The crisis signal is different in its magnitude and firms in the sample are not a homogeneous group of firms. This measurement error can be controlled for by incorporating the variable abnormal return into the statistical analysis.

Among 147 executive members in the sample, 123 agreed to answer questions about their demographic profiles, human capital, social capital and compensation schemes. In the regression analysis 111 individual managers' answers are incorporated.

Information about the respondent's social background was traced by asking about the father's occupation at the time of the respondent's upbringing. The SEI classification (1984) was used for socioeconomic classification. The SEI classification of persons in the labor force is based primarily on their occupation. Distinctions between self-employed persons and employees, and between employees with and without subordinates must, however, be based on additional information, which is not available in the present study.

The variable 'Social Back' is defined as 0 = workers, 1 = white-collar workers, independent professionals and higher ranked white-collar workers.

Human capital was measured by the traditional variables, 'schooling experience' and 'tenure'. The tenure indicator was measured by the year of entrance into the team (TENURETEAM), and experience measured by the total number of working years (EXPERIENCE). Two sets of schooling variables are applied. Education level (EDUC): 0 = less than university education, where 22.7 percent of the managers are found; 1 = university education, where 72.3 percent of the managers are found; more basic training in university, i.e., master's or a doctoral qualification, where 5 percent of the managers belong.

The second schooling measurement contains five dummy variables expressing level and type of education: HCNOACAD = no academic qualification; HCECON = qualification in economics; HCLAW = Law qualification; HCENG = in engineering; HCOTHER = other qualifications. The idea behind the exchange of education indicators is that, since the variance in the education variable EDUC is small, the dummy variables for education categories can provide more information. One of the education categories is excluded from the regression and used as a base category. Two criteria are used to pick the base group. The first is that the group should consist of educationally homogeneous members and the second is that the group should be fairly large. The managers with a bachelor's or master's qualification in economics (HCECON) are chosen as a base group for the HC variables.

Since external or internal recruitment to the firm may influence the level of the individual's attained income this is captured by number of years in the firm (INTERNRECRUIT). Finally, it is also argued that changing workplace and employer increases your wage since it shows your bargaining power (you get offers on a continued basis and hence your reservation salary rises). The number of moves from one firm to another in a manager's professional career is captured (JOBCH).

Boxman, De Graaf & Flap (1991) report that both social capital and human capital explain the variation in Dutch managers' incomes. The level of explained variance increases dramatically when position is accounted for, which is of course not surprising. Their choice of measuring social capital, however, is bound to reflect positional aspects. Social capital in the study was captured by two indicators. The first was work contacts in other organizations external to the firm. The other indicator was membership in elite clubs such as Rotary and Lions and other professional associations. Both of these indicators are logically coupled with professional position.

Boxman et al. 1991 argue that the direct relationship between a manager's social capital as a resource variable and his career as a manager has to be interpreted with caution. Measuring social capital, human capital and income in the same period (my sample is from 1985) may imply that the relationship between social capital and income may not be due to a direct effect of social capital on income. An alternative explanation of this association may be found in a mutual dependence on the attained position of the managers. When the careers of managers proceed they might gain social capital and income simultaneously. With prestigious positions come a number of ties and hence the size of the social capital.

The suggested regression model is based on the assumption of recursivity. It is assumed that it is plausible that position, wage and mix of tie strength are not simultaneously determined. It is possible to suggest theoretical arguments for both of the two models. This is, however, not the issue in the present article. Hence, I have to apply a practical solution to this theoretically interesting question.[9]

It is difficult empirically to assess the ordering of wage, position and ties with a cross-sectional data. However, the sample provides information on the length of time the manager has known the reported contact. There is a strong and positive correlation between the time of acquaintance and the strength of the tie.

Furthermore, the study focuses on a homogeneous group: managers, a specific profession, and managers in leadership teams, i.e., in a fixed position. Although the position is similar for all individuals, there is a variation of tie mix among them. Hence, I choose the more practical assumption of recursivity.

In our case the measure of social capital is the number of strong ties. It takes time for a strong tie to develop. A test of the idea that the strength of ties takes time to build up was performed. The correlation between time for first contact with a person that eventually became a strong tie was found to be positive.

---

[9] But first. one clarification. I ask the respondent manager about his relationship to external contacts. These contacts are not interviewed about their opinion of the character of the relationship. Hence, the character of the tie is characterized by one side, the one in the prestigious position. Whether that person has a tendency or not to connect him or herself to strong or weak ties is an interesting question that we know little about. Does the movement upwards in a hierarchy increase the attraction for strong ties? And if so, why?

Also, it was found that managers' strong ties tended to develop earlier than the members' entry into the executive team.

Instead, in order to capture the team's connection to an external resource network, i.e., their social capital, information about each member's most important external ties was collected. Each team member was asked about his ties to resource persons outside the firm and the executive team. Information was collected about these persons concerning their age, their profession and whether the members and these persons socialized with and/or confided in one another. To distinguish between strong and weak ties, the respondents were asked if they socialized with and/or discussed private and personal matters with, i.e., confided in the person they were connected to. Depending on whether the respondent both socializes with and confides in the contact, the tie is considered strong or weak.[10] The number of total ties per member is measured by the number of external ties per member. NUMBERTIES. The variable used for strength of ties in the regression is STRONG and defined as the share of strong ties out of a total number of external ties.[11]

The degree of overlap of one team member's network is measured by the number of overlapping ties in the team's total number of ties. An overlapping tie is a non-redundant tie. A non-redundant tie is one tie that nobody else in the team or any tie connected to a team member is connected with. A manager's share of non-redundant ties in his external network is labelled

[10] Numerous measures have been used in the aftermath of Gravonetter's first article on the strength of ties. The most common measure used has been the indicators 'closeness of a relationship'; thus close friends are coded as strong ties while acquaintances are weak ties. Other measures are not only the closeness of two parties but also the source of the tie, such as relatives or neighbors. Granovetter (1973, 1982) has used frequency of contact in combination with closeness. Friedkin (1980) used mutual acknowledgement of contact as a measure of strong ties in a scientific community. Marsden & Campbell (1984) came to the conclusion that closeness or emotional intensity of a relationship is on balance the best indicator. The measures duration and frequency of contact were badly contaminated by the foci around which ties can be organized. These two measures are suggested by Marsden & Campbell (1984) to be avoided. The variable 'personal confiding' is little used as a measure of tie strength and hence cannot be well evaluated in the Marsden and Campbell study. In this study the three indicators of strength are all aspects of closeness, socializing, mutual confiding, i.e., the respondent's opinion on the degree of intimacy he entertains with the party.

[11] There is a problem connected to the use of number of strong respectively weak ties instead of the share of strong or weak ties. The respondent had the opportunity to report on the 15 most important external ties. The fact that cut off the tail in the distribution of number of ties distorts the variation of the size of the external network. Hence, the variable share of strong ties gives an indication of the tendency in the particular individual's network. The number of external ties is taken in for the sake of providing as much information as possible. Leaving it out of the regression does not change any results.

NONREDUNDTIE.[12] The interaction term of social capital and human capital is measured by STRONG* EDUC and labelled ISOEDUC.

In order to obtain compatibility with Boxman, De Graaf & Flap's study, the explained variable, income, is measured by the gross yearly fixed income in Swedish Kronor, FIXSAL, for the executive respondent in 1985.[13]

From an incentive perspective executive compensation schemes can be composed in many different ways. If there is a risk component in a risk-averse manager's compensation he is likely to receive a compensation for that (Milgrom & Roberts 1992). In Meyerson (1994) it was found that a larger share of firm shares was compensated for by a higher level of total income. Hence, to make managers' incomes compatible the degree of risk in their compensation contracts must be taken into account.

Three outcome-related compensation measures are accounted for. The first is the return on firm shares a manager is in possession of. Firm stock compensation is measured by a 10 percent return on firm shares divided by the total income, SHAREAND, that a manager possess.[14] The second type of outcome-related compensation to be considered is the share of tantieme, defined as the total value of tantieme divided by the total income. TANBOAND. Finally, the third type is the share of stock options and convertibles defined as 10 percent on stock options and convertibles divided by the total income. CONOPAND. The first type of outcome-related compensation is more risky than the other two because with stocks you can actually lose money.

Other control variables in the regression analysis model are ownership structure and the firm size. Ownership structure is measured by ownership concentration ration, OWNERCONCENTR: the largest shareholder's percentage of votes. Firm size is measured by the market value of the firm (MARKETVALUE)[15].

The second and third hypotheses contain the explanatory variables 'ownership structure' and 'firm size'.

The selection variable 'abnormal return' is incorporated in all three regressions. The difference in the magnitude of the crisis signal is controlled for.

---

[12] There may be a problem with the link between reported secondary contacts of the team members. (A primary contact is someone to whom you are connected through weak non-redundant ties while a secondary tie is an indirect tie that one is connected to through primary ties.) (See Burt 1991). The secondary contacts may know each other and hence limit the uniqueness of these contacts. This we do not know from the collected data.

[13] Other pecuniary and non-pecuniary rewards are collected in the database; however, the size of those rewards was rather small during the 1980s and thus treated as negligible in the analysis.

[14] Owing to the Swedish tax laws during the 1980s it was beneficial to give managers profitable loans to buy firm shares.

[15] Because of the aggregation bias problem with non-individual attributes such as ownership structure and market size, the beta coefficients for owner concentration and market value are interpreted as indication of trends. In a statistical hierarchical LISREL model the effects of these indicators are better modelled and give more reasonable information.

Abnormal return is defined as the difference between the expected and the actual return for a firm's share. Regression analyses in log form are performed and presented below. Paraphrasing Mincer's wage equation the regression equation is derived from:

$$Y = Y_0 * e^{aHC + \beta 2HNURI + \beta 3EXP + u}$$

The results from the testing of the empirical support of hypotheses 1–3 are presented in a step-wise form. The base form for the regression equations takes the following form:

$$\begin{aligned} \ln y = {} & \ln y_0 + a\text{EDUC} + \beta_1\text{TENURETEAM} + \beta_2\text{EXPERIENCE} \\ & + \beta_3\text{INTERNRECRUIT} + \beta_4\text{STRONG} + \beta_5\text{NUMBERTIE} \\ & + \beta_6\text{NONREDUNTIE} + \beta_7\text{JOBCHANGE} + \beta_8\text{SHAREAND} \\ & + \beta_9\text{CONOPAND} + \beta_{10}\text{TANBOAND} + \beta_{11}\text{SOCIALBACK} \\ & + \beta_{12}\text{ABNORMALRETURN} + \beta_{13}\text{MARKETVALUE} \\ & + \beta_{14}\text{OWNERSCONCENTR} + u. \end{aligned}$$

The first step is to analyze hypothesis 1 with a simple model containing the human capital variables EDUC, EXPERIENCE and TENURETEAM (model 1, Table 12.1). A modification of this model incorporates the interaction factor of social capital (STRONG) and human capital (EDUC): ISOCEDUC (model 2, Table 12.1).

In Model 2, Table 12.1 where the interaction term 'strong ties and education' (ISOCEDUC) is shown, there is no empirical support of the hypothesis. In the consecutive regression analysis the interaction term is left out, the reason being that the interpretation of the factor is difficult because of a selection bias in managers' education. The variation in education is small, which restricts a meaningful interpretation of the incorporated interaction term. Furthermore, the interaction term does not contribute very much to the explained variance as shown in Table 12.1 regression model 1 with the interaction factor where R^2 is 0.38 percent and in regression model 2 without the interaction factor where R^2 is 38 percent. The variables in regression model 1 explain 77 percent of the interaction term.[16]

The second step is to analyze hypothesis 1 where instead of using the educational level indicator the education categories are applied (model 3, Table 12.2).

Table 12.1, model 1 and Table 12.2, model 3 show that the Hypothesis 1 is supported empirically by the data; social capital (STRONG) exhibits a positive

[16] In an SAS collin analysis it is shown that there is a difference in the quotas of min. and max. eigen values. A high value of a quota of eigen values means a collinearity problem; however, since it is difficult to decide high respectively low value a collin analysis of a regression with and without the interaction term is applied. With the interaction term the value is 7264.28 and without the value is 6502.69.

TABLE 12.1 Regression Models 1 and 2. The Impact of Social Capital on Income.

Exogenous variables	Model Ifixsal 1	Model Ifixsal 2
Intercept	3.9918**	4.2166**
	(5.759)	(5.781)
EDUC	0.1745*	0.0790
	(1.733)	(0.567)
EXPERIENCE	−0.0019	−0.0024
	(−0.314)	(−0.384)
TENURETEAM	−0.0066	−0.0083
	(−0.970)	(−1.184)
INTERNRECRUIT	0.0004	0.0058
	(0.060)	(0.088)
JOBCH	0.0207	0.0229
	(0.749)	(0.824)
SOCIAL BACK	0.0289	0.0296
	(0.493)	(0.506)
STRONG	0.3968**	0.2033
	(2.826)	(0.845)
NONREDUNDTIE	−0.1512	−0.1580
	(−0.705)	(−0.737)
NUMBERTIES	0.0073	0.0066
	(0.761)	(0.686)
SHAREAND	−0.0495	−0.0383
	(−0.242)	(−0.187)
TANBOAND	0.2923	0.2570
	(0.798)	(0.699)
CONOPAND	−0.6088	−0.6559
	(−0.906)	(−0.974)
OWNERCONCENTR	0.0007	0.0007
	(0.259)	(0.260)
MARKETVALUE	0.0002**	0.0002**
	(5.053)	(4.956)
ABNORMALRETURN	−0.5777	−0.5152
	(−0.840)	(−0.746)
ISOCEDU		0.2942
		(0.991)
R^2	0.3616	0.3681
adj R^2	0.2618	0.2617
Total observations	111	111

** significant 5%
* significant 10%
Note: 1-values shown within parentheses.

TABLE 12.2 Regression Model 3. The Impact of Social Capital, Market Value and Ownership Concentration on Income.

Exogenous variables	Model 3
Intercept	3.9865^{**}
	(5.944)
HCNOACAD	0.0879
	(−0.828)
HCOTHER	0.1931
	(1.371)
HCENG	0.2222^{**}
	(2.092)
HCLAW	0.0473
	(0.400)
EXPERIENCE	−0.0019
	(−0.305)
TENURETEAM	−0.0073
	(−1.086)
INTERNREC	0.0006
	(0.103)
JOBCH	0.0353
	(1.257)
STRONG	0.3979^{**}
	(2.854)
NONREDUNDTIE	−0.1055
	(−0.527)
NUMBERTIES	0.0093
	(0.987)
SOCIAL BACKGROUND	0.0768
	(1.273)
OWNERCONCENTR	0.0009
	(0.352)
MARKET VALUE	0.0002^{**}
	(4.675)
ABNORMAL RETURN	−0.5758
	(−0.854)

$R^2 = 0.39$
adj $R^2 = 0.29$
Total observations 111

** significant 5%
Note: t-values shown within parentheses.

and significant effect on income (FIXSAL). Consequently, a mobilization-oriented network seems to be more efficient in providing a high salary than do information-oriented networks based on weak ties. As mentioned above, in terms of exerting influence strong ties are instrumental in mobilizing or restraining others' actions, whereas the networks based on weak ties are efficient in accruing information. (See Meyerson 1992, the leadership paradox for a discussion of why you cannot have access to both information-efficient and mobilization-oriented networks.)

The third and the fourth hypotheses concerning the relative importance of the ownership structure of the firm (OWNERCONCENTR) and the firm size (MARKETVALUE) for income attainment are presented in regression model 3 in Table 12.2.

Social capital (STRONG) together with firm size (MARKETVALUE) exhibit a significant positive effect on fixed income. Ownership concentration shows no significant effect on fixed income. Hence, the empirical data do not support hypothesis 2 but support hypothesis 3. It can be noted that the correlation between ownership structure and firm size shows that large firms often have a dispersed ownership (see Meyerson 1992). Furthermore, no apparent evidence is found of collinearity between the variables market value and ownership structure (the correlation between market value and ownership concentration is -0.27).

4. DISCUSSION AND CONCLUSIONS

The results are partly in agreement with the findings of Boxman, De Graaf & Flap (1991): given the level of schooling there is a strong positive effect of social capital on managers' income attainment. Social capital adds explained variation in income when incorporated into a human capital model.

However, results here that were not in accordance with Boxman et al. (1991) had to do with the kind of tie that provides the most instrumental type of social capital. Top managers' reservation wages increase with the presence of strong ties, not weak ones. Consequently, social capital does not necessarily have to be based on weak non-redundant ties in order to be instrumental. The type of social capital that is the most beneficial depends on the social context. These results give a hint of the general notion of the relative efficiency of the weak tie in attaining resources such as jobs, information and income.

Examining social capital as a general concept opens up interesting paths to understanding not only issues such as how individuals benefit from their social networks or how income is distributed but also how society is stratified. It sheds light on the mechanisms that allocate resources in a society. Are the most talented individuals the highest paid and are these people positioned at the top of the largest firms? The study shows that the highest paid managers are found in the largest firms and lack social networks that are information efficient. The networks of these managers consists mainly of strong and overlapping ties (redundant ties). On the other hand, over the course of a long career, these managers have developed a social capital that is beneficial for mobilization and for restraining others' actions. What benefits this ability brings to society in the long run is an open question.

APPENDIX 1. THE SAMPLE CRITERION

The selection criterion of a public firm confronting a crisis signal from the stock market was a strong negative abnormal return. The 106 public firms on the stock market in both in 1980 and 1988 were ranked according to their strongest negative abnormal return during any month in 1985. From that list 32 firms were selected and where 28 executive teams participated. The characteristics of the univariate distribution of the 106 firms and 28 firms are presented in Table 12.A 1:1.

Since no assumption is made about the variable being normally distributed, a complement to the mean (Mean) and the standard deviation (Sd) is given by the median (Md), the skewness (Skew) Kurtosis (Kurtos) and the minimum (MIN) and maximum (MAX) values.[17]

Abnormal return (AR) is a measure taken from the field of financial theory. It is postulated that individuals make consistent and rational decisions, and that all expectations are realized since no one acts on the wrong premises (Hansson & Högfeldt 1988: 636). Financial theory analyzes the economic effects of both time and risk on resource allocation and gives a rational economic explanation for seemingly random changes in stock prices using stochastic theory. Three major ideas are incorporated in financial theory: information efficiency, diversification and arbitrage principles. The idea of information efficiency is of relevance in our study.

From Hansson & Högfeldt (1988) the following description on the information efficiency assumption is drawn: when new information enters the market, investors evaluate it and change their portfolio to exploit potential profits from

TABLE 12.A 1:1 Characteristics of the Univariate Distribution for the Variables Negative Abnormal Return for 106 Firms and Negative Abnormal Return for 28 Firms.

	Mean	Sd	Md	Skew	Kurtos	MIN	MAX
Negative abnormal return (population of 106 firms)	−0.12	0.09	−0.11	−2.61	12.61	−0.68	0.12
Negative abnormal return (Sample of 28 firms)	0.05	0.05	0.05	−0.27	12.37	−0.27	0.008

[17] Under the normal distribution assumption skewness is equal to 0 and kurtosis is equal to 0 (see definition and computation of kurtosis in SAS Elementary Statistics Procedure (p. 11) from SAS Procedures Guide. Release 6.03 Edition).

the new knowledge. The new equilibrium prices therefore contain the information. Prices are an efficient information bearer and price changes reflect the market's joint evaluation and response to new information. This implies that investors base their decisions only on the information that has already been exploited by the market. This intuition is called the market-efficiency hypothesis: market prices reflect all relevant information. The analysis testing the hypothesis shows that the Swedish market is at least semi information-efficient.

It is assumed that the investors not only base their actions on historical information (weak information efficiency), but also on economic information that is accessible to the public. For example, announcements revealing a firm's specific information are easily and quickly processed by the actors, and the stock market prices reflect this process. However, empirical analysis shows that insider information is not reflected in the stock prices. Trading with insider information may give abnormal returns. In general, previous studies have been interpreted to support the information-efficiency hypothesis because insider information cannot give an ongoing abnormal return for long, since other investors will discover the abnormal returns and try to exploit them.

The expected rate of return is given by the CAPM approach, Capital Asset Pricing Model (Sharpe 1964) or the more general model of APT, the Arbitrage Pricing Theory (Copeland & Weston 1983). The CAPM predicts that security rates of return will be linearly related to a single common factor, the asset's systematic risk. The APT is based on similar intuition but it is more general. CAPM can be viewed as a special case of the APT when the market rate of return is assumed to be the single relevant factor.

Investors put together portfolios by evaluating the stock's expected rate of return and its risk. Risk is defined as the volatility in the returns. A share with high variability is classified as a share with high risk and vice versa. Because the variability of risk for different shares is not perfectly correlated, investors may reduce risk by diversifying their portfolio. Risk may be divided into unsystematic (or firm-specific) risk and systematic risk (variation due to the market return). The latter is compensated for by investors diversifying their portfolio (Hansson & Högfeldt 1988).

Even though there is a theory behind the CAPM, and not behind the market model, the latter is chosen. The market model is easier to compute (DeRidder 1988: 16). Furthermore, a data set of firms on the stock market during 1980–85 already exists, as does a program for computing abnormal return values based on the market model. Also, there is evidence that the output from the two models, the market model and the CAPM, yields the same results (DeRidder 1988).

Abnormal return for a particular share is defined as the difference between the actual and the expected return. A share's expected return is evaluated by the CAPM as:

$$R_{i,t} = \alpha_i + \beta_i R_{m,t} + \varepsilon_{i,t}$$

where

$R_{i,t}$ = the share's return in period t
$R_{m,t}$ = return of the market porfolio, R_m, at the period t
α_i, β_i = the share specific parameters
ε_i = error term with the expected value of zero

The expected rate of return given by the model is determined by the unsystematic risk, alpha, and the product of $ß_i R_{m,t}$, determined by the market. The market factor beta indicates how much a share's return is expected to change given a certain change in the market portfolio (approximated by Affärsvärldens 'general index'). Given the use of the model the abnormal return is expressed by

$$ar_{i,t} = R_{i,t} - (\hat{\alpha}_i + \hat{\beta}_i R_{m,t})$$

where $\hat{\alpha}_i$ and $\hat{\beta}_i$ are estimates of the share-specific parameters. $\hat{\beta}_i$ is defined as the covariance between R_i and R_m divided by the variance of the market portfolio

$$\beta_i = Cov(R_i, R_m) / var(R_m)$$

Summing all the single observations of AR and dividing by the total gives us an average abnormal return AR_t.

Some shortcomings of the selected measures and computation are (a) abnormal return- and information-efficient markets, (b) the problem of estimating betas, and (c) the problem of thin trading (DeRidder 1988; Hansson & Högfeldt 1988; Claesson 1989; Berglund, Liljeblom & Löflund 1989) The problem with adjusting betas is especially worth noting. A crisis signal as defined here, contains some radical new information which of course could change the risk of the firm's share, i.e., the true beta. However, this is not taken into account in our estimation, which is a drawback.

ACKNOWLEDGMENTS

Valuable comments from Erik Mellander, Anders Björklund and four anonymous referees are gratefully acknowledged.

Received July 1994
Final version accepted October 1994

REFERENCES

Akerlof, & Yellon. 1986. *Efficiency Wage Models of the Labor Market*. Cambridge: Cambridge University Press.

Anderson, B. 1979. Cognitive Balance Theory and Social Network Analysis: Remarks on Some Fundamental Theoretical Matters. In P. W. Holland & S. Lemhardht (eds.). *Perspectives on Social Networks Research*, pp. 453–469.

Anderson, B. & Carlos, M. L. 1979. A Political Brokerage and Network Politics in Mexico. In B. Anderson & D. Willer (eds.). *Social Exchange Networks: The Elementary Theory and its Applications*. pp. 1–32. New York: Elsevier Press.

Boxman, E. A. W., De Graaf, P. M., and Flap, H. D. 1991. The Impact of Social and Human Capital on the Income Attainment of Dutch Managers. *Social Networks* 13. 51–73.

Becker, G. 1964. *Human Capital. A Theoretical and Empirical Analysis with Special Reference to Education*, New York: Columbia University.

Becker, G. 1992. *Nobel Lecture*, Stockholm, December.

Becker, G. & Tomes, N. 1986. Human Capital and the Rise and Fall of Families. In S. Lindenberg et al. (eds.). *Approaches to Social Theory*. New York: Russel Sage.

Berglund, T., Liljeblom, E., & Löflund, A. 1989. Estimating Betas on Daily Data for a Small Stock Market, *Journal of Banking and Finance* 13:41–64.

Berndt, E. 1992. *The Practice of Econometrics Classic and Contemporary*, Reading, Mass: Addison-Wesley Publishing Company.

Bordieu, P. 1980. Le Capital Social, Notes Provisoirs, *Actes de la Recherche en Sciences Sociales* 3:2–3.

Burt, R. S. 1990. Tertius Gaudens. A Study of Structural Holes as Social Capital. Paper presented at the Interdisciplinary Perspectives on Organization Studies held at NIAS. May-June, in Wassenaar.

Burt, R. 1991. Structural Holes. In R. Swedebergs (ed.). *Explorations in Economic Sociology. The Social Structure of Competition*.

Burt, R. S. 1992. *Structural Holes. The Social Structure of Competition*, Harvard Cambridge: University Press.

Bridges, W. P. & Villemez, W. J. 1986. Informal Hiring and Income in the Labor Market. *American Sociological Review* 51, 574–582.

Claesson, K. 1989. Anomalies på aktiemarknaden. Skandinaviska Enskilda Banken Kvartalsskrift 1.

Coleman, J. S. 1965. *Adolescents and the Schools*. New York: Basic Books.

Coleman, J. S. 1988. Social Capital, in the Creation of Human Capital. *American Journal of Sociology* 94, S95–120.

Coleman, J. S. 1992. *Foundation of Social Theory*, Belknap Harvard.

Copeland E. E. and J. F. Weston. 1983. *Financial Theory and Corporate Policy*, Massachusetts: Addison-Wesley Publishing Company, second edition.

Dasgupta, P. 1990. Trust as a Commodity. In D. Gambetta (ed.). *Trust-Making and Breaking Cooperative Relations*. Oxford: Basil Blackwell.

DeRidder, A. 1988. Börsstopp och kursut-veckling på Stockholmsbörsen. Stockholms Fondbörs. Industriförbundets skriftserie nr 5.

Festinger, L. A. 1957. *A Theory of Cognitive Dissonance*. Paolo Alto: Stanford University Press.

Freidkin, N. 1980. A Test of Structural Features of Granovetters Strength of Weak Ties Theory. *Social Networks* 2, 411–422.

Frey, D. 1982. Different Levels of Cognitive Dissonance, Information Seeking, and Information Avoidance. *Journal of Personality and Social Psychology*, 43, 1175–1183.

Gilad, B., Kaish, S. & Loeb, P. D. 1987. Cognitive Dissonance and Utility Maximization. A General Framework. *Journal of Economic and Organization*. 8, 61–73.

Granovetter, M. S. 1973. The Strength of Weak Ties. *American Journal of Socioloᵒy* 78, 1360–1380.

Granovetter, M. S. 1974. *Getting a Job: A Study of Contacts and Careers*, Cambridge: Harvard University Press.

Granovetter, M. S. 1982. The Strength of Weak Ties Revisited. In P. V. Marsden & N. Lin (eds.). *Social Structure and Networks Analysis*, pp. 131–145. Beverly Hills: Sage.

Hanson, B. and Högfeldt, P. 1988. Finansiell ekonomi: Tre grundläggande principer. *Ekonomisk Debatt* 8, 635–647.

Hedlund, G., Hägg, I., Hörnell, E. & Rydén, B. 1985. *Institutioner som aktieägare: Förvaltare? Industrialister? Klippare?* Stockholm: SNS Förlag.

Kazamaki Ottersten, E., Mellander, E., Meyerson, E. M. & Nilsson, J. 1994. Pitfalls in the Measurement of the Return to Education: An Assessment Using Swedish Data. IUI working paper No. 414.

Lin, N. 1982. Social Resources and Instrumental Action. In P. V. Marsden & N. Lin (eds.). *Social Structure and Networks Analysis*. pp. 131–145. Beverly Hills: Sage.

Lin, N. and Dumin, M. 1986. Access to Occupations Through Social Ties. *Social Networks* 8, 365–385.

Lindbeck, A. 1992. Gary Becker. *Ekonomisk Debatt*, or 8, 694–657.

Lindbeck, A. and Snower, D. J. 1988. *The Insider Outsider Theory of Employment and Unemployment*, Cambridge: MIT Press.

Lazeat, E. P. 1993. *The Economies of Personnel*. Wicksell Lectures, Stockholm, Sweden, Match.

Lomy, G. 1977. A Dynamic Theory of Racial Income Differences. In P. A. Wallace & A. Le Mund (eds.). *Women, Minorities and Employment Discrimination*, ch. 8, Lexington. Mass: Lexington Books.

Loury, G. 1987. Why Should We Care About Group Inequality? *Social Philosophy and Policy* 5, 249–271.

Lucas Jr. R. E. 1988. On the Size Distribution of Business Firms. *Bell Journal of Economics*, 508–523.

McCain, B. E., O'Reilly III, C. A. & Pfeffer, J. 1983.The Effects of Departmental Demography on Turnover: The Case of a University, *Academy of Management Journal*, 26, 626–641.

Marsden P. V. & Campbell, K. E. 1984. Measuring Tie Strength. *Social Forces*, 63, 482–501.

Meyerson, E. M. 1992. *The Impact of Ownership Structure and Team Composition on Firm Performance*, Stockholm IUI.

Meyerson, E. M. 1994. *Compensation Contracts in Firms on the Swedish Stock Market*, Working Paper, Stockholm.

Meyerson, E. M. & Lang, H. 1993. *Ownership Structure and Team Composition. An Application of Proposive Action on Managers' Risk Behavior*. IUI Working Paper no. 396. Stockholm.

Merton, R. K. 1968. *Social Theory and Social Structure*, second edition. New York: Free Press.

Mincer, J. 1974. *Schooling, Experience and Earnings*. New York: Columbia University Press.

Milgrom P. & Robert, J. 1992. *Economics, Organization and Management*. New Jersey: Prentice Hall International.

Mitchell, L. C. 1969. *Social Networks in Urban Situations*, Manchester: University Press.

Montgomery, J. 1988. Social Networks and Labor Market Outcomes: Toward an Economic Analysis, Ph.D. dissertation, MIT Cambridge.

Montgomery, J. 1992. Job Search and Network Composition: Reconsidering the Implication of the Strength-of-Weak-Ties Hypothesis. *American Sociological Review* 57(5).

Newcomb, T. M. 1961. *The Acquaintance Process*. New York: Holt, Rinehart and Winston.

Pinard, M. 1968. Mass Society and Political Movements: A New Formulation. *American Journal of Sociology* 73, 683–690.

SEB, Socioekonomisk indelning SEI, MIS 1982:4 Nytryck 1984.

Sharpe, W. F. 1964. Capital Asset Prices: A Theory of Market Equilibrium under Conditions of Risk. *Journal of Finance* 19, 425–442.

Simon, C. J. & Warner, J. T. 1992. Matchmaker, Matchmaker: The Effect of Old Boy Networks on Job Match Quality, Earnings, and Tenure. *Journal of Labor Economics* 10, 306–329.

Wagner, W. G. Pfeffer, J. & O'Reilly III, S. A. 1984. Organizational Demography and Turnover in Top-Management Groups. *Administrative Science Quarterly* 29, 74–92.

Williamson, O. E., 1992. Calculativeness, Trust, And Economic Organization. Paper presented at the ASA meeting in Pittsburgh, USA.

Index

Butterworth-Heinemann Business Books . . .
for Transforming Business

*5th Generation Management: Co-creating Through Virtual
Enterprising, Dynamic Teaming, and Knowledge
Networking, Revised Edition,*
> Charles M. Savage, 0-7506-9701-6

*After Atlantis: Working, Managing, and Leading in
> Turbulent Times,*
> Ned Hamson, 0-7506-9884-5

*The Alchemy of Fear: How to Break the Corporate Trance
> and Create Your Company's Successful Future,*
> Kay Gilley, 0-7506-9909-4

*Beyond Business as Usual: Practical Lessons in Accessing
> New Dimensions,*
> Michael W. Munn, 0-7506-9926-4

*Beyond Strategic Vision: Effective Corporate Action with
> Hoshin Planning,*
> Michael Cowley and Ellen Domb, 0-7506-9843-8

Beyond Time Management: Business with Purpose,
> Robert A. Wright, 0-7506-9799-7

*The Breakdown of Hierarchy: Communicating in the
> Evolving Workplace,*
> Eugene Marlow and Patricia O'Connor Wilson,
> 0-7056-9746-6

*Business and the Feminine Principle: The Untapped
    Resource,*
    Carol R. Frenier, 0-7506-9829-2

Choosing the Future: The Power of Strategic Thinking,
    Stuart Wells, 0-7506-9876-4

Conscious Capitalism: Principles for Prosperity,
    David A. Schwerin, 0-7506-7021-5

Corporate DNA: Learning From Life,
    Ken Baskin, 0-7506-9844-6

*Cultivating Common Ground: Releasing the Power of
    Relationships at Work,*
    Daniel S. Hanson, 0-7506-9832-2

*Flight of the Phoenix: Soaring to Success in the 21st
    Century,*
    John Whiteside and Sandra Egli, 0-7506-9798-9

*Getting a Grip on Tomorrow: Your Guide to Survival and
    Success in the Changed World of Work,*
    Mike Johnson, 0-7506-9758-X

Innovation Strategy for the Knowledge Economy: The Ken
    Awakening,
    Debra M. Amidon, 0-7506-9841-1

Innovation through Intuition: The Hidden Intelligence,
    Sandra Weintraub, 0-7506-9937-X

The Intelligence Advantage: Organizing for Complexity,
    Michael D. McMaster, 0-7506-9792-X

Intuitive Imagery: A Resource at Work,
    John B. Pehrson and Susan E. Mehrtens, 0-7506-9805-5

The Knowledge Evolution: Expanding Organizational Intelligence,
    Verna Allee, 0-7506-9842-X

Leadership in a Challenging World: A Sacred Journey,
    Barbara Shipka, 0-7506-9750-4

Leading Consciously: A Pilgrimage Toward Self Mastery,
    Debashis Chatterjee, 0-7506-9864-0

Leading from the Heart: Choosing Courage over Fear in the Workplace,
    Kay Gilley, 0-7506-9835-7

Learning to Read the Signs: Reclaiming Pragmatism in Business,
    F. Byron Nahser, 0-7506-9901-9

Leveraging People and Profit: The Hard Work of Soft Management,
    Bernard A. Nagle and Perry Pascarella, 0-7506-9961-2

Marketing Plans That Work: Targeting Growth and Profitability,
    Malcolm H.B. McDonald and Warren J. Keegan, 0-7506-9828-4

Time to Take Control: The Impact of Change on Corporate Computer Systems,
Tony Johnson, 0-7506-9863-2

The Transformation of Management,
Mike Davidson, 0-7506-9814-4

What Is the Emperor Wearing? Truth-Telling in Business Relationships,
Laurie Weiss, 0-7506-9872-1

Who We Could Be at Work, Revised Edition,
Margaret A. Lulic, 0-7506-9739-3

Working From Your Core: Personal and Corporate Wisdom in a World of Change,
Sharon Seivert, 0-7506-9931-0

Business Climate Shifts: Profiles of Change Makers,
Warner Burke, and William Trahant, 0-7506-7186-6

Large Scale Organizational Change: An Executive's Guide,
Christopher Laszlo and Jean-Francois Laugel,
0-7506-7230-7

To purchase any Butterworth-Heinemann title,
please visit your local bookstore or call 1-800-366-2665.